Contemporary Human Resource Management

Improving Performance in the Workplace

Contemporary Human Resource Management

Improving Performance in the Workplace

Mohd. Shahbaz Alam
Anita

ATLANTIC
PUBLISHERS & DISTRIBUTORS (P) LTD

Published by
ATLANTIC
PUBLISHERS & DISTRIBUTORS (P) LTD
7/22, Ansari Road, Darya Ganj,
New Delhi-110002
Phones : 40775252, 23273880, 23275880, 23280451
Fax : +91-11-23285873
Web : www.atlanticbooks.com
E-mail : orders@atlanticbooks.com

Branch Office
5, Nallathambi Street, Wallajah Road,
Chennai-600 002
Phones : +91-44-64611085, 32413319
E-mail : chennai@atlanticbooks.com

Printed in India at Nice Printing Press, A-33/3A, Site-IV, Industrial Area, Sahibabad, Ghaziabad, U.P.

ACKNOWLEDGEMENTS

We wish to put on record our gratefulness to Dr. Rattan Sharma, the excellent management guru, MBA (IIM), Ph.D. and Director of Bharatiya Vidya Bhavan's Usha & Laxmi Mittal Institute of Management (BULMIM), New Delhi for being especially helpful in this project and providing invaluable professional expertise.

We are thankful to the many academicians and professionals, especially, Ashraf Jaffrey, Dr. S.B. Vyas, Ph.D. and Dr. Nalin Jain, Ph.D., who were our advocates when this book was but a concept in our mind.

We are indebted to the research assistants who offered so much encouragement, especially Ayaz from Caledonian University, Scotland; Shaista Yasmin from Jamia Millia Islamia, India; Inderjeet Singh, Hamdard University, India; Anurag Singh, Pune University, India; Mansi Dholakia, Sheffield Hallam University, UK; and Vijay Kumar, Campbell University, USA.

To our wonderful associates Mumtaz, Tasneem, Simon, Arshi and Ayesha whose presence helped us the sanity and stability to get through it all, we are especially thankful.

We are indebted to our kids—Meher and Anis, for freeing us to focus on this endeavor. Their sense of coordination and shared passion contributed a lot in this project in ways they will never know.

We also thank our bosses Sanjeev Jain, MD and D.C. Jain, CMD of Akums Drugs and Pharmaceuticals Ltd., Delhi for their wizardry in pulling it all together at the eleventh hour.

We are indebted to our parents Azhar Alam and Sarwari Afzalur Rahman, and Jaikishan and Kailasho for their blessings, inspiration, guidance and insightful contributions. We are thankful to our cherished friends, especially Ranjeet, Birender, Basit, Moqeem, Jawed, Nishat, Nyla, Altamash and Renu who helped us maintain a sense of balance during the busy schedule.

We are indebted to Imtiyaz, Ejaz, Nawaz and Taj for their sweet encouragement and direction all the way from day one.

We are eternally grateful to supreme power Almighty Allah or Ishwar for always being the best supporter.

Mohd. Shahbaz Alam

Anita

PREFACE

In a highly competitive world, selecting the right personnel is extremely important for companies, corporations and industrial houses to survive. The onus of managing, retaining and moulding the careers of employees is to a large extent on Human Resource Managers.

Contemporary Human Resource Management: Improving Performance in the Workplace attempts to provide useful information for skills upgradation to do better in a highly competitive arena with full confidence. It is the first of its kind book based on theory coupled with experience of managing human resources.

The main objectives of conceptualizing this book are: to provide updated management concepts, theories and techniques that enable managers to make bold business decisions; to equip them with need-of-the-hour business tools and terminologies to match with the unmet need of the business world; to empower them and raise their confidence in mentoring, brainstorming, talent management, face reading, career mapping, interview technique, learning, loyalty, counseling, hiring, firing, *Chanakya niti* and exit interview for perfect delegation, negotiation, authority and autonomy; and to encourage and update the knowledge of non-MBAs in easy-to-understand language.

The book has touched upon all existing management concepts, theories and techniques along with newer ones as well. It deals with such concepts as Retention Management, Absenteeism Management, Happiness Quotient, Metamorphosis in HRM, HR calculation, Social Security benefits, etc. It is designed in such a way that it is easy to understand and remember. Every bit of information is written clearly so that readers can feel motivated and confident. The book will help the readers to take bold decisions in day-to-day business management practices and will be particularly useful to those who manage human resources. It will prove immensely beneficial to students and teachers of Human Resource Management and researchers in this field.

Mohd. Shahbaz Alam
Anita

CONTENTS

Chapter one

CAREER MAPPING

A career map is a tool used to explore your future career development in the short and long term. It is a tool to help you consider your personal skills and values as they relate to your career goals and a specific job. The questioning involved is very open ended because individuals will vary greatly in the way they respond to questioning. Skills and values are left up to personal interpretation. Other exercises focus on brainstorming and reflection. The map is yours to create.

Why We Need Career Map?

Would you start a home business without first writing a business plan? Would you enroll in a degree program without reviewing a degree audit? No, before making a huge investment of your time and money, you need to know what will be required and determine if the expectations are reasonable and feasible. Similarly, before entering the workforce, you should have a career map.

How to Use a Career Map?

Career mapping exercises are designed to be thought provoking, so complete these exercises when you are not distracted. If you find the career mapping exercises intimidating, use as a part of a discussion group or coaching session. Mission, objective and goals are time bound. Therefore, you write in pencil, as goals and priorities change with time.

Good Decision-making in Career Mapping

Good decision-making is very important for an employee and employer to get success in career path. Dhirubhai Ambani when started his venture, initially it was incurring huge loss and that is why his partner left him in between. Why Dhirubhai became a global business honcho, it is because he was having a planned vision and he used to make bold decision then and there fearlessly? His two sons are among top 10 global billionaires and not only this, daughter of Mukesh Ambani, elder son of Dhirubhai has become one of the top 10 global teen billionaires.

L.N. Mittal allowed his son to work in a merger and acquisition company just after finishing MBA education in finance. His son worked in America one year only to know about practical world and then joined bandwagon of his father's company. Duo created history and within a few span of time, L.N. Mittal became one of the top 5 global billionaires specific with the application of merger and acquisition technique. His daughter has also become one of the top 10 global teen billionaires.

DLF is the largest real estate company in the world and it has been created within one and half decade. DLF has now become international brand and his promoter is K.P. Singh. He was neither a qualified person nor a rich businessman but his vision made him the owner of DLF, the largest global real estate company. His daughter also created history and she has entered into global teen billionaire club. She ranks under top 10 global teen billionaires.

Narayan Murthy, the founder director of Infosys created a history by launching software venture when most of his colleagues were targeting their career in American job market. When he started his business, he couldn't do well and few of his partners left him in between and made a move towards America, but few of them remained with him. His decision made a small company into global software company and now India is recognized with Infosys. It is very surprising that now, most of the employees of America want to work with Infosys. Working with Infosys has become a standard and proud for both Americans and Indians.

Azeem Premji is a respected name like Gandhi ji in Indian and global corporate world. Premji used to sell dalda but now he is owner of one the top 10 software solution companies in the world. He is innovative, creative and a very good decision-maker. His decision made him billionaire in one decade only.

Visionary Attitude in Career Mapping

You can earn lots of money, respect and global recognition even to be an employee whole of your life. The best example is of my ideal man Jack Welch, the most admired chairman and CEO of the most admired company in the world, General Electrical of USA. He started his career with GE and retired with GE. He was the most admired chairman and CEO of the world and made GE, the most admired global company. He is also known for introducing 360° appraisal system and six sigma quality. He has not only made GE a global most admired company but also he has given a career path. He has proven himself as the most successful employee on this earth.

Success story of Jack Welch has been summarized in a book *Straight from the Gut* written by John A. Bryne. Jack always remained worried about his stammer but his strong mind and confidence made the super duper corporate business honcho. His ideal who made him so bold and confident is no one but his own mother. His mother was a great judge of character. She always had opinions of the people she met. She could smell a phoney, a mile away. Jack accepted perhaps the greatest single gift she gave him was self-confidence. The insight she drilled into him never faded. *Straight from the Gut* is highly appreciated from all corners of the world and this book ranked the international bestseller.

If you have your career map with you, then you can surely get whatever you have planned or even more than that but remember one thing; you have to put efforts honestly and tactfully. You should have self-confidence and self-starter with you. Your designed vision, mission, objective and target will help in craving need for accomplishment.

Role of Vision in Career Mapping

Vision helps you to visualize your career in whole life and it is not attached with time. You may or may not achieve whatever you have planned because there is no security of life even for a second. Even then, you have to design your vision well in advance. Vision will give you motivational energy and make you a self-starter. You will be self-directed and self-controlled if you will attach a dream with your career vision. If there is no dream attached with your vision, then you will be controlled by others and in your whole life, you have to depend on others for career growth and for the moment of happiness. Vision is static and it cannot be changed.

Role of Mission in Career Mapping

What is your next five years plan is nothing but your mission. Mission is time bound and you have to achieve in a stipulated time period. In today's global free trade arena, your first mission will be how to penetrate your product and services everywhere in the world. For this, you have to have international accreditation. For example, if you are in a pharmaceuticals industry, your need be accreditation of WHO-GMP, UKMHRA and USFDA. These certifications are mandatory and prerequisite to launch your brand into international market. You cannot get all certification in a day or two. Firstly, you will get permission of plant audit and if things go smoothly, then within six months or one year, you might get certification. Before audit, you have to install latest approved machinery with fully centrally air-condition plant. All these will take not less than 3-5 years. Finally, you have to achieve you mission by providing quality brands to global healthcare customers. Similarly, you can plan your study or career in a time bound schedule. Mission changes after every accomplishment.

Role of Objective in Career Mapping

Objective is nothing but to achieving desired accomplishment. It could be salary increment, promotion or admission in part time MBA. For example, I will not marry till I get Rs. 50,000 per month or I will not go back to hometown until I get my first promotion or I will work hard to change my designation and reputation in the company. For timely achievement of objective, you need to invest an extra honest effort.

Role of Target in Career Mapping

Target varies from junior level to senior level and skilled worker to non-skilled worker. Target of a rickshaw puller is based on daily basis. He has to pay Rs. 20 daily to rickshaw owner and the rest he will utilize in food and lodging. For sales executive, it could be monthly, but for a sales manager, it could be monthly, quarterly, half yearly and annually. It is strictly time bound. Target of January month cannot be achieved in the month of February. By hook or crook, you have to achieve target on monthly basis.

Stages of Professional Life

Like product life cycle, professional career cycle has five stages. All stages have its own importance and we should know prior to start our career, so that we could do better in professional life.

Exploratory: The moment we start our professional career, exploratory stage starts and it goes up to 30 years in totality. Here, generally, lot of switch over in job happens because of instability in nature and lesser amount of patience and decision making capability. In this stage, any one can change job for some small amount of money or due to small rift with colleague or boss.

Development: We can say this stage after 30th year because in this stage, most of the professionals settle down and become more responsible for family. In this stage, before making any job change, we think thousand times because we have to run family and due to this responsibility, we change our switchover attitude.

Growth: This stage starts after the age of 40 and goes up to 50 years. In this stage, we become more responsible and more visionary. Here, job changing attitude and chances of getting job also decreases. We concentrate here more and more on skills and accomplishment of target both, personal and professional.

Maturity: This is the prime time of job and here our attitude becomes like an employer and we get some highly satisfactory position such as CEO or department head. Here we make decision very carefully. We hardly think of changing job in this stage. We think more and work less here. Because we have to think to earn more and more money for the augmentation of profitability of organization. In this stage, we do best contribution for the family and society. This stage ranges from 50 to 60.

Decline: It is an old adage "Good start is half done" and the second proverb is "all well if end well". Here, in this stage, we should attach with some social work or academic institution to trend new comers into the job market.

Career Mapping Strategy

The career mapping plan is made up of nine specific steps as follows:

Know Yourself

Deciding on a career is easy for some people and hard for some, but planning can help make it easier. The first part of planning can help you to decide on career options, and then the rest can help you to achieve the career goals you set after making the decision.

The first step in the decision process is to know yourself.

Know what you are interested in. Do you love to solve math equations or write stories, study biology or paint? Beyond knowing what you are fascinated by, you need to evaluate your skills. Include both your academic strengths and others like athletics and communication. Could you work in a cubicle or do you need to be outdoors? Do you prefer working by yourself or in a team? What sort of pace is best for you: slow, moderate, fast or frenzied?

Many companies and career centres, including those on college campuses, offer career assessment tests that ask you all sorts of questions in order to analyze your interests and your strengths. Then, they will provide you with a list of possible careers to pursue.

After determining your strengths and interests, which may give you a handful of career options, do some exploration. Research the careers you are still considering on the internet or go to your local library. The reference section will have books that explain jobs with information about salaries, hours, skill requirements, etc. Another better way to actually learn about jobs you are interested in is to talk to people working in them if you can, or arrange to shadow them. But the best way is to intern if you can.

Now that you are down to the decision-making process, you should consider your options in the way that you make decisions. If you are a logical decision maker, use a pro and con list for each. If you go with your instincts, listen to what your gut is telling you. Once you have made your decision, make your plan.

Creating a support system including a career counselor may be particularly helpful at this juncture.

Starting Over or Refocusing

If you are already in mid-career, but seeking to make a career change, you should go through a slightly different process.

The first step is still know yourself, but at a mid-point in your career, there are other questions that need to be answered. What things have you liked about your career so far? Working alone, or in a team? Do you like being incharge or being left alone? What paced environment do you need? At this point, you will also have to make decisions based partly on income needs as well. Do you have family to support? House payments or other large bills? What skills have helped make you successful to this point? Are you a persuasive speaker or a peacemaker at work? Do you have a head for great ideas, or for laying out the plans to make them reality?

Soliciting help from a career counselor may also help you through this process. Before making a career change, try talking to people in the field you want to pursue. A switch will take hard work and time, but after making your decision and mapping, a plan to get there it is possible.

Identifying Your Market

The next step is to identify who your market is. It's the same step a business goes through. Decide which industries or companies are most likely to continue to grow and need you.

The Marketing Plan

If you are working long hours, not making the money you want, and are quite unhappy, it may be a matter of focus. Decide which aspect of your profession is the most appealing for you and develop a plan to market your knowledge, skills and experience to get the position you want.

Identifying Your Strengths and Weaknesses

The idea is to maximize your strengths and minimize your weaknesses. But first, you have to know what they are. Ask the people in your life you most respect to help you with this one. Put them down on paper. It may give you a new understanding of you.

The Positioning Statement

In order to be good at what we do, we have to know what business we are in. The positioning statement is no more than one paragraph long. It spells out here who I am, and here how I'm going to position myself going forward, and here are my capabilities, and here, how I fit into my industry or company.

The Action Plan

Now that you know what you want to do for the next year or two, you need to identify the tactics you use to carry it out. You might include research, talking to experts in your industry, and mirroring people who are already successful doing what you plan to do.

The Financial Plan

The key here is to understand that a change in career direction may have an impact of your finances. I recommend you determine up-front what could happen, good or not so good, and have a plan to deal with it.

The Review

How often should you stop along your journey? Take a look at where you are on your map: check weather patterns and road conditions. If you are new to "mapping", I suggest you to do it once a week. Once you are more comfortable with the process, once a month is probably enough. The key is to set a pattern for regularly looking at your progress.

Today's job market is changing so rapidly that the people who hope to do well are those who have an idea about where they are going and how they are going to get there. I see too many of us making career decisions without a real strategy behind them. It's a little like ready.... Fire! ... Aim! Occasionally, you'll get lucky and hit the target. Most often you won't.

Creating a Personal Career Map

Whether you are unemployed or have an unfulfilling job, you probably suffer from an ailment that plagues many people: career disorientation. You are not where you want to be professionally. Somewhere along the road to professional happiness, you veered off course and lost your way. If you are driving and become lost, a map is a handy tool to help get back on course. A career map is just as useful in curing career disorientation. Once you know the path you want to take, it is much easier to get where you want to go. These four key elements will be covered:

1. Finding the Big Picture,
2. Do Some Research,
3. Start Marketing Yourself,
4. Plan for the Unexpected.

1. *Finding the Big Picture*

To create a career map, you must be able to take a step back and examine your position. More often than not, you may need to take many steps before the big picture becomes visible. The whole purpose of a career map is to create a path to your end goal. Being able to envision the entire path is crucial. As you step back to examine your situation, ask yourself these questions:

- How far into the future do you want to plan? One year? Five years? Ten years?
- What job characteristics are most important to you? Location? Salary? Room for Promotion?
- Is there flexibility for unexpected detours? You never know when a spouse will find a job in another city or when a new boss will make your current job unbearable.

2. *Do Some Research*

Planning should not be a stationary act. A vital part of effective career mapping is gathering information. After all, you cannot fully prepare for a journey unless you have a detailed understanding of the places you want to go. Determining the path you want to take for the next few years requires a lot of legwork. You must identify the specific actions you need to take on the road to success and fulfillment. There are numerous methods to obtain all the information necessary for creating a sound career map. Some of the most popular choices include:

- Reading trade magazines and professional industry analysis.
- Interviewing industry experts.
- Finding a mentor who is already successful in the job you hope aspire to be in one day.

3. *Start Marketing Yourself*

As you examine your path to success, you must determine how to get yourself on that path. This means you need to be in contact with the companies and/or industries you see in your future. As you already know, landing the job you want is not an easy task. That is why, marketing is an essential part of career mapping. Above all else, a self-marketing strategy for career mapping should address these three issues:

- *Market Identification*: Just, like a business must decide on the customers to whom it will sell its product, you must decide on the companies and industries to which you will sell yourself. Be specific, having only a general idea will leave you unfocused. Make a list of specifics so that you can properly allocate your time and effort.
- *Strength/Weakness Identification*: When a business sells its product, it does not just to tell you the product's name. Advertisements emphasize the advantages of a product. You need emphasize your strengths and downplay your weaknesses as you market yourself. Have your closest friends and colleagues help you compile a list of your positive and negative characteristics.
- *Mission Statement*: It may seem trivial to actual develop a mission statement for yourself, but they perform a very valuable function. Creating a mission statement requires you to concisely explain your goals. In doing this, you remove frivolous details and better focus yourself.

4. *Plan for the Unexpected*

Often times, as a person develops their career map he or she realizes that they are far off course. This is perfectly normal, but it also means that getting on the right road will require a change of direction.

What the future holds is always a mystery. Drastically changing your life can only complicate things. A very important concern to have is your financial stability. A career map is only valuable when it is realistic, so it should address any of your financial concerns. As you plan for the future, ensure you have a financial plan to tackle the worst-case scenario. With each step along the way, your career map should answer the question "Can I afford to continue on?" And the answer must be yes.

Career Path

Career path is a great way because it provides us with the most direct way of measuring the return on the time and talent investment we are doing in current job. However, this raises the question: how do I create the map of my career path so that I can track my progress against it. Easier said than done, right? Here are the ingredients I have used to map my own career and of people who have asked me for career advice:

1. ***Your value system***: These are the set of values you live your life with (or want to live with). They define who you are, and what are acceptable and unacceptable paths of life for you.
2. ***Your life goal***: Every career map needs a rallying point: the major objective of life, the reason you want to live and feel motivated to work at all. Defining this takes effort, but this needs to be a clearly defined (and mentally visible) goal 'significantly' down the road.
3. ***Your strengths and weaknesses***: These are the foundations on which you will build your career, so, it is essential you know them well. A good career map uses the strengths and avoids the weaknesses.
4. ***Your likes and dislikes***: A great career path is sustainable only when you do what you like to do, at least most of the time. So, it is useful to know them in advance.

5. ***Your current and desired skills***: What skills you possess and are working towards are necessary to determine a starting point of the career as well as direction of career change at any given point of time.

If you know all of these aspects of your life, mapping a career path can be broken like this:

1. Break the goal into 1-2 year milestones, each milestone should be defined in a SMART way. This is the hardest part because this needs to take care of your value system as well as your strength profile. A project management approach will help here, with the involvement of a career counsellor or a mentor.
2. For the immediate milestone, figure out what you need to be doing now in order to reach there. This may mean changing your role or company or both, so, this is a careful decision. Also, this needs to make sure your likes and dislikes are taken care of, because this will involve learning new skills and it better be in an area you like.
3. Write down your plan for next 12 months and make sure you discuss with your manager so that he/she understands your aspirations. If he/she is not bought in, it may be much more difficult to achieve.

Make sure you review this entire plan as well as the ingredients above every quarter or so (depends on the pace at which your company/project/life is moving). Be open for changing any of these. Typically, the value system will not change at all, goal will change very slowly, and others can change rapidly. What has been your recipe for career planning? Do you think career can be planned? I will be interested in knowing your thoughts about this.

Summary

Planning before you act allows you to make focused moves. Once you've plotted your course, you must act without hesitation. Don't forget to check your career map regularly to ensure you have not veered off course. Make forecasts and continue to plan. When the job market is rough, the people that do well are those that have a strong idea of where they are trying to go. Remember, driving is a lot easier when you keep your eyes on the road. Happy planning.

Career mapping is nowadays a very important tool to be successful in highly competitive professional career. Whole career path can be divided into four stages, exploratory, development, growth, maturity and finally decline. This career path can be defined by linking with vision, mission, objective and target.

You can plan your career either you want to be an employee whole of life or in mid of your employment, you will start your own venture. Starting a new venture requires lot of experience, capital and correct selection of business. Failure in business is majorly due to unplanned expansion, unknowingly or knowingly violation of legal documentation that decrease control and business in partnership. It is an old proverb, "partnership in wife is better than partnership in business". Apart from this, it requires lots of risk if you have not done feasibility study in advance.

Career mapping is charting an employee's path to success. Just as companies who use a business plan as a "road map", find the path easier to negotiate, people who use a "career map", have a much better chance of reaching their destination. Making a career map can be beneficial at initial stage of the career.

If you're just entering/re-entering the job market, or perhaps been in the fray for decades, career mapping can prove to be an invaluable tool. Particularly, if you are thinking of switching fields. More importantly, the "C-Map" is necessary to help you better navigate the rapidly changing workplace rules.

Chapter two

INTERVIEW TECHNIQUE

An interview is a conversation between two or more people (the interviewer and the interviewee) where questions are asked by the interviewer to obtain information from the interviewee. This takes off some of the performance pressure, but be intentional nonetheless. Come prepared with thoughtful questions about the field and the company. Interviews are an important and a crucial part of recruitment process. The person taking the interview of the candidate has to be well prepared in advance. Concerns like the location of the interview, the time table, the structure of the question strategy, style of taking the interview needs to be decided beforehand so that nothing is left ambiguous in.

Job Interview

A job interview is a process in which a potential employee is evaluated by an employer for prospective employment in their company, organization, or firm, and was established in the late 16th century.

Role

A job interview typically precedes the hiring decision, and is used to evaluate the candidate. The interview is usually preceded by the evaluation of submitted résumés from interested candidates, then selecting a small number of candidates for interviews. The job interview is considered one of the most useful tools for evaluating potential employees. It also demands significant resources from the employer, yet has been demonstrated to be notoriously unreliable in identifying the optimal person for the job.

Multiple rounds of job interviews may be used where there are many candidates or the job is particularly challenging or desirable. Earlier rounds may involve fewer staff from the employers and will typically be much shorter and less in-depth. A common initial interview form is the phone interview, a job interview conducted over the telephone. This is especially common when the candidates do not live near the employer and has the advantage of keeping costs low for both sides.

Once all candidates have been interviewed, the employer typically selects the most desirable candidate and begins the negotiation of a job offer.

Preparation

It is very important to be well prepared for an interview. According to the University of Delaware's career centre, a common reason employers give for not hiring an applicant is the inability of the applicant to fully explain the contents of his or her résumé. Therefore, it is paramount to be able to discuss in detail every item listed in one's resume, and if possible, to give examples when appropriate. It is also wise to research the company before the interview. To avoid being nervous, the applicant should practice answering difficult questions. Good sources of interview questions can be found by searching the Internet.

Process

A typical job interview has a single candidate meeting with between one and three persons representing the employer; the potential supervisor of the employee is usually involved in the interview process. A larger interview panel will often have a specialized human resources worker. While the meeting can be over in as little as 15 minutes, job interviews usually last less than two hours. The bulk of the job interview will entail the interviewers asking the candidate questions about his or her job history, personality, work style and other factors relevant to the job. The candidate will usually be given a chance to ask any questions at the end of the interview. These questions are strongly encouraged since they allow the interviewee to acquire more information about the job and the company, but they can also demonstrate the candidate's strong interest in them. A candidate should follow up the interview with a thank you letter, expressing his or her appreciation for the opportunity to meet with the company representative. The thank you letter ensures that the candidate will stay fresh in the interviewer's mind. The primary purpose of the job interview is to assess the candidate's suitability for the job, although the candidate will also be assessing the corporate culture and demands of the job.

Candidates for lower paid and lower skilled positions tend to have much simpler job interviews than do candidates for more prestigious positions. For instance, a lawyer's job interview will be much more demanding than that of a retail cashier. Most job interviews are formal; the larger the firm, the more formal and structured the interview will tend to be. Candidates generally dress slightly better than they would for work, with a suit (called an interview suit) being appropriate for a white-collar job interview.

Types of Interview

- Behavioural interview.
- Stress interview.
- Technical interview.
- Case interview.
- Informational interview.
- Screening interview.
- Specific job opening.
- Directive style.
- Meandering style.
- Audition.
- Group interview.
- Tag-Team interview.
- Mealtime interview.
- Follow-up interview.
- Exit interview.
- Cognitive interview.
- Computer-assisted personal interviewing.
- Ladder interview.

- Mall-intercept personal interview.
- Mock interview.
- Parent-teacher interview.
- Structured interview.
- Semi-structured interview.
- Unstructured interview.

Behavioural Interview

A common type of job interview in the modern workplace is the behavioural interview or behavioural event interview. This type of interview is based on the notion that a job candidate's previous behaviours are the best indicators of future performance. In behavioural interviews, the interviewer asks candidates to recall specific instances where they were faced with a set of circumstances, and how they reacted. Typical behavioural interview questions:

- "Tell me about a project you worked on where the requirements changed midstream. What did you do?"
- "Tell me about a time when you took the lead on a project. What did you do?"
- "Describe the worst project you worked on."
- "Describe a time you had to work with someone you didn't like."
- "Tell me about a time when you had to stick by a decision you had made, even though it made you very unpopular."
- "Give us an example of something particularly innovative that you have done that made a difference in the workplace."
- "What happened the last time you were late with a project?"

A bad hiring decision nowadays can be immensely expensive for an organization—cost of the hire, training costs, severance pay, loss of productivity, impact on morale, cost of re-hiring, etc. (Gallup international places the cost of a bad hire as being 3.2 times the individual's salary). Structured selection techniques have a better track record of identifying the soundest candidate than the old-style "biographical" interview.

Stress Interview

Stress interviews are still in common use. One type of stress interview is where the employer uses a succession of interviewers (one at a time or en masse) whose mission is to intimidate the candidate and keep him/her off-balance. The ostensible purpose of this interview: to find out how the candidate handles stress. Stress interviews might involve testing an applicant's behaviour in a busy environment. Questions about handling work overload, dealing with multiple projects, and handling conflict are typical.

Another type of stress interview may involve only a single interviewer who behaves in an uninterested or hostile manner. For example, the interviewer may not make eye contact, may roll his eyes or sigh at the candidate's answers, interrupt, turn his back, take phone calls during the interview, or ask questions in a demeaning or challenging style. The goal is to assess how the interviewee handles pressure or to purposely evoke emotional responses. This technique was also used in research protocols studying Stress and Type A (coronary-prone) behaviour because it would evoke hostility and even changes in blood pressure and heart rate in study subjects. The key to success for the candidate is to de-personalize the process. The interviewer is acting a role, deliberately and calculatedly trying to "rattle the cage". Once the candidate realizes that there is nothing personal behind the interviewer's approach, it is easier to handle the questions with aplomb. Example of stress interview questions:

- ***Sticky situation:*** "If you caught a colleague cheating on his expenses, what would you do?"
- ***Putting you on the spot:*** "How do you feel this interview is going?"
- ***Popping the balloon:*** "(deep sigh) Well, if that's the best answer you can give...(shakes head) Okay, what about this one...?"
- ***Oddball question:*** "What would you change about the design of the hockey stick?"

- ***Doubting your veracity:*** "I don't feel like we're getting to the heart of the matter here. Start again—tell me what really makes you tick."

Candidates may also be asked to deliver a presentation as part of the selection process. The "Platform Test" method involves having the candidate make a presentation to both the selection panel and other candidates for the same job. This is obviously highly stressful and is therefore useful as a predictor of how the candidate will perform under similar circumstances on the job. Selection processes in academic, training, airline, legal and teaching circles frequently involve presentations of this sort.

Technical Interview

This kind of interview focuses on problem solving and creativity. The questions aim at your problem-solving skills and likely show your ability and creativity. Sometimes, these interviews will be on a computer module with multiple-choice questions.

Case Interview

A case interview is a job interview in which the applicant is given a question/situation/problem/challenge and asked to resolve the situation. The case problem is often a business situation or a business case that the interviewer has worked on in real life.

After the applicant is given information about the case, the applicant is expected to ask the interviewer logical and sequential questions that will enable the applicant to understand the situation, probe deeper into relevant areas, gather pertinent information and arrive at a solution or recommendation for the question or situation at hand.

Case interviews are mostly used in hiring for management consulting and investment banking jobs. Firms use case interviews to evaluate analytical ability and problem-solving skills; they are looking not for a "correct answer" but for an understanding of how the applicant thinks and how the applicant approaches problems. During case interviews, interviewers are generally looking for the following skills:

- Numerical and verbal reasoning skills.

- Communication and presentation skills.
- Business skills and commercial awareness.

Candidates are often asked to estimate a specific number, often a commercial figure (such as market size or profitability). Candidates are expected to demonstrate reasoning rather than produce the exact answer.

A case interview can also be conducted as a group exercise. Here, several candidates are given some briefing materials on a business problem and asked to discuss and agree upon a solution. The interviewers normally sit around the exterior of the room as silent observers. They assess candidates' communication and interaction as well as analytical thinking and commercial awareness.

Informational Interview

An informational interview is a meeting in which a job seeker asks for advice rather than employment. The job seeker uses the interview to gather information on the field, find employment leads and expand their professional network. This differs from a job interview because the job seeker asks the questions. There may or may not be employment opportunities available. Informational interviews are initiated by the job seeker. There are many avenues the job seeker may pursue to obtain the informational interview. Career and social networking, newspaper want ads, job boards, placement services, company websites, human resource contacts, job search engines, and professional recruiters.

While the job seeker initiates the interview, he must follow the basic guidelines for interview etiquette. He must arrive promptly, dress appropriately, prepare informational questions, and make a good first impression.

Screening Interview

Companies use screening tools to ensure that candidates meet minimum qualification requirements. Computer programs are among the tools used to weed out unqualified candidates. (This is why you need a digital resume that is screening-friendly.) Sometimes, human professionals are the gatekeepers. Screening interviewers often have honed skills to determine whether there is anything that might disqualify you for the position. Remember, they do not need to know whether you are the best fit for the position, only whether you are not a match. For this reason, screeners tend to dig for dirt. Screeners will hone in on gaps in your employment history or pieces of information that look inconsistent. They also will want to know on the outset, whether you will be too expensive for the company.

Some tips for maintaining confidence during screening interviews:

- Highlight your accomplishments and qualifications.
- Get into the straightforward groove. Personality is not as important to the screener as verifying your qualifications. Answer questions directly and succinctly. Save your winning personality for the person making hiring decisions.
- Be tactful about addressing income requirements. Give a range, and try to avoid giving specifics by replying, "I would be willing to consider your best offer."
- If the interview is conducted by phone, it is helpful to have note cards with your vital information sitting next to the phone. That way, whether the interviewer catches you sleeping or vacuuming the floor, you will be able to switch gears quickly.

Specific Job Opening

This takes off some of the performance pressure, but be intentional nonetheless:

- Come prepared with thoughtful questions about the field and the company.
- Gain references to other people and make sure that the interviewer would be comfortable if you contact other people and use his or her name.
- Give the interviewer your card, contact information and resume.
- Write a thank you note to the interviewer.

Directive Style

In this style of interview, the interviewer has a clear agenda that he or she follows unflinchingly. Sometimes, companies use this rigid format to ensure parity between interviews; when interviewers ask each candidate the same series of questions, they can more readily compare the results. Directive interviewers rely upon their own questions and methods to tease from you what they wish to know. You might feel like you are being steam-rolled, or you might find the conversation develops naturally. Their style does not necessarily mean that they have dominance issues, although you should keep an eye open for these if the interviewer would be your supervisor.

Either way, remember:

- Flex with the interviewer, following his or her lead.
- Do not relinquish complete control of the interview. If the interviewer does not ask you for information that you think is important to proving your superiority as a candidate, politely interject it.

Meandering Style

This interview type, usually used by inexperienced interviewers, relies on you to lead the discussion. It might begin with a statement like "tell me about yourself", which you can use to your advantage. The interviewer might ask you another broad, open-ended question before falling into silence. This interview style allows you tactfully to guide the discussion in a way that best serves you.

The following strategies, which are helpful for any interview, are particularly important when interviewers use a non-directive approach:

- Come to the interview prepared with highlights and anecdotes of your skills, qualities and experiences. Do not rely on the interviewer to spark your memory. Note down some notes that you can refer throughout the interview.
- Remain alert to the interviewer. Even if you feel like, you can take the driver's seat and go in any direction

you wish, remain respectful of the interviewer's role. If he or she becomes more directive during the interview, adjust.

- Ask well-placed questions. Although the open format allows you significantly to shape the interview, running with your own agenda and dominating the conversation means that you run the risk of missing important information about the company and its needs.

Audition

For some positions, such as computer programmers or trainers, companies want to see you in action before they make their decision. For this reason, they might take you through a simulation or brief exercise in order to evaluate your skills. An audition can be enormously useful to you as well, since it allows you to demonstrate your abilities in interactive ways that are likely familiar to you. The simulations and exercises should also give you a simplified sense of what the job would be like. If you sense that other candidates have an edge on you in terms of experience or other qualifications, requesting an audition can help level the playing field.

To maximize on auditions, remember to:

- Clearly understand the instructions and expectations for the exercise. Communication is half the battle in real life, and you should demonstrate to the prospective employer that you make the effort to do things right the first time by minimizing confusion.
- Treat the situation as if you are a professional with responsibility for the task laid before you. Take ownership of your work.
- Brush up on your skills before an interview if you think they might be tested.

Group Interview

Interviewing simultaneously with other candidates can be disconcerting, but it provides the company with a sense of your leadership potential and style. The group interview helps the company get a glimpse of how you interact with peers—are you timid or bossy, are you attentive or do you seek attention, do others turn to you instinctively, or do you compete for authority? The interviewer also wants to view what your tools of persuasion are: do you use argumentation and careful reasoning to gain support or do you divide and conquer? The interviewer might call on you to discuss an issue with the other candidates, solve a problem collectively, or discuss your peculiar qualifications in front of the other candidates. This environment might seem overwhelming or hard to control, but there are a few tips that will help you navigate the group interview successfully:

- Observe to determine the dynamics the interviewer establishes and try to discern the rules of the game. If you are unsure of what is expected from you, ask for clarification from the interviewer.
- Treat others with respect while exerting influence over others.
- Avoid overt power conflicts, which will make you look uncooperative and immature.
- Keep an eye on the interviewer throughout the process so that you do not miss important cues.

Tag-team Interview

Expecting to meet with Ms. Glenn, you might find yourself in a room with four other people: Ms. Glenn, two of her staff, and the Sales Director. Companies often want to gain the insights of various people when interviewing candidates. This method of interviewing is often attractive for companies that rely heavily on team cooperation. Not only does the company want to know whether your skills balance that of the company, but also whether you can get along with the other workers. In some companies, multiple people will interview you simultaneously. In other companies, you will proceed through a series of one-on-one interviews. Some helpful tips for maximizing on this interview format:

- Treat each person as an important individual. Gain each person's business card at the beginning of the meeting, if possible, and refer to each person by name. If there are several people in the room at once, you might wish to scribble down their names on a sheet of paper according to where each is sitting. Make eye contact with each person and speak directly to the person asking each question.

- Use the opportunity to gain as much information about the company as you can. Just as each interviewer has a different function in the company, they each have a unique perspective. When asking questions, be sensitive not to place anyone in a position that invites him to compromise confidentiality or loyalty.
- Bring at least double the anecdotes and sound-bites to the interview as you would for a traditional one-on-one interview. Be ready to illustrate your main message in a variety of ways to a variety of people.
- Prepare psychologically to expend more energy and be more alert than you would in a one-on-one interview. Stay focused and adjustable.

Mealtime Interview

For many, interviewing over a meal sounds like a professional and digestive catastrophe in the making. If you have difficulty chewing gum while walking, this could be a challenge. With some preparation and psychological readjustment, you can enjoy the process. Meals often have a cementing social effect—breaking bread together tends to facilitate deals, marriages, friendships, and religious communion. Mealtime interviews rely on this logic, and expand it.

Particularly when your job requires interpersonal acuity, companies want to know what you are like in a social setting. Are you relaxed and charming or awkward and evasive? Companies want to observe not only how you handle a fork, but also, how you treat your host, any other guests, and the serving staff. Some basic social tips help ease the complexity of mixing food with business:

- Take cues from your interviewer, remembering that you are the guest. Do not sit down until your host does. Order something slightly less extravagant than your interviewer. If he badly wants you to try a particular dish, oblige him. If he recommends an appetizer to you, he likely intends to order one himself. Do not begin eating until he does. If he orders coffee and dessert, do not leave him eating alone.

- If your interviewer wants to talk business, do so. If she and the other guests discuss their upcoming travel plans or their families, do not launch into business.
- Try to set aside dietary restrictions and preferences. Remember, the interviewer is your host. It is rude to be finicky unless you absolutely must. If you must, be as tactful as you can. Avoid phrases like: "I do not eat mammals," or "Shrimp makes my eyes swell and water."
- Choose manageable food items, if possible. Avoid barbeque ribs and spaghetti.
- Find a discrete way to check your teeth after eating. Excuse yourself from the table for a moment.
- Practice eating and discussing something important simultaneously.
- Thank your interviewer for the meal.

Follow-up Interview

Companies bring candidates back for second and sometimes third or fourth interviews for a number of reasons. Sometimes, they just want to confirm that you are the amazing worker they first thought you to be. Sometimes, they are having difficulty deciding between a short-list of candidates. Other times, the interviewer's supervisor or other decision makers in the company want to gain a sense of you before signing a hiring decision.

The second interview could go in a variety of directions, and you must prepare for each of them. When meeting with the same person again, you do not need to be as assertive in your communication of your skills. You can focus on cementing rapport, understanding where the company is going and how your skills mesh with the company vision and culture. Still, the interviewer should view you as the answer to their needs. You might find yourself negotiating a compensation package.

Alternatively, you might find that you are starting from the beginning with a new person. Some tips for managing second interviews:

- Be confident. Accentuate what you have to offer and your interest in the position.
- Probe tactfully to discover more information about the internal company dynamics and culture.
- Walk through the front door with a plan for negotiating a salary.
- Be prepared for anything: to relax with an employer or to address the company's qualms about you.

Exit Interview

An exit interview is an interview conducted by an employer of a departing employee. They are generally conducted by a relatively neutral party, such as a human resources staff member, so that the employee will be more inclined to be candid, as opposed to worrying about burning bridges. For this reason, some companies opt to employ a third party to conduct the interviews and provide feedback. The purpose of an exit interview is usually to gather data for improving working conditions and retaining employees. Common questions asked in exit interviews are, "What are your primary reasons for leaving", "What did you find most satisfying about your job", "What did you find most frustrating about your job", "Were there any company policies or procedures that made your work more difficult", etc. Many career advisers recommend treating an exit interview like a hiring interview, in that criticism of the past employer should be limited to statements about the company as a whole, rather than specific individuals.

Schools may also conduct exit interviews with students before graduation, or even as a requirement of it. This is sometimes called a graduation interview.

Cognitive Interview

A cognitive interview is a procedure designed for use in police interviews that involve witnesses. There were two main forces behind the development of the CI. The first was the need to improve the effectiveness of police interviews when questioning witnesses. The second was to apply the results of psychological research to this area, particularly the work of Elizabeth Loftus, whose research had already dispelled the myth that eyewitnesses memory operates like a video camera. 'Psychology, The Complete Companion'.

Cognitive interviewing is less effective on eyewitness accounts than the courts would prefer as the witnesses can be easily persuaded or lead into believing certain details which are not true, especially if they are more believable or expected from the situation. This can be due to even simple aspects of the questioning such as tones or choice of phrase or wording.

For example, if one was to ask 'did you see a broken headlight?' when referring to a car accident, the witness is more likely to state there was none than if they were asked 'did you see the broken headlight?' which could lead the witness to believe that there was one which they had not noticed, and so they are less likely to counter the interviewer by stating there was none. Subconsciously, most witnesses wish to please their interviewer and so, this will also contribute to their recall or willingness to be persuaded.

Computer-assisted Personal Interviewing

Computer-assisted personal interviewing (CAPI) is an interviewing technique similar to computer-assisted telephone interviewing, except that the interview takes place in person instead of over the telephone. The respondent or the interviewer sits in front of a computer terminal and enters the answers into the computer. If an emphasis is put on the fact, that no personal interviewer is present, sometimes the term Computer-assisted self-interviewing (CASI) is also used:

- The respondent sits in front of a computer terminal and answers a questionnaire on the screen by using the keyboard or a mouse.
- Help screens and courteous error messages are provided.
- The colourful screens and on and off-screen stimuli add to the respondent's interest and involvement in the task.

- This method has been classified as a personal interview technique since an interviewer is usually present to serve as a host and to guide the respondent as needed.
- This approach is used in shopping malls, preceded by the intercept and screening process.
- It is also used to conduct business-to-business research at trade shows or conventions. For example, CAPI is used as the method of data collection for the British Crime Survey.

Advantages

This form of interview is substantially cheaper when a large number of respondents is required, because

- There is no need to recruit or pay surveyors.
- There is no need to transcribe the results into a computer form. The computer program can be constructed so as to place the results directly in a format that can be read by statistical analysis programs such as PSPP or DAP.
- The program can be placed on a website, potentially catching a worldwide audience.

Disadvantages

- The survey is likely to attract only respondents who are "computer savvy", thus introducing potential bias to the survey.

Ladder Interview

A ladder interview is an interviewing technique where a seemingly simple response to a question is pushed by the interviewer in order to find subconscious motives. It begins with a simple question, and then another question is asked about that response. For example, an interviewer may ask: "How come you skipped class?" and the response may be: "I went out with my friends". The next question would be something like "Why did you go out with your friends?"

The first responses are generally functional justifications, like "I went out with my friends because I wanted some pizza", or "I wanted some pizza because I used to eat it as a child"; but eventually the interviewer hopes to reach a virtue justification like "It's good to be childish". Then it is fair to conclude that the interviewee skipped class because he valued childishness. This technique is used for marketing in order to see what values inspire the consumption of the particular product. A chocolate bar producer would do this test so they can match the most common terminal virtue to their product in an advertisement. For example, the virtue of justice, or a virtue of efficiency, or in the above example, the virtue of childhood.

Mall-intercept Personal Interview

A mall-intercept personal interview is a survey whereby respondents are intercepted in shopping in malls. The process involves stopping the shoppers, screening them for appropriateness, and either administering the survey on the spot or inviting them to a research facility located in the mall to complete the interview. While not representative of the population in general, shopping mall customers do constitute a major share of the market for many products.

Mock Interview

A mock interview is sometimes a videotaped interview, and one of the very best ways to prepare for a real life employment interview. [neutrality disputed] It allows you to gain experience and practice in answering questions which you are likely to be asked by the recruiter. After the interview, you can watch the videotape to see yourself as others see you, and in academic career's offices, you may be given constructive feedback regarding your interviewing style and how you responded to the questions.

Preparing for a Mock Interview

You need to make a checklist of requirements for the interview:

1. Have an updated copy of your CV—preferably the same, as the one forwarded to the employer.
2. When planning for the interview, see also you need to think (and remember...!) what you have put on the

application form. As part of your pre-interview planning, it might be an idea to take a copy of the application you submitted to the organization, so you can see what you have written.

3. Make sure you know the correct directions and venue—find a map if need be.
4. Make a note of the person who is interviewing you.
5. If you have a list of questions you are going to ask, ensure they are included with your information you are taking to the interview.

Interview Preparation—What to Wear?

Make sure the outfit you have selected is clean and ironed. Select clothes that you feel comfortable in the clothes and manner in which you present yourself do reflect an aspect of your personality. Interview preparation includes your wardrobe!

Interview Preparation—Do You have the Answers?

Have you thought about the impression you wish to convey during the interview?

Part of your interview preparation is to think about the qualities your prospective employer will be looking for possibly: Responsibility, Honesty, Loyalty, Initiative, Drive.

In summary, someone who would be an asset to the organization. Think about how you can convey these qualities during your interview preparation, if you think they are qualities that you possess!

As part of your interview preparation, also prepare for behavioural questions. A behavioural question is one that asks the interviewee for an example of a specific time when a certain behaviour or skill has been applied. The underlying philosophy is "past behaviour predicts future behaviour"—so think of actual examples that support your skills and knowledge. Telephone interview.

Interview Preparation—Who?

Important general questions to research during your interview preparation are:

1. What is the core business of this organization?
2. Who are their strategic clients?
3. Has there been any publicity around the organization lately that you should be aware of?
4. Is the organization involved in any form of social responsibility projects?

Interview Preparation—Questions About the Job

During your interview preparation, think about questions that might be important to your specific interests/skills/ requirements. For example:

Is overtime required in the job?

What computer skills are required?

What interaction with customers—internal and external is required?

What workflow systems are in place?

Does the organization have a flexi-time policy?

What training is provided on the job?

And many more. Remember—your interview preparation is just as important as the interview itself!

Parent-teacher Interview

A parent-teacher interview (also a parent-teacher conference) is a once per term, short conference between students, parents and teachers. The interview is a chance for parents to meet their child's teachers and review any issues or concerns the parents or teachers may have with child/student's performance. These interviews are usually between five to fifteen minutes long. Parent-teacher interviews are a tradition in Western school systems.

Structured Interview

A structured interview (also known as a standardized interview or a researcher-administered survey) is a quantitative research method commonly employed in survey research. The aim of this approach is to ensure that each interviewee is presented with exactly the same questions in the same order. This ensures that answers can be reliably aggregated and that comparisons can be made with confidence between sample subgroups or between different survey periods.

Structured interviews are a means of collecting data for a statistical survey. In this case, the data is collected by an interviewer rather than through a self-administered questionnaire. Interviewers read the questions exactly as they appear on the survey questionnaire. The choice of answers to the questions is often fixed (close-ended) in advance, though open-ended questions can also be included within a structured interview.

A structured interview also standardizes the order in which questions are asked of survey respondents, so the questions are always answered within the same context. This is important for minimizing the impact of context effects, where the answers given to a survey question can depend on the nature of preceding questions. Though context effects can never be avoided, it is often desirable to hold them constant across all respondents.

Semi-structured Interview

A semi-structured interview is a method of research used in the social sciences. While a structured interview has a formalized, limited set questions, a semi-structured interview is flexible, allowing new questions to be brought up during the interview as a result of what the interviewee says. The interviewer in a semi-structured interview generally has a framework of themes to be explored.

Unstructured Interview

Unstructured interviews are a method of interviews where questions can be changed or adapted to meet the respondent's intelligence, understanding or belief. Unlike a structured interview, they do not offer a limited, pre-set range of answers for a respondent to choose, but instead advocate listening to how each individual person responds to the question.

The method to gather information using this technique is fairly limited, for example, most surveys that are carried out via telephone or even in person tend to follow a structured method. Outside of sociology, the use of such interviews are very limited.

How will You Conduct Interview of Executives?

Q.1. Introduce yourself and your family.

(You should know the earning and non-earning family members and their qualifications that will give you insight about the family status and their need.)

Q.2. What is your career plan and what do you want to achieve within five years from now?

(This input will give you either the person is planned or not and how much salary hike and promotion he wants to get within the stipulated time period.)

Q.3. When you are supposed to marry?

(This question is important for hiring female candidate because if she will marry within the probation period or even within one year, then don't hire.)

Q.4. Will it be convenient for you to come every day after travelling more than one hour journey?

(Try to hire people who reside nearby because it will be comfortable for the candidate and it retains employee for long time.)

Q.5. What is your expectation about salary package?

Q.6. Why do you expect this much salary, why not more than this?

(This will guide you about the convincing skills and justification skills.)

Q.7. How soon you want to join?

(If he is ready to join immediately and he is working, then he is not an ethical professional because he should take care of notice period which is generally one month in India.)

Q.8. Do you want to study further for professional growth?

(This will give about his ambition and planning and you can plan his performance accordingly.)

Q.9. Who is your reporting manager?

(You can cross-check the background and reality of data provided to you.)

Q.10. Do you know something about this company?

(This will guide you about his planning. If he doesn't know this company very well, then he is weak in survey, therefore he can't hit the target on the head.)

Q.11. What is your next promotion plan and how will you achieve that plan?

(This will give you insight about his career planning and his vision. If he can plan his career, that means he is capable to design others career too.)

Q.12. Why do you want to leave your present company?

(You must ask question if he says my boss is very rude or I am getting lots of pressure of target or not getting increment or confirmation. If he is not having good coordination with boss, then boss will naturally rude. If he cannot take pressure of target in present company then he will do the same here. If he is a non-performer then he couldn't get increment and promotion on time.)

Q.13. Why do you want to join this company?

Q.14. Can I talk to your immediate boss?

(If he boldly says yes then he is confident. But you must check the reality because sometime you will get wrong contact number or he might give you his friend's contact number. In this case, you must take landline number only.)

Q.15. How many papers did you study in graduation?

(This question is good to know that really he is a graduate or he has arranged false degree.)

Q.16. Why don't you start your own business?

(Here he can share with you if he directly or indirectly involve in family business. If he is directly or indirectly involved in family business or he has plan in short run then don't hire.)

Q.17. What is your current CTC (Cost to the Company)?

Q.18. Do you have copy of appointment and current salary slip?

Q.19. How do you know this company?

Q.20. Have you ever applied to this company earlier?

Q.21. What is your current job profile?

How will You Conduct Interview of a Manager?

Q.1. What is your current job profile?

Q.2. Who is your reporting?

Q.3. How many subordinates you have?

Q.4. In which levels are you working, middle management or top management?

Q.5. What is your achievement till now with the current organization?

Q.6. What is your current CTC?

Q.7. Do you have copy of appointment and current salary slip?

Q.8. How do you know this company?

Q.9. Have you ever applied to this company earlier?

Q.10. How many customers do you have to whom you can get business from very first month?

Q.11. Do you have top 10 customer's mobile no in your mobile phone right now?

Q.12. How will you motivate your subordinate to achieve their target and objective?

(For a good manager, it is mandatory that he must have skills how to design career map of subordinate, how to increase professional attitude, management skills and product knowledge.)

Q.13. How will you develop managerial skills in your team mates?

(Give them slowly and slowly authority to delegate, make decision, negotiate with customers. Guide him to develop presentation skills, strategy formulation skills and projects presentation skills for lets say marketing and sales planning for his region with pros and cons.)

Q.14. How many kids do you have?

Q.15. Your wife is also working?

Q.16. What is your next promotion plan and how will you achieve that plan?

Q.17. Why do you want to join this company?

Q.18. Can I talk to your immediate boss?

Q.19. Why do you want to leave your present company?

Q.20. How much salary do you expect from us?

Repertory Grid

The repertory grid is an interviewing technique which uses factor analysis to determine an idiographic measure of personality. It was devised by George Kelly in around 1955 and is based on his Personal Constructs theory of personality.

The repertory grid is a technique for identifying the ways that a person construes his or her experience. It provides information from which inferences about personality can be made, but it is not a personality test in the conventional sense. It is underpinned by a strong theory, the Personal Construct Theory developed by George Kelly first published in 1955.

A grid consists of four parts:

1. *A Topic*: It is about some part of the person's experience.
2. ***A set of elements, which are examples or instances of the Topic***: Working as a clinical psychologist, Kelly was interested in how his clients construed people in the roles they adopted towards the client, and so, originally, such terms as 'my father', 'my mother', 'an admired friend' and so forth were used. Since then, the grid has been used in much wider settings (educational, occupational, organizational) and so any well-defined set of words, phrases, or even brief behavioural vignettes can be used as elements. For example, to see how I construe the purchase of a car, a list of vehicles within my price range could make an excellent set of elements.
3. ***A set of constructs***: These are the basic terms that the client uses to make sense of the elements, and are always expressed as a contrast. Thus, the meaning of 'Good' depends on whether you intend to say 'Good versus Poor', as if you were construing a theatrical

performance, or 'Good versus Evil', as if you were construing the moral or ontological status of some more fundamental experience.

4. ***A set of ratings of elements on constructs***: Each element is positioned between the two extremes of the construct using a 5- or 7-point rating scale system; this is done repeatedly for all the constructs that apply and thus, its meaning to the client is captured, and statistical analysis varying from simple counting, to more complex multivariate analysis of meaning is made possible.

Constructs are regarded as personal to the client, who is psychologically similar to other people depending on the extent to which s/he would tend to use similar constructs, and similar ratings, in relating to a particular set of elements. And it is the way that the constructs are identified that makes a Repertory Grid unique.

The client is asked to consider the elements three at a time, and to identify a way in which two of the elements might be seen as alike, but distinct from, contrasted to, the third. For example, in considering a set of people as part of a topic dealing with personal relationships, a client might say that the element 'my father' and the element 'my boss' are similar because they are both fairly tense individuals, whereas the element 'my wife' is different because she is 'relaxed'. And so, we identify one construct that the individual uses when thinking about people: whether they are 'Tense as distinct from Relaxed'. (in practice, good grid interview technique would delve a little deeper and identify some more behaviourally explicit description of 'Tense versus Relaxed'.) All the elements are rated on the construct, further triads of elements compared and further constructs elicited, and the interview would continue, until no further constructs are obtained.

Using the Repertory Grid

Behavioural specificity is important. Careful interviewing to identify what the individual means by the words initially proposed, and careful consideration of the ratings the client wishes to use to position elements on constructs in order to express that meaning precisely, are required.

For example, when using a 5-point rating system to characterize the way in which a group of fellow-employees are viewed on the construct 'Keen and committed versus Energies elsewhere', a 1 indicating that the left pole of the construct applies ('Keen and committed') and a 5 indicating that the right pole of the construct applies ('Energies elsewhere') might be used. On being asked to rate all of the elements, our interviewee might reply that Tom merits a 2 (fairly keen and committed), Mary a 1 (very keen and committed), and Peter a 5 (his energies are very much outside the place of employment). The remaining elements (another five people in our example) are then rated on this construct.

Typically (and of course depending on the topic), people have a limited number of genuinely different constructs for any one topic: 6 to 16 are common when they talk about their job or their occupation, for example. The richness of our meaning structures comes from the many different ways in which a limited number of constructs can be applied to individual elements. We might discover that Tom is fairly keen, very experienced, lacks social skills, is a good technical supervisor, can be trusted to follow complex instructions accurately, has no sense of humour, will always return a favour, and only sometimes help his co-workers; while Mary is very keen, fairly experienced, has good social and technical supervisory skills, needs complex instructions explained to her, appreciates a joke, always returns favours, and is very helpful to her co-workers. Two very different and complex pictures, using just 8 constructs about one's co-workers.

Analysis of Results

Interesting and important information can be obtained by including self-elements such as 'Myself as I am now'; 'Myself as I would like to be' among other elements, where the topic permits.

A single grid can be analyzed for both content (eyeball inspection) and structure (cluster analysis, principal components analysis, and a variety of structural indices relating to the complexity and range of the ratings being the chief techniques used). Sets of grids are dealt with using one or other of a variety of content analysis techniques. A range of associated techniques can be used to provide very precise, operationally defined expressions of an interviewee's constructs, or a detailed expression of the interviewee's personal values, and all of these techniques are used in a collaborative way. The repertory grid is emphatically not a psychological 'test'; it is an exercise in the mutual negotiation of a person's meanings.

The repertory grid has found favour among both academics and practitioners in a great variety of fields because it has one unique characteristic. It provides a way of describing people's construct systems (loosely, understanding people's perceptions) without prejudging the terms of reference.

Unlike a conventional rating-scale questionnaire, it is not the investigator but the interviewee who provides the constructs on which a topic is rated. Market researchers, trainers, teachers, guidance counsellors, new product developers, sports scientists, and knowledge capture specialists are among the users who find the technique (originally developed for use in clinical psychology) helpful.

Interview of IIM Ahmedabad Passed Out

Intas is one of the leading pharmaceuticals company in India. Once upon a time it had planned to take IIM graduate to augment the profitability of the company. Interviewer asked one question which was very easy but confusing. Interviewer had given permission to management student to design salary package of his choice if his answer will be correct and fully convincing. Question was a case study, suppose you are a project manager of Intas and you are going to start your project with survey and all feasibility study but your subordinates are not happy with your decision. Your subordinates don't want to start project because they feel that project will be a big failure. In the last moment, you come to know that this project would be a big failure. Now do you think that you should take a U turn and ultimately you should follow the decision taken by your subordinates?

What will be your decision? He was selected because he said he would take back his decision and can save a huge loss of the company. But in this situation, any one will say no to have some ego.

Survey on Interview

This is my very common question that I ask frequently why did you chose bachelor study as art or commerce or science but no one had given satisfactory answer. Mostly said their marks were not up to the mark, that is why there was no choice but to arts. Even I asked so many questions with job seekers after bachelor of pharmacy, why didn't you join masteriate in pharmacy and why did you join MBA. Even in this, I got unsatisfactory and unplanned answer. In most of the cases, I find students need planning in advance so that they can do wonder after entering into the professional career but till now, students are taking subjects of arts and that hardly has significance in the professional era.

Sanjeev Jain, MD, Akums Drugs & Pharmaceuticals Ltd. Management colleges are not making aware to the passing out students about the common current salary package offered by the employer. This is a big challenge for fresher and employers take advantage of this weak point but in long-run retaining of under paid executive becomes problem some for the company as well. When employer asks where you want to see yourself after five years, then students say general manager or CEO but he is not well aware what could be the average salary of a general manager or a CEO?

In another way around, if employer asks what is your expectation now and what will be your expectation after five years. Even in this case, students answers remain unexplained and unsatisfactory because they don't know how much salary increment should be every year and how salary increment should be calculated for five years. If students answer wrong, then he or she lose a chance and for this, management college is totally responsible and not the students. Therefore, if ready students will be entering into the job market then, it will be good for both employer and employee because time is money. Another point getting job is tough and retaining good employee is very challenging. Hence, be ready like a fast food, then you can sell yourself as per you wish.

Daya K. Kaul, AGM, Akums Drugs & Pharmaceuticals Ltd.

Summary

In this fastest moving world of laptop, palm top, mobile and internet, processing time has shrunken and we are now accustomed to do the things fast. Management College should train the students according to the need of the hour and student should get more practical project work rather than mugging up theories. Role play is the best tool to develop practical exposure to the students. More and more guest lecture should be call upon by the management colleges for updating the student about whats happening into the professional fraternity. Not only to this, through corporate guest lecture student can make prior professional relation and interaction for better placement. Students should be ready for both offensive and defensive queries. Only going through with interview chapter, you cannot make yourself confident at the time of interview. Remember, you have to develop knowledge and negotiation skills for the success in interview today and always.

Chapter three

COUNSELING

Counseling is a behavioural control technique used by the supervisor to solve performance problems. As a counselor, the supervisor is a helper, discusses the employee's personal problems that are affecting his or her job performance, aiming to resolve them. Supervisory counseling is guidance of the employee's behaviour.

In other words, counseling is a process through which one person helps another by purposeful conversation in an understanding atmosphere. It seeks to establish a helping relationship in which the one counseled can express their thoughts and feelings in such a way as to clarify their own situation, come to terms with some new experience, see their difficulty more objectively, and so face their problem with less anxiety and tension. Its basic purpose is to assist the individual to make their own decision from among the choices available to them.

Role of Counselor

Supervisors use controls to help employees achieve objectives. An employee's problem performance is often related to non-job factors. Yet, personal problems generally get worse, not better without professional help. The supervisor is in the best position to spot and handle problems when they arise. He or she can use counseling to provide relief for the troubled employee.

An employee should be counseled when he or she has personal problems that affect job performance. Supervisors should recognize early signs. Signs of a troubled employee include: personal rifts with colleagues, pre-occupation, sudden change of behaviour due to work load or weak coordination, irritability due to family disputes, excessive drinking, difficulty in absorbing training, poor performance, weak coordination and control, demotivation and depression due to underpaid salary package, increment and promotion.

In the role of the counselor, the supervisor listens, limits, and refers. The supervisor uses active listening and reflective listening skills. By listening the supervisor helps the employee to feel valued and understood. The employee is encouraged to talk and explore and to understand more about how he or she feels and why. The employee can consider options and examine alternatives and may be able to choose a solution to his or her problems. The supervisor can help the employee develop clear objectives; to form specific action plans and to do, with support what needs to be done. The supervisor helps employees help themselves. In counseling, the supervisor limits comments to the employee's job performance, since the supervisor is not an expert in the problem area. The supervisor refers or gives information to the employee. Informing mainly passes along data and information.

Why do You Need Counseling?

Professionals are not problem creator, they are problem solver but few so-called professionals create problems and incur huge loss of organization. In other way around, problems can be created by the professionals, one, if you are a fresher in career and two, if you are highly experienced and highly qualified working under some manager who is lower than you in terms of experience and education. Sometimes, it happens when you get good hike in package and it remains convenient in other sense.

You need counseling when you have extra marital relation with your personal secretary or subordinates and you are not taking care of your family members as per their need and expectation. You need counseling if not reaching office on time or taking frequent leave with or without intimation.

You need counseling when your colleague or subordinate leaves the organization due to personal dispute and he writes down something bad about you or fact of past incidents. One day your employer asks about incidents once again, then you become hypersensitive and loose your emotion and even sometime you try to cry out to prove your loyalty.

You need counseling when you get scolded by your employer or boss due to loose coordination or loose controlling. Immature professional sometime submits resignation to the respective head. Here, emotion overrules the professionalism. Remember, professionalism is above all and requires lot of patience and control on emotion.

Types of Counseling

Counseling should be looked upon in terms of the amount of direction that the counselor gives the counselee. This direction ranges from full direction (directive counseling) to no direction (non-directive counseling). Non-directive counseling reflects what is said and felt. For example, a supervisor using the non-directive approach would say, "You feel frustrated because you don't meet Rob's approval." Directive counseling tells and advises. For example, a supervisor using the directive approach would say, "I want you to concentrate on your work and not worry about what the other employees do." Interactive counseling combines them. Apart from these, there are many more types of counseling depending upon the situation.

Directive Counseling

Directive counseling is the process of listening to a member's problem, deciding with the member what should be done, and then encouraging and motivating the person to do it. This type of counseling accomplishes the function of advice; but it may also reassure, give emotional release, and, to a minor extent, clarify thinking. Most everyone likes to give advice, counselors included, and it is easy to do. But is it effective? Does the counselor really understand the member's problem? Does the counselor have the technical knowledge of human behaviour and the judgement to make the "right" decision? If the decision is right, will the member follow it? The answer to these questions is often no, and that is why advice-giving is sometimes an unwise act in counseling. Although advice-giving is of questionable value, some of the other functions achieved by directive counseling are worthwhile. If the counselor is a good listener, then the member should experience some emotional release. As the result of the emotional release, plus ideas that the counselor imparts, the member may also clarify thinking. Both advice and reassurance may be worthwhile if they give the member, more courage to take a workable course of action that the member supports.

Non-directive Counseling

Non-directive, or client-centered, counseling is the process of skillfully listening to a counselee, encouraging the person to explain bothersome problems, and helping him or her to understand those problems and determine courses of action. This type of counseling focuses on the member, rather than on the counselor as a judge and advisor; hence, it is "client-centered". This type of counseling is used by professional counselors, but non-professionals may use its techniques to work more effectively with service members. The unique advantage of non-directive counseling is its ability to cause the member's re-orientation. It stresses changing the person, instead of dealing only with the immediate problem in the usual manner of directive counseling. The counselor attempts to ask discerning questions, restate ideas, clarify feelings, and attempts to understand why these feelings exist. Professional counselors treat each counselee as a social and organizational equal. They primarily listen and try to help their client discover and follow improved courses of action. They especially "listen between the lines" to learn the full meaning of their client's feelings. They look for assumptions underlying the counselee's statements and for the events the counselee may, at first, have avoided talking about. A person's feelings can be likened to an iceberg. The counselor will usually only see the revealed feelings and emotions. Underlying these surface indications is the true problem that the member is almost always initially reluctant to reveal.

Personal Counseling

All personal problems should not be referred to a specialist. Your first duty as a chief is to recognize whether the problem is beyond your ability to help or not. Many times you can solve personal problems with a telephone call. If the problem is beyond your ability to solve, then give the division officer a chance to solve the problem. Stay informed of the progress made towards solving the problem. If the problem requires assistance from outside the command, you can smooth the process by making appointments and ensuring the counselee gets help. Keep informed of progress and follow-up! As a CPO, you may encounter situations in which persons being counseled must be referred to other sources for assistance. There will be times when a person will have special problems that will require special help. These problems should be handled by such specialists as the chaplain, legal officer, and medical officer. The effective CPO should be able to recognize situations in which referral is necessary and to assist the counselee in obtaining maximum benefit from these referrals. Examples of situations in which referral would be appropriate include drug and alcohol abuse, psychological problems or behavioural disorders, medical problems, personal limitations, such as a personality conflict with the counselor and the inability of the counselor to relate to or comprehend a counselee's problem. In each instance, the key to successful referral lies not in the ability to diagnose a problem but rather in the ability to recognize those signs or symptoms that indicate referral to appropriate sources. To assist CPOs in fulfilling their advising and counseling responsibilities with regard to referral, the Navy has developed an impressive array of helping resources. A listing of these helping resources is provided for reference.

Crisis Intervention Counseling

In cases of emergency (such as rape, spouse abuse, running away and suicide), the counselor will help you get through the crisis and refer you to further counseling or medical care, if needed. These services are provided by community health agencies, helplines and hotlines.

Individual Counseling

You meet one-on-one with the counselor. This type of counseling works well when problems come mainly from you and your thinking patterns and behaviours. In addition, some problems are very personal and difficult to confront with others present. Some examples include grieving, anxiety disorders, depression and phobias.

Family Counseling

Sometimes, a problem isn't part of just one person, but has roots in close relationships with others, especially family members. For instance, alcoholism is called a "family disease" because it affects the alcoholic's life and the life of those around him.

Family therapy can help family members resolve issues among each other. It also can help them adopt ways to help another family member get well. Family members can learn how actions and ways of communicating can worsen problems. With help, new and improved ways of communicating can be explored and practised. Family therapy often is used when an adolescent has a problem with alcohol and substance abuse.

Group Counseling

In group therapy, people join in a group and discuss their problems together. The session is guided by a counselor. Members in the group often share the same problem, but not always. The group session provides a place where people can confide with others who understand their struggles. They also can learn how they see themselves and how they are seen by others. Members gain strength in knowing that they are not alone with their problems. Group therapy is useful for a variety of problems.

Career Counseling

Career counseling is a common supervisory activity. In addition to job knowledge and skills, employees need to be punctual, diligent, responsible, and receptive to supervision. Supervisors have an opportunity to help employees understand that developing these behaviours can improve their future success. Development is preparing employees for future jobs. Bringing out the best in employees is the most powerful and most available resource for supervisors to do more with less. Employee development produces "win-win" agreements between supervisor and employee.

Long-term, Residential Treatment

The person lives at a treatment centre. The length of stay can vary, depending on the treatment program and progress of therapy. A program can last more than a year or just a week or two. Settings include hospitals, home-like structures and clinics.

In the case of residential treatment, you would focus on your problem and on getting well. Other activities such as work, school, family and hobbies take a backseat to treatment. In most programs, you receive counseling daily and participate in regular group therapy. Additional counseling after residential treatment has ended may be needed.

Alcoholics Anonymous, Al-Anon

Alateen and Overeaters Anonymous are examples of self-help groups. These groups provide support and understanding to participants who share the same problem, such as a chemical dependency or overeating. These groups usually meet regularly without a therapist or counselor. There are self-help groups for many mental and physical problems.

The Counseling Process

Step 1. Describe the changed behaviour. Let the employee know that the organization is concerned with work performance. The supervisor maintains work standards by being consistent in dealing with troubled employees. Explain in very specific terms what the employee needs to do in order to perform up to the organization's expectations. Don't moralize. Restrict the confrontation to job performance.

Step 2. Get employee comments on the changed behaviour and the reason for it. Confine any negative comments to the employee's job performance. Don't diagnose; you are not an expert. Listen and protect confidentiality.

Step 3. Agree on a solution. Emphasize confidentiality. Don't be swayed or misled by emotional please, sympathy tactics, or "hard-luck" stories. Explain that going for help does not exclude the employee from standard disciplinary procedures and that it does not open the door for special privileges.

Step 4. Summarize and get a commitment to change. Seek commitment from the employee to meet work standards and to get help, if necessary, with the problem.

Step 5. Follow up. Once the problem is resolved and a productive relationship is established, follow up is needed.

Overcoming Depression—Counseling and Therapy

Having come this far along the Depression Learning Path, you should understand the difference between simply treating the symptoms of depression with drugs and overcoming depression for good. Here we're going to look at what research has shown to be the best type of depression counseling for overcoming depression permanently. You should already know the types of depression counseling to avoid from the last step.

Many professionals advocate a combination of drug therapy and psychotherapy, but more and more studies show that medication is unnecessary if the sufferer receives the right sort of help. Overcoming depression if you have it now, knowing exactly what depression is means you can recognize the onset of future episodes, if they occur. Gaining new skills, or being able to challenge depressive thinking and behaviour at the onset, means you can be confident about leading a depression-free life. Good depression counseling will help you learn these skills. Counseling or therapy that is effective in overcoming depression focuses on:

- What we do. (Behavioural therapy)
- How we think about things. (Cognitive therapy)
- How we relate to others. (Interpersonal therapy)
- How things are going to be better in the future. (Solution focused therapy)
- Getting our basic emotional needs met in the wider world.
- Helping you find solutions to your immediate problems.

And *not* on why you are depressed, or what went wrong in the past. These types of therapy, far from overcoming depression, will tend to make it worse. A combination of these above approaches has been shown to work best. Here's a quick description of the types of therapy found to be effective in beating depression. Therapy and counseling are the same thing, although counseling is more often the non-directive stuff to avoid if you're depressed.

Behavioural therapy for depression. The basic idea of behavioural theory is that everything amounts to behaviour and inner processes are of little or no account. So if people feel miserable, it is because of their behaviour. Traditional behavioural therapists are less interested in the thoughts and emotions of their patients and more concerned with their behaviour as can be observed. Changing peoples' behaviour can have dramatic results but it is now known that people's perceptions and thought processes are also vitally important when overcoming depression.

Cognitive therapy for depression. Cognitive therapy works on the basic premise that all emotions come from thoughts. For example: If you think about something scary, you will feel fear. Basically, the idea behind cognitive therapy is that people learn to 'catch' their thoughts and challenge them so that they can feel differently. Working on your thinking styles is absolutely essential if you suffer from depression. Any therapist or counselor who does not address this with you is going about it the wrong way! Recent studies of how the brain works have shown that certain emotions occur before thoughts and it is possible to be afraid of something before we can think what it is. However, cognitive therapy, if applied skillfully, has done very well in the research for lifting and preventing relapse of depression. (The danger with cognitive therapy is that it becomes too complex for the patient to understand, so it must be applied with skill, and with consideration for the patient's way of learning.)

Interpersonal therapy for depression. This approach focuses on the way people relate with other people in their lives—how they communicate and express themselves. Whether a person is assertive, aggressive or timid or has 'social skills' is seen as key. Extremely common in depression sufferers is the lack of satisfaction in various relationships: family, work, social. Depression can cause us to lose access to the skills and the desire to sustain these relationships successfully. Whether it be feelings of wanting to be alone, not knowing what to say, or just feeling wretched and not wanting to be in company, a large percentage of depression sufferers exhibit what is crudely called "poor social skiils" such as:

- Being less assertive.

- Being less positive.
- Showing negative facial expressions and poor eye contact.
- Displaying less interaction in group situations.
- Unwittingly carrying out 'off-putting' social behaviour such as inappropriate questioning, too much or too little self-disclosure, or missing out small-talk.

Again, this therapy can be seen as practical, sensible and very helpful for some people as communication skills are 'teachable'. However, like all the other approaches, it's not the whole story.

Solution focused therapy for depression. As it's name suggests, the emphasis here is on finding solutions to current problems and focusing on future wellness rather than past hurts. This is not to say that the past is ignored but the main emphasis is on teaching new skills and keeping therapy brief and focused. It is an extremely hopeful and motivational form of therapy when applied skillfully. Each therapy type contributes greatly to overcoming depression. Good depression counseling uses all these approaches in a skillful blend. In Getting Help with Depression, we'll look at the core elements of successful help for depression.

Getting Help with Depression

Help for depression varies wildly in terms of what it considers depression to be, how it treats it and therefore ultimately, how effective it is. The idea that depression can simply be treated as a chemical imbalance is rapidly losing ground. You will know why if you have not completed the rest of the Depression Learning Path. Therefore, the first incredibly important stage of getting help for depression is to understand what depression is. If you have reached this page without completing the rest of the Depression Learning Path, it would be a good idea to go to the start. It will help you get the complete picture. In summary, we'll give here:

- an indication of the best way to get help with depression,
- an assessment of depression help in terms of overcoming, depression and preventing relapse,

- the common features of successful therapies for depression,
- what to look for when seeking help for your depression through therapy.

Antidepressants as help for depression. As we have seen on the Learning Path, no one type of depression medication has been shown to be significantly more effective than any other. Antidepressants are also very poor at preventing relapse, and more often than, not require a long course of treatment.

Self help for depression. Effective therapy needs to incorporate everything that works in lifting depression. You may be able to help yourself effectively, although often, it is useful to get the help of a professional. Here, we'll go through what you can do, as well as what you should look for in any therapy you choose to undergo.

What can You Do to Help Yourself?

(1) ***Know about your condition.*** What you know about your depression has been shown to have an effect on how well you respond to treatment. Take the Depression Learning Path—it's the best way to start helping yourself.

(2) ***Cut down on rumination.*** Do whatever you can to decrease the amount of rumination you are doing. (Ruminating is 'chewing over' emotional issues in your mind without coming to any decision to act.) If possible, decide to put off difficult decisions for 1 or 2 weeks while you get your energy back. Ways to cut down rumination are to:

   (a) Stop yourself when you spot yourself doing 'all or nothing' thinking.

   (b) Read novels when you have nothing to do, to occupy your mind. (Make them exciting novels, not romance or self-help books.)

   (c) Do exercise. (see 5)

   (d) Work if you can.

   (e) Keep yourself occupied as much as possible in ways that stop you thinking too much.

(3) ***Find ways to assess and monitor your depressive episodes.*** The way depression makes us adopt all or nothing thinking is a unique and crucial part of understanding depression. The way depression makes us generate seemingly hopeless outcomes to our situation can make it almost impossible to see a way out of it. Finding ways to gauge your depression can help to show the shades of gray that will ultimately defeat the black and white thinking on which depression thrives. This is often done in the form of a diary, where you grade how bad your days have been on a scale of 1 to 10, where 1 is the worst and 10 is the best. Then, after 2 weeks or so, you can look back and see how things have varied over that time.

(4) ***Lower your emotional arousal levels.*** Calming down emotions such as anxiety and anger helps your brain function more subtly and decreases the amount of catastrophising you do. Along with getting proper rest, being able to relax is incredibly important.

Relaxation therapies are effective in overcoming some of the other issues that can co-occur with depression. The effects of panic attacks, anxiety and anger, etc. can be lessened and overcome with the ability to relax properly and deeply. Physical disciplines such as Tai Chi, which occupy the mind whilst performing gentle, relaxing exercise can be useful, as can relaxation training such as guided imagery or self-hypnosis.

(5) ***Get exercise if you can.*** If you can increase the amount of physical exercise you get, it can be a great self help for depression. The results of the physical exertion will lift your depression temporarily at least, in addition to the other benefits of exercise. (As always, consult your medical practitioner before starting any strenuous exercise regime.)

(6) ***Do what you enjoy.*** Do what you used to enjoy doing, even if you don't particularly feel like it. Even complete small tasks within the home if you don't feel like meeting other people. Seemingly mundane tasks, if they have an

end result, can result in a feeling of satisfaction, and actually increase your serotonin levels.

(7) ***Maintain a regular sleep pattern.*** Do not lie in if you feel exhausted in the morning. All that happens is that you dream a large amount if you sleep through the morning, because your REM periods get longer the longer you have been asleep. Set a time to get up every morning, and get up. Try to spend 8-9 hours in bed, and get up regardless.

(8) ***Important.*** Check that you are meeting your basic emotional needs.

Counseling and Psychotherapy

Modern counseling and psychotherapy provide wide range of options for addressing many different kinds of psychological distress. The decision to seek counseling is an important step. Too often, people don't get help because they feel guilt, shame or embarrassment. By deciding to get help, you have made a choice to feel better and to improve your life.

Counseling services should be chosen to meet your needs. This information describes common types of counseling. Working with a trained mental health care provider, you can develop the right treatment plan. Keep in mind that all counseling services are confidential. Counselors are bound by law to keep your problems private.

Where do I Start?

First, you will receive an "assessment", a review of your mental health. The assessment is done by a person trained in mental health care. Mental health care specialists include family therapists, social workers, psychologist, psychiatrists and other professionals. (Your health care provider can refer you to a mental health care professional.) The assessment is used to diagnose the problem and determine the best treatment. You will be asked to describe why you want counseling, any symptoms you have had (emotional, mental and physical) and your medical history. You may be given a question-and-answer survey. For substance abuse problems, a drug screening may be required.

What Happens after the Assessment?

Once the assessment is complete, you and your mental health professional can develop a treatment plan. At this time, you and your counselor can discuss:

- The best type of counseling.
- The best setting for counseling (counselor's office, outpatient clinic, hospital, residential treatment centre).
- Who will be included in your treatment (you alone, family members, others with similar problems).
- How often you should go to counseling.
- How long counseling may last.
- Any medications that will be needed.

Substance Abuse

Some problem performance stems from substance abuse. In handling alcohol or drug abuse situations, the supervisor must avoid inferences and stick to actual clues. He or she avoids giving advice. The supervisor gives support and information, if needed, and makes clear that rehabilitation is the employee's responsibility.

Career Guidance

Career counseling is a common supervisory activity. In addition to job knowledge and skills, employees need to be punctual, diligent, responsible, and receptive to supervision. Supervisors have an opportunity to help employees understand that developing these behaviours can improve their future success. Development is preparing employees for future jobs. Bringing out the best in employees is the most powerful and most available resource for supervisors to do more with less. Employee development produces "win-win" agreements between supervisor and employee.

Clarified Thinking

Clarified thinking tends to be a normal result of emotional release. The fact is that not all clarified thinking takes place while the counselor and counselee are talking. All or part of it may take place later as a result of developments during the counseling relationship. The net result of clarified thinking is that a person is encouraged to accept responsibility for problems and to be more realistic in solving them.

Reorientation

Reorientation is more than mere emotional release or clear thinking about a problem. It involves a change in the member's emotional self through a change in basic goals and aspirations. Very often it requires a revision of the member's level of aspiration to bring it more in line with actual attainment. It causes people to recognize and accept their own limitations. The counselor's job is to recognize those in need of reorientation before their need becomes severe, so that they can be referred to professional help. Reorientation is the kind of function needed to help alcoholics return to normalcy or to treat those with mental disorders.

Tips to be a Matured Professional

1. Be a good listener and response accordingly.
2. Be ethical in approach what may come the situation.
3. Put your boneless vital organs in control like eyes, tongue and sex organs.
4. Appraise in group and scold in loneliness.
5. Don't share corporate share with colleagues.
6. Don't share your future plan with your colleagues.
7. Don't abuse your company infront of your colleagues or others.
8. Avoid arguments that creates only tension and no gain.
9. Follow hierarchy for information flow.
10. Be ready to work for organization without regard to days and hours.

How will You Downsize Your Boss or Colleague?

This is a negative strategy that needs lot of maturity level and patience but it is a Ram wan or stick of mosses to use sometime in professional life. Suppose your boss or your colleague is not a good professional and always takes thing in personal. They might be jealous to you due to your professional acumen, good performance, better recognition and that is why they disturb you in routine job.

You have to identify two attacking points to destroy his or her image in one shot. Point one that creates strong feeling of demotion or disrespect or irritation. You do it through your office friend without informing him. He or she will burst and will loose emotional control and will break professional ethics. Oh this is a fine time for you. You take these abusive incidents as a discussion points with the employer and your boss or colleague will be call upon for clarification and finally they will be penalized accordingly. Now, you counsel the targeted person and advise him or her to switch over to some where else. If possible, help him or her to get job immediately in another organization.

Our aim shouldn't be to spoil the career of any one but in the forest, there shouldn't be two lions of different motive. Dead fish can infect the river water and thus we should throw out deadly colleague or boss prior to the infection and revengeful action.

Summary

Performance is the key criteria to judge any professional. For desired performance apart from required qualification, training and experience, you need good cooperation, coordination inside the office and with family members. During establishment stage (20s-25s), generally we don't accept responsibility wholeheartedly and that is why we invest our valuable time towards useless affairs. Concentration deviation plays a vital role in non-performance and deviation depends on justified and non-justified personal and professional need.

When we join any organization, we should make up our mind that we have to perform from very first week or first month, then only we can hit the nail on the head. If you will perform in very first organization, you can get recognition with this organization and you can encash your performance somewhere else. Therefore, first you have to prove how good performer are you and how competent are you in grasping the professional skills.

In initial stage of professional life, we generally get motivated or demotivated with the behaviour of girl friend and off course, on pay package. If you have girl friend, then you cannot save your salary and you will always be in depression because you cannot save money for your parents and family. Professionally, our best girl friend should be our profession only and we should whole-heartedly concentrate on our performance with good cooperation, coordination with peer groups. Our aim should be to earn more and more professional skills so that we can apply those skills to augment the profitability of the organization.

We should try being away from the office politics and unnecessary personal and professional sharing view with office colleague because it will always pull you down and can create depression. If you cannot solve your problem, you should directly reach to the concerned personnel and then discuss in detail with the aim to solve the problem. In the office, you should have only professional relation and no personal relation. You must develop habit of how to make others happy but remember you cannot make happy to every one. You should give plastic smile when you meet some one and give respect to everone. You should develop how to think positive for others because if you will do this, then you will get rewarded with the same positive vibration. Always try to position yourself as a neutral employee and this is the best way to be away from office politics.

Chapter four

MENTORING

Mentoring has become a widespread talent development tool with a long standing form of training, learning and development and an increasingly popular tool for supporting personal development.

Mentor = Trusted friend or advisor

"Mentoring is advising, teaching, counseling and role modeling. Formal mentoring matches a senior or more experienced person—the mentor—to a junior or less experienced person-the mentee.

Mentors focus on a mentee's achievements, success in school and preparation for the workforce through a one-to-one relationship that is non-threatening and non-judgmental to both parties. It is a relationship that changes over time as each grows, learns, and gains experiences in the relationship."

Quoted From: Brainard, S.G. (1998) *Mentors and Mentees*, University of Washington, Western Regional WEPAN Centre.

In management context, Mentoring is a process of developing perfect managerial and leadership qualities in mentee by a mentor. Mentoring helps mentee to do a job more effectively and/or to progress in their career with full perfection. Ultimately, the goal of mentoring improves efficiency level of employees and generates more profits for the organization. The mentor was probably someone who had "been there, done that" before. A mentor might use a variety of approaches, e.g., coaching, training, discussion, counseling, etc. Today, there seems to be much ongoing discussion and debate about the definitions and differences regarding coaching and mentoring. Amitabh Bachchan, the bollywood superstar is mentor for his son Abhishek Bachchan, Yoginder

Bindra is mentor for his son Abhinav Bindra, Sonia Gandhi is mentor for her son Rahul Gandhi, Dhirubhai Ambani is mentor for his sons Mukesh and Anil Ambani, etc.

'Behind every successful person, there is one elementary truth: somewhere, somehow, someone cared about their growth and development. This person was their mentor.'

Dr. Beverley Kaye, *Up is Not the Only Way*, 1997.

What do You Understand by the Term "Mentoring"?

- Support.
- Listening.
- Empathy.
- Guidance.
- Scenario planning.
- Setting goals.
- Having experience.
- Communicating.
- Understanding.
- Knowledge of situations.

Why do You have a Mentor?

- To learn about how your company works—culture and how do things get done.
- To develop your functional knowledge—Technical advise and to learn about other functions (Marketing, Sales, etc.).
- To get advice-based on mentor's experience.
- For growth and development.

Why are Mentoring Programs so Popular?

The number of mentoring programs has grown dramatically in recent years. This popularity results in part from compelling testimonials by people—youth and adults alike—who have themselves benefited from the positive influence of an older person who helped them endure social, academic, career, or personal crises.

How do They Work?

Mentoring programs are established to match a suitable adult or older youth, the mentor with a younger person. Potential mentors are recruited from various sources including corporate, professional, and religious communities as well as neighborhood citizens. Nominations for mentors are sought formally and informally through flyers, posters, mailings, and word-of-mouth.

Appropriately matching mentors with youths is at the heart of all programs. Matching can be done formally and informally through interviews, personal profiles, comparative interest inventories, and get-acquainted sessions. In programs where mentors and youths are given a chance to choose each other, planned mentoring takes on many aspects of natural mentoring.

Why are They Needed?

Data clearly show many youths have a desperate need for positive role models. The most compelling data describe changes to the American family structure: the number of single-parent homes has radically increased, as have two-parent working families. More preventive care is needed, as are support networks to fill the void left by busy or absent parents. Other statistics are equally troubling: each day in the United States, 3,600 students drop out of high school, and 2,700 unwed teenage girls get pregnant (Petersmeyer, 1989).

What are They For?

Mentoring programs generally serve the following broad purposes:

- Educational or academic mentoring helps mentored youth, improve their overall academic achievement.
- Career mentoring helps mentored youth develop the necessary skills to enter or continue on a career path.
- Personal development mentoring supports mentored youth during times of personal or social stress and provides guidance for decision-making.

What Makes a Good Mentor?

- Helps mentee his or her own goals, not the mentor's goal.

- Makes time for the mentee.
- Good listener.
- Treats mentee with respects.
- Prepared to give constructive criticism.
- Shows faith in the mentee.
- No judgement.
- Has the ability to get things done.
- Reliability.
- Positive attitude.
- Patient.
- Empathetic.
- Experience and knowledgeable.

Difference between Mentoring and Coaching

There is some confusion about what exactly mentoring is and how it differs from coaching. Broadly speaking, the CIPD defines coaching as 'developing a person's skills and knowledge so that their job performance improves, hopefully leading to the achievement of organizational objectives. It targets high performance and improvement at work, although it may also have an impact on an individual's private life. It usually lasts for a short period and focuses on specific skills and goals.'

Traditionally, mentoring is the long-term passing on of support, guidance and advice. In the workplace it has tended to describe a relationship in which a more experienced colleague uses their greater knowledge and understanding of the work or workplace to support the development of a more junior or inexperienced member of staff. This comes from the Greek myth where Odysseus entrusts the education of his son to his friend Mentor. It's also a form of apprenticeship, whereby an inexperienced learner learns the tricks of the trade from an experienced colleague, backed-up as in modern apprenticeship by offsite training.

Mentoring is used specifically and separately as a form of long-term tailored development for the individual which brings benefits to the organization. The characteristics of mentoring are:

- It is essentially a supportive form of development.
- It focuses on helping an individual manage their career and improve skills.
- Personal issues can be discussed more productively unlike in coaching where the emphasis is on performance at work.
- Mentoring activities have both organizational and individual goals.

The following table, adapted from Alred et al., highlights the differences between mentoring and coaching. It is separate and distinct from coaching, but coaching and mentoring can often overlap.

Mentoring	*Coaching*
Ongoing relationship that can last for a long-time.	Relationship generally has a short duration.
Can be more informal and meetings can take place as and when the mentored individual needs some guidance and or support.	Generally more structured in nature and meetings scheduled on a regular basis.
More long term and takes a broader view of the person. Often known as the 'mentee' but the term client or mentored person can be used.	Short-term (sometimes time bounded) and focused on specific development areas/issues.
Mentor usually passes on experience and is normally more senior in organization.	Not generally performed on basis that coach needs direct experience of clients formal occupational role.
The focus is on career and personal development.	Focus generally on development/ issues at work.
Agenda is set by the mentored person with the mentor providing support and guidance to prepare them for future roles.	Agenda focused on achieving specific, immediate goals.
Revolves more around developing the mentee professionally.	Revolves more around specific development areas/issues.

Finally, mentoring is an excellent management tool for an employee to make him confident decision maker in day to day professional career and we should have firm confidence that it will also increase retention of human capital. You can call mentor as a godfather.

Methods of Mentoring

There are multiple approaches to mentoring, based on how informal or how formal the relationship. Generally, mentoring will fall into three types: Formal, Informal, and Self-Mentoring. Informal mentoring is something which takes place through a "natural" connection—one which is based on friendship, personal relationships or common background (academic, hometown, hobbies, etc.). And a formal mentoring is based upon an organized mentoring-focused organizational program. In addition to the two approaches to mentoring, there are several "types" of mentoring:

One-on-One—This is the most commonly utilized approach to mentoring and it involves a mentoring relationship between one mentor and one individual being mentored. This type of mentoring can be established either through a formal or informal mentoring approach, and it tends to be a relationship that lasts longer than other types of mentoring. It is also not uncommon for this type of mentoring to be based on specific needs of the mentoring candidate—meaning, they form a relationship based on a specific need of the candidate, based on the ability of the mentor to address or meet that need.

Team Mentoring—Involves a group of at least two mentors who work together to mentor one candidate. The specific contributions of each mentor may vary based upon unique experiences and such, or it may be that the two mentors capabilities overlap and are then used to further reinforce the contribution of each. It is also not unusual for a Team Mentoring approach to be utilized based on work schedules or geographic locations/constraints.

Group Mentoring—Involves one mentor that then works with a group of candidates. This type of mentoring relationship is useful when dealing with, for example, groups of new workers who all would tend to have the same needs and requirements, need access to the same basic levels of knowledge, etc. In addition to the two approaches and three types of mentoring, there are also two modes of mentoring:

Face-to-Face—Involves a relationship between the mentor and the candidate which relies at least to some degree upon an ability to meet face-to-face.

Virtual—Virtual mentoring allows for mentors to be involved via e-mail, teleconferencing, and other online forms of collaboration.

And in addition to the two approaches, three types of mentoring, and two modes of mentoring, there are also two durations of commitments typical to mentoring relationships: Short-term—Mentoring relationship that generally lasts for one year or less. Long-term—Mentoring relationship that generally lasts longer than one year.

One important point—regarding to the trend towards the "virtual mentoring" that is taking place as far as I know there is no definitive study out there which addresses the effectiveness of this approach.

Another important aspect of mentoring, is in establishing that formal mentoring program. I believe that to maximize the effectiveness of mentoring that sooner or later, every organization should consider establishing a formal program. And probably the most important step there is to identify a potential champion. I'd posted a summary of the considerations for that in an answer in another post, so I'll "re-use" that knowledge a bit here in talking to the steps of identifying and working with a potential champion of a formal mentoring program.

Types of Mentoring

1. ***Pal or Buddy Mentoring***: An informal "mentoring" when someone shows a new member of staff or team the way things are done. The Pal/Buddy is usually someone familiar with the procedures but not far in advance of the newcomer.

2. ***Peer Mentoring***: Peer mentoring is when people mentor someone of a similar age or experience to themselves. So in a school context, older pupils support younger ones by meeting regularly and passing on their experience and advice. Peer mentoring offers young people the opportunity to develop their skills and qualities in a way that will prove beneficial to them.
3. ***E-mentoring***: Mentors provide support to local school students through regular e-mail contact.
4. ***Business Mentoring***: Business mentors advise and support start-up businesses or assist those new to a trade or profession. Some businesses have workplace mentors. They offer a positive role-model for young people who have come off track, helping them to return to education or training.
5. ***School Mentoring***: School mentors work with schools and parents to raise standards and expectations, either one-to-one or in small groups. They work in the classroom; help with homework and coursework and support work experience.
6. ***Care Leave Mentoring***: Care-leave mentors help young people just leaving care with practical advice as well as emotional support like confidence building.
7. ***Learning Mentoring***: A Learning Mentor is a paid mentor, mainly employed by primary or secondary schools, to provide support in raising pupils' attainment, improving attendance and reducing exclusions and were originally funded through the 'Excellence in Cities' initiative. Learning Mentors come from a wide range of backgrounds including volunteer mentoring, teaching, social services and youth work but all have experience of working with young people and with the ability to build a rapport with them.
8. ***Executive Mentoring***: Executive Mentoring is a specialist form of management development and education. It is particularly suited to senior executives who have risen above the scope of formal management development

programmes and require highly focused development and support tailored to the particular challenges facing them in their business. Executive Mentoring stimulates and manages the individual growth necessary to deliver business performance beyond present levels and beliefs of what is possible. It does this by helping executives:

- Build a solid personal foundation and demonstrate strong confidence in self and others.
- Develop their personal vision and uncover their value priorities.
- Think strategically and inspire shared vision, mission and values.
- Determine appropriate goals, strategies, tactics and action plans.
- Enhance their management and leadership skills.
- Identify their personal winning strategies.
- Uncover self sabotage, recognise repeating patterns and introduce change to interrupt habitual responses.
- Elicit high commitment to personal change and development.

9. *Role Model Mentoring*: This is often the form of mentoring that is envisaged. A successful person with experience gives support, guidance and help to someone who wishes to succeed in a similar or the same career. Both mentor and mentee are trained so that they can both gain from the mentoring relationship.
10. *Coaching for Confidence*: This is usually a short one on one mentoring situation where the mentee has a specific issue. A trained mentor is found who can give advice and guidance in the area in question. It could develop into Role Model mentoring.

Purpose of Mentoring

Being mentored can therefore be a challenging and stretching experience, inviting executives to draw on and develop hidden personal resources and qualities. And it can be an exciting, stimulating journey of self discovery and development which opens up new opportunities for personal fulfillment and achievement. In either case, it involves a journey into the unknown and into unfamiliar ways of being and doing; we may have to confront our fear of failure and, paradoxically, our fear of success; we may have to cast aside long held beliefs about who we are and what we are capable of; and we may have to resist strong pressure from family and colleagues to lapse back to our habitual ways. Thus, to create and then sustain change in the face of the many forces which may pull us back, a powerfully motivating context is necessary. That context is Purpose.

Purpose

Your purpose expresses who you are, who you are becoming, and what contribution you can make. You have a sense of purpose when your life has a direction and meaning which you have chosen. (Purpose differs from Vision which is about what you want to create and achieve. You choose a Vision but discover your Purpose.)

When our lives, at home and at work, are aligned with our Purpose, then our lives are meaningful and we connect to deep wells of energy within ourselves.

A prime reason why a sense of purpose is important is that it provides the strong container or context through which we can manage our inner experience of change. But to create that change, we must be able to express that purpose in the world, that is, to be purposeful.

You are being purposeful when you are fully living your purpose, that is when you are expressing your purpose in the moment rather than working towards achieving it in the future. Purposefulness can also be described as wilfulness (in its sense of 'full of Will') and has the following qualities:

- energy, dynamic power, intensity,
- mastery, control, discipline,
- concentration, attention, focus,
- determination, decisiveness, resoluteness, promptness,
- persistence, endurance, patience,
- initiative, courage, daring,
- organization, integration, synthesis (Assagioli 1973).

Bringing Purpose into the present requires the ability to be present—or to have Presence. Put simply:

Purpose + Presence = Purposefulness

Presence is the ability to be with another person with such inner self-knowledge that the other person is able to ponder the depths of who he or she is with awareness and clarity. It is the single most important skill the mentor requires. Marianne Williamson describes presence rather more poetically: "We are all born to shine, as children do. We were born to make manifest the glory of God that is within us. It's not just in some of us; it's in everyone. And as we let our own light shine, we unconsciously give other people permission to do the same. As we are liberated from our own fear, our presence automatically liberates others" (Williamson, 1992). This is also an excellent description of the essence of mentoring.

The Mentoring for Change model provides a framework and methodology for mentoring. This model and the four elements of the mentoring process—Freeing Up, Envisioning, Implementing, and Sustaining—are described elsewhere (Turner, 1995). Figure 1 shows the corresponding elements of mentoring on purpose—Satisfying Needs, Uncovering Purpose, Being Purposeful, and Realising Purpose.

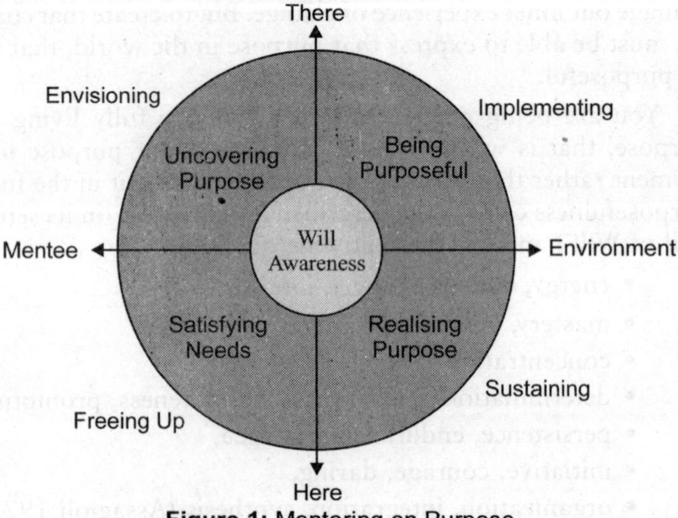

Figure 1: Mentoring on Purpose

1. *Satisfying Needs*

Needs are those things which must be satisfied for us to have a solid foundation to our lives. For this reason, mentoring on purpose will often start in this quadrant of the model.

When we are driven by our needs (e.g., for appreciation, self-worth, security, love, success), it is difficult to express and live by our purpose because our energy and attention are devoted to getting our needs met. In developing a sense of our purpose, it is therefore important to determine whether our behaviour is being driven by our needs. If it is, then we must find ways to get those needs satisfied once and for all so that their fulfilment no longer gets in the way of our purpose. So, for example, we may be a team-leader and have a strong need to belong. If we try to get our belonging needs met from the team when we are supposed to be challenging its members to new levels of performance, we are likely to fail both to provide the leadership the team requires and to get our own needs met. More appropriate ways of getting this need met must be found.

Sometimes, mere awareness that a need is being met in inappropriate ways is sufficient to enable people to drop the pattern. But often the need's function has been to protect the individual from the challenge of embracing their sense of purpose and then more wide ranging work is required.

2. *Uncovering Purpose*

As we release ourselves from the hold of our needs, so we create the opportunity for our sense of purpose to begin to emerge more fully into our lives. This emergence can be facilitated by looking at the course of our lives, distinguishing the themes and patterns, becoming aware of what is unfolding, noticing the qualities of those times when we have felt most alive, recalling what it was we especially enjoyed as a six year old, considering the Tombstone Test ("What would you like your epitaph to be?"), and by other explorations of the wider context of our lives.

Steve Jobs, trying to lure John Sculley, then CEO of PepsiCo, to Apple famously and ultimately successfully evoked Sculley's sense of purpose by asking "Do you want to spend the rest of your life selling sugared water or do you want a chance to change the world?" (Sculley, 1988).

A more analytical approach to working with both purpose and needs is to work with value priorities. Values sit at the gateway between our inner and outer worlds. They describe what is fundamentally important, and hence meaningful to us and so are directly related to our sense of purpose and to our needs. Instrumentation, such as the VMI from Values Technology Inc which can be used to uncover individual and organizational values and place them in a developmental framework of 125 global values (Figure 2), can be used to measure value priorities. This can be a particularly effective way to identify those values which are just emerging into our lives and which point us towards our unfolding purpose.

3. *Being Purposeful*

A sense of purpose does not necessarily lead to purposeful behaviour. Purpose is passive; purposefulness is active and emerges out of a process in which we express ourselves through what we do. Connecting our sense of purpose to the actions we take involves clarifying our values, developing our intention, deliberating on the possible ways of realising our purpose, choosing one or more, affirming the choice, formulating plans, and finally acting.

In being purposeful, we must mobilise our mind and our feelings at the intellectual level our sense of purpose provides a powerful reason for making the changes; and at the emotional level our purposefulness provides the motive force to bring our purpose into existence.

4. *Realising Purpose*

Once we are taking purposeful action we must ensure that this is creating the outcomes we seek to achieve. To do this, we have to learn to perceive clearly our impact on our environment (e.g., organization, family, team) and be able to sense the intricate web of connections in which we exist, and to see the whole as well as the parts.

We have to develop the ability to sustain our new behaviours and ways of being, to develop new habits, to learn from our experience, and to be sensitive to what we are creating. These are systems skills and they emerge most fully when our instrumental, interpersonal and imaginal skills become integrated. In essence, they involve a shift from seeing a world made up of things to seeing a world that's open and primarily made up of relationships.

Linking Individual and Corporate Purpose

The traditional psychological contract between employer and employee has involved a trade of time for pay. But many people are now looking for more from their work than just financial rewards; they are seeking the opportunity to develop and fulfil themselves. Increasingly, it will be those organizations which are able to satisfy this desire for more fulfilling work which will be able to attract and retain the best staff. Thus, the challenge that organizations face is how to provide their staff with the opportunity for more personally meaningful work whilst simultaneously enabling the organization to meet its goals.

In fact, organizations too can be described as having purpose, although it is more usually referred to as the organizational mission. An organization's mission expresses itself in a variety of ways—through the structures, polices processes, etc. of the organization—but predominantly, it comes from the sense of purpose of the people who make up the organization. And just as individual purpose can be accessed through personal values, so organizational mission can be accessed through corporate values. It is values that provide the link between the individual's purpose and the organization's mission. This is not to say that the individual should have the same value priorities as the organization—though there does need to be a core of shared values—but that the stage of development of the individual's value system should match that of the organization.

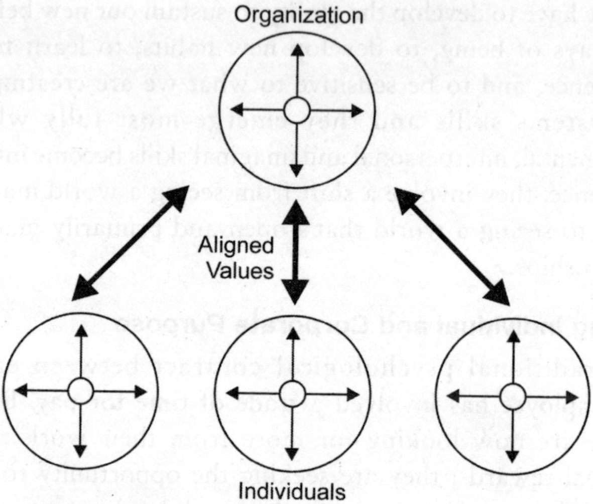

Figure 2: Individual and Organizational Values

Conclusion

Living our purpose consistently is a profound challenge. It requires high levels of self-awareness, a firm commitment, a strong sense of our own self-worth, a willingness to take risks, and the emotional discipline to travel outside our comfort zone. In essence, it requires that we develop the skills of self-leadership. The role of the mentor in this is to help the mentee continually deepen their understanding of reality, develop their sense of self, learn to listen for what is emerging, and to encourage them to live their purpose.

Ten Commandments of Leadership Qualities

1. **Be technically proficient**—As a leader, you must know your job and have a solid familiarity with your employees' tasks.
2. **Seek responsibility and take responsibility for your actions**—Search for ways to guide your organization to new heights. And when things go wrong, they always do sooner or later—do not blame others. Analyze the situation, take corrective action, and move on to the next challenge.

3. **Make sound and timely decisions**—Use good problem solving, decision making, and planning tools.
4. **Set the example**—Be a good role model for your employees. They must not only hear what they are expected to do, but also see. *We must become the change we want to see*—Mahatma Gandhi.
5. **Know your people and look out for their well-being**—Know human nature and the importance of sincerely caring for your workers.
6. **Keep your workers informed**—Know how to communicate with not only them, but also seniors and other key people.
7. **Develop a sense of responsibility in your workers**—Help to develop good character traits that will help them carry out their professional responsibilities.
8. **Ensure that tasks are understood, supervised, and accomplished**—Communication is the key to this responsibility.
9. **Train as a team**—Although many so-called leaders call their organization, department, section, etc. a team; they are not really teams; they are just a group of people doing their jobs.
10. **Use the full capabilities of your organization**—By developing a team spirit, you will be able to employ your organization, department, section, etc. to its fullest capabilities.

Leadership Style

The Enneagram is the single most powerful tool I have encountered to help leaders face and work through their limitations in order to achieve their full potential. I agree with Robert Kaplan (*Beyond Ambition*) that we are all somewhat ambivalent about knowing ourselves better because we're invested through long habit—however unfortunate its outcomes—in the self-image we find familiar. But coming to know your Enneagram style can be a powerful catalyst for personal change, that will also enhance your effectiveness as a leader.

Because this is a *motivational* model, however, and not a *behavioural* model, it is best to determine your character type through a process of discovery, focusing on the *compulsion* or "driving force" of each style (vs. relying on any of the available questionnaires). If you focus only on the *behaviours* that are emphasized for each, you will see yourself in a number of them, which would be unnecessarily confusing. Friends and co-workers may offer useful feedback about behaviours that *seem* to identify your style. But only you can make the final judgement—one of the styles will characterize these key aspects more fully than the others:

- What is your **driving force** or "compulsion"?
- What is the **behaviour set** or "fixation" that arises from your driving force?
- What **talk style** is typical of you?
- How do you react **under stress**?
- What is your key **development** need?

Once you make those distinctions, you will understand why Michael Goldberg (*The Nine Ways of Working*) suggests that the nine styles might come from different planets: each views the world differently and wants something different from life. At work, each has a characteristic agenda and operates within a particular decision-making frame. My book with Clarence Thomson, *Out of the Box: Coaching with the Enneagram*, is full of business-related cases that bring all nine Enneagram styles to life.

In my experience as a leadership development coach, all of the Enneagram styles, when driven by compulsive forces, protect their self-image at great cost to their full potential as organizational leaders. With awareness of their underlying character and a commitment to self-development, all of the nine are also capable of great contributions and gifts to the organization and to the people they manage.

Leadership Style One: The Idealist

A self-observing *Idealist* can be a wonderful leader: wise, tolerant, balanced, and focused on standards of excellence in ways that provide an exemplary vision for followers. Ones are often the purveyors of quality in an organization.

When less well-developed, they show their *fixation* on perfectionism. They carry an internal judging voice, which chastises themselves (or others) for falling short of perfection (preaching) or, in a very healthy individual, invokes higher attainment (teaching). Their *driving force* is anger, which is typically over-controlled until it erupts as resentment when someone has failed to live up to their expectations. They're good at moral tirades, yet they also show a "running amok" side that allows them to escape their own high standards.

Developmental skills include reducing the power of their internal critic, channeling anger more effectively, learning to respond to criticism non-defensively, and moving away from black-and-white thinking with positive reframing and creative problem-solving. The key development need for this leadership style is patience, the willingness to accept conditions that do not conform to one's ideal.

Leadership Style Two: The Mentor

The most interpersonally oriented of all the leadership styles, healthy *Mentors* are unconditionally caring leaders who derive deep satisfaction from seeing and encouraging the development of others; they are typically great supporters of customer service. Well-developed Twos will also be aware of their own needs, which provides balance in their lives and allows them to give freely, without expectation of return.

Their *driving force* is pride, which is attached to their self-image as helper; out of this they tend to be in the middle of things, giving help and advice whether others want it or not. When less developed they have a *fixation* on entitlement and can use manipulation to influence people. If they feel betrayed they may even become vindictive ("after all I've done for you!"). Their key development need is humility, which accompanies true compassion without expectation.

Developmental skills include acknowledging their own needs, seeing how they contribute to their own workload and saying no, setting clearer boundaries, and asserting their interpersonal power more directly.

Leadership Style Three: The Star

Star leaders are often expansive, risk-taking go-getters who ensure high productivity for their organizations. Formidable models for others, they are efficient and supremely goal-oriented; consequently, they tend to rise to top organizational levels, or to run their own companies.

What under-developed threes personify for *all* of us is our image-making. They're good at self-promotion and can be perceived as showcasing themselves at the expense of the team. Threes tend to look outward for their reflection in the eyes of others—and their inner life can be lacking. Their *driving force* is vanity, which shows up in the *fixation* of self-deception (e.g., convincing oneself that a failure to involve the team in a major business coup was not important because of the results achieved).

Developmental skills include learning to collaborate instead of compete, clarifying their own values/developing internal criteria (vs. external validation), learning from failure, and accessing their feelings. Their key development need is truthfulness, speaking from the essential self and not through personality needs.

Leadership Style Four: The Innovator

Innovators are vital to the health of an organization because they are able to view things from a new slant and are not bound by tradition; they can keep an organization from slowly dying out of untested and outdated assumptions.

More in touch with their feelings than other types, they are in danger of sinking into moodiness if they meet with resistance to their ideas. The same talent that allows Fours to "look outside the box" can lead them to wonder why they never see things the way others do, and subsequently to question if they are flawed—their conversation is ripe with sad stories. Their *driving force* is envy, which shows up in the *fixation* of dissatisfaction, a perception that "the grass is always greener somewhere else".

Developmental skills include focusing more on strengths and resources and less on the "tragedy" of life, learning to develop the possibilities of their current jobs, shifting their moods through physical exercise or creative outlets, reframing self-criticism in more positive ways, and championing a program or process they believe in. Their key development need is equanimity, the ability to live in the moment.

Leadership Style Five: The Synthesizer

Because of their ability to take in the whole picture and integrate its components in creative ways, well-developed *Synthesizers* can be consummate strategists and visionaries. Often very bright, they are extremely capable of influencing others through their knowledge.

Sometimes, they sound like they're giving a dissertation. Although Fives can be profound and passionate leaders, they tend to disdain the role of emotions in human interaction. They are the most independent of the nine styles and prefer to be surrounded by other highly capable people who need no direction or external reinforcement. Their *driving force* is hoarding, which shows up particularly in their *fixation* on detachment from emotions, a "stinginess" of feelings.

Developmental skills include debating less and probing/listening more with the goal of mutually satisfying solutions, taking their role as coach more seriously—including giving attention to group process (meetings, teamwork, etc.), and affirming others' positive efforts. Their key development need is *non-attachment*, engaging with others without fear of being overwhelmed.

Leadership Style Six: The Partner

Partners at their best are highly team-oriented leaders and excellent managers who bring out the best in everyone. These are energetic executives who attend to interdependent organizational needs, which shows up in their language as thoughts about the group.

Their *driving force* is fear, which is manifested in less well-developed Sixes as a *fixation* on accusation of others (particularly those in authority). Sixes also look for hidden agendas, and experience self-doubt. They may procrastinate and/or blurt out their feelings with a kind of reckless courage (driven by their anxieties), and then worry that they've shot themselves in the foot—and they may have. The good news is that they challenge others in ways that hold them accountable; the bad news is that they're always looking for the bad news!

Developmental skills include getting a reality check on their fears, empowering themselves vs. blaming others, focusing more on possibilities vs. worries, and centering their verbal presentations on a central theme and several key points. Their key development need is courage, consistent with a certain kind of "morality": recognizing their own contribution to situations instead of playing "victim".

Leadership Style Seven: The Futurist

Charming and easy to talk to, highly evolved *Futurists* are the organization's cheerleaders because of their natural optimism. They focus on long-term perspective and possibilities. Equality is important to them, so Sevens sometimes have to work around organizational constraints.

Less developed leaders of this type can seem egotistical because they love to tell anecdotes and may forget to invite others to talk. They're sometimes perceived as lacking analytical ability because of oversimplifying or skating over the surface. The Seven's *driving force* is gluttony, a seeking of pleasure in order to avoid pain; consequently they are overfocused (*fixated*) on enthusiasm (the "bad" news is that they only want to hear the good news) and uneasy activity.

Developmental skills include contingency planning for problems, eliciting and accepting feedback, using negative reframing to counter their optimism, and—particularly—disciplining themselves to follow through on their own development (it's hard work)! Their key development need is temperance: seeking moderation and letting go of materialism.

Leadership Style Eight: The Advocate

Advocate leaders who have paid attention to their own development are able to shoulder huge responsibility without having to control everything. Right beneath the surface they are soft-hearted; when this is tempered with their typical self-confidence, they have loyal followers and can truly move mountains.

Unfortunately, Eights have the reputation of power mongers and tyrants because it is difficult for them to feel enough trust to acknowledge any vulnerability. Their *driving force* is lust/excess. Often, they feel it is their responsibility to intervene in and direct situations, and they pursue power and control (their *fixation*) aggressively. They hold a value for justice—as self-defined. *Advocates* can have a "bull-in-the-china-shop" approach because they speak in imperatives.

Developmental skills include enhancing their ability to put themselves in others' shoes, collaborative negotiation and active listening skills, and respecting and mentoring others. Their key development need is innocence—a regaining of the child they never were, accompanied by a shift to more altruistic and benign modes of operating, a focus on service to the world.

Leadership Style Nine: The Diploma

Serene and centered, well-developed *Diplomats* bring cooperation to any organization; they are highly capable of dealing with others' problems and building consensus. They have a natural tendency to honor diversity, and can get along with almost anyone.

Unexamined Nines tend to merge with others' preferences, however, and to forget their own. Taking a strong position is particularly difficult for them, because they see all sides of an issue and because they are essentially non-aggressive. Their *driving force* is indolence—not that they're lazy (they're very hard workers) but that they are out of touch with their own wishes, a *fixation* on self-forgetting. Though quiet, once they get started they tend toward epic tales (they hold so many alternative views it's hard to focus).

The Mentoring Process

- Goal setting
- Observation
- Analysis
- Providing feedback
- Action planning
- Review

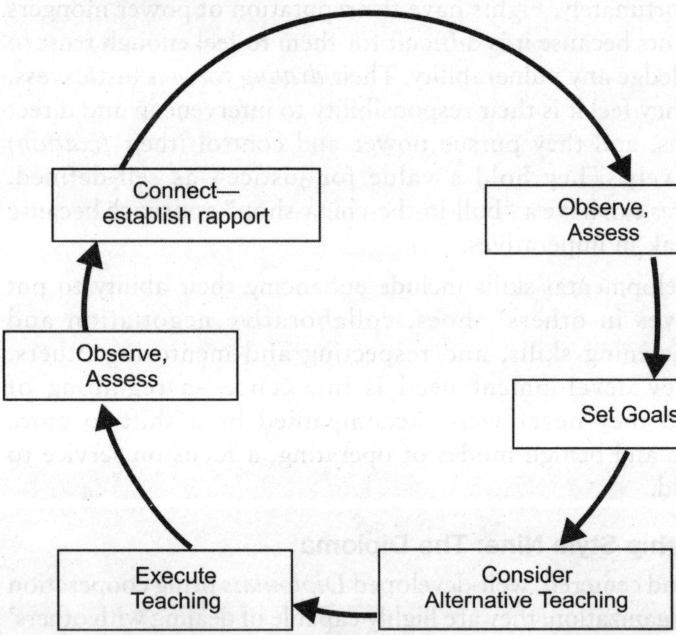

Mentoring Purposes

- Professional Development
- Accreditation
- Updating
- Fast tracking

Mentoring Program in Indian Pharmaceutical Industry

Dr. Reddy's laboratories have its own in-house learning centre, "Ankur". Ankur stands for SPROUT, which means beginning of growth or germination from a bud. The symbolism of SPROUT stands for growth with transformation and is an apt representation of Human Potential Development. Ankur acts as a node, to ensure that the learning process is accelerated throughout the group. The activities of Ankur are steered by a Supervisory Board consisting of Heads of the Strategic Business Units. This Supervisory Board is led by a Director.

The Vision of Ankur is to: Involve people to enable Dr. Reddys' Family to be the best learning organization. The Mission of Ankur is to:

- To provide a space where employees can study and reflect.
- To provide resources for intellectual stimulation.
- To enable an individual to grow as a person.
- To provide learning resources for self development and potential enfoldment, to make the difference so that one can become more valuable to the Self-Organization and Society.

Dr. Reddy's organizes events to encourage holistic employee development. Some of the plans and programs outlined by Dr. Reddy's are:

Leadership Development Program

The Leadership Development Program (LDP) has been initiated as part of the overall talent management program in the company. The top 50 executives of the company are included in this process which consists of workshops on company strategy and values, 360 degree feedback, development of coaching skills, etc. Every individual in the Leadership Group also prepares his/her development plan which is discussed with the CEO and the COO. Based on the LDP, structured development programs are being rolled out including training, job rotation, special projects, etc. The program also includes formal methods of assessing leadership competencies and providing career growth for senior executives.

Management Development Program

Management Development Program (MDP) is one of the programs in the Overall Talent Management initiative. It is an Annual program that helps identify leaders capable of shouldering responsibility in future. MDP creates a talent pool of those employees who rank high on performance in their present position and also have the potential to handle challenges and greater responsibility. MDP creates a career path for promising executives by offering options for growth and development, besides providing opportunities for moving into leadership positions.

Mentoring Roles

- Coach
- Facilitate
- Counsel
- Sponsor
- Support

Characteristics of a Good Mentor

"Mentoring is to support and encourage people to manage their own learning in order that they may maximise their potential, develop their skills, improve their performance and become the person they want to be."

Mentoring is a powerful personal development and empowerment tool. It is an effective way of helping people to progress in their careers and is becoming increasing popular as its potential is realised. It is a partnership between two people (mentor and mentee) normally working in a similar field or sharing similar experiences. It is a helpful relationship based upon mutual trust and respect.

A mentor is a guide who can help the mentee to find the right direction and who can help them to develop solutions to career issues. Mentors rely upon having had similar experiences to gain an empathy with the mentee and an understanding of their issues. Mentoring provides the mentee with an opportunity to think about career options and progress.

A mentor should help the mentee to believe in herself and boost her confidence. A mentor should ask questions and challenge, while providing guidance and encouragement. Mentoring allows the mentee to explore new ideas in confidence. It is a chance to look more closely at yourself, your issues, opportunities and what you want in life. Mentoring is about becoming more self aware, taking responsibility for your life and directing your life in the direction you decide, rather than leaving it to chance. The points under as follows are the main characteristics of a good mentor:

- Approachable and welcoming.
- Shares information and experiences openly.
- Good communication skills.
- Trustworthy.
- Provides accurate and appropriate feedback.
- Technical expertise.
- Motivating, encouraging, positive and empowering.
- Allocates appropriate time to mentoring.
- Sensitive to the needs of the coach/official.

Characteristics of a Good Coach

- Drives the process and take responsibility for solving problems, personal growth and development.
- Motivated and willing to develop a good relationship.
- Listens and accepts guidance and feedback.
- Sets realistic and appropriate goals.
- Reliable, trustworthy and maintains confidentiality.
- Looks to be challenged.
- Flexible and open to new ideas.
- Shows initiative and enthusiasm but has reasonable expectations.
- Recognizes, acknowledges and appreciates mentor.

Foundations for Successful Mentoring Relationships

- Develop and communicate clear goals and expectations at the beginning.
- Set the ground rules and develop an agreement.
- Clarify the roles of the mentor and mentee.
- Work out when and how feedback will occur.
- Review the relationship at regular intervals.

Tips for Mentors

In an effort to be helpful, some mentors go too far. They offer to do things we believe are unwise. Here are some examples along with what we believe are preferable steps to take.

Investing Financially in Mentee's Business or Life Pursuits

Occasionally you may be invited by your mentee to buy something, invest in his/her business, pay his/her bills, or otherwise bring money into the relationship. Doing so in a formal mentoring partnership changes the relationship and causes a conflict of interest. In counseling, this is called a "dual relationship". No longer can you be neutral and objective about the mentee's performance. He/she won't be as open with you about problems, concerns, and mistakes for fear you'll withdraw (or regret) your support. The mentee could even become inappropriately dependent upon you, something to avoid in all mentoring relationships.

Preferred response: I'm honoured that you asked, but I have to say no. I'd like to keep our relationship strictly a mentoring partnership at this time. Once our formal partnership has ended, I'd be glad to entertain a discussion about options like that. How about, if we identify some other sources for you.

"Working" for Your Mentee

In this case, your mentee "hires" you (with or without pay) to do an actual work task. Examples: write his/her resume, complete a scholarship application, inventory Web-based degree programs, interview his/her fellow employees about how the mentee is performing on the job. In each of these situations, you're doing the work the *mentee* should be doing (or paying someone else to do).

Preferred response: I appreciate your faith in my ability to do that task. However, this is a step I'd rather not take. I prefer working behind the scenes with you and helping you do this important task yourself. I'll be very glad to give you feedback as you go along.

Playing Personal Counselor

This one can happen before you even realize it, so discuss some boundaries when you're setting up the partnership. Effective mentors don't limit their helping to work-related issues. In fact, the best mentors help mentees with their total life issues and challenges. Yet, they pay attention to "the line". They resist giving critical personal advice and counseling especially when the mentee is experiencing big psychological challenges. These can include major marital or family difficulties, drug or alcohol misuse, depression, and other potentially complex and even life-threatening situations.

Preferred response: I'm glad you mentioned about my talent. I care very much about you and want to support you as you deal with this. As we discussed, when we set up our relationship, we may run into something I'm not an expert on. I believe this is one of those situations. How about if we talk with confidence on this and come up with a way you can get the assistance you need?

If you're in a work setting, by all means get advice from your human resources or personnel experts anytime you believe your mentee is heading into difficult areas. If you're on your own, make an anonymous call to a local or national mental health hotline or consult another expert for some guidance.

When you're starting out as a mentor, you won't always be clear about where to set your boundaries. Whenever possible, check with your program coordinator or someone else you trust to develop limits that are right for you.

A sense of purpose and the ability to be purposeful are key to personal and organizational success. Mentoring can be a highly effective means of evoking purposefulness, and so generate high levels of motivation and corporate intent. Now it explores how mentoring can be used to uncover purpose, what the impact on the individual of increased purposefulness can be, and how individual and organizational purpose can be aligned to the benefit of both.

Interestingly, organizations need to be able to continuously reinvent themselves so as to stay aligned with and responsive to their customers and other stakeholders. Creating the necessary changes can involve a wide range of programs and initiatives such as culture change, process re-engineering, benchmarking, total quality management, values alignment, and so forth. What all these have in common is that, to be successful, they have to be accompanied by behavioural change by the organization's stakeholders and, in particular, by the organization's senior executives. Executive mentoring is an intervention designed to support such senior executives and other key staff in making the necessary behaviour changes.

Summary

In ancient time, there was a tradition of guru and shish (Mentor and mentee) in almost all the fields such as education, wrestling, spiritualism, politics, etc. That time mentor was very much diehard and devoted for the mentee and so was the mentee. In that era, both of them remain ready to sacrifice the nearest and dearest things of life without taking a second thought. In *Mahabharata*, Arjun was a famous archer and he was trained by his Guru Dronacharya. Eklavya was a schedule caste fellow and he was eager to learn archery with Guru Dronacharya. Dronacharya had refused to accept him as student because he belongs to schedule caste. Interestingly, Eklavya was used to learn the art of archery without attending the class of Guru Dronacharya. In *Mahabharata* fight, Eklavya was standing against Arjun and he was far superior to Arjun in hitting the target. Guru Dronacharya demanded *guru dakshna* and he demanded his right thumb. Eklavya had given his right thumb to Guru Dronacharya because he had accepted him as imaginary *guru* but he had spoiled his career and sacrificed his right thumb as *guru dakshna*.

Mentoring is the key to developing top talent and visionary acumen in professional career. Mentoring in an individual career significantly enhances the ability to advance compared to non-method peers. Significant improvement in the performance of individuals and in both skills and knowledge for participants and mentors. Organizations with formal mentoring have significantly higher employee performance, morale and commitment. Mentoring increases organization commitment for customers, vendors, employees and associates. It is an old proverb "guru bina gyan nahi" (Knowledge transfer is not possible without mentor).

Chapter five

BRAINSTORMING

Brainstorming is a process for developing innovative solutions to problems by a group of people. The method was first popularized in the late 1930s by Alex Faickney Osborn, an advertising executive and one of the founders of BBDO, in a book called *Applied Imagination*.

It works by focusing on a problem, and then deliberately coming up with as many solutions as possible and by pushing the ideas as far as possible. One of the reasons it is so effective that the brainstormers not only come up with new ideas in a session, but also spark off from associations with other people's ideas by developing and refining them.

This method improves the service that you offer, or when existing approaches just aren't giving you the results you want. This increases the richness of solutions explored (meaning that you can find better solutions to the problems you face, and make better decisions). It can also help you get buy in from team members for the solution chosen—after all, they have helped create that solution.

For example, how will you control terrorism 100 per cent globally? In my opinion, terrorism stems from injustice, and simultaneously backed by known and unknown rival. You can stop separatist terrorism such as terrorism in Punjab and North-East and you really did that but controlling terrorism backed by religious group is a tough task and the burning example is J&K. Indian Mujahideen is one of the top Indian religious terrorist groups and it is believed that they are communal riot hybrid terrorist group.

There are few reasons for formation of terrorist groups in India:

- Involvement of political parties for the justice of religious rights and religious place (Ram janam bhumi and Babri masjid disputed issue).

- Involvement of political parties for vote benefits by using sentiments of caste and creed (formation of sunlight sena and Ranbeer sena in Bihar).
- Weak control of government if communal riot take place (communal riot of 1984, Bhagalpur riot and Gujarat riot).
- Fueling the issue by media.
- Huge delay in justice and compensation reimbursement of deprived group.

What are the measures to control religious terrorism in India? We have to follow strictly the following points:

- Honest and ethical role of media in cooling down the pulse of citizen so that hatred wave cannot go beyond control.
- Government should be honest and ethical in providing safety and security in time.
- Strict and honest behaviour of judiciary is required and justice should be as early as possible.
- Compensation should be paid to the victim then and there.
- Those who remain alone aftermath of riot incidence that person should be taken care by the government authority with love and affection so that no one can take advantage of his or her hatred.
- Regular counseling should be given to the affected people with full dedication.

Rules of Brainstorming Session

Brainstorming with a group of people is a powerful technique. Brainstorming creates new ideas, solves problems, motivates and develops teams. Brainstorming motivates because it involves members of a team in bigger management issues, and it gets a team working together. However, brainstorming is not simply a random activity. Brainstorming needs to be structured and it follows brainstorming rules. There are four basic rules in brainstorming. These are intended to reduce the social inhibitions that occur in groups and therefore stimulate the generation of new ideas. The expected result is a dynamic synergy that will dramatically increase the creativity of the group.

1. ***Focus on quantity***: This rule is a means of enhancing divergent production, aiming to facilitate problem solving through the maxim, *quantity breeds quality*. The assumption is that, the greater the number of ideas generated, the greater the chance of producing a radical and effective solution.
2. ***No criticism***: It is often emphasized that in group brainstorming, *criticism* should be put 'on hold'. Instead of immediately stating what might be wrong with an idea, the participants focus on extending or adding to it, reserving criticism for a later 'critical stage' of the process. By suspending judgment, one creates a supportive atmosphere where participants feel free to generate unusual ideas.
3. ***Unusual ideas are welcome***: To get a good and long list of ideas, unusual ideas are welcomed. They may open new ways of thinking and provide better solutions than regular ideas. They can be generated by looking from another perspective or setting aside assumptions.
4. ***Combine and improve ideas***: Good ideas can be combined to form a single very good idea, as suggested by the slogan "1+1=11". This approach is assumed to lead to better and more complete ideas than merely generating new ideas alone. It is believed to stimulate the building of ideas by a process of association.

Methods of Brainstorming Session

Brainstorming can help you choose a topic, develop an approach to a topic, or deepen your understanding of the topic's potential. If you consciously take advantage of your natural thinking processes by gathering your brain's energies into a "storm", you can transform these energies into written words or diagrams that will lead to lively, vibrant writing. Below you will find a brief discussion of what brainstorming is, why you might brainstorm, and suggestions for how you might brainstorm.

Whether you are starting with too much information or not enough, brainstorming can help you to put a new writing task in motion or revive a project that hasn't reached completion.

What follows are great ideas on how to brainstorm—ideas from professional writers, novice writers, people who would rather avoid writing, and people who spend a lot of time brainstorming about well, how to brainstorm.

Try out several of these options and challenge yourself to vary the techniques you rely on; some techniques might suit a particular writer, academic discipline, or assignment better than others. If the technique you try first doesn't seem to help you, move right along and try some others.

Set the Problem

One of the most important things to do before a session is to define the problem. The problem must be clear, not too big, and captured in a definite question such as "What service for mobile phones is not available now, but needed?". If the problem is too big, the chairman should divide it into smaller components, each with its own question. Some problems are multi-dimensional and non-quantified, for example, "What are the aspects involved in being a successful entrepreneur?" Finding solutions for this kind of problem can be done with morphological analysis (problem-solving).

Create a Background Memo

The background memo is the invitation and informational letter for the participants, containing the session name, problem, time, date, and place. The problem is described in the form of a question, and some example ideas are given. The ideas are solutions to the problem, and used when the session slows down or goes off-track. The memo is sent to the participants at least two days in advance, so that they can think about the problem beforehand.

Select Participants

The chairman composes the brainstorming panel, consisting of the participants and an idea collector. Ten or fewer group members are generally more productive than larger groups. Many variations are possible but the following composition is suggested:

- Several core members of the project who have proved themselves.
- Several guests from outside the project, with affinity to the problem.
- One idea collector who records the suggested ideas.

Create a List of Lead Questions

During the brainstorm session, the creativity may decrease. At this moment, the chairman should stimulate creativity by suggesting a lead question to answer, such as *Can we combine these ideas?* or *How about a look from another perspective?* It is advised to prepare a list of such leads before the session begins.

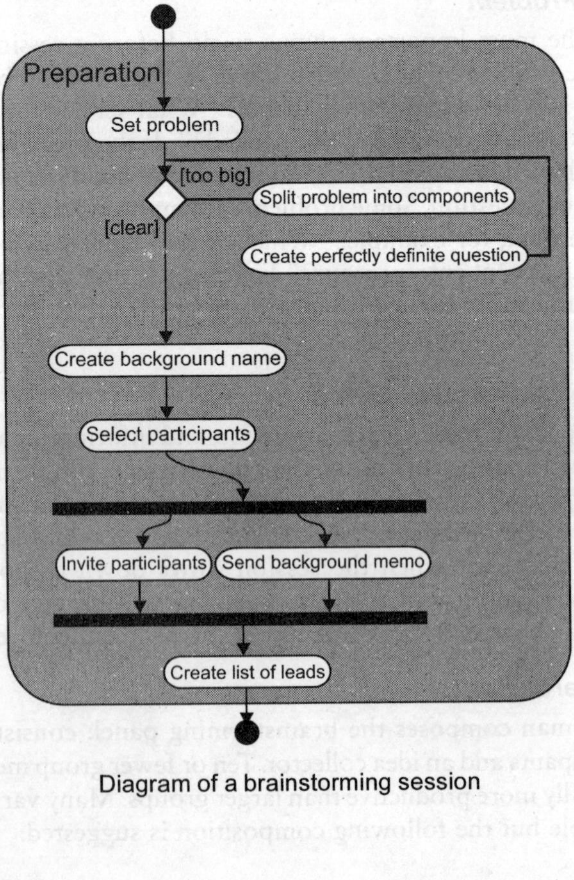

Diagram of a brainstorming session

Process of Brainstorming Session

The brainstorming process is described below, for which you will need a flip-chart or alternative. This is crucial as Brainstorming needs to involve the team, which means that everyone must be able to see what's happening. Brainstorming places a significant burden on the facilitator to manage the process, people's involvement and sensitivities, and then to manage the follow up actions. Use Brainstorming well and you will see excellent results in improving the organization, performance, and developing the team. The *chairperson* leads the brainstorming session and ensures that the basic rules are followed. The activities of a typical session are:

1. A warm-up session, to expose novice participants to the criticism-free environment. A simple problem is brainstormed, for example, *what should be the next corporate Christmas present?* Or *what can be improved in Microsoft Windows?*
2. The chairman presents the problem and gives a further explanation if needed.
3. The chairman asks the brainstorming panel for their ideas.
4. If no ideas are coming out, the chairman suggests a lead to encourage creativity.
5. Every participant presents his or her idea, and the idea collector records them.
6. If more than one participant has ideas, the chairman lets the most associated idea be presented first. This selection can be done by looking at the body language of the participants, or just by asking for the most associated idea.
7. The participants try to elaborate on the idea, to improve the quality.
8. When time is up, the chairman organizes the ideas based on the topic goal and encourages discussion. Additional ideas may be generated.
9. Ideas are categorized.

10. The whole list is reviewed to ensure that everyone understands the ideas. Duplicate ideas and obviously infeasible solutions are removed.
11. The chairman thanks all participants and gives each a token of appreciation.

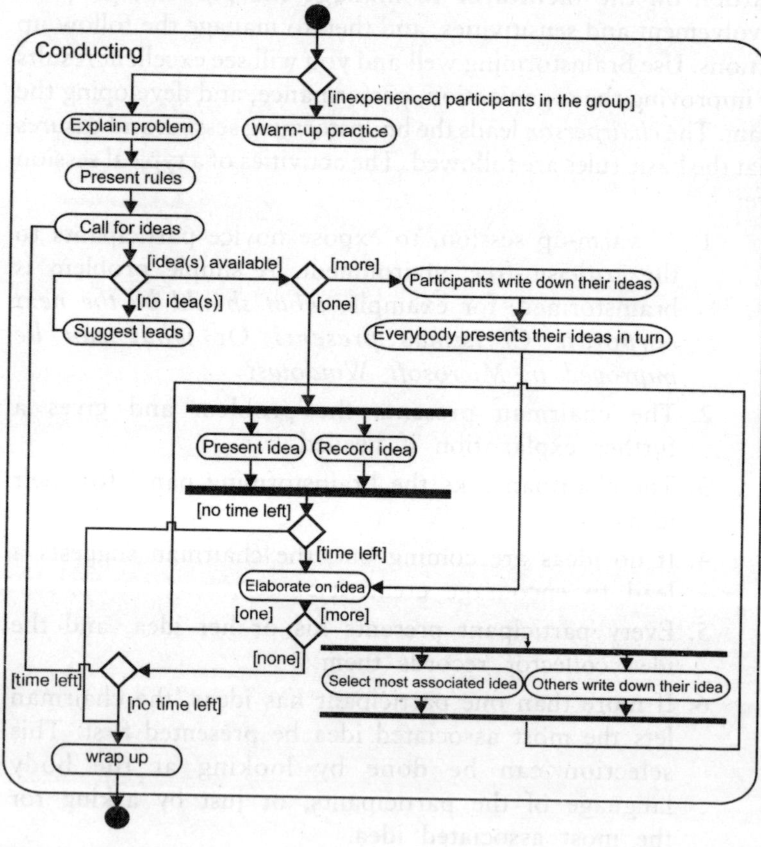

The Process

- Participants who have an idea but no possibility to present it are encouraged to write down their idea and present it later.

- The idea collector should number the ideas, so that the chairperson can use the number to encourage quantitative idea generation, for example: *We have 46 ideas now, let's get it to 50.*
- The idea collector should repeat the idea in the words he or she has written it, to confirm that it expresses the meaning intended by the originator.
- When more participants are having ideas, the one with the most associated idea should have priority. This to encourage elaboration on previous ideas.
- During the brainstorming session the attendance of managers and superiors is strongly discouraged, as it may inhibit and reduce the effect of the four basic rules, especially the generation of unusual ideas.

Brainstorming Process Steps Include

1. Define and agree the objective.
2. Brainstorm ideas and suggestions having agreed a time limit.
3. Categorize/condense/combine/refine.
4. Assess/analyse effects or results.
5. Prioritise options/rank list as appropriate.
6. Agree action and timescale.
7. Control and monitor follow-up.

Evaluation of Brainstorming Session

Brainstorming is not just about generating ideas for others to evaluate and select. Usually the group itself will, in its final stage, evaluate the ideas and select one as the solution to the problem proposed to the group.

- The solution should not require resources or skills the members of the group do not have or cannot acquire.
- If acquiring additional resources or skills is necessary, that needs to be the first part of the solution.
- There must be a way to measure progress and success.

- The steps to carry out the solution must be clear to all, and amenable to being assigned to the members so that each will have an important role.
- There must be a common decision-making process to enable a coordinated effort to proceed, and to reassign tasks as the project unfolds.
- There should be evaluations at milestones to decide whether the group is on track toward a final solution.
- There should be incentives to participation such that participants maintain their efforts.

Types of Brainstorming

Brainstorming can be an effective way to generate lots of ideas on a specific issue and then determine which idea is the best solution. Brainstorming is most effective with groups of 8-12 people and should be performed in a relaxed environment. If participants feel free to relax and joke around, they'll stretch their minds further and therefore produce more creative ideas.

A brainstorming session requires a facilitator, a brainstorming space and something on which to write ideas, such as a white-board a flip chart or software tool. The facilitator's responsibilities include guiding the session, encouraging participation and writing ideas down.

Brainstorming works best with a varied group of people. Participants should come from various departments across the organization and have different backgrounds. Even in specialist areas, outsiders can bring fresh ideas that can inspire the experts.

There are numerous approaches to brainstorming, but the traditional approach is generally the most effective because it is the most energetic and openly collaborative, allowing participants to build on each others' ideas. Creativity exercises, relaxation exercises or other fun activities before the session can help participants relax their minds so that they will be more creative during the brainstorming session.

Personal Brainstorming

Personal brainstorming just by yourself is very useful for the start of any new project, especially if you can be prone to put things off until tomorrow.

Planning a new venture, a presentation, or any new initiative, is generally much easier if you begin simply by thinking of ideas in no particular order or structure and jotting them down on a sheet of paper or in a notebook. Basically this is personal brainstorming, and it can follow the same process as described above for groups, except that it's just you doing it.

Sometimes, it's very difficult to begin planning something new because you don't know where and how to start. Brainstorming is a great way to begin. The method also generates lots of possibilities which you might otherwise miss by getting into detailed structured planning too early. A really useful tool for personal brainstorming and note-taking generally is the wonderful Luxar 4-colour ball pen. The pen enables you quickly to switch colours between red, blue, black and green, without having to walk around with a pocket-full of biros.

Using different colours in your creative jottings and written records helps you to make your notes and diagrams clearer, and dramatically increases the ways in which you can develop and refine your ideas and notes on paper. To prove the point, review some previous notes in black or blue ink using a red pen—see how you can organize/connect the content, still keeping it all clear and legible. This simple pen is therefore a brilliant tool for organizing your thoughts on paper much more clearly and creatively than by being limited to a single colour—especially if you think in visual terms and find diagrams helpful.

For example, using different colours enables you to identify and link common items within a random list, or to show patterns and categories, or to over-write notes without making a confusing mess, and generally to generate far more value from your thoughts and ideas. Keeping connected notes and ideas on a single sheet of paper greatly helps the brain to absorb and develop them. Try it; you'll be surprised how much more useful your notes become.

The principle is the same as using different colours of marker pens on a flip-chart. Other manufacturers produce similar pens, but the Luxar is reliable, widely available, and very inexpensive.

The usefulness of different colours in written notes is further illustrated in a wider organizational sense in the health industry. Apparently, black is the standard colour; green is used by pharmacy services, red is used after death and for allergies, and blue tends to be avoided due to poorer reprographic qualities. As I say, correct me if this is wrong, and in any event *please let me know* any other examples of different coloured inks being used to organize or otherwise clarify written communications within corporations, institutions or industries.

When you brainstorm on your own, you will tend to produce a wider range of ideas than with group brainstorming—you do not have to worry about other people's egos or opinions, and can therefore be more freely creative. You may not, however, develop ideas as effectively as you do not have the experience of a group to help you. When Brainstorming on your own, it can be helpful to use *Mind Maps* to arrange and develop ideas.

Nominal Group Technique

The nominal group technique is a type of brainstorming that encourages all participants to have an equal say in the process. It is also used to generate a ranked list of ideas.

Participants are asked to write down their ideas anonymously. Then the *moderator* collects the ideas and each is voted on by the group. The vote can be as simple as a show of hands in favour of a given idea. This process is called distillation.

After distillation, the top ranked ideas may be sent back to the group or to sub-groups for further brainstorming. For example, one group may work on the colour required in a product. Another group may work on the size, and so forth. Each group will come back to the whole group for ranking the listed ideas. Sometimes, ideas that were previously dropped may be brought forward again once the group has re-evaluated the ideas.

It is important for the moderator to have received training in this process before attempting to take on the moderating task.

The group should be primed and encouraged to embrace the process. Like all team efforts, it may take a few practice sessions to train the team in the method before tackling the important ideas.

Group Passing Technique

Each person in a circular group writes down one idea, and then passes the piece of paper to the next person in a clockwise direction, who adds some thoughts. This is repeated until everybody gets their original piece of paper back. By this time, it is likely that the group will have extensively elaborated on each idea.

A popular alternative to this technique is to create an "Idea Book" and post a distribution list or routing slip to the front of the book. On the inside cover (or first page) is a description of the problem. The first person to receive the book lists his or her ideas and then routes the book to the next person on the distribution list. The second person can log new ideas or add to the ideas of the previous person. This continues until the distribution list is exhausted. Follow-up "read out" meeting is then held to discuss the ideas logged in the book. This technique takes longer, but allows individual thought whenever the person has time to think deeply about the problem.

Group brainstorming can be very effective as it uses the experience and creativity of all members of the group. When individual members reach their limit on an idea, another member's creativity and experience can take the idea to the next stage. Therefore, group brainstorming tends to develop ideas in more depth than individual brainstorming.

Brainstorming in a group can be risky for individuals. Valuable but strange suggestions may appear stupid at first sight. Because of this, you need to chair sessions tightly so that uncreative people do not crush these ideas and leave group members feeling humiliated.

Team Idea Mapping Method

This method of brainstorming works by the method of *association*. It may improve collaboration and increase the quantity of ideas, and is designed so that all attendees participate and no ideas are rejected.

The process begins with a well-defined topic. Each participant creates an individual brainstorm around the topic. All the ideas are then merged into one large idea map. During this consolidation phase, the participants may discover a common understanding of the issues as they share the meanings behind their ideas. As the sharing takes place, new ideas may arise by the association. Those ideas are added to the map as well. Then ideas are generated on both individual and group levels. Once, all the ideas are captured, the group can prioritize and/or take action.

Electronic Brainstorming

Electronic brainstorming is a computerized version of the manual brain writing technique. It can be done via email. The chairman or facilitator sends the question out to group members, and they contribute independently by sending their ideas directly back to the facilitator. The facilitator then compiles a list of ideas and sends it back to the group for further feedback. Electronic brainstorming eliminates many of the problems of standard brainstorming, such as production blocking and evaluation apprehension. An additional advantage of this method is that all ideas can be archived electronically in their original form, and then retrieved later for further thought and discussion. Electronic brainstorming also enables much larger groups to brainstorm on a topic than would normally be productive in a traditional brainstorming session.

Other forms of electronic brainstorming could be browser based client/server, or peer to peer related software.

Directed Brainstorming

Directed brainstorming is a variation on electronic brainstorming (brainwriting) described above. It can be done manually or with computer technology. Directed brainstorming works when the solution space (that is, the criteria for evaluating a good idea) is known prior to the session. If known, that criteria can be used to intentionally constrain the *ideation* process. In directed brainstorming, each participant is given one sheet of paper (or electronic form) and told the brainstorming question. They are asked to produce one response and stop. At that point, all of the papers (or forms) are randomly swapped among the participants. Each, then, has possession of someone else's form containing a single response. The participants are asked to look at the idea in front of them and create a new idea that is better than that idea on the first criterion dimension. For example, if the first criterion was "low cost" the participants might be asked to improve upon the idea in front of them by creating an idea that is lower in cost. The forms are then swapped again and respondents are asked to improve upon the ideas against the second criterion. The process is repeated for three or more rounds.

In the laboratory, directed brainstorming has been found to almost triple the productivity of groups over electronic brainstorming.

Individual Brainstorming

"Individual Brainstorming" is the use of brainstorming on a solitary basis. It typically includes such techniques as *free writing*, free speaking, word association, and the "spider web", which is a visual note taking technique in which a people diagram their thoughts. Individual brainstorming is a useful method in *creative writing* and has been shown to be superior to traditional group brainstorming.

Other Variations

One of the problems can be to find the best questions to ask. This has been called *questorming*. Another of the problems for brainstorming can be to find the best evaluation methods for a problem.

Brainstorming and Lateral Thinking

Brainstorming is a lateral thinking process. It asks that people come up with ideas and thoughts that seem at first to be a bit shocking or crazy. You can then change and improve them into ideas that are useful, and often stunningly original.

During brainstorming sessions, there should therefore be no criticism of ideas: You are trying to open up possibilities and break down wrong assumptions about the limits of the problem. Judgements and analysis at this stage will stunt idea generation.

Ideas should only be evaluated at the end of the brainstorming session. You can then explore solutions further using conventional approaches.

If your ideas begin to dry up, you can 'seed' the session with, for example, a random word (see *Random Input*).

Delphi Decision-making

In Delphi decision groups, a series of questionnaires are sent to selected respondents (Delphi group). The group does not meet face-to-face. All communications are normally in writing (normally letters or email). Members of the groups are selected because the are experts or they have relevant information. Steps include:

- Members are asked to share their assessment and explanation of a problem or predict a future state of affairs.
- Replies are gathered, summarized, and then fed back to all the group members.
- Members then make another decision based upon the new information.
- The process may be repeated until the responses converge satisfactory.

The success of this process depends upon the member's expertise and communication skill. Also, each response requires adequate time for reflection and analysis. The major merits of the Delphi process are:

- Elimination of interpersonal problems.
- Efficient use of expert's time.
- Diversity of ideals.
- Accuracy of solutions and predictions.

Dialectic Decision-making

The dialectic decision method (DDM) traces its roots back to Socrates and Plato. It helps to overcome such problems as converging too quickly one solution while overlooking others, participants dislike of meetings, incomplete evaluations, and the failure to confront tough issues. The steps of DDM are:

- Issue a clear statement of the problem to be solved.
- Two or more competing proposals are generated.
- Members identify the explicit or implicit assumptions that underlie each proposal.
- The team then breaks into advocacy sub, who examine and argue the relative merits of their positions.

The group reassembles and makes a decision:

- Embrace one of the alternatives.
- Forge a compromise.
- Generate a new proposal.

The process looks like this:

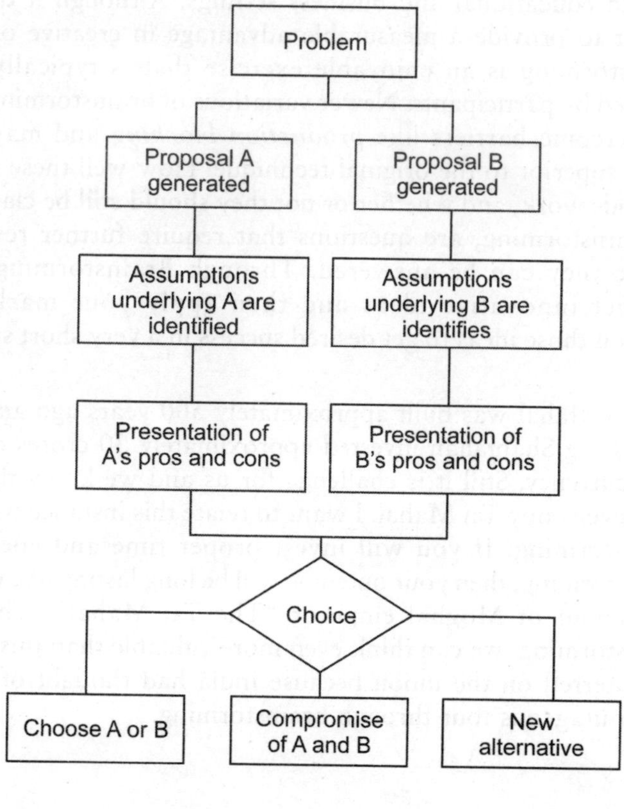

This process helps the members to better understand the proposals along with their pros and cons. The main disadvantage is the tendency to forge a compromise in order to avoid choosing sides.

Summary

It is an old adage "Always there is an idea problem and not the money problem." Once a group of management students asked Pitter Drucker, father of management, in America, sir what is key to earn money, he replied "you can earn lots of money through innovation and marketing". You can't get recognition if you will think like an average people. You have to create storm in your brain to think something useful, something new, something valuable.

Brainstorming is a popular method of group interaction in both educational and business settings. Although it doesn't appear to provide a measurable advantage in creative output, brainstorming is an enjoyable exercise that is typically well received by participants. Newer variations of brainstorming seek to overcome barriers like *production blocking* and may well prove superior to the original technique. How well these newer methods work, and whether or not they should still be classified as brainstorming, are questions that require further research before they can be answered. Through Brainstorming, you will get innovative ideas and then apply your marketing skills on those ideas to get desired success in a very short span of time.

Taj Mahal was built approximately 500 years ago and that time, King Shahjahan invested approximately 30 crores of that time currency. Still it is challenge for us and we know that we can't even copy Taj Mahal. I want to relate this instance with the brainstorming. If you will invest proper time and energy in brainstorming, then your outcome will be long lasting like unique monument of Moghal emperor "The Taj Mahal". Through brainstorming, we can think even more valuable than this. India has interred on the moon because India had thought of doing this courageous tour through brainstorming.

We can apply brainstorming technique in our day-to-day professional career, office management, customer relationship management, retention of employees, performance management, total quality management, project management, personal and professional dispute solving, better coordination with boss and colleagues etc.

Chapter six

LOYALTY

Loyalty is a "non-negotiable or unconditional relationship between employer and employee in which both of them have willingness to make an investment or personal sacrifice to strengthen a relationship".

If, someone has worked for your organization for ten years or twenty years it does not necessarily mean he or she is loyal. May be he is unhappy but doesn't feel like looking for another job, or may be she doesn't have marketable skills and can't find another employer to hire her. It is important to identify your loyal (not your longstanding) employees.

On some fine day, one of your good performer employees comes to you and says, he is ready to work with you whole of life. But it is up to you if you are ready to contract with him with prior condition of increment and promotion or even profit sharing basis etc. Mind it, this is not at all a loyalty from the end of employee or if you contract with him, then you have developed a mutual agreed contractual relationship. Therefore, loyalty is always a non-negotiable relationship between employer and employee and loyalty goes a long way in whole of life. The best example is Jack Welch, the most admired chairman and CEO of the most admired company of the world GE. Jack started his career with GE with $300 per month salary and retired from GE with global recognition, respect and many more assets. He is so valuable that his autobiography is the best seller.

In this era of globalization and liberalization, employees are becoming the competitive advantage for business. A business may manage with mediocre employees but competent employees can propel an average business to greater heights. Likewise, bad employees can cause flourishing business empires to collapse. In a tight labour market, keeping good employees and developing employee loyalty becomes increasingly important and a continuing challenge.

With the tight labour market, employers therefore need a strategy to retain their key experts and crucial skilled workers. As prospective employers continuously bid for top performers, management strategies must therefore give due consideration and sufficient resource allocation to keep employees motivated and satisfied. The idea is that the satisfied employee is less likely to pursue greener pastures. Thus, implementing desirable human resource management policies will have a positive effect on employee loyalty.

Human resource management places great emphasis on the internal labour market to fill promotion opportunities, long-term development programs and job security, among others. All these are contributory factors for employee loyalty. For India and other part of the world to sustain economic growth, appropriate human resource management policies that promote employee loyalty are essential.

Continuous and systematic approach to training and development, recruitment policies that reduce job-hopping and ensure long-term employment, internal promotion practices with a little recognition given to seniority and the implementation of the productivity-linked wage system would create a more committed employee towards the company. As most of these elements are representative of Japanese style of human resource management which enhance employee loyalty and encourages long-term employment, the hypothesis for this study is employee loyalty would be higher in companies where elements of Japanese style of human resource management are present.

Loyalty and Ethics

The concept of loyalty is an important part of *ethics*. *Plato* originally said that only a man who is just can be loyal, and that loyalty is a condition of genuine *philosophy*. The philosopher Josiah Royce said it was the supreme moral good, and that one's devotion to an object mattered more than the merits of the object itself.

Loyalty in the *Bible*

Jesus said, "No one can serve two masters. Either he will hate the one and love the other, or he will be devoted to the one and despise the other" (Matthew 6:24 NIV). Attempting to serve two masters leads to "double-mindedness" (James 4:8), undermining loyalty to a cause.

Employees Loyalty

In a tight labour market, keeping employees and developing employee loyalty becomes increasingly important and a long-term challenge. Your employees serve as the face of your organization on a daily basis. Whether they interact with clients by telephone or e-mail, or meet customers face-to-face every day, you need loyal employees in order to have loyal clients. If an employee is not happy at your organization, that fact will come across to customers; if he is loyal, that will come across too. Employees who are loyal and enthusiastic will encourage your customers to also feel loyal and enthusiastic towards your organization.

Loyal employees represent a cost savings over recruiting and training new hires, and loyal employees can be incredible assets to a growing company. Furthermore, there is a direct relationship between customer loyalty and a company's growth and profitability. You can't have loyal customers without loyal employees. Employee loyalty is evident to your customers and it's nearly impossible to generate loyal customers without strong internal loyalty. There's no way around it.

How to Build Employee Loyalty?

Many human resource specialists cite employee satisfaction and retention as main concerns of today's employers. One way a business can retain key employees is by offering creative alternatives to standard HR benefits that better meet employees' professional, and personal, needs.

Over time, companies have increased the level of HR support they give their employees. In the past, employees who had health insurance and any type of retirement plan considered themselves fortunate. Now businesses offer a variety of benefits that go far beyond basic health care and retirement. In today's workforce, employees can expect added or supplemental health benefits that can include dental, vision, chiropractic, and employee-assistance programs, as well as a series of retirement and pension programs that give a multitude of options for adapting the plan to meet an employee's specific needs.

The idea of alternative benefits has also expanded to include a variety of perks from flexible scheduling to telecommuting options. The list of common alternative benefits includes the following:

- Educational assistance and management training.
- Paid time off (other than vacation and sick leave).
- Health club memberships.
- Leave bank/leave donation program.
- Attendance incentives.
- Various health benefit options.
- Supplemental retirement plans.
- Pension systems.
- Employee credit unions.
- Outside recreational activities.

Once thought to be a benefit appealing mostly to working mothers or parents, flex scheduling has recently become one of the most popular perks a business can offer. A study by the Families and Work Institute found that 73 per cent of employees take advantage of flexible-scheduling benefits when available. Businesses use flex scheduling in four basic ways:

- ***Flex time***: Employees are given control over setting their daily schedules.
- ***Compressed work weeks***: Employees work longer hours but fewer days.
- ***Job sharing***: Two part-time employees share the same full-time position.
- ***Flex place***: Employees work from home (or a location closer to home).

In addition, businesses increasingly provide benefits such as employee-assistance programs (tuition reimbursement, counseling), wellness programs (sleep breaks, massages), and fitness programs (free health club memberships).

Some innovative benefits include the following:

- Educational assistance and tuition reimbursement.
- Sleep breaks.
- Onsite day care.
- Onsite fitness center.
- Partial reimbursement for buying a hybrid vehicle.
- Onsite massage.
- Fully paid luxury retreats for all employees.

Employees are the most important resource your company has. Treat your employees well and they will become invaluable assets that can help make your business be a success.

Life Partner Loyalty

You can enjoy your success professional life in a better way if you have good personal relation with your life partner. It is common story in India that God has first created plant Kingdome and slept away. He then created animal Kingdome and slept away. He created man and again slept away. Finally He created woman and from then neither God slept nor the man. Some says a woman loves gold, diamond, money and always ready to make a move for shopping and outing. It is also very famous that lion is the only fearless animal on the earth but it is also true that a lion bows his head only before a lioness. There is many more myth about a woman and all myths are created or cooked by a man only.

In reality you can develop a loyal relationship with your life partner. First you have to identify the needs and wants of your life partner and satisfy those need and wants in such a manner that he or she becomes addict of your service. A female partner can lure the heart of her partner if she is competent in cooking tasty dishes and can respect the ego as well. A male partner can win the beautiful heart of his partner if he can support in shopping and outing with full emotion and devotion. She wants possessiveness, cares, emotional love and not the costly ornaments and money. You must say your partner "love you" morning and evening without hesitation and without ego clash. If you will really follow the above-mention strategy, then obviously, your relation will be loyal life partner relationship.

Customer Loyalty

The term *customer loyalty* is used to describe the behaviour of repeat customers, as well as those that offer good ratings, reviews, or testimonials. Some customers do a particular company a great service by offering favourable word of mouth publicity regarding a product, telling friends and family, thus adding them to the number of loyal customers. However, customer loyalty includes much more. It is a process, a program, or a group of programs geared toward keeping a client happy so he or she will provide more business.

Customer loyalty can be achieved in some cases by offering a quality product with a firm guarantee. Customer loyalty is also achieved through free offers, coupons, low *interest rates* on financing, high value trade-ins, extended warranties, rebates, and other rewards and incentive programs. The ultimate goal of customer *loyalty programs* is happy customers who will return to purchase again and persuade others to use that company's products or services. This equates to profitability as well as happy stakeholders.

Customer loyalty may be a one-time program or incentive, or an ongoing group of programs to entice consumers. Buy-one-get-one-free programs are very popular, as are purchases that come with rebates or free gifts. Another good incentive for achieving customer loyalty is offering a risk free trial period for a product or service. Also known as *brand name loyalty*, these types of incentives are meant to ensure that customers will return, not only to buy the same product again and again, but also to try other products or services offered by the company.

Excellent customer service is another key element in gaining customer loyalty. If a client has a problem, the company should do whatever it takes to make things right. If a product is faulty, it should be replaced or the customer's money should be refunded.

This should be standard procedure for any reputable business, but those who wish to develop customer loyalty on a large-scale basis may also go above and beyond the standard. They may offer even more by way of free gifts or discounts to appease the customer.

Customer loyalty is the practice of finding, attracting, and retaining your customers who regularly purchase from you. Customer loyalty is not customer satisfaction. Customer satisfaction is the basic entry point of good business practices. Your small business should provide satisfaction to all your customers.

Loyalty cards and programs have their rewards and pitfalls. Rewarding customers for spending more dollars can create a vicious cycle of creating customers who want rewards and will look anywhere to obtain them. With loyalty cards and programs reaching a saturation point, how can a small business stand out?

Without loyal customers, it is harder to grow your business and more costly to service the customers you have. It is harder to grow your business, because the best sources of new customers are referrals and positive comments from existing customers. If this source of new business dries up, your company either does not grow or must acquire new customers in a more costly fashion (i.e. expensive advertising, larger sales force, etc.). It is more costly to service disloyal customers because they are the ones who keep your employees busy with their complaints. Additionally, unhappy customers become more price-sensitive.

So, to sum it up, loyal customers are simply more profitable than customers who are not loyal and it is easier to grow your company when you retain loyal customers. And it is easier to have loyal customers when you have loyal employees.

"It takes a lot less money to increase your retention of current customers than to find new ones, but I know I don't give it as much effort as I should, because it does take a lot of energy and effort."

Strategize and Plan for Loyalty—Do you even have a specific plan for building customer loyalty? I bet you haven't given it as much thought as you should, because to tell the truth I need to give it more effort also. If you currently retain 70 per cent of your customers and you start a program to improve that to 80 per cent, you'll add an additional 10 per cent to your growth rate. Particularly, because of the high cost of landing new customers versus the high profitability of a loyal customer base, you might want to reflect upon your current business strategy. These four factors will greatly affect your ability to build a loyal customer base:

1. Products that are highly differentiated from those of the competition.
2. Higher-end products where price is not the primary buying factor.
3. Products with a high service component.
4. Multiple products for the same customer.

Market to Your Own Customers—Giving a lot of thought to your marketing programs aimed at current customers is one aspect of building customer loyalty.

When you buy a new car, many dealers will within minutes try to sell you an extended warranty, an alarm system, and maybe rust proofing. It's often a very easy sale and costs the dealer almost nothing to make. Are there additional products or services you can sell your customers?

Three years ago, my house was painted, and it's now due for another coat. Why hasn't the painter called or at least sent a card? It would be a lot less expensive than getting new customers through his newspaper ad, and since I was happy with his work, I won't get four competing bids this time. Keep all the information you can on your customers and don't hesitate to ask for the next sale.

Use Complaints to Build Business—When customers aren't happy with your business they usually won't complain to you—instead, they'll probably complain to just about everyone else they know—and take their business to your competition next time. That's why an increasing number of businesses are making follow-up calls or mailing satisfaction questionnaires after the sale is made. They find that if they promptly follow-up and resolve a customer's complaint, the customer might be even more likely to do business than the average customer who didn't have a complaint.

In many business situations, the customer will have many more interactions after the sale with technical, service, or customer support people than they did with the sales people. So if you're serious about retaining customers or getting referrals, these interactions are the ones that are really going to matter. They really should be handled with the same attention and focus that sales calls get because in a way they are sales calls for repeat business.

Reach Out to Your Customers—Contact...contact...contact with current customers is a good way to build their loyalty. The more the customer sees someone from your firm, the more likely you'll get the next order. Send Christmas cards, see them at trade shows, stop by to make sure everything's okay.

Send a simple newsletter to your customers. Tell them about the great things that are happening at your firm and include some useful information for them. Send them copies of any media clippings about your firm. Invite them to free seminars. The more they know about you, the more they see you as someone out to help them, the more they know about your accomplishments, the more loyal a customer they will be.

Loyal Customers and Loyal Workforces—Building customer loyalty will be a lot easier if you have a loyal workforce. It is especially important for you to retain those employees who interact with customers such as sales people, technical support, and customer-service people. Many companies give a lot of attention to retaining sales people but little to support people. I've been fortunate to have the same great people in customer service for years, and the compliments from customers make it clear that they really appreciate specific people in our service function.

The increasing trend today is to send customer-service and technical-support calls into queue for the next available person. This builds no personal loyalty and probably less loyalty for the firm. Before you go this route, be sure this is what your customers prefer. Otherwise, I'd assign a specific support person to every significant customer. One last thing—don't tell your customers your 800 line phone number is for orders only!

Can Customer Loyalty be Bought?

Forget about customer relationship management software, customer loyalty programs and cards. Customer loyalty can't be bought. It must be earned. Learn the 8 ways your small business can earn customer loyalty.

There is no shortage of lip service in corporate America these days about customer loyalty. The advent of the loyalty movement began in the 80's in the airline industry and expanded to cover every major industry. Research firm Gartner estimates American businesses spent more than 1 billion dollars on loyalty programs in the year 2003. Over 75 per cent of consumers have at least one loyalty card, according to Jupiter Research. My wallet alone has 12 loyalty cards. But does it pay?

Does Customer Loyalty Pay?

A mere 5 per cent increase in customer retention can result in a 75 per cent increase in customer value according to Fred Reichheld, author of *Loyalty Rules*. A great reason to pay attention to loyalty. Here are more benefits:

- grab more sales from existing customer base,
- helps pread word of mouth marketing,
- identify product/service problems earlier,
- improve profitability,
- provide a competitive advantage.

Eight Ways for Small Business to Earn Customer Loyalty

Software, card programs, and loyalty schemes are the tools of customer loyalty programs but they aren't the essence of loyalty. To build loyalty, you must earn it. Look at these 8 ways to earn more customer loyalty for your small business:

Company Loyalty First: Customer loyalty is a 2-way street. How can you expect customer loyalty if you don't practice company loyalty? Are you loyal to your best customers or are you giving discounts and extra attention to new customers?

Loyalty is about being fanatical with devotion to your best customers.

Employee Loyalty Second: Any customer loyalty program must factor in the front line of the business. It's the point of contact between customer and employee that sets the foundation of repeat business. "Hire for attitude, train for skill. Hire nice people. As a customer, I'm always amazed when small businesses put unfriendly, surly people in front of their customers. Loyalty is often the direct result of the relationships your employees build and maintain," says Ben McConnell of marketing consulting firm Wabash and Lake and co-author of *Creating Customer Evangelists*.

Quench the Thirst: Consumers are thirsty for trust following corporate scandals and the general distrust of corporations. If your small business is not trustworthy, your odds of establishing customer loyalty are diminished. Establish good business ethics and practices.

Finding Loyalty: Any small business wishing to start a customer loyalty initiative needs first to identify important customers and understand their customer's behaviours. Use whatever tools, software, and data-mining techniques to locate your repeat, regular customers. Equally vital is to know your profit margins. Don't offer discounts until you know the impact on your bottom line.

Reward Customer Retention: The key metric to track in your customer loyalty program is customer retention. How many customers are defecting? How many clients are retained? Measuring customer retention is half the battle. Your staff must be rewarded for retention. Your small business doesn't have to be like big corporations who talk retention but reward sales people for bringing in new customers only.

Use Customer-centric Language: It's easy to think you put the customer first. However, take a closer look at your marketing communications. How many times does your literature refer to "we" the company versus "you" the customer? Go back and speak from the customer's perspective.

Bolster Customer Communications: Part of customer loyalty and retention are maintaining regular contact with your most profitable customers. Communication to your best customers should take the form of showing your appreciation and providing new learning experiences to add value to your customer's life. Send special thank-you notes, surprise gifts, and regular communications such as newsletters to connect with them.

Use the Small Business Advantage: Small business will always have the advantage in connecting with customers and building a solid relationship. Your passion for helping customers with your products and services is difficult for large companies to replicate. As customer evangelist guru Ben McConnell states, "Small businesses thrive on outstanding customer loyalty. It's their currency of growth and their best differentiator. Without loyalty, small businesses are destined to compete on a playing field with larger competitors where they are outnumbered and outwitted." Win the customer service game by putting customer loyalty to work in your small business. Just remember, it's more than cards and software. It's more about earning trust and relationship building.

Ten Tips to Build Customer Loyalty

The key to a successful business is a steady customer base. After all, successful businesses typically see 80 per cent of their business come from 20 per cent of their customers. Too many businesses neglect this loyal customer base in pursuit of new customers. However, since the cost to attract new customers is significantly more than to maintain your relationship with existing ones, your efforts toward building customer loyalty will certainly payoff. Here are ten ways to build customer loyalty:

1. ***Communicate.*** Whether it is an e-mail newsletter, monthly flier, a reminder card for a tune up, or a holiday greeting card, reach out to your steady customers.
2. ***Customer Service.*** Go the extra distance and meet customer needs. Train the staff to do the same. Customers remember being treated well.

3. ***Employee Loyalty.*** Loyalty works from the top down. If you are loyal to your employees, they will feel positively about their jobs and pass that loyalty along to your customers.
4. ***Employee Training.*** Train employees in the manner that you want them to interact with customers. Empower employees to make decisions that benefit the customer.
5. ***Customer Incentives.*** Give customers a reason to return to your business. For instance, because children outgrow shoes quickly, the owner of a children's shoe store might offer a card that makes the tenth pair of shoes half price. Likewise, a dentist may give a free cleaning to anyone who has seen him regularly for five years.
6. ***Product Awareness.*** Know what your steady patrons purchase and keep these items in stock. Add other products and/or services that accompany or compliment the products that your regular customers buy regularly. And make sure that your staff understands everything they can about your products.
7. ***Reliability.*** If you say a purchase will arrive on Wednesday, deliver it on Wednesday. Be reliable. If something goes wrong, let customers know immediately and compensate them for their inconvenience.
8. ***Be Flexible.*** Try to solve customer problems or complaints to the best of your ability. Excuses—such as "That's our policy"—will lose more customers then setting the store on fire. Read our 60-Second Guide to Managing Upset Customers for more information.
9. ***People over Technology.*** The harder it is for a customer to speak to a human being when he or she has a problem, the less likely it is that you will see that customer again.

10. ***Know Their Names.*** Remember the theme song to the television show *Cheers*? Get to know the names of regular customers or at least recognize their faces.

Customer Retention

Customer retention marketing is a tactically-driven approach based on customer behaviour. It's the core activity going on behind the scenes in *Relationship Marketing, Loyalty Marketing, Database Marketing, Permission Marketing*, and so forth. Here's the basic philosophy of a retention-oriented marketer:

1. ***Past and current customer behaviour is the best predictor of future customer behaviour.*** Think about it. In general, it is more often true than not true, and when it comes to action-oriented activities like making purchases and visiting websites, the concept really shines through.

We are talking about actual behaviour here, not implied behaviour. Being a 35-year-old woman is not a behaviour; it's a demographic characteristic. Take these two groups of potential buyers who surf the Net:

- People who are a perfect demographic match for your site, but have never made a purchase online anywhere.
- People who are outside the core demographics for your site, but have purchased repeatedly online at many different websites.

If you sent a 20 per cent off promotion to each group, asking them to visit and make a first purchase, response would be higher from the buyers (second bullet above) than the demographically targeted group (first bullet above). This effect has been demonstrated for years with many types of Direct Marketing. It works because actual behaviour is better at predicting future behaviour than demographic characteristics are. You can tell whether a customer is about to defect or not by watching their behaviour; once you can predict defection, you have a shot at retaining the customer by taking action.

2. ***Active customers are happy (retained) customers; and they like to "win".*** They like to feel they are in control and smart about choices they make, and they like to feel good about their behaviour. Marketers take advantage of this by offering promotions of various kinds to get consumers to engage in a behaviour and feel good about doing it.

These promotions range from discounts and sweepstakes to loyalty programs and higher concept approaches such as thank-you notes and birthday cards. Promotions encourage behaviour. If you want your customers to do something, you have to do something for them, and if it's something that makes them feel good (like they are winning the consumer game), then they're more likely to do it.

Retaining customers means keeping them active with you. If you don't, they will slip away and eventually, no longer be customers. Promotions encourage this interaction of customers with your company, even if you are just sending out a newsletter or birthday card. The truth is, almost all customers will leave you eventually. The trick is to keep them active and happy as long as possible, and to make money doing it.

3. ***Retention Marketing is all about*: Action—Reaction—Feedback—Repeat.** Marketing is a conversation, as the *Clue Train Manifesto* and *Permission Marketing* have pointed out. Marketing with customer data is a highly evolved and valuable conversation, but it has to be back and forth between the marketer and the customer, and you have to *listen* to what the customer is saying to you.

For example, let's say you look at some average customer behaviour. You look at every customer who has made at least 2 purchases, and you calculate the number of days between the first and second purchases. This number is called "latency"—the number of days between two customer events. Perhaps you find it to be 30 days. Now, look at your One-Time buyers. If a customer has not made a second purchase by 30 days after the first purchase, the customer is not acting like an "average" multi-purchase customer. The customer data is telling you something is wrong, and you should react to it with a promotion. This is an example of the data speaking for the customer; you have to learn how to listen.

This site and the *Drilling Down book* are all about how to discover, manage, and listen to customer data. The data is speaking for the customer, telling you by its very existence (or non-existence), there has been an action (or non-action) waiting for a reaction.

4. ***Retention marketing requires allocating marketing resources.*** You have to realize some marketing activities and customers will generate higher profits than others. You can keep your budget flat or shrink it while increasing sales and profits if you continuously allocate more of the budget to highly profitable activities and away from lower profit activities. This doesn't mean you should "get rid" of some customers or treat them poorly.

It means when you have a choice, as you frequently do in marketing, instead of spending the same amount of money on every customer, you spend more on some and less on others. It takes money to make money. Unless you get a huge increase in your budget, where will the money come from?

For example, let's say you have 1,000 customers, and you have an annual budget of $1,000. You spend $1 on each customer each year, and for that $1, you get back $1.10 in profits. That's an ROI of 10 per cent; you got back $1,100 for spending $1,000. Now, what if you knew spending $2 each year on a certain 50 per cent of customers would bring back $8 in profits. That's a 400 per cent ROI. Where do you get the extra $1? You take it away from the other 50 per cent of customers. You spend the same $1,000 total and you make back 500 (half the customers) × $8 = $4,000.

If you always migrate and reallocate marketing dollars towards higher ROI efforts, profits will grow even as the marketing budget stays flat. You have to develop a way to allocate resources to the most profitable promotions, deliver them to the right customer at the right time, and not waste time and money on unprofitable promotions and customers. This is accomplished by using the data customers create through their interactions with you to build simple models or rules to follow. These models are your listening system, like the "30 day latency" model *above*. They allow the data to speak to you about the customer.

Outlook of Loyalty

Employee loyalty isn't gone, it's just different. Today, people in their 20s change jobs within a year, in 25s every one-to-two years and so on till 30s. This frustrates employers, who say, "Why should I hire someone who is going to leave? I need someone who is loyal." At the same time, employees look at the work they are given and say, "How can I spend my days doing work that doesn't mean anything to me?"

Ironically, the way to make your work more meaningful is to be more loyal. This doesn't mean you can't quit in three months. It means that you have to be loyal while you are there. And in this way, the idea of workplace loyalty is changing: Loyalty is not dead, but you have to ask yourself, what are you loyal *to*?

It's a great job market for young people today. Among college graduates, the unemployment rate is less than 2 per cent. The problem is finding meaningful work. But this task doesn't need to be as hard as people make it. You don't need to be saving lives. You need to work at a place that contributes to your core needs, in a way that gives you the opportunity to express passions in significant ways.

One of the most common ways of finding meaning at work is through personal development. "Loyalty as a function of time is a dated idea." "Work is only appealing if there's constant learning." But loyalty is a layered concept, and for many, this includes the power of a company's brand.

"Organizations are not a source of security but they are a source of identity." So, find a company that you want to attach your identity to. In this way, you are searching for a company that deserves your loyalty. Its brand will be in line with your own values and the image you have of yourself.

Loyalty doesn't always satisfy image-building. If you want to help homeless kids, you can work at many different types of organizations that fight homelessness, and while you might not feel huge dedication to a particular organization, your enthusiasm to the cause will keep you loyal to the work. You can carry your loyalty from company to company.

"People can [also] be loyal to a cause or to a technology. For example, Shanta biotech has developed hepatitis-B vaccine in collaboration with Oman and it is a great contribution for both the country because earlier they were used to buy it from inventor. They can also be loyal to team and country."

The common thread in all this loyalty, though, is being part of something bigger than yourself. You cannot give up everything for your company, but being loyal to nothing is equally disconcerting. "People are their best when they have obligations not only to themselves, but to other people as well. People do their best work when they identify themselves as part of a team or a project."

What can employers do to attract new loyalists? Find a mission that they believe in. If they don't believe in it, they'll never be able to convince other people. And remember that people can feel affiliated to an organization without having to work 70 hours a week. We need to understand what the company's goals are and need to share that vision.

In fact, some of the most loyal employees are those whose company arranged working situations to accommodate very strong loyalties such as family or athletic endeavours. Even a company that has little mission to speak of can gain extreme loyalty from employees by easing the employee's individual mission. Among *Microsoft* loyalists, for example, are those who rely on its outstanding insurance coverage for children with autism. So, figure out your needs and passions, and cast a wide net for the company that could fill them. You'd be surprised at the number of companies that can make you feel like work is meaningful. Similarly, employers will be surprised at the intense loyalty there is to be had from this generation of job hopers.

Mixed Opinion About Loyalty

Employees aren't loyal because they know their employers can—and will—lay them off at the drop of a hat—entirely due to forces completely outside of the employee's control. If employers want more loyalty, they shouldn't be slaves to the next quarterly earnings report from *Wall Street*.

Loyalty absolutely must begin on the side of the employer, and not the other way around. Employees are a company's first customers, buying money from the employer in exchange for their own currency: work. Like any other customer, they are human beings who want respect, courtesy, and value for their currency. If they don't get what they pay for, they will leave the company. And their replacements, even if easy to find, will eventually do the same. And bottom line? Happy employee-customers will also work to give you happy customer-customers.—*Yukti Bhargava,* Delhi University, India

Companies don't really care about most employees except star employees. Therefore there is a huge shift in loyalty from years ago. However as stated here, learning is a great loyalty bone. If a person is learning he at least feels like he is advancing. That is one reason why Toyota is so incredibly successful. Their employees are learning everyday while doing continuous improvement.—*Junaind*, Product Manager, Alhayat, UAE

"Time spend by Company thinkfing about an employee" is proportional to "Time spend by employee thinking about company". Is this equation is matched you can convert a lot of normal employees to loyal group.—*Gaurav*, Manager City Financial, UAE

In India, we have a bigger problem when it comes to changing jobs. Mostly it's for people in IT and the call centre related jobs. There are so many opportunities available so people are jumping around just for a nominal increase in the pay package. Employers are not being able to hold on to employees for more than an year or two, with hikes available as high as 30-50% of your current package outside, its tough to hold on to people. People too have got into the mode of make as much as you can very bad trend. I have 4 years of work experience and changes 2 companies, first one I lasted for 10 months and have been in the current company since more than 3 years.—*J.S. Gill*, GM Sales Synchrom, India

In my experience as an employee and as a manager, sharing the company values is nice and may encourage you to do some PR for your company among friends but it won't keep you loyal when a better job opportunity comes along. I like the way you said it—employees are loyal when companies help them be loyal to others, e.g. their family, friends etc. In other words, when the company takes employees needs into account.—*Ayaz*, Research Scholar, Caledonian University, Scotland.

You bring up another interesting aspect of the loyalty discussion: If companies create environments that help employees to be loyal, then the employees will be, in effect, publicists for the company. A great way for companies to hire great people is to turn their employees into publicists. Word of mouth is so powerful when you decide which company to work for.—*Sanjay Verma*, AGM, Planteous, India

It is a good equation to evaluate the scenario when a person is leaving. I wanted to created a chain where an employee (can't call him a mentor but I can call him a personal HR) will think about other employee atleast 15 mins a week and will also report the opinion to HR. This will bring many hidden issues to the visible surface. Most of the times there is no one to care about other member or no one to spare some exclusive time to think about other member. Even a 15 mins thinking a week can change the scene.—*Sanjeev Kapila*, AGM, Planteous, India

Attitudes about company and employee loyalties are definitely changing. My own father worked 35 years for one company. I followed his lead and worked 25 years for one company but they went through a corporate merger and eliminated my department. So I tried again with another company and stayed 10 years. This second company bought out a competitor and eliminated the group I worked in. I am now working for a third company but feel NO loyalty to this company and doubt that I ever will. I followed my father's work ethic but I tell my daughter to be cautious about becoming too loyal to any one workplace.—*Imtiyaz*, Manager, Waleed Pharmacy, Oman

I do think we need to be mindful of the tendency to rename things in their best possible light. When Imtiyaz is advising his daughter not to be too loyal to any one workplace, is that because he really thinks loyalty is a bad thing, or because he's renaming stability (stasis) as loyalty. I think Penelope draws an important distinction between loyalty to an abstract concept (personal development, company's brand being in line with personal values, etc.) versus defining loyalty in a really linear, time-driven way. Loyalty is not tolerance for being ill-used.—*Kusum Sharma,* Manager HR, Akums, India

Those of us who worked in high-tech in the 1980's and 1990's were in the vanguard of the "don't get too attached to your company" trend. What each individual needs to do is work out their own balance between need for stability, need for workplace attachment, ability to withstand whatever amount of time without a paycheck, desire to always be on to something new. There may be different times in your life when different elements appeal more than others.—*Harish*, AGM, Akums, India

Having worked in a couple of places where some people did believe that they were going to be there "for life", and seeing how crushed they were when they lost their jobs, I know it was a lot easier for those of us who had the attitude of "as long as it's interesting/fun/challenging or whatever, I'll work hard and enjoy my stay," knowing that when it was over, that was fine, too.—*Sanjya Sood*, MD, Intomed, India

I like the notion of loyalty to a company's brand. I think when I have felt disconnected from an organization that I worked for, it was because I couldn't be loyal to its brand, or in my case, its mission. The one job I found truly fulfilling had a brand/mission that I valued. Then I got laid off. BUT, I like the distinction between loyalty and stability. This helps me further explore why I feel I can't find the right job, and my discomfort with leaving jobs frequently.—*Priyanka*, HLL, India

In order to prepare for a recent position, I had to read the Toyota Way by Liker. It provided a very interesting perspective right from the beginning about loyalty. I don't have the book with me, but the passage boils down to something like this: The

Company will never lay off employees because of a bad quarter. Toyota feels that doing so based on a bad quarter would be similar to an individual employee telling one of their kids they have to leave because they had a bad quarter with their stock market portfolio. Until we get away from the quarter to quarter philosophy and adopt a longer term perspective (which is healthier anyways), employee loyalty is going to be hard to find.—*Ejaz*, Royal Labs, India

As a project assistant in my young 20s, I must admit that it's a feeling of loyalty in higher management (or in 'corporate' as many of my fellow workers would call it) that helps me to feel loyal. I personally feel and act loyal to the company when I start to feel that I have a place and future with the company, and that they are doing what they can to stay afloat in a currently volatile business (forestry, natural resource related). I feel that and act that partly in my own attempts at tenure, which I feel can benefit the company just fine. If I didn't think that those working above me believed in their work, and it's effect and growth—my own beliefs won't be sparked.—*Renu Sharma*, Shreya Life Sciences, Mumbai

If we speak about loyalty of employees, we speak about commitment of organization as I understood, but there are so many different contracts with organizations, for example, employer hired me for layout of a book and I have performed good that task, result—the organization left satisfied. But my next work will be in another organization, so here arise question: Will I be disloyal? Just because of concept of loyalty.—*M.M. Khan*, Caddice, India

How do You Foster Employee Loyalty?

Since each employee is a unique individual, no single approach works for everyone, but here are ten ideas that I have put into practice in my own business to improve loyalty:

1. ***Offer more than just a job***: Employees who view their current job as part of a rewarding career path with their employer are naturally more motivated and invested in their work. They may also be more

likely to view necessary but tedious parts of the job in the context of the bigger picture.

2. ***Generate goodwill through good deeds***: Being involved with a company that "does good" makes employees feel good about their jobs and their employer. In some way, each employer supports the larger community. Develop and communicate your company's outreach efforts and community support philosophies. Then offer employees the opportunity to participate in those efforts or to have their own involvement in charitable causes supported by the company.
3. ***Get out the checkbook***: While you can't buy loyalty, you can destroy loyal ties if you're not paying someone what he or she is worth.
4. ***Empower employees***: Providing a channel for employees to communicate ideas and influence company practices gives them a stake in the business' success and promotes team spirit.
5. ***Invest in training and development***: If you invest in your employees, they are more likely to invest in your company. They'll also have a better understanding of your organization's business goals and practices, which can likely translate to improved performance.
6. ***Share your vision***: Communicate your company's direction and decisions. Employees feel trusted and are more trusting when they know about company decisions.
7. ***Challenge employees***: My experience is that setting and meeting high expectations makes employees feel more positive about their jobs.
8. ***Recognize and reward often***: Employees appreciate positive feedback and tend to be more productive after receiving it. Additionally, giving praise to an employee is like tipping over a row of dominos: a productive employee tends to inspire and motivate

co-workers by example. By giving marriage anniversary gift you can lure the heart of your employee and this give feeling of family members.

9. ***Find common ground***: Align career development with company goals. If a concession that you make for an employee is not good for both the employee and the company, it will not be good for long.
10. ***Get to know your employees***: An employee's relationship with his/her boss and co-workers is one of the most important factors in determining how loyal that employee is. Treat employees as individuals and look for ways to foster solid relationships.

I'm excited about the subject of loyalty and how adopting a loyalty initiative can improve the employment experience for your staff and simultaneously enhance your company's growth and profitability.

Advantages/Disadvantages of Loyalty

There are many advantages to loyalty. Often, whomever you have loyalty towards will reciprocate with loyalty, protection, or other benefits. Examples include friendship, government, and pet ownership. Loyalty is a strong bond. Though it isn't easy to measure, in intense/difficult situations it's easier to gauge.

On the flip side of the coin, loyalty can have some disadvantages. Loyalty towards a cause/person one doesn't like, or towards someone/something that one used to like but doesn't like anymore, can be personally dissatisfying. Sometimes a person can't be friendly with one group because he's already loyal to another group, if these groups are of conflicting ideas. For example, if a person is loyal to a Pro-Choice group, a Pro-Life group might be hostile towards him.

Also, the defining disadvantage of loyalty is that it requires a person to 'take a position'. Anyone who is loyal to anything, by the very merit of his loyalty, takes a stance on different positions. Often, a friend of Person A is automatically involved in an argument if Person A gets in an argument with Person B. If a person doesn't want this, he must avoid being loyal to anyone or anything. A person with no loyalties owes nothing to nobody, but often has enemies and, because he has no loyalties, he also has no help dealing with these enemies. Think of an outlaw against the government.

Why Loyalty Works?

Successful loyalty programs can have a huge impact on a customer's purchasing habits. One program put in place by a popular hotel chain doubled the number of repeat guests in the first 18 months, and increased the average stay duration by 25 per cent. A loyalty program can encourage your customers to book earlier, stay longer, and vacation more often.

What are the Benefits to Having a Loyalty Program?

Loyalty programs perform several functions that are critical to your rental management business.

1. They help to set you apart from other rental management companies for that crucial first impression.
2. Website visitors reading about coupons that you offer for point redemptions are automatically learning about the attractions and fun things to do in your area.
3. Points and rewards can be used to incentivize renters to book earlier and save you last minute marketing costs and discounts as well as incentivize them to book targeted properties.
4. Once renters begin earning points, they are much less likely to waste a trip with a competitive rental management company where their points do not grow.
5. Discounts and specials can be targeted towards long-term renters as rewards and extra incentives to keep them coming back, instead of diluting the benefits of discounting by offering them to the general public.
6. Administrative points can be awarded as non-monetary compensation for those occasional problems that renters have with a property.

7. Loyalty programs provide an opportunity to learn about your customers' preferences and expectations when vacationing in your area, as well as their long-term vacation trends year after year.

Loyalty programs provide another channel for developing a long-term relationship with your renters and for reaping all the benefits that a good relationship entails. As the premier loyalty program in the rental vacation market, Guest Advantage™ provides a mature, complete toolset for crafting and managing a custom program that addresses your unique business needs.

Key Elements of a Winning Employee Retention Strategy

A comprehensive people strategy is *not* comprehensive if it does not include a proven retention strategy for holding onto the employees you've worked hard to recruit into your organization.

That may sound logical, but many if not most small firms overlook this critical component in their human resources program. In a recent Watson Wyatt survey, over 50 per cent of the responding companies said they did not have a formal strategy for retaining employees once they have been successfully recruited.

Why? I think the answer lies in a misperception about what actually drives retention.

Most business owners and managers think retention keys off of compensation issues—wage and salary levels, incentives and golden handcuffs—when in reality the drivers go much deeper into the human psyche to the actions and attitudes that make employees feel successful, secure and appreciated. As a result, a sound retention strategy should focus on and tactically address four key elements—performance, communication, loyalty and competitive advantage.

Performance

The benefit of having measurable objectives for individuals, teams and for the company as a whole is fairly obvious to most managers, but this perception usually stops short of relating performance metrics to employee retention. Study after study confirms that people have a deep desire to feel they are succeeding, and that their talents and capabilities are being used in a way that makes a difference to the organization. When people sense their actions are fulfilling this desire, they begin to develop a sense of belonging and a feeling that your company is their company.

Human beings are often the happiest when they are in the process of achieving a goal. Clear, achievable objectives that gauge personal, team and company performances provide the feedback employees need to confirm that they are making valuable contributions and accomplishing goals.

Communication

The second element in a retention strategy is communication, specifically a communication process that is structured to inform, emphasize and reaffirm to employees that their workplace contributions are having an impact. Since we are dealing very directly with how employees feel about their performance, the company, and their work environment, the question becomes, "How do you *know* how they feel about these matters?" Properly done, communication with your staff will provide you with the insights you need in order to know how your employees feel about working in your organization. Do you communicate in an ongoing fashion with your employees? Do you have regular meetings with your people? Is it two-way communication, and do you have a non-threatening channel for them to offer comments and suggestions? Do you conduct employee surveys to gather opinions on company issues and activities? Are your managers and supervisors good listeners? An effective and sensitive communications plan can provide you with insight on what is driving employee morale and how your workers feel about your company.

Loyalty

The third element in a successful employee retention strategy is employee loyalty. True loyalty is not an enforced requirement, but an earned response to the trust, respect and commitment shown to the individuals in your organization. When you demonstrate loyalty to your employees, they will reciprocate with commitment and loyalty to your company. Remember that people do not begin their employment with you as loyal employees, but will develop loyalty over time as they are trusted, respected and appreciated by you. So, how are you going to demonstrate your commitment to them? How loyal are you to your employees? Are you more concerned about their success or their contributions to your company's success? In actuality, these two considerations are not mutually exclusive, but are both essential and should work together.

Competitive Advantage

The fourth and final element in your strategy to retain employees has to do with your competitive advantage. While that may seem odd at first, think about it; people want to work for a winner. What sets your company apart from your competition? How are you, and as a result, your employees, making a difference in your industry, in your community, and for your customers and clients? Take the time to identify and inform your clients and your employees about your unique competitive advantage. If your product is similar to others in the market place, your service can be what distinguishes you (and probably should in any case). People want to be with a winner; and that includes employees.

Together, these four elements can provide you with a retention strategy capable of producing amazing results. You may even have some of them already in place, such as performance metrics and a communications process. The key is to make sure you have integrated all four elements into a strategy for retaining employees that is grounded in a genuine commitment to serving your clients and employees over time.

Loyalty and Employee Satisfaction

- Service is the key to employee loyalty.
- Satisfied customers will spread the word.
- Make a difference with an extra-special touch.
- Use rewards to strengthen the value proposition.
- Change employee behaviour.
- Learn more about your employee: the learning relationship.

Components of Loyalty System

- The right customers
- Lifetime products and services
- Loyal employees
- Measures of loyalty

The Virtuous Circle of Loyalty

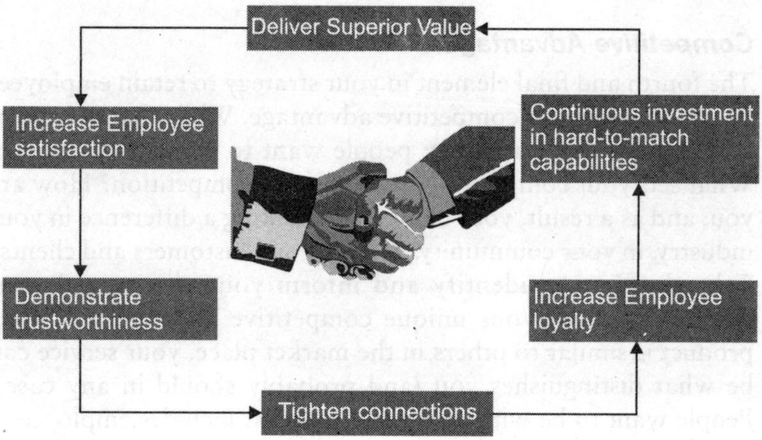

Hot Facts

1. Nearly 70 per cent of organizations report that staff turnover has a negative impact.
2. Approximately, retention of 50 per cent of organizations experience regular problems with employee.
3. Over 50 per cent of the people recruited into an organization will leave within 2 years.
4. 1 in 4 people recruited will leave within 6 months.
5. Over 70 per cent of all employees respond to competitors' job offers during work hours?
6. Voluntary resignations are at the highest level in over 20 years?
7. Nearly 50 per cent of all middle managers are either currently looking for another job or plan to do so?

Top Ten Talent Retention Tips

1. What do employees really wants?
2. Work environment.
3. Challenging work.
4. Recognition and rewards.
5. Grow competencies, situationally. Look for opportunities to put people into challenging situations where their skills and competencies will grow.
6. Meet one-on-one, routinely. Conduct regular, but brief one-on-one meetings between manager/leaders and direct reports. Begin by asking, "What's on your mind?"—then listen and act.
7. Make retention everyone's responsibility. Encourage all members of the work group to feel responsible for the retention of their peers and to be alert to problems that can be fixed.
8. Be a career builder. Talk to people about their long-term career aspirations and help them use or build the skills and competencies they need for the future.
9. Help people get an "A". Give the gift of being clear about what an "A" level performance looks like.
10. Walk your talk. Be aware that people are always watching and assessing you and your actions as a leader.

Rewarding Talent

- Be careful here. While rewarding good performance, one should ensure that it nourishes healthy competition.
- An organization should try to create balance while encouraging people to perform better.
- An employee's performance should be appreciated and rewarded, but in such a manner that is motivates his peers.

- It often happens that an employee is rewarded and it becomes a bone of contention between another employee and the organization.
- So don't go overboard, but also try not to be parsimonious.

Summary

The great challenge of teaching is not about having a million students. It is about giving every child exactly what he or she needs to grow into a confident, self-loving profession who can offer something back to the world. A teacher is essentially a dispeller of darkness and one who throws light on your professional road map.

You cannot teach loyalty. It is a natural phenomenon which comes directly from the heart. You can name it affair between employer and employee over the time. In management context, loyalty is a non-contractual agreement between both the parties. Loyalty is the faith and those who get loyal people are luck by chance.

One loyal employee begets 11 loyal employees and one loyal employee can develop 100 loyal customers. Employee is the face value of the company and our behaviour plays vital role in generating, developing, and retaining customers for whole of life. Any employee is the first customer of employer; therefore, employer should take every employee with full love and devotion.

Loyalty is a three step process and it is very simple to understand and analyze who is loyal for you. You can judge to whom you can make loyal in the long-run. The first step is trust and yes, you begin with trust and try him or her on routine basis. Second step is faith and it develops on the basis of your past data but it takes time. The last step is confidence and this confidence initially remains in the scan and finally, it becomes blind. Thus, you have given your own organization a very strong pillar to take care in good and bad days.

TRUST = FAITH = LOYALTY

Chapter seven

LEARNING

Learning is acquiring new knowledge, behaviours, skills, values, preferences or understanding, and may involve synthesizing different types of information. Progress over time tends to follow learning curves.

Human learning may occur as part of education or personal development. It may be goal-oriented and may be aided by motivation. The study of how learning occurs is part of neuropsychology, educational psychology, learning theory, and pedagogy.

Learning may occur as a result of habituation or classical conditioning, seen in many animal species, or as a result of more complex activities such as play, seen only in relatively intelligent animals and humans. Learning may occur consciously or without conscious awareness. There is evidence for human behavioral learning prenatally, in which habituation has been observed as early as 32 weeks into gestation, indicating that the central nervous system is sufficiently developed and primed for learning and memory to occur very early on in development.

Play has been approached by several theorists as the first form of learning. Children play, experiment with the world, learn the rules, and learn to interact. Vygotsky supports that play is pivotal for children's development, since they make meaning of their environment through play.

Steps of Learning

Learning occurs in four major ways-transmission, acquisition, accretion and emergence. Transmission is the process by which information, knowledge, ideas and skills are taught to others through purposeful, conscious telling, demonstration, and guidance. Over the course of a lifetime, this method accounts for only about 10 per cent of learning. Unfortunately, this is the most traditional and, currently, the most predominate method of instruction. However, we are finding out it is not very effective and moving toward acquisition and emergence, and examining the lessons of accretion. Acquisition is the conscious choice to learn. Material in this category is relevant to the learner. This method includes exploring, experimenting, self-instruction, inquiry, and general curiosity. Currently, acquisition accounts for about 20 per cent of what we learn. Accretion is the gradual, often subconscious or subliminal, process by which we learn things like language, culture, habits, prejudices, and social rules and behaviors. We are usually unaware that the processes involved in accretion are taking place, but this method accounts for about 70 per cent of what we know. Social learning certainly plays into this type of learning, as does the hidden or covert curriculum.

Emergence is the result of patterning, structuring and the construction of new ideas and meanings that did not exist before, but which emerge from the brain through thoughtful reflection, insight and creative expression or group interactions. This form of learning accounts for the internal capacities of synthesis, creativity, intuition, wisdom, and problem-solving. This method is greatly dependent on the allocation of time, and opportunities to reflect and construct new knowledge. This method plays an important role in inspiration and originality. In the context of current educational practices, we learn only 1-2 per cent by this method.

Types of Learning

Non-associative Learning

Habituation

In psychology, habituation is an example of non-associative learning in which there is a progressive diminution of behavioral response probability with repetition of a stimulus. It is another form of integration. An animal first responds to a stimulus, but if it is neither rewarding nor harmful the animal reduces subsequent responses. One example of this can be seen in small song birds—if a stuffed owl (or similar predator) is put into the cage, the birds initially react to it as though it were a real predator. Soon the birds react less, showing habituation. If another stuffed owl is introduced (or the same one removed and re-introduced), the birds react to it again as though it were a predator, demonstrating that it is only a very specific stimulus that is habituated to (namely, one particular unmoving owl in one place). Habituation has been shown in essentially every species of animal, including the large protozoan *Stentor Coeruleus.*

Sensitization

Sensitization is an example of non-associative learning in which the progressive amplification of a response follows repeated administrations of a stimulus (Bell et al., 1995). An everyday example of this mechanism is the repeated tonic stimulation of peripheral nerves that will occur if a person rubs his arm continuously. After a while, this stimulation will create a warm sensation that will eventually turn painful. The pain is the result of the progressively amplified synaptic response of the peripheral nerves warning the person that the stimulation is harmful. Sensitization is thought to underlie both adaptive as well as maladaptive learning processes in the organism.

Associative Learning

Operant Conditioning

Operant conditioning is the use of consequences to modify the occurrence and form of behaviour. *Operant conditioning* is distinguished from Pavlovian conditioning in that operant conditioning deals with the modification of voluntary behaviour. Discrimination learning is a major form of operant conditioning. One form of it is called Errorless learning.

Classical Conditioning

The typical paradigm for classical conditioning involves repeatedly pairing an unconditioned stimulus (which unfailingly evokes a particular response) with another previously neutral stimulus (which does not normally evoke the response). Following conditioning, the response occurs both to the unconditioned stimulus and to the other, unrelated stimulus (now referred to as the "conditioned stimulus"). The response to the conditioned stimulus is termed a *conditioned response.*

Imprinting

Imprinting is the term used in psychology and ethology to describe any kind of phase-sensitive learning (learning occurring at a particular age or a particular life stage) that is rapid and apparently independent of the consequences of behaviour. It was first used to describe situations in which an animal or person learns the characteristics of some stimulus, which is therefore said to be "imprinted" onto the subject.

Observational Learning

The most common human learning process is imitation; one's personal repetition of an observed behaviour, such as a dance. Humans can copy three types of information simultanesouly: the demonstrators goals, actions and environmental outcomes [results, see Emulation (observational learning)]. Through copying these types of information (most) infants will tune into their surrounding culture.

Play

Play generally describes behaviour which has no particular end in itself, but improves performance in similar situations in the future. This is seen in a wide variety of vertebrates besides humans, but is mostly limited to mammals and birds. Cats are known to play with a ball of string when young, which gives them experience with catching prey. Besides inanimate objects, animals may play with other members of their own species or other animals, such as orcas playing with seals they have caught. Play involves a significant cost to animals, such as increased vulnerability to predators and the risk of injury and possibly infection. It also consumes energy, so there must be significant benefits associated with play for it to have evolved. Play is generally seen in younger animals, suggesting a link with learning. However, it may also have other benefits not associated directly with learning, for example improving physical fitness.

Enculturation

Enculturation is the process by which a person learns the requirements of the culture by which he or she is surrounded, and acquires values and behaviours that are appropriate or necessary in that culture. The influences which as part of this process limit, direct or shape the individual, whether deliberately of not, include parents, other adults, and peers. If successful, enculturation results in competence in the language, values and rituals of the culture.

Multimedia Learning

The learning where learner uses multimedia learning environments (Mayer, 2001). This type of learning relies on dual-coding theory (Paivio, 1971).

E-Learning and M-Learning

Electronic learning or e-learning is a general term used to refer to Internet-based networked computer-enhanced learning. A specific and always more diffused e-learning is mobile learning (m-Learning), it uses different mobile telecommunication equipments, such as cellular phones.

Rote Learning

Rote learning is a technique which avoids understanding the inner complexities and inferences of the subject that is being learned and instead focuses on memorizing the material so that it can be recalled by the learner exactly the way it was read or heard. The major practice involved in rote learning techniques is *learning by repetition,* based on the idea that one will be able to quickly recall the meaning of the material the more it is repeated. Rote learning is used in diverse areas, from mathematics to music to religion. Although it has been criticized by some schools of thought, rote learning is a necessity in many situations.

Informal Learning

Informal learning occurs through the experience of day-to-day situations (for example, one would learn to look ahead while walking because of the danger inherent in not paying attention to where one is going). It is learning from life, during a meal at table with parents, Play, exploring.

Formal Learning

A depiction of the world's oldest university, the University of Bologna, Italy. Formal learning is learning that takes place within a teacher-student relationship, such as in a school system.

Non-formal Learning

Non-formal learning is organized learning outside the formal learning system. For example: learning by coming together with people with similar interests and exchanging viewpoints, in clubs or in (international) youth organizations, workshops.

Non-formal Learning and Combined Approaches

The educational system may use a combination of formal, informal, and non-formal learning methods. The UN and EU recognize these different forms of learning (cf. links below). In some schools students can get points that count in the formal-learning systems if they get work done in informal-learning circuits. They may be given time to assist international youth workshops and training courses, on the condition they prepare, contribute, share and can proof this offered valuable new insights, helped to acquire new skills, a place to get experience in organizing, teaching, etc.

In order to learn a skill, such as solving a Rubik's cube quickly, several factors come into play at once:

- Directions help one learn the patterns of solving a Rubik's cube.
- Practising the moves repeatedly and for extended time helps with "muscle memory" an therefore speed.
- Thinking critically about moves helps find shortcuts, which in turn helps to speed up future attempts.
- The Rubik's cube's six colors help anchor solving it within the head.
- Occasionally revisiting the cube helps prevent negative learning or loss of skill.

Tangential Learning

Tangential learning is the process by which some portion of people will self-educate if a topic is exposed to them in something that they already enjoy.

Domains of Learning

The three domains of learning are:

- Cognitive such as learning to recall facts, to analyze, and to solve a problem.
- Psychomotor such as learning to perform the correct steps in a dance, learning to swim, learning to ride a bicycle, or drive a car.
- Affective such as learning how to like someone, "to hate sin", to love one's country (patriotism), to worship God, or to move on after a failed relationship.

These domains are not mutually exclusive. For example, in learning to play chess, the person will have to learn the rules of the game (cognitive domain); but he also has to learn how to set up the chess pieces on the chessboard and also how to properly hold and move a chess piece (psychomotor). Furthermore, later in the game the person may even learn to love the game itself, value its applications in life, and appreciate its history (affective domain).

Learning Styles

This approach to learning emphasizes the fact that individuals perceive and process information in very different ways. The learning styles theory implies that how much individuals learn has more to do with whether the educational experience is geared toward their particular style of learning than whether or not they are "smart". In fact, educators should not ask, "Is this student smart?" but rather "How is this student smart?"

The concept of learning styles is rooted in the classification of psychological types. The learning styles theory is based on research demonstrating that, as the result of heredity, upbringing, and current environmental demands, different individuals have a tendency to both perceive and process information differently. The different ways of doing so are generally classified as:

1. *Concrete and abstract* perce/Vers—Concrete perceivers absorb information through direct experience, by doing, acting, sensing, and feeling. Abstract perceivers, however, take in information through analysis, observation, and thinking.
2. *Active and reflective* processors—Active processors make sense of an experience by immediately using the new information. Reflective processors make sense of an experience by reflecting on and thinking about it.

Traditional schooling tends to favour abstract perceiving and reflective processing. Other kinds of learning aren't rewarded and reflected in curriculum, instruction, and assessment nearly as much.

How the Learning Styles Theory Impacts Education

Cuw'cu/um-Educators must place emphasis on intuition, feeling, sensing, and imagination, in addition to the traditional skills of analysis, reason, and sequential problem solving.

Instruction—Teachers should design their instruction methods to connect with all four learning styles, using various combinations of experience, reflection, conceptualization, and experimentation. Instructors can introduce a wide variety of experiential elements into the classroom, such as sound, music, visuals, movement, experience, and even talking.

Assessment—Teachers should employ a variety of assessment techniques, focusing on the development of "whole brain" capacity and each of the different learning styles.

Brain-based Learning

This learning theory is based on the structure and function of the brain. As long as the brain is not prohibited from fulfilling its normal processes, learning will occur. People often say that everyone can learn. Yet, the reality is that everyone does learn. Every person is born with a brain that functions as an immensely powerful processor. Traditional schooling, however, often inhibits learning by discouraging, ignoring, or punishing the brain's natural learning processes. The core principles of brain-based learning state that:

1. The brain is a parallel processor, meaning it can perform several activities at once, like tasting and smelling.
2. Learning engages the whole physiology.
3. The search for meaning is innate.
4. The search for meaning comes through patterning.
5. Emotions are critical to patterning.
6. The brain processes wholes and parts simultaneously.
7. Learning involves both focused attention and peripheral perception.
8. Learning involves both conscious and unconscious processes.
9. We have two types of memory: spatial and rote.
10. We understand best when facts are embedded in natural, spatial memory.
11. Learning is enhanced by challenge and inhibited by threat.
12. Each brain is unique.

The three instructional techniques associated with brain-based learning are:

1. **Orchestrated immersion**—Creating learning environments that fully immerse students in an educational experience.
2. **Relaxed alertness**—Trying to eliminate fear in learners, while maintaining a highly challenging environment.
3. **Active processing**—Allowing the learner to consolidate and internalize information by actively processing it.

How Brain-based Learning Impacts Education?

Curriculum—Teachers must design learning around student interests and make learning contextual.

Instruction—Educators let students learn in teams and use peripheral learning. Teachers structure learning around real problems, encouraging students to also learn in settings outside the classroom and the school building.

Assessment—Since all students are learning, their assessment should allow them to understand their own learning styles and preferences. This way, students monitor and enhance their own learning process.

What Brain-based Learning Suggests?

How the brain works has a significant impact on what kinds of learning activities are most effective. Educators need to help students have appropriate experiences and capitalize on those experiences. As Renate Caine illustrates on p. 113 of her book *Making Connections,* three interactive elements are essential to this process:

- Teachers must immerse learners in complex, interactive experiences that are both rich and real. One excellent example is immersing students in a foreign culture to teach them a second language. Educators must take advantage of the brain's ability to parallel process.
- Students must have a personally meaningful challenge. Such challenges stimulate a student's mind to the desired state of alertness.
- In order for a student to gain insight about a problem, there must be intensive analysis of the different ways to approach it, and about learning in general. This is what's known as the "active processing of experience."

A few other tenets of brain-based learning include: Feedback is best when it comes from reality, rather than from an authority figure. People learn best when solving realistic problems. The big picture can't be separated from the details. Because every brain io different, educators should allow learners to customize their own environments. The best problem solvers are those that laugh!

Designers of educational tools must be artistic in their creation of brain-friendly environments. Instructors need to realize that the best way to learn is not through lecture, but by participation in realistic environments that let learners try new things safely.

Multiple Intelligences

This theory of human intelligence, developed by psychologist Howard Gardner, suggests there are at least seven ways that people have of perceiving and understanding the world. Gardner labels each of these ways a distinct "intelligence" in other words, a set of skills allowing individuals to find and resolve genuine problems they face. Gardner defines an "intelligence" as a group of abilities that is somewhat autonomous from other human capacities. Has a core set of information-processing operations. Has a distinct history in the stages of development we each pass through. Has plausible roots in evolutionary history. While Gardner suggests his list of intelligences may not be exhaustive, he identifies the following seven:

1. **Verbal-Linguistic**—The ability to use words and language.
2. **Logical-Mathematical**—The capacity for inductive and deductive thinking and reasoning as well as the use of numbers and the recognition of abstract patterns.
3. **Visual-Spatial**—The ability to visualize objects and spatial dimensions, and create internal images and pictures.
4. **Body-Kinesthetic**—The wisdom of the body and the ability to control physical motion.
5. **Musical-Rhythmic**—The ability to recognize tonal patterns and sounds, as well as a sensitivity to rhythms and beats.
6. **Interpersonal**—The capacity for person-to-person communications and relationships.
7. **Intrapersonal**—The spiritual, inner states of being, self-reflection, and awareness.

How Multiple Intelligences Impact Learning?

Curriculum—Traditional schooling heavily favours the verbal-linguistic and logical-mathematical intelligences. Gardner suggests a more balanced curriculum that incorporates the arts, self-awareness, communication, and physical education.

Instruction—Gardner advocates instructional methods that appeal to all the intelligences, including role playing, musical performance, cooperative learning, reflection, visualization, story telling, and so on.

Assessment—This theory calls for assessment methods that take into account the diversity of intelligences as well as self-assessment tools that help students understand their intelligences.

Right Brain vs. Left Brain

This theory of the structure and functions of the mind suggests that the two different sides of the brain control two different "modes" of thinking. It also suggests that each of us prefers one mode over the other.

Experimentation has shown that the two different sides, or hemispheres of the brain are responsible for different manners of thinking. The following table illustrates the differences between left-brain and right-brain thinking:

Left Brain	Right Brain
Logical Sequential	Random
Rational	Intuitive
Analytical	Holistic Synthesizing
Objective	Subjective
Looks at parts	Looks at wholes

Most individuals have a distinct preference for one of these styles of thinking. Some, however, are more whole-brained and equally adept at both modes. In general, schools tend to favour left-brain modes of thinking, while downplaying the right-brain ones. Left-brain scholastic subjects focus on logical thinking, analysis, and accuracy. Right-brained subjects, on the other hand, focus on aesthetics, feeling, and creativity.

How Right-Brain vs. Left-Brain Thinking Impacts Learning?

Curriculum—In order to be more "whole-brained" in their orientation, schools need to give equal weight to the arts, creativity, and the skills of imagination and synthesis.

Instruction—To foster a more whole-brained scholastic experience, teachers should use instruction techniques that connect with both sides of the brain. They can increase their classroom's right-brain learning activities by incorporating more patterning, metaphors, analogies, role playing, visuals, and movement into their reading, calculation, and analytical activities.

Assessment—For a more accurate whole-brained evaluation of student learning, educators must develop new forms of assessment that honor right-brained talents and skills.

Communities of Practice

This approach views learning as an act of membership in a "community of practice". The theory seeks to understand both the structure of communities and how learning occurs in them.

Basic Elements

The communities of practice concept was pioneered by the Institute for Research on Learning, a spin-off of the Xerox Corporation in Palo Alto, CA. The Institute pursues a cross-disciplinary approach to learning research, involving cognitive scientists, organizational anthropologists, and traditional educators. Communities of practice is based on the following assumptions:

Learning is fundamentally a social phenomenon. People organize their learning around the social communities to which they belong. Therefore, schools are only powerful learning environments for students whose social communities coincide with that school.

Knowledge is integrated in the life of communities that share values, beliefs, languages, and ways of doing things. These are called communities of practice. Real knowledge is integrated in the doing, social relations, and expertise of these communities.

The processes of learning and membership in a community of practice are inseparable. Because learning is intertwined with community membership, it is what lets us belong to and adjust our status in the group. As we change our learning, our identity-and our relationship to the group-changes.

Knowledge is inseparable from practice. It is not possible to know without doing. By doing, we learn.

Empowerment or the ability to contribute to a community-creates the potential for learning. Circumstances in which we engage in real action that has consequences for both us and our community create the most powerful learning environments.

How Communities of Practice Impact Education?

This approach to learning suggests teachers understand their students' communities of practice and acknowledge the learning students do in such communities. The communities of practice theory also suggests educators structure learning opportunities that embed knowledge in both work practices and social relations, for example, apprenticeships, school-based learning, service learning, and so on. Plus, educators should create opportunities for students to solve real problems with adults, in real learning situations.

Control Theory

This theory of motivation proposed by William Glasser contends that behaviour is never caused by a response to an outside stimulus. Instead, the control theory states that behaviour is inspired by what a person wants most at any given time: survival, love, power, freedom, or any other basic human need.

Responding to complaints that today's students are "unmotivated", Glasser attests that all living creatures "control" their behaviour to maximize their need satisfaction. According to Glasser, if students are not motivated to do their schoolwork, it's because they view schoolwork as irrelevant to their basic human needs.

Boss teachers use rewards and punishment to coerce students to comply with rules and complete required assignments. Glasser calls this "leaning on your shovel" work. He shows how high percentages of students recognize that the work they do—even when their teachers praise them—is such low-level work.

Lead teachers, on the other hand, avoid coercion completely. Instead, they make the intrinsic rewards of doing the work clear to their students, correlating any proposed assignments to the students' basic needs. Plus, they only use grades as temporary indicators of what has and hasn't been learned, rather than a reward. Lead teachers will "fight to protect" highly engaged, deeply motivated students who are doing quality work from having to fulfill meaningless requirements.

How the Control Theory Impacts Learning?

Curriculum—Teachers must negotiate both content and method with students. Students' basic needs literally help shape how and what they are taught.

Instruction—Teachers rely on cooperative, active learning techniques that enhance the power of the learners. Lead teachers make sure that all assignments meet some degree of their students' need satisfaction. This secures student loyalty, which carries the class through whatever relatively meaningless tasks might be necessary to satisfy official requirements.

Assessment—Instructors only give "good grades"—those that certify quality work—to satisfy students' need for power. Courses for which a student doesn't earn a "good grade" are not recorded on that student's transcript. Teachers grade students using an absolute standard, rather than a relative "curve".

Learning Theory (Education)

In psychology and education, a common definition of learning is a process that brings together cognitive, emotional, and environmental influences and experiences for acquiring, enhancing, or making changes in one's knowledge, skills, values, and world views (Illeris, 2000; Ormorod, 1995). Learning as a process focuses in what happens when the learning takes place. Explanations of what happens are called learning theories. A learning theory is an attempt to describe how people and animals learn, thereby helping us understand the inherently complex process of learning. Learning theories have two chief values according to Hill (2002). One is in providing us with vocabulary and a conceptual framework for interpreting the examples of learning that we observe. The other is in suggesting where to look for solutions to practical problems. The theories do not give us solutions, but they do direct our attention to those variables that are crucial in finding solutions.

There are three main categories or philosophical frameworks under which learning theories fall: behaviourism, cognitivism, and constructivism. Behaviourism focuses only on the objectively observable aspects of learning. Cognitive theories look beyond behaviour to explain brain-based learning. And constructivism views learning as a process in which the learner actively constructs or builds new ideas or concepts.

It is also important to take account of the Sudbury Model learning theory, that adduces that learning is a process you do, not a process that is done to you, and shows that there are many ways to learn without the intervention of a teacher being imperative, of informal learning theories, and to consider the philosophical anthropology implied by any theory.

Behaviourism

Behavourism as a theory was most developed by B.F. Skinner. It loosely includes the work of such people as Thorndike, Tolman, Guthrie, and Hull. What characterizes these investigators is their underlying assumptions about the process of learning. In essence, three basic assumptions are held to be true. First, learning is manifested by a change in behaviour. Second, the environment shapes behaviour. And third, the principles of contiguity (how close in time two events must be for a bond to be performed) and reinforcement (any means of increasing the likelihood that an event will be repeated) are central to explaining the learning process. For behaviourism, learning is the acquisition of new behaviour through conditioning. There are two types of possible conditioning:

(1) Classical conditioning, where the behaviour becomes a reflex response to stimulus as in the case of Pavlov's Dogs. Pavlov was interested in studying reflexes, when he saw that the dogs drooled without

the proper stimulus. Although no food was in sight, their saliva still dribbled. It turned out that the dogs were reacting to lab coats. Every time the dogs were served food, the person who served the food was wearing a lab coat. Therefore, the dogs reacted as if food was on its way whenever they saw a lab coat. In a series of experiments, Pavlov then tried to figure out how these phenomena were linked. For example, he struck a bell when the dogs were fed. If the bell was sounded in close association with their meal, the dogs learned to associate the sound of the bell with food. After a while, at the mere sound of the bell, they responded by drooling.

(2) Operant conditioning where there is reinforcement of the behaviour by a reward or a punishment. The theory of operant conditioning was developed by B.F. Skinner and is known as Radical Behaviourism. The word 'operant' refers to the way in which behaviour 'operates on the environment'. Briefly, a behaviour may result either in reinforcement, which increases the likelihood of the behaviour recurring, or punishment, which decreases the likelihood of the behaviour recurring. It is important to note that, a punisher is not considered to be punishment if it does not result in the reduction of the behaviour, and so the terms punishment and reinforcement are determined as a result of the actions. Within this framework, behaviourists are particularly interested in measurable changes in behaviour. Educational approaches such as applied behaviour analysis, curriculum based measurement, and direct instruction have emerged from this model.

Cognitivism

The earliest challenge to the behaviourists came in a publication in 1929 by Bode, a Gestalt psychologist. He criticized behaviourists for being too dependent on overt behaviour to explain learning. Gestalt psychologists proposed looking at the patterns rather than isolated events. Gestalts views of learning have been incorporated into what have come to be labeled *cognitive theories.* Two key assumptions underlie this cognitive approach: (1) that the memory system is an active organized processor of information and (2) that prior knowledge plays an important role in learning. Cognitive theories look beyond behaviour to explain brain-based learning. Cognitivists consider how human memory works to promote learning. For example, the physiological processes of sorting and encoding information and events into short-term memory and long-term memory are important to educators working under the cognitive theory. The major difference between Gestaltists and behaviourists is the locus of control over the learning activity. For Gestaltists, it lies with the individual learner; for behaviourists it lies with the environment.

Once memory theories like the Atkinson-Shiffrin memory model and Baddeley's Working memory model were established as a theoretical framework in Cognitive Psychology, new cognitive frameworks of learning began to emerge during the 1970s, 80s, and 90s. Today, researchers are concentrating on topics like Cognitive load and Information Processing Theory. These theories of learning are very useful as they guide the Instructional design. Aspects of cognitivism can be found in learning how to learn, social role acquisition, intelligence, learning and memory as related to age.

Constructivism

Constructivism views learning as a process in which the learner actively constructs or builds new ideas or concepts based upon current and past knowledge. In other words, "learning involves constructing one's own knowledge from one's own experiences." Constructivist learning, therefore, is a very personal endeavour, whereby internalized concepts, rules, and general principles may consequently be applied in a practical real-world context. This is also known as *social constructivism* (see social constructivism). Social constructivists posits that knowledge is constructed when individuals engage socially in talk and activity about shared problems or tasks. "Learning is seen as the process by which individuals are introduced to a culture by more skilled members" (Driver et al., 1994). Constructivism itself has many variations, such as Active learning, discovery learning, and knowledge building. Regardless of the variety, constructivism promotes a student's free exploration within a given framework or structure. The teacher acts as a facilitator who encourages students to discover principles for themselves and to construct knowledge by working to solve realistic problems. Aspects of constructivism can be found in self-directed learning, transformational learning, experiential learning, situated cognition, and reflective practice.

Informal and Post-modern Theories

Informal theories of education deal with more practical breakdown of the learning process. One of these deals with whether learning should take place as a building of concepts toward an overall idea, or the understanding of the overall idea with the details filled in later. Modern thinkers favour the latter, though without any basis in real world research. Critics believe that trying to teach an overall idea without details (facts) is like trying to build a masonry structure without bricks.

Other concerns are the origins of the drive for learning. To this end, many have split off from the mainstream holding that learning is a primarily self-taught thing, and that the ideal learning situation is one that is self-taught. According to this dogma, learning at its basic level is all self-taught, and class rooms should be eliminated since they do not fit the perfect model of self-learning. However, real world results indicate that isolated students fail. Social support seems crucial for sustained learning.

Informal learning theory also concerns itself with book vs. real-world experience learning. Many consider most schools severely lacking in the second. Newly emerging hybrid instructional models combining traditional classroom and computer enhanced instruction promise the best of both worlds.

Other Learning Theories

Other learning theories have also been developed. These learning theories may have a more specific purpose than general learning theories. For example, andragogy is the art and science to help adults learn.

Connectivism is a recent theory of networked learning which focuses on learning as making connections.

Multimedia learning theory focuses on principles for the effective use of multimedia in learning.

Basic Theories of Adult Learning

When it comes to adult learning strategies, it's best to know about the background of adult learning theories, sometimes referred to as andragogy, so the instructor knows what best practices have been proven to work in the past.

Three main theories have influenced adult learning programs. Malcolm Knowles created one such theory, commonly referred to as the Knowles Theory, and other adult learning professionals have applied the learning theories of behaviourism and constructivism to adult learning. Here is a brief overview of each theory.

Knowles's Theory

Malcolm Knowles published the book *The Adult Learner: A Neglected Species* in 1973, building on the snippets of adult learning theory that were already starting to take form by John Dewey and Eduard C. Lindeman. He borrowed the term andragogy, which he initially defined as "the art and science of helping adults learn". The term now refers to learner-focused education for all ages of learners, although many educational texts use the term to refer to adult learning theory. Knowles's theory states that five issues should be addressed in formal adult learning:

1. Learners should know why something is important to learn.
2. Learners should be shown how to direct themselves through information.
3. Instruction should relate the topic to the learners' experiences.
4. People will not learn until they are ready and motivated to learn.

5. This requires some help in overcoming inhibitions, behaviours and beliefs about learning.

Knowles has said himself that all but the above point no. 3 can also apply to children. Because children have fewer experiences than adults, it can be hard for them to relate the topic to their experiences.

Speck has expanded on Knowles's theory and stated that adults will commit to learning when the goals and objectives are important to them and they can use the knowledge in the "real world". Also, adult learning differs from how children learn when it comes to the ego factor. Adults don't like to be told they don't know as much as another adult that they see as their equal. Adult learning "must be structured to provide support from peers and to reduce the fear of judgement during learning". Speck also states that feedback is important to adults, so learning activities must have some kind of helpful feedback involved.

The Learning Organization

The 'learning organization' has its origins in companies like Shell, where Arie de Geus described learning as the only sustainable competitive advantage. The Learning Organization is seen as a response to an increasingly unpredictable and dynamic business environment. Here are some definitions by key writers:

"The essence of organizational learning is the organization's ability to use the amazing mental capacity of all its members to create the kind of processes that will improve its own" (Nancy Dixon, 1994).

"A Learning Company is an organization that facilitates the learning of all its members and continually transforms itself (M. Pedler, J. Burgoyne and Tom Boydell, 1991). "Organizations where people continually expand their capacity to create the results they truly desire, where new and expansive patterns of thinking are nurtured, where collective aspiration is set free, and where people are continually learning to learn together" (Peter Senge, 1990).

Learning organizations are those that have in place systems, mechanisms and processes, that are used to continually enhance their capabilities and those who work with it or for it, to achieve sustainable objectives—for themselves and the communities in which they participate. The important points to note about this definition are that learning organizations:

- Are adaptive to their external environment.
- Continually enhance their capability to change/adapt.
- Develop collective as well as individual learning.
- Use the results of learning to achieve better results.

Why the Interest in 'Learning Organizations'?

Basically, it's the search for the (unattainable) Holy Grail. Companies are seeking to improve existing products and services (continuous improvement), and innovation (breakthrough strategies). This has resulted in a plethora of initiatives such as TQM (Total Quality Management) and BPR (Business Process Re-engineering). But companies are finding that such programmes succeed or fail depending on human factors, such as skills, attitudes and organizational culture. It also appears that many implementations are geared to highly specified processes, defined for anticipated situations. The current interest in the 'learning organization' stems from the recognition that these initiatives, by themselves, often do not work. Something more is needed to:

- Cope with rapid and unexpected changes where existing 'programmed'—responses are inadequate.
- Provide flexibility to cope with dynamically changing situations.
- Allow front-line staff to respond with initiative based on customer needs vs. being constrained by business processes established for different circumstances.

As various management writers put it:

"Organizations must develop a capacity for fast-paced innovation, learn to love change" (Peters).

"As the competitive environment becomes more complex and variegate, the need for greater genetic variety—a broader range of managerial beliefs, and a greater repertoire of managerial actions—grows apace" (Hamel and Prahaled).

"Top companies seem to organise around people honouring these needs—feeling of control, something to believe in, challenge, lifelong learning, recognition" (Waterman). With the pace of change ever quickening, the need to develop mechanisms for continuous learning and innovation is greater than ever.

Types of Learning

A learning organization is not about 'more training'. While training does help develop certain types of skill, a learning organization involves the development of higher levels of knowledge and skill. We have developed a 4-level model:

Level 1 - Learning facts, knowledge, processes and procedures. Applies to known situations where changes are minor.

Level 2 - Learning new job skills that are transferable to other situations. Applies to new situations where existing responses need to be changed. Bringing in outside expertise is a useful tool here.

Level 3 - Learning to adapt. Applies to more dynamic situations where the solutions need developing. Experimentation, and deriving lessons from success and failure is the mode of learning here.

Level 4 - Learning to learn. Is about innovation and creativity; designing the future rather than merely adapting to it. This is where assumptions are challenged and knowledge is reframed.

Furthermore, this model (or adaptation of it) can be applied at three levels—to the learning of individuals, of teams and of organizations. Organizations that achieve learning to Level 4 will "reinvent not just their organization but their industry" (Hamel and Prahaled in *Competing for the Future*).

Characteristics of a Learning Organization

Observation and research identifies four types of factor:

Learning Culture—An organizational climate that nurtures learning. There is a strong similarity with those characteristics associated with innovation.

Processes—Processes that encourage interaction across boundaries. These are infrastructure, development and management processes, as opposed to business operational processes (the typical focus of many BPR initiatives).

Tools and Techniques—Methods that aid individual and group learning, such as creativity and problem-solving techniques.

Skills and Motivation—To learn and adapt.

Here are some additional points on the first three of these.

A Learning Culture

- **Future, external orientation**—These organisations develop understanding of their environment; senior teams take time out to think about the future. Widespread use of external sources and advisors, e.g. customers on planning teams.
- **Free exchange and flow of information**—Systems are in place to ensure that expertise is available where it is needed; individuals network extensively, crossing organizational boundaries to develop their knowledge and expertise.
- **Commitment to learning, personal development**—Support from top management; people at all levels encouraged to learn regularly; learning is rewarded. Time to think and learn (understanding, exploring, reflecting, developing).
- **Valuing people**—Ideas, creativity and "imaginative capabilities" are stimulated, made use of and developed. Diversity is recognised as a strength. Views can be challenged.
- **Climate of openness and trust**—Individuals are encouraged to develop ideas, to speak out, to challenge actions.
- **Learning from experience**—Learning from mistakes is often more powerful than learning from success. Failure is tolerated, provided lessons are learnt ("learning from fast failure", Peters).

Key Management Processes

- **Strategic and Scenario Planning**—Approaches to planning that go beyond the numbers, encourage challenging assumptions, thinking 'outside of the box'. They also allocate a proportion of resources for experimentation.

- **Competitor Analysis**—As part of a process of continuous monitoring and analysis of all key factor in the external environment, including technology and political factors. A coherent competitor analysis process that gathers information from multiple sources, sifts, analyses, refines, adds value and redistributes is evidence that the appropriate mechanisms are in place.
- **Information and Knowledge Management**—Using techniques to identify, audit, value (cost/benefit), develop and exploit information as a resource (known as IRM—information resources management); use of collaboration processes and groupware, e.g. Lotus Notes, First Class to categorise and share expertise.
- **Capability Planning**—Profiling both qualitatively and quantitatively the competencies of the organisation. Profiling these on a matrix can be helpful to planning adjustment.
- **Team and Organisation Development**—The use of facilitators to help groups with work, job and organisation design and team development—reinforcing values, developing vision, cohesiveness and a climate of stretching goals, sharing and support.
- **Performance Measurement**—Finding appropriate measures and indicators of performance; ones that provide a 'balanced scorecard' and encourage investment in learning (for example, Measuring Intellectual Capital).

Reward and Recognition Systems—Processes and systems that recognize acquisition of new skills, team-work as well as individual effort, celebrate successes and accomplishments, and encourages continuous personal development.

Tools and Techniques

Too numerous to cover in detail, but include a wide range of learning and creativity skills in the following groups:

- Inquiry—interviewing, seeking information.
- Creativity—brainstorming, associating ideas.
- Making sense of situations—organizing information and thoughts.
- Making choices—deciding courses of action.
- Observing outcomes—recording, observation.
- Reframing knowledge—embedding new knowledge into menta memorizing.

Collective (i.e. team and organizational) learning require skills for sharing information and knowledge, particularly implicit knowledge, assumptions and beliefs that are traditionally "beneath the surface". Key skills here are:

- Communication, especially across organizational boundaries.
- Listening and observing.
- Mentoring and supporting colleagues.
- Taking a holistic perspective—seeing the team and organization as a whole.
- Coping with challenge and uncertainty.

Many (but not all) of these will be found described in *The Fifth Discipline Fieldbook* by Peter Senge et. al. The five disciplines are Personal Mastery, Systems Thinking, Team Learning, Shared Vision, Mental Models. Another useful source is *Techniques for Structured Problem Solving* by Arthur B. van Gundy.

Inhibitors to becoming a Learning Organization

These are some of the most common obstacles to becoming a learning organization:

- operational/fire fighting preoccupation—not creating time to sit back and think strategically,
- too focused on systems and process (e.g. ISO 9000) to exclusion of other factors (bureaucratic vs. thinking),

- reluctance to train (or invest in training), other than for obvious immediate needs,
- too many hidden personal agendas,
- too top-down driven, overtight supervision—lack of real empowerment.

Getting Started

As with many 'interventions', there are many good places to start, depending on the specific context. Some ones often recommended are: **Start at the top**—helpful to give an impetus.

Start with a chronic problem—always a good place to get the thinking caps on.

Initiate a Task Force—a common response, but they will need drive and vision.

Start with an Organizational Diagnosis—the HR consultants favour this one.

Link to an existing process or initiative—go where there is existing energy.

Review existing systems and processes—an audit to identify a 'capability' gap.

New Product Development

We particularly favour the latter. It is tangible, is an opportunity to be innovative, and needs a lot of 'boundary crossing' to succeed. It draws on many of the processes, tools and techniques to become effective at learning.

The Role of Systems

It is our belief that many learning organization initiatives are high-jacked by the HR function or outside specialists. This should not be the case. Developing a learning organization is about doing it from within and taking a holistic systems perspective. MIS departments and IS professionals have a major contribution to make.

- They have a systems approach and mind-set: a strong background in logical methods and process and are generally capable of developing creative solutions and holistic views.

- They often provide some of the best project managers within an organization, capable of co-ordinating multiple activities across several functions and involving significant change in work processes.
- An information infrastructure that enables information flows, including networked connections between internal systems and access to external networks and databases.
- Likely to be "early adopters" of important learning enabling technologies, such as groupware, computer conferencing, videoconferencing, Internet exploration, multimedia.
- Have systems integration knowledge, essential aspect of making efficient connections between information, and more importantly knowledge.

In conjunction with library information services function, they play a key part in the management of information and knowledge resources Providing the systems and processes for the management of knowledge and flow of information is, we believe, a crucial and underrated aspect of the learning organization, using techniques such as Information Resources Management (IRM).

The Management Challenge

The challenge facing managers today is to make the effort needed to learn some of the new skill and techniques, and to put in processes that engage their workforce in programs of continuous capability development. Learning should be integrated into the doing, as part and parcel of everyday work. It should also be energising, stimulating and fun. Getting the best out of everybody, including yourself to meet the challenges ahead.

Learning Strategies

Studying strategies, also called learner strategies, are ways of learning. Good learners use these strategies to make their learning more efficient.

There are two main types of learning strategies, the first are strategies for planning how to learn, and secondly strategies for learning.

Strategies for Planning How to Learn

Advance Organization

Doing a preview of what you are going to learn. For example, if you want to improve your pronunciation, you can read the introduction to different pronunciation books, and find out that you need to study the sounds of consonants, vowels, intonation, stress and linking.

Directing Attention

This means paying attention to studying something, and not doing other things like surfing the Internet.

Selective Attention

This means studying things that you can remember more easily, for example, because they are useful for your university course or for your job. If you need to do a presentation for your course you can study presentations, if you need to write a report at work, you can learn how to write a report.

Self-management

This is understanding the conditions that help you learn, and organizing them. For example, if you like music, learning in a place with music. You will also need materials like books and may be a computer. CILL has good learning conditions (but no coffee!).

Advance Preparation

Planning and learning English that you will need for something, for example, learning the correct pronunciation of important words in a presentation.

Self-monitoring

Correcting yourself if you make a mistake when you are using English. This is good for accuracy, but not for fluency.

Delayed Production

When you first start to learn a new language, you may decide not to try speaking until you have learned some vocabulary, grammar and pronunciation. You may just want to try listening first, before speaking.

Self-evaluation (Self-assessment or testing)

Deciding if you have finished learning a topic because your English is good enough to do the things you need. Click here for more details on how to test yourself.

Self-reinforcement

This means giving yourself a present when you have successfully learned something.

For example, chocolate or 10 minutes playing computer games.

Working Alone or with Other People

There are sections in the reading, writing, listening, speaking, grammar, vocabulary and pronunciation pages on this as well. With other people you can compare ideas, criticise ideas, get more ideas, and therefore think about things in more detail than you can alone.

Thinking Strategies

Grouping: Putting things in groups and in order helps you to build a framework for learning. Grouping also reflects the way your brain organises information. For example, you can group vocabulary words together according to categories like furniture, animals, office equipment, etc. Using mind-maps is one type of grouping.

Imagery: This means making pictures in your mind to help you remember things. For example, a 'hamburger paragraph'.

Speaking Strategies

Questions for Clarification: This means talking to English-speakers and asking for them to repeat, paraphrase (summarise in different words), explain or give examples. You can say:

Repeat: "I'm sorry, I didn't catch that, can you say that again?"

Paraphrase: "I'm sorry, I'm not sure what you mean. Can you tell me again?"

Recording yourself: Record yourself speaking, either on your own, or with other people. Later you can review the recording, listen for problems such as saying "Urn" too much, and research anything that you didn't know how to say.

Form a group of people to practise speaking English: In CILL, you can join the SAP to do this with a teacher. The English Club also runs the Big Mouth Corner for speaking practice.

Sing: You can sing English songs that you like, either alone, or with friends; e.g. karaoke. Click here for videos of current British hits.

Act: You can join a drama club or group that puts on English plays. The ELC has a Drama Club.

Imagine: Imagining that you are in a situation where you need to speak English; e.g. as a character you like in a movie. Try to imagine what you would say. Do you know what to say? If you are not sure, you can research it later.

Pronunciation Strategies

Repetition: You can repeat a word out loud or silently to practice pronunciation. Be careful to listen to a model to make sure that you pronunciation is correct.

Sound: This means remembering English sounds by using sounds in your own language. For example, the English sound is very similar to the Chinese (Putonghua) sound of the word that means 'one'.

Writing Strategies

Note-taking: It's a good idea to write down the main ideas, important points, an outline or a summary of a topic.

Organization: You can use a mind-map, organization tool or pros and cons calculator to help you organize the information.

Proofreading: You can use this program to automatically check for some common mistakes.

Peer-review: Ask a friend to read your text and comment on it. Do they understand it? Can they suggest any improvements?

To-do list: Write a list of 10 specific problems you have with your writing. Put them in order of seriousness or solvability. Work on the highest priority problems until you solve them. When you have solved them, cross them out, and add new problems to the bottom of the list.

Reading Strategies

Transfer: This means using ideas that you already have to make learning easier. For example, if you know that a paragraph (like a hamburger) usually has an introduction, a middle containing supporting detail, and a conclusion, you can use this knowledge to skim (read very quickly, by missing out non-important information, to understand the general topic) a text because you know that you only have to read the introduction and conclusion of both the whole text and the paragraphs.

Translation: You can read a story in a newspaper in your own language first, then read the same story in an English newspaper. Most of the story will probably be the same, so the story in your own language will help you to prepare for reading in English. For example, it will give you vocabulary, and when you read the English story and there is some vocabulary that you don't know, then you can use your knowledge of the story to guess what the new vocabulary is.

Inferencing: You can also use the strategy of reading a newspaper story in your own language first for prediction. You can predict the contents of the same story in an English newspaper. Reading to confirm your predictions is easier than reading with no background information. Click here for more information on reading newspapers.

Prediction: As well as predicting from newspaper stories in your own language, you can predict from your knowledge of the world, you knowledge of how people think, write and talk, and your knowledge of what the writer is like. For example, if you are reading a book it is a good idea to read about the author and the contents (on the cover or at the front of the book) to help you make predictions about what he or she believes.

Listening Strategies

Physical Response: You can listen to instructions about how to do something, and follow the instructions. Relating sounds to movements helps you remember the sounds.

So does listening to the sounds many times and repeating the movements. For example, you can buy an English fitness video and listen and follow the instructions, and get fit at the same time.

Prediction: You can predict what someone is going to say by the topic of the conversation and your knowledge of that person's opinions. Listening to confirm what you predict is easier than listening and trying to understand everything. For example, if you are watching a film or TV program about lawyers, you can predict that the defense lawyer will say that his client is "not guilty", and give reasons.

Preparation: You can listen to the news in your own language, then listen to it in English. Listening in your own language will help to predict what topics and vocabulary will be in the English news.

Motivate yourself: For example, if you like movies or music, you can practise listening to them. CILL has a large collection of movies, and some songs on CD.

Grammar Strategies

Deduction: This means using rules to work out the answer or how to do something. It is especially useful for grammar, for example, *Rule: To change normal speech to reported speech; eg. for writing minutes of a meeting, move the tenses back one past tense. Example: Mr. Chan—"I will see her tomorrow." Reported speech—'Mr. Chan said that he would see her the next day.'*

Recombination: This means joining together things you already know to make new things. For example, if you know that the simple past tense is used to describe things that happened in the past which have finished, and you know that the present perfect tense is used to describe experience, you can make a sentence that includes both of them:

"I first visited America in 1990. Last summer, I went there again, so I have been there twice."

Writing your own grammar book: This can contain rules, examples (e.g. from newspapers or magazines), your notes (e.g. on things you don't understand), lists of exceptions, etc.

Using new grammar: After you learn some new grammar, use it in conversation or writing, and see what your listener's or reader's reaction is: do they understand you. You can ask "Did I say that right?"

Get a grammar book: Come to CILL or go to a bookshop and look at the different grammar books. Choose one that you understand.

Read and listen: To see how writers and speakers use English grammar to communicate their ideas.

Vocabulary Strategies

Contextualisation: This means putting new vocabulary words into sentences to help you remember them and to test if you are using them correctly. You can use these sentences when talking to an English-speaker to see if they understand, you can write these sentences in your learner portfolio for the tutors to see, or you can e-mail the tutors and ask them to check these words in your sentences. The most independent ways are talking to an English speaker, and searching the Internet to find examples of the word being used in sentences.

Elaboration: This means relating new information to information you already know. For example, if you know the meaning of 'information', it is easy to remember that the verb is 'to inform', and that 'informative' is an adjective, and that 'an informant' is someone who gives information.

Inferencing: This means using available information to predict or guess the meanings of, e.g. new vocabulary items. For example, if you know that you are reading about football, and you know that a field is often a large area covered in grass, then you can guess that a football field is a large, grassy area for playing football.

Translation: You can read a story in a newspaper in your own language first, then read the same story in an English newspaper. Most of the story will probably be the same, so the story in your own language will help you to prepare for reading in English. For example, it will give you vocabulary, and when you read the English story and there is some vocabulary that you don't know, then you can use your knowledge of the story to guess what the new vocabulary is.

Personalisation: You can write down why the vocabulary item (i.e. the word or phrase) is important to you, where you first saw it, and when you used it, for example, you may have heard the item in a movie you liked (click here for list of movies and famous phrases in them), and used the item when you talked about the movie with your friends.

Keeping your own dictionary/vocabulary book: Writing entries for the dictionary will help you to learn words, and using your own dictionary can be faster than a normal dictionary. Click here for more details and examples.

Grouping: You can group words into different areas, such as words in the different courses you study. For example, business students could group vocabulary items into marketing vocabulary, accounting vocabulary, and human resources vocabulary.

Summary

Learning is an ongoing process and habit of learning is positive symbol for professional to grow in a highly competitive corporate environment. We are into a total quality management era and we are ready to pay for six sigma quality but we are not ready to face error in day to day business arena.

A doctor or a pharmacist can save life or give death because both of them have authority to prescribe medicine. We know that medicine is double edged sword and if we don't know how to use the medicine, then surely a doctor or a pharmacist can give death instead of life. For a management graduate business management tool is very important and if they don't know the updated business management tool then it is very tough to face the competitive environment.

The golden age of learning is up to the age of 25 and the learning interest decreases if you are not habitual learner. You will find few people study book at bed time and few read newspaper regularly. This is because, they want to invest time on study and they enjoy as well. Thus, we increase our knowledge bank on daily basis. The concepts of the Learning Organization and Knowledge Management are increasingly seen as two sides of the same coin—as you learn you gain knowledge which you apply and learn more.

Chapter eight

RETENTION MANAGEMENT

Retaining employees, especially high-performing employees, can be challenging in this fast-paced employment world. Help your organization retain seasoned employees through communicating support and appreciation with the help of these training programs and resources.

When your new employee starts the job, it takes him/her a while to adjust to new surroundings, new rules and new expectations. Begin your successful retention efforts with a proper orientation. New employee orientation efforts can help new team members feel more at home and let them know what others expect of them.

Current Scenario of Employee Turnover (Attrition)

Nothing can be more frustrating to a small business owner or manager than the constant aggravation of employee turnover. High or low employee turnover can be detrimental to your company. Learn what you need to know to calculate and curtail the revolving employee exit door in your business.

Employee turnover can vary as a result of the industry and location of your business. For instance, the food service industry typically experiences turnover of 100-300 per cent. The stress of employee turnover is much greater on smaller businesses than larger corporations. Before you can take effective measures to reduce turnover, you first need to find the price your business pays in lost employees.

What are the key motivating factors in today's job market? Most business owners initially think money is the key issue. However, many employees state that they are looking for challenges, recognition, and empowerment. Despite the current softness in the economy and the rise in the unemployment rate, the shortage of skilled insurance workers is still restraining growth for many agencies. Given this environment, what can a firm do to retain and attract the best and brightest employees, while challenging them to achieve the business' goals?

First, recognize that money, by itself, will not do it. High performing employees are searching for something more than just a high salary. The typical employee compensation plan should include a total package of rewards, recognition and environment. Some of the elements are "satisfiers" that allow a firm to attract and retain employees such as benefits, flex-time and training. Other elements of compensation are "motivators" such as bonuses, incentives, challenge and opportunity. A well-designed plan will have long-term and short-term compensation components.

The key to attracting and retaining the best people to the firm is the use of a "total compensation" approach. A firm that takes the time to carefully customize a "total compensation" package will transform individual employees into high performing, and committed employees.

The Indian FMCG sector demonstrated a steady rise in the attrition rate over the past three years. The attrition rate was 9.8 per cent in 2004. It moved up to 10.8 per cent in 2005. In 2006, the attrition rate became 17 per cent. The pharma sector—which employs a total of 500,000 people in India across domestic and global firms—is losing at least 30 per cent of its workforce annually, primarily in sales and marketing, for reasons ranging from low salaries to lack of growth opportunities and a new perception of it being an unstable industry. Merck Ltd., the Indian arm of the German drug maker and one of the oldest multinational pharma companies operating in India, suffered 20 per cent attrition last year. Aventis Pharma Ltd., the Indian unit of French drug maker Sanofi-Aventis, loses around 22 per cent of its 2,177—strong workforce annually.

The increasingly competitive drug market and the patent regime have also spread the impression that pharma companies are not very stable, he says.

"The vast opportunities available in the market and the rising trend of salaries offered by different sections of the market have resulted in the company losing good employees," Merck said in its last annual report released in September. Merck employs around 2,100 people in India. P.B. Padmajakshan, a former marketing manager with the country's sixth largest drug maker Wockhardt Ltd., is currently working with a Hyderabad-based lifestyle products firm. "First line marketing managers, who earn around Rs. 2.5 lakh a year in a large pharmaceutical company, earn more than double in an insurance company, which pays around Rs. 6.5-7 lakh a year at present," he says.

Consequently, pharma companies are being forced to recruit people who don't have enough experience at low salaries, Padmajakshan says. Shrinking profitability because of rising competition and a narrowing pipeline of new drugs mean that pharma companies are in no position to offer competitive salaries and other benefits. "Pharma industry lost its glamour as an attractive job destination after the emergence of information technology and a few other new generation services sector(s)," says R.D. Joshi, executive director, Interlink Marketing Consultancy Pvt. Ltd., a Mumbai-based pharma marketing consultancy firm.

Attrition rates in voice-based BPO service providers in India are as high as 60 per cent. The reasons cited for high attrition are,

- HR challenges.
- The industry is looked at as a stop-gap arrangement by youngsters.
- Career path not well defined and not strong.
- Lifestyle issues.
- Lack of bonding with peers and the organization.
- Perception-based problem.
- Unorganized BPO labor market.

The fall in attrition rate is directly related to the paucity of opportunities and a general slowdown in employment rate within the industry. Many companies across sectors including industry majors have put a break on their recruiting process in an effort to fight out the economic crisis. The corporations are definitely feeling the heat, and amidst uncertainty, they are treading cautiously and hence have deferred almost all of their recruitment decisions to a later date. By adding manpower, companies don't want to increase their cost. As a result, the job opportunities have reduced drastically, as the companies are not in a mood for expansion.

Cost of Employee Turnover

The following is a comprehensive checklist of items to include when calculating the cost of turnover in any organization. To determine the costs, have the hourly and weekly cost of fully loaded payroll costs (i.e. salary plus benefits) of the vacant position, the management staff, the recruitment staff and others as outlined below.

It should be noted that the costs of time and lost productivity are no less important or real than the costs associated with paying cash to vendors for services such as advertising or temporary staff. These are all very real costs to the employer.

These calculations will easily reach 150 per cent of the employees annual compensation figure. The cost will be significantly higher (200% to 250% of annual compensation) for managerial and sales positions.

To put this into perspective, let's assume the average salary of employees in a given company is $50,000 per year. Taking the cost of turnover at 150 per cent of salary, the cost of turnover is then $75,000 per employee who leaves the company. For the mid-sized company of 1,000 employees who has a 10 per cent annual rate of turnover, the annual cost of turnover is $7.5 million.

Do you know any CEO who would not want to add $7.5 million to their revenue? And, by the way, most of that figure would be carried over to the profit line as well. What about the company with 10,000 employees? The cost of turnover equals $75 million.

Here is the list:

Costs Due to a Person Leaving

1. Calculate the cost of the person(s) who fills in while the position is vacant. This can be either the cost

of a temporary or the cost of existing employees performing the vacant job as well as their own. Include the cost at overtime rates.

2. Calculate the cost of lost productivity at a minimum of 50 per cent of the person's compensation and benefits cost for each week the position is vacant, even if there are people performing the work. Calculate the lost productivity at 100 per cent if the position is completely vacant for any period of time.
3. Calculate the cost of conducting an exit interview to include the time of the person conducting the interview, the time of the person leaving, the administrative costs of stopping payroll, benefit deductions, benefit enrollments, COBRA notification and administration, and the cost of the various forms needed to process a resigning employee.
4. Calculate the cost of the manager who has to understand what work remains, and how to cover that work until a replacement is found. Calculate the cost of the manager who conducts their own version of the employee exit interview.
5. Calculate the cost of training your company has invested in this employee who is leaving. Include internal training, external programs and external academic education. Include licenses or certifications the company has helped the employee obtain to do their job effectively.
6. Calculate the impact on departmental productivity because the person is leaving. Who will pick up the work, whose work will suffer, what departmental deadlines will not be met or delivered late. Calculate the cost of department staff discussing their reactions to the vacancy.
7. Calculate the cost of severance and benefits continuation provided to employees who are leaving that are eligible for coverage under these programs.

8. Calculate the cost of lost knowledge, skills and contacts that the person who is leaving is taking with them out of your door. Use a formula of 50 per cent of the person's annual salary for one year of service, increasing each year of service by 10 per cent.
9. Calculate the cost impact of unemployment insurance premiums as well as the time spent to prepare for an unemployment hearing, or the cost paid to a third party to handle the unemployment claim process on your behalf.
10. Calculate the cost of loosing customers that the employee is going to take with them, or the amount it will cost you to retain the customers of the sales person, or customer service representative who leaves.
11. Subtract the cost of the person who is leaving for the amount of time the position is vacant.

Recruitment Costs

1. The cost of advertisements (from a $200 classified to a $5,000 or more display advertisement); agency costs at 20-30 per cent of annual compensation; employee referral costs of $500-$2,000 or more; internet posting costs of $300-$500 per listing.
2. The cost of the internal recruiter's time to understand the position requirements, develop and implement a sourcing strategy, review candidates backgrounds, prepare for interviews, conduct interviews, prepare candidate assessments, conduct reference checks, make the employment offer and notify unsuccessful candidates. This can range from a minimum of 30 hours to over 100 hours per position.
3. Calculate the cost of a recruiter's assistant who will spend 20 or more hours in basic level review of resumes, developing candidate interview schedules and making any travel arrangements for out of town candidates.

4. The cost of the hiring department (immediate supervisor, next level manager, peers and other people on the selection list) time to review and explain position requirements, review candidates background, conduct interviews, discuss their assessments and select a finalist. Also include their time to do their own sourcing of candidates from networks, contacts and other referrals. This can take upwards of 100 hours of total time.
5. Calculate the administrative cost of handling, processing and responding to the average number of resumes considered for each opening at $1.50 per resume.
6. Calculate the number of hours spend by the internal recruiter interviewing internal candidates along with the cost of those internal candidates to be away from their jobs while interviewing.
7. Calculate the cost of drug screens, educational and criminal background checks and other reference checks, especially if these tasks are outsourced. Don't forget to calculate the number of times these are done per open position as some companies conduct this process for the final 2 or 3 candidates.
8. Calculate the cost of the various candidates pre-employment tests to help assess candidates' skills, abilities, aptitude, attitude, values and behaviours.

Training Costs

1. Calculate the cost of orientation in terms of the new person's salary and the cost of the person who conducts the orientation. Also include the cost of orientation materials.
2. Calculate the cost of departmental training as the actual development and delivery cost plus the cost of the salary of the new employee. Note that the cost will be significantly higher for some positions such as sales representatives and call centre agents

who require 4-6 weeks or more of classroom training.

3. Calculate the cost of the person(s) who conduct the training.
4. Calculate the cost of various training materials needed including company or product manuals, computer or other technology equipment used in the delivery of training.
5. Calculate the cost of supervisory time spent in assigning, explaining and reviewing work assignments and output. This represents lost productivity of the supervisor. Consider the amount of time spent at 7 hours per week for at least 8 weeks.

Lost Productivity Costs

As the new employee is learning the new job, the company policies and practices, etc. they are not fully productive. Use the following guidelines to calculate the cost of this lost productivity:

1. Upon completion of whatever training is provided, the employee is contributing at a 25 per cent productivity level for the first 2-4 weeks. The cost therefore is 75 per cent of the new employees full salary during that time period.
2. During weeks 5-12, the employee is contributing at a 50 per cent productivity level. The cost is therefore 50 per cent of full salary during that time period.
3. During weeks 13-20, the employee is contributing at a 75 per cent productivity level. The cost is therefore 25 per cent of full salary during that time period.
4. Calculate the cost of co-workers and supervisory lost productivity due to their time spent on bringing the new employee "up to speed".
5. Calculate the cost of mistakes the new employee makes during this elongated indoctrination period.
6. Calculate the cost of lost department productivity caused by a departing member of management who

is no longer available to guide and direct the remaining staff.

7. Calculate the impact cost on the completion or delivery of a critical project where the departing employee is a key participant.
8. Calculate the cost of reduced productivity of a manager or director who looses a key staff member, such as an assistant, who handled a great deal of routine, administrative tasks that the manager will now have to handle.

New Hire Costs

1. Calculate the cost of bring the new person on board including the cost to put the person on the payroll, establish computer and security passwords and identification cards, business cards, internal and external publicity announcements, telephone hookups, cost of establishing e-mail accounts, costs of establishing credit card accounts, or leasing other equipment such as cell phones, automobiles, pagers.
2. Calculate the cost of a manager's time spent developing trust and building confidence in the new employee's work.

Lost Sales Costs

1. For sales staff, divide the budgeted revenue per sales territory into weekly amounts and multiply that amount for each week the territory is vacant, including training time. Also use the lost productivity calculations above to calculate the lost sales until the sales representative is fully productive. Can also be used for telemarketing and inside sales representatives.
2. For non-sales staff, calculate the revenue per employee by dividing total company revenue by the average number of employees in a given year. Whether an employee contributes directly or indirectly to the generation of revenue, their purpose

is to provide some defined set of responsibilities that are necessary to the generation of revenue. Calculate the lost revenue by multiplying the number of weeks the position is vacant by the average weekly revenue per employee.

Reducing Employee Turnover

With today's baby boomer generation beginning to retire from the labour market, many companies are finding it increasingly difficult to retain employees. Turnover is becoming a serious problem in today's corporate environment. The employment culture is changing as well. It is now relatively common to change jobs every few years, rather than grow with one company throughout the employment life as was once commonplace. In addition, employees are increasingly demanding a balance between work and family life.

Turnover costs for many organizations are very high and can significantly affect the financial performance of an organization. Direct costs include recruitment, selection, and training of new people. Much time and expense go into this process. Indirect costs include such things as increased workloads and overtime expenses for co-workers, as well as reduced productivity associated with low employee morale. Estimated costs vary from organization to organization, some as low as a few hundred dollars to as high as four times the annual salary of the employee.

It has been estimated that, on average, it costs a company one-third of a new hire's annual salary to replace an employee. Therefore, at minimum wage, the cost to replace an employee is estimated at $3,700.

There are many potential causes for turnover. Area economic conditions and labour market conditions affect general turnover rates and can be very difficult to manage. However, certain causes associated with turnover in any specific job or organization can be managed. These include such things as non-competitive compensation, high stress, working conditions, monotony, poor supervision, poor fit between the employee and the job, inadequate training, poor communications, and organization practices.

For a company to develop a retention strategy, several steps must be taken. First, they must assess the current situation and measure the turnover rate in their company. Turnover is calculated simply by dividing the number of annual terminations by the average number of employees in the work force. The average employee turnover rate is 14.4 per cent annually, according to the Bureau of National Affairs. *How does your company compare?*

A company must also measure the cost of turnover, develop retention strategies, and plan for some expected turnover and a changing workforce culture. Employers must recognize that quality of work life is becoming more and more important to employees.

What initial steps can be taken to reduce turnover? **First, hire the right people and continue to develop their careers.** Does your company have an ongoing career development program, tuition reimbursement, or skills training program? An investment in upgrading the workforce is one of the best investments a company can make when looking at long-term growth. Hiring the people that are a good "fit" with the culture of the organization—meaning that their values, principles, and goals clearly match those of the company—and then training as necessary will go a long way toward ensuring employee loyalty and retention.

Second, most companies with low turnover rates are very employee oriented. They solicit input and involvement from all employees and maintain a true "open-door" policy that avoids closed-door meetings. Employees are given an opportunity for advancement and are not micro-managed. Intrinsic rewards are critical. Employees must believe they have a voice and are recognized for their contribution. Remember that "trust" and "loyalty" are a two-way street. Does your company's culture encourage open communication and employee input?

Third, develop an overall strategic compensation package that includes not only base and variable pay scales, but long-term incentive compensation, bonus and gain-sharing plans, benefit plans to address the health and welfare issues of the employees, and non-cash rewards and perks as well. To be competitive in today's labour market, most companies find it necessary to offer a standard benefit package, including health, dental, and life insurance, vacation and leave policies, and investment and retirement plans. But what more could be done that would be cost effective toward creating an employee-oriented work environment?

Creativity in compensation and benefits can make quite a difference to the welfare of the employee. A company should assess overall employee needs when addressing retention issues.

If employee welfare is a genuine concern, what about child care? How much employee absenteeism is attributable to not having a dependable babysitter? Although the costs and liabilities involved in providing onsite day care can be prohibitive, perhaps a company could subsidize childcare in some manner. Sometimes, just negotiating rates for your employees with area childcare providers could be very helpful. May be, some kind of a company match would be possible. Household chore assistance is another possibility that is being used by some companies.

Consider other options—such as alternative work schedules or flextime, or perhaps preventative health care and wellness programs such as fitness centre memberships—as possible cost-effective benefits. Don't forget that perks or non-cash rewards to recognize exceptional performance can be critical. Service recognition, event tickets, trips, and public recognition can send strong messages to the public regarding company culture and values. Simply examine the issues and needs of your employees and try to develop creative programs to address these needs.

Although many costs associated with these suggestions may seem prohibitive, as well they may be, the company must evaluate the costs of current turnover, analyze the reasons for the individual organization, and develop strategies that in the long-term are less costly than continued turnover. Some of these suggestions may not be so costly in comparison.

Just a word of caution: Be fair and consistent in establishing compensation. Promote from within if possible. Attempt to avoid bringing new people on board at a higher rate than current employees. Policies to prevent discussion of wages simply do not work. Furthermore, such policies are in complete opposition of "open-door" communications.

Although many companies use contract employees to address fluctuations in business, working side by side with someone who is making twice the rate of pay without any commitment or loyalty to the company can be a real morale killer. Avoid this if at all possible.

If your company follows these steps and shows a genuine concern for the well being of your employees, you may not have to pay the highest wages n town to have the lowest employee turnover rate.

Fighting Employee Turnover Costs

Calculating Employee Turnover Cost—A general approach to calculate employee turnover cost is to use 50 per cent to 200 per cent of an employee's annual salary. This calculation uses the cost of hiring and training new staff. We will adjust some variables to match the needs of small business. Total employee turnover cost = Costs of hiring new employees + Costs of training new employees.

Tips for Reducing Employee Turnover

***Hire the Right Demographic*:** Is your small business properly recruiting the right age group? Match your company profile with your target hiring group. If you can't offer career advancement to your workforce, then avoid hiring young career oriented staff. Consider hiring older employees who are less concerned with advancement.

***Understand Employee Motivation*:** Retaining staff requires learning what's important to your employees. Look to the external motivators like recognition and rewards. Remember the internal motivators of purpose and passion.

***Read Between the Lines*:** The real cause of employee turnover usually won't be found in your typical exit interview. Departing employees will provide the usual response of leaving for more pay or a better job. Inquire for deeper meaning. Was it a lack of support? Was the commission structure unreasonable? Take the time to get to the bottom of the turnover.

These three tips to reduce turnover are a good start to understanding your employee loss issue. Be critical and always look inward. You may be the source of the turnover. Make certain your management style is the way you would want to be managed. High turnover can be a signal your business is in trouble. Low turnover can also be a negative.

The Price of Low Employee Turnover

You aren't immune to the costs of employee turnover because your turn rate is low. Low turnover can be a bad sign. Over 40 per cent of distressed businesses have very low employee turnover, according to a study by Getzler & Company, Inc.

Employee turnover costs impact your bottom line and the culture of your business. "The organizations that achieve the most dramatic reductions in turnover and maintain those lower levels are usually the ones where the top executive or owner makes it a priority" says F. Leigh Branham, author of *Keeping the People Who Keep You in Business: 24 Ways to Hang on to Your Most Valuable Talent*. Addressing the issue rests on your shoulders.

Pay Systems and Benefits

Benefits are also a vital consideration in attracting and retaining good people into our industry, but many shop owners/managers think it is strictly the paycheck. Research done many times over has proven this otherwise. Benefits also have become an extremely critical concern for businesses, especially in regard to health care costs ("Health Insurance Can Help Attract, Retain Employees", p. 37).

When asked, almost all staff members who left the repairer ranks say the reason they left was for a better work environment and benefits.

There are a number of programs out there that can put money back into the employee's pockets, which have minimal costs to you as the employer. They include:

- Pre-tax cafeteria plans for medical and child care expenses.

- Medical discount plans (not health insurance but discounted services).
- All of these can reduce costs to the employees, which translates to more disposable income.

The tool reimbursement programs actually reduce the company's expenses as well. I suggest you research tool reimbursement programs. There is a good informational Web site at www.tool reimbursement.net that provides a clear understanding of how it can be beneficial, both in costs and retaining good employees.

ASA offers two benefit providers—Pro-Check National and Solutions Now, that provide tool reimbursement programs. Both companies provide ASA members with special pricing on their tool expense reimbursement programs.

One important and underutilized benefit is training. We have analyzed facilities worldwide, and too often the commitment to training is more of a verbal one. Companies say they "train their employees", but when their training is reviewed it is not supported with actual expenses. In other words, I often see less than 5.5 per cent of sales budgeted for employee training.

Employee performance evaluations, pay plan, incentive system, training and benefits combine to attract, motivate and retain employees. Along with clear communication and a good company presentation, this will certainly improve your market area and organization. What's stopping you?

Career or Temporary Job?

Part of motivating and retaining good employees is distinguishing between whether a position you have is a career or a temporary job. If you don't know which it is, it will certainly be unclear to your employee as well.

Many studies show the No. 1 reason employees leave a position is that they didn't feel they knew what was expected of them. There is a saying I use often—I call it the "Law of Communication":

- If you don't tell someone what you want, it's likely it won't be what you expect.

- If you don't write down what you want, it's likely no one will remember the same.
- If you don't train for what you want, it's likely no one will know how.
- If you don't have incentives tied in, it's likely no one will have time to do it.

Richard Flint has a good definition of communication: "If both participants do not understand the same thing, it is not communication." Simply put, do you provide a clear path for candidates/new hires to understand their role and expectations within your company? Most do it by verbal communication and believe that is sufficient. As the Law of Communication says, you will not get the results you expect consistently.

The key difference between a mentorship program and an apprenticeship program is that the latter is usually managed by an association or governmental body. The mentorship program is an internal program designed for your business.

A good mentorship program outlines the technical skills and tasks needed for each position of the collision or mechanical repair industries. It also trains and manages the mentors and their relationship to apprentices. This is a key component since many previous mentorships failed because the skills needed to manage, train and coach an apprentice were not skills our best techs possessed (or were even interested in obtaining).

Attracting Good Candidates

To attract good candidates, your company's presentation must also be considered. Presentation refers to how your business looks, runs and feels to an outsider. Do you have the appearance of a state-of-the-art mechanical or collision repair facility? Or does the dust, grease and clutter present a stereotypical picture of our industry?

Another important component in attracting good candidates is to always be looking. Don't wait until a crisis forces you to hire the first person who can fog up a mirror. Evaluate your workforce monthly and determine its strengths and weaknesses.

How to Retain Good Employees?

1. Determine what motivates your individual employees. For most employees, money is not the key issue; relationships, fulfillment and recognition are.
2. Notice how much recognition an employee needs. Some employees can go years without praise, whereas others will leave after six months.
3. Understand that many employees are motivated by their social network at work. Encourage activities that make your employees feel like valued members of a team.
4. Realize that incentives don't have to be huge. A surprise gift certificate for the local ice cream parlor in the weekly paycheck will generate positive feelings.
5. Make benefits more accessible. If your company reimburses tuition for college courses, have a college administrator come to your company, so employees can find out about classes and programs.
6. Consider telecommuting, job sharing and other flexible working arrangements.
7. Offer profit sharing incentives to encourage longevity.
8. Create clear career paths at the company.

Ten Ways to Attract and Retain Great Employees

(1) ***Challenging work***. The old system of directing and monitoring every task that an employee performs is out. Employees with multiple skills and authority are in. For example, a major retailer has a one-paragraph employee handbook that states: "Use your judgment in all situations. There will be no additional rules." To truly perform at this level, requires enormous trust in the employees. However, if a business is able to perform at this level it will reach incredible heights.

Provide additional opportunities for learning and skill development to spice work up. Encourage the staff to take classes to get licensed and for courses to earn the necessary CEUs. But, an expansion of training could provide more flexibility through a higher skilled workforce. Send the employees to Dale Carnegie, Microsoft software training, business skills seminars, team building sessions or a sales class (such as Dynamics of Sales sponsored by CIC).

(2) ***Work environment.*** Today's workforce is looking for flexibility on the job and balance in their life. Management needs to evaluate ways to realistically provide this sought after flexibility in work. For example, tradition has it that the employees' work in an office with established work hours. Could the firm allow for variations, such as 4-day workweeks, working at home two days a week or job sharing? Flexible work hours are becoming a common tool to attract and retain good employees.

(3) ***Recognition and rewards.*** Non-cash recognition awards are a very effective way to reinforce the agency's values. They can be a low-cost, high-impact element of the total compensation package. For example, employees who provide outstanding or innovative customer service receive special awards. One way is for employees to be nominated by customers or their peers.

Management needs to think about the types of awards that make sense for employees. Here are some examples:

- Provide a day off with pay.
- Provide tickets to sports, music or cultural events.
- Take out an advertisement in the local newspaper thanking your employees for their contributions.
- Provide a donation in an employee's name to the charity of his or her choice.
- Pay for tutoring for the winner's child.
- Have the winner's car detailed during work.
- Pay for the winner's house to be cleaned.
- Pay for an evening out for the winner and their spouse—dinner and babysitting.

Once the basic ingredients are established, the firm can then look into advanced tools to attract and retain employees. The following are some of the approaches that owners should also consider:

(4) ***Profit sharing***. Although money is not always king, it still has a lot of clout. Firms that establish a bonus plan based on the business profitability will have employees that strive to increase sales and cut expenses. Profit sharing can be based on the profitability of the overall business or by profit centers such as commercial lines versus personal lines versus life and health. The pool of bonus money can then be distributed to the staff based on management's discretion.

A variation of profit sharing is to reduce the employees' base compensation while providing quarterly bonuses based on a department's performance. A plan that tracks employee performance will then allow them to see a direct correlation between their effort and their compensation.

(5/6) ***Phantom stock and stock appreciation rights***. Stock appreciation rights (SARs) and phantom stock are both specialized deferred compensation techniques designed to provide an employee with the economic benefits of stock ownership without the employee actually owning any company stock. When an owner cannot or will not change the existing ownership structure, SARs and phantom stock are often used, to provide an employee with some sort of incentive compensation based on the actual business performance.

A SAR is simply a grant to an employee which gives that person a right, at some specific time in the future, to receive a cash award equal to the appreciation in value of a certain number of shares of company stock. In concept, SARs are similar to stock options, but different in several points. Stock options require the employee to purchase the company's stock at the grant price. However, SARs do not require a cash outlay from the employee. The employee only receives the appreciation in value of the stock.

Phantom stock on the other hand can be viewed as units of value, which directly correspond to an equivalent number of shares of company stock. These phantom stock units are then granted to an employee for a specific period of time. When the maturity period is reached, the employee is then compensated directly in cash, based on the value of the phantom stock. Unlike SARs, the amount of compensation with phantom stock usually includes the underlying value of the stock as well as any appreciation above the grant price. Another difference is that SARs are typically paid out when the employee chooses to exercise the SAR, while phantom stock typically has a fixed award date.

(7) ***Deferred compensation***. Deferred compensation is a method for producers to build long-term value for their efforts directly related to their books of business. We recommend using deferred compensation instead of ownership in the producer's book of business. The plan is often phased in overtime until the producer is fully vested in the plan.

The agency benefits by having a system that encourages the producers to build their books as well as remain with the firm. It must be noted that a deferred compensation plan (as well as SARs and phantom stock) creates a contingent liability for the firm, which does negatively affect agency value. However, deferred comp is also "consideration", which helps uphold the covenant not-to-compete in a producer contract.

(8) ***Split-dollar life policies***. A split-dollar plan is a way to provide life insurance for an employee or their spouse at a reduced cost to that individual. The premium for the insurance is shared by the employee and his or her employer (thus the name "split-dollar").

It is an effective way to retain key employees while the business is reimbursed for every dollar it advances. From the employer's perspective, split-dollar is an inexpensive method of buying life insurance for any personal or business needs of select employees. It enhances employee loyalty by providing substantial insurance benefits. Some split dollar policies can provide funds which may be used for additional employee benefits in the future (deferred compensation, salary continuation, stock redemption, or retirement income).

From the employee's perspective, split-dollar can help replace needed family income that would be lost at the employee's death or help pay any estate taxes. If the employee owns the policy and collaterally assigns the policy to the employer, the employer can borrow against the cash value to the extent allowed by the collateral assignment form.

(9) ***ESOPs***. Employee Stock Ownership Plans (ESOPs) are a way for business owners to sell shares in the company or to provide an additional benefit to all qualified company employees. These plans were initially created as a win-win for business owners and employees. ESOP contributions are tax deductible as are dividends if they are paid to employees directly, on their behalf to the ESOP or applied to the loan payments of a leveraged plan. Because the ESOP is funded with pre-tax dollars, the company's tax savings may increase even further.

The selling shareholder can also defer the capital gains on stock sold to an ESOP as long as the ESOP owns 30 per cent or more of the company's stock and the seller rolls over the sale proceeds into qualified replacement property (stocks or bonds of domestic companies). Employees pay no tax on the contributions until they are entitled to receive the stock when they leave the company or retire. At this point, the company generally buys back the stock through a buyback provision in the ESOP.

ESOPs are expensive to set up and maintain. Businesses need to be a certain size before it makes financial sense. We recommend that agency owners do their homework before seriously considering this option.

(10) ***Stock equity***. Stock ownership usually conjures up visions of importance and respect. Producers and employees feel that having the word "Owner" on their business card will improve sales and stature. Often the employees only understand the benefits of

stock ownership and the drawbacks are ignored or not understood.

Agency owners are often unclear themselves whether or not they should offer stock to an employee. They usually first think about it either when a current employee is about to walk out the door and may not come back. Owners might often feel that they are forced to offer stock in order to entice a new producer to join the firm or to retain the employee, such as a producer with a book of business.

We recommend that owners think long and hard before offering stock to an employee. The decision whether or not to make an employee an owner needs to be based on a review of many factors. The right decision can propel the agency forward for many years to come. The wrong decision can mire the firm in unimportant muck.

Ways to Show Appreciation

These are my top eleven ways to show appreciation to employees and co-workers. Stretch your imagination. There are hundreds of other employee and co-worker appreciation ideas just waiting to be found. They'll bring you success in employee motivation, employee recognition and in building a positive, productive workplace.

From Food to Favours for Employee and Co-worker Appreciation.

You can tell your colleagues, co-workers and employees how much you value them and their contribution any day of the year. Trust me. No occasion is necessary. In fact, small surprises and tokens of your appreciation spread throughout the year help the people in your work life feel valued all year long.

Looking for ideas about how to praise and thank co-workers and employees? Here are eleven ways to show your appreciation to employees and co-workers:

- Praise something your co-worker has done well. Identify the specific actions that you found admirable.
- Say "thank you". Show your appreciation for their hard work and contributions. And, don't forget to

say "please" often as well. Social niceties do belong at work. A more gracious, polite workplace is appreciated by all.

- Ask your co-workers about their family, their hobby, their weekend or a special event they attended.
- Your genuine interest—as opposed to being nosey—causes people to feel valued and cared about.
- Offer staff members flexible scheduling for the holidays, if feasible. If work coverage is critical, post a calendar so people can balance their time off with that of their co-workers.
- Know your co-worker's interests well enough to present a small gift occasionally. An appreciated gift, and the gesture of providing it, will light up your co-worker's day.
- If you can afford to, give staff money. End of the year bonuses, attendance bonuses, quarterly bonuses and gift certificates say "thank you" quite nicely. *TechSmith* staff received a percentage of their annual salary for their end of year bonus.
- Almost everyone appreciates food. Take co-workers or staff to lunch for a birthday, a special occasion or for no reason at all. Let your guest pick the restaurant.
- Create a fun tradition for a seasonal holiday. *ReCellular* employees draw names for their Secret Santa gift exchange. Alison Doyle, About's Guide to *Job Searching*, also works in *Career Services* at Skidmore College where they do a "gift grab" at their holiday party.

  LuAnn Johnson who works in Human Resources at the *Schaller Anderson Mercy Care Plan* says, "We celebrate Treat Tuesday, every Tuesday between Thanksgiving and Christmas. We match up departments or people who don't normally work together as a unit and assign a day to provide gooey, healthy or scrumptious treats for the other groups.

It's a great mixer, an opportunity to show off our culinary skills and a morale builder—to say nothing of the sugar high!"

- Bring in bagels, doughnuts or another treat for staff and co-workers. Offerings such as cookies or cupcakes, that you've baked personally, are a huge hit. (Have you tried baking cupcakes in ice cream cones? People love them.) Another hit? Bring chocolate—chocolate anything.
- Last, but not least, provide opportunity. People want chances for training and cross-training. They want to participate on a special committee where their talents are noticed. They like to attend professional association meetings and represent your organization at civic and philanthropic events.

Attracting and Retaining Talent

It has been observed a rapidly-growing trend by leadership in every industry to attract and retain good people who are capable of creating and maintaining a very competitive, creative, and cutting-edge culture. After two decades of corporate downsizing, middle-management layoffs, merger-mania, and hostile takeovers, companies in every industry are waking up to the reality that they must make the management and motivation of their employees their number one strategic priority—or risk falling behind the competition.

Organizations are investing more time, energy, talent and dollars in this area than ever before—and with good cause. Obviously, without a responsive, top-notch workforce, it is impossible for management to fully execute and sustain a strategic plan. Without your people enthusiastically supporting your goals, your plan is likely to remain just that: a plan, and not a reality. Those who decline to invest in those areas mentioned above are certainly destined to pay even higher costs in the future.

Today's workers are an entirely new breed: more demanding, more diverse, more technically astute, and less likely than workers of a generation ago to believe that the employer has their best interests at heart. They obviously want fair compensation. They know what they're worth and they're going to get it somewhere. However, that isn't all they want. Today's employees expect more than a job and a paycheck;

- They expect meaningful work.
- They expect to be challenged.
- They want to see the "big picture" and know where they fit in.
- They require expectations and guidance.
- They want to contribute.
- They demand feedback.
- They crave on-going training (education).

First, leadership and middle-management define, discuss, and then rate their organization on each element of the checklist. After arriving at average scores, they brainstorm to identify areas of immediate concern and develop action plans to address each area. This feedback will not only provide targeted feedback for future action plans but will also send a message to employees of concern and action on behalf of leadership. This is just one of several steps your organization can take in attracting and retaining talent.

Employee Engagement Survey Program

The **Employee Engagement Survey** program measures your company's retention health to provide a clear picture of strengths and opportunities for development. The program has two main components:

1. *Employee Engagement Survey*

Program participants complete this on-line survey, which measures organizational systems, climate/culture factors, and managerial behaviours that impact retention, including:

- Organizational systems.
- Group/departmental factors.
- Management practices.
- Overall employee satisfaction.
- The likelihood employees will leave your company within the next twelve months.

2. *Retention Profile Report*

ITS analyzes the survey results to produce a report that identifies your organization's attrition vulnerabilities and strengths and provides general and specific recommendations for improving employee retention.

Demographic information gathered in the survey is used to focus recommendations on those employee populations most in need of intervention. Report findings and recommendations address:

- Current state of retention health.
- Key retention risk factors.
- Status of existing organizational systems.
- Recommended strategies for improvement.

Supplementary Program Components can be used to enhance the analysis, findings and recommendations presented in the Retention Profile Report:

- *Focus Groups* for specific departments or populations to explore why those employees stay with or leave the company; early warning signals that have been observed; and retention best practices currently in use.
- *An Organizational Systems Review* to assess the strengths and potential vulnerabilities of existing

systems for: recruitment and hiring, orientation and assimilation, performance management, learning and professional growth, career development, quality of work/life balance, and compensation and benefits.

- *Review and analysis of exit interview data*, gathered either with the *Out Takes Exit Interviewing Service* or via your organization's existing HR processes.

Out Takes Exit Interviewing System

The Out Takes Exit Interviewing System provides continuous tracking of the root causes of unwanted attrition at your company, to reveal attrition trends and the reasons behind them, and to help direct organizational efforts to increase employee commitment.

The Out Takes Exit Interviewing System has three primary components as well as an optional Re-Recruiting Protocol:

1. Out Takes On-line Exit Interview

As part of your organization's exit process, departing employees complete this on-line survey anywhere from three to nine months following their departure. This standardized interview collects valuable data about employee demographics, job conditions and organizational systems, the departing employee's manager, your organization's culture, and the new employer. ITS can customize the standard interview content to meet your unique organizational requirements.

2. Data Collection and Compilation

Out Takes data collection is managed by the ITS service bureau. Depending on the level of detail needed to meet your diagnostic needs, ITS can compile your data by division/department, level of responsibility, length of tenure, and/or other demographic specifications most relevant to your retention goals.

3. Out Takes Retention Reports

The ITS service bureau generates OutTakes reports whenever you need them—monthly, quarterly, annually, or as required. Out Takes reports include:

- A summary of the most critical retention factors impacting your organization.
- Survey results organized by retention factor, with overall and item-level results for each factor.
- The top reasons why departed employees have left your organization.
- New employer data.
- Analysis and recommendations from our Senior Retention Consultants on changes or enhancements to existing organizational systems or management practices.

Out Takes Re-recruiting Protocol

An increasing number of employees who have voluntarily terminated their employment are discovering that the grass isn't always greener on the other side. The Out Takes Re-recruiting Protocol allows you to augment your existing recruiting efforts by targeting these potential "boomerangers" for re-recruitment into your organization.

Linked to the *Out Takes on-line exit interview*, the Re-recruiting Protocol asks former employees if they are interested in returning to your company. If they are interested, the on-line re-recruiting process collects relevant data on the former employee's work history and current contact information; asks the former employee specific questions on their skill set and their interest in specific positions or career paths; and identifies what it would take for them to return to the organization.

Managing Employee Emotion—Individual reaction to performance feedback messages relating to pay or bonuses.

Understanding self-esteem is critical in determining individual reactions to performance feedback messages. Performance feedback messages employees receive from managers or supervisors are among the most important types of organizational communication. But what supervisors say about pay or bonuses may affect employees more than what is said in a performance review. Such feedback is designed to motivate future performance as well as recognize and reward employees for productive past behaviour. However, different people rarely react in the same way to the same messages, partly because of differences in self-esteem. Understanding self-esteem is critical in determining individual reactions to performance feedback messages. Self-esteem is clearly linked to a variety of job-related behaviours, including performance, job satisfaction and interpersonal skills. Consider, for example, the following illustrations:

- Bill Porter was given significant responsibilities in an important project late last year. Traditionally, employees working on such projects have received generous bonuses when the project was completed. However, a recession and supplier problems affected some of the project outcomes. While everyone did receive a bonus, it was smaller than bonuses others had received previously. Since then, Bill has been quite depressed and has mentioned to co-workers that he felt he really let the project team down. He has confided to several close friends that he just doesn't think he has the skills and ability that are needed in his job. Yesterday, Bill told his boss that he was thinking of quitting since "he wasn't doing much good around here anyway."
- Three years ago, Julie Kandel spent 18 months completely overhauling her company's computer network system. After many 12-hour days and 60-hour weeks, she completed the job on time and under budget. Julie's manager expressed a great deal of appreciation for her performance and told her it was the best work he had seen anyone do. However, at the same annual review, Julie was recommended for what she considered a "normal" raise. Unknown to Julie, the department's budget, which included the merit pay pool, had been reduced. During the year since her last merit review, Julie has worked on two similar, though smaller, projects and has done a mediocre job at best. She has become reluctant to take on new responsibilities. Her manager has complained that Julie seems "really unmotivated."

Both examples involve an employee's negative reaction to a feedback message about pay.

Self-esteem affects performance

Employees with low self-esteem are particularly vulnerable to the negative feedback that occurs when their expectations about pay are not met, making it difficult for them to sustain acceptable levels of performance. Research indicates that employees with low self-esteem are generally less productive, less creative and less motivated than employees with higher self-esteem.

In addition, individuals with low self-esteem are not as skilled as those with high self-esteem in interpersonal relations or conflict resolution. Indeed, they may often try to raise their own chronically low self-esteem by creating conflict, abusing sick or personal leave policies, or directing their anger at managers or peers. Furthermore, when given a negative feedback message, individuals with low self-esteem tend to react in much more dysfunctional ways than do individuals with higher self-esteem.

Differences in self-esteem are also associated with differences in "reactance"—the ways individuals respond to situations that initially appear to be uncontrollable—and "attribution"—the ways people assign causality.

Whenever people are confronted with a performance or task situation that is viewed as unacceptable, they make some attempt to regain control over the event in order to perform as others desire or expect. Research by Joel Brockner at Columbia University, has shown that individuals with low self-esteem exhibit less of this reactance than do individuals with high self-esteem.

Therefore, employees with high self-esteem make significant efforts to improve performance and gain control over outcomes. Employees with low self-esteem do not exhibit a significant change in effort or improvement in performance; in fact, decrease in both may occur. These employees may be viewed as chronically poor performers or lacking sufficient motivation.

Alternatively, such employees may show some reactance, but in areas unrelated to performance. They may initiate conflict with others, insult the work or performance of other employees, or abuse sick or personal leave policies. Since they are unable to control the outcome of their own performance, these employees may try to build or maintain their self-esteem by seeking control over other aspects of the work situation, for example, interpersonal relations and attendance.

Individuals who differ in self-esteem also differ in how they attribute a particular outcome to external or internal causes. Individuals with high self-esteem attribute positive outcomes to internal causes and negative outcomes to external causes. They view success as a result of their own talent or effort; failure, as a consequence of events outside their control—the economy, the boss, the competition, the sales force. The result is that they maintain and protect their own self-esteem.

People with low self-esteem attribute successes to external factors: "I got lucky", "The job was easy", or "So-and-so really did all the work". To make matters worse, they attribute negative outcomes to internal causes: "I'm really not very good at my job" or "I don't know what I'm doing". By blaming themselves for negative outcomes, people with low self-esteem can maintain consistently negative perceptions of their own worth. They also believe that they lack the skills or lack the ability to "control" the situation.

Pay Decisions and Self-esteem

Because decisions about pay or bonuses are among the most significant feedback messages employees receive, managers need to pay special attention to two facts that complicate the sending and receiving of these powerful messages:

- Employees measure pay in both referent and absolute terms.
- Budget constraints limit resources available for merit pay, bonuses and so forth.

Employees evaluate pay increases or bonuses not only in absolute terms, but also by using referent persons or points. Referent individuals include fellow employees—and, to some extent, employees of other organizations—who are or are perceived to be similar in experience, job classification, skill, contribution to the organization and effort. Referent points include the employee's contribution to the organization, the cost of living, the state of the economy, and the financial position of the organization. When a pay decision is not consistent with employee expectations, the employee may view the decision as negative feedback regarding his or her performance.

Of course, performance-related rewards given to employees are not totally a function of individual performance. Budgets also constrain pay decisions. While employee expectations may stay constant overtime, the resources available for merit pay or raises can vary from year to year, and even from quarter to quarter. If management fails to explain how resources constrain decisions, employees may view unmet expectations regarding pay as negative feedback.

Consider the first case of Bill Porter. Bill's behaviour is typical for an individual with low self-esteem reacting to a negative feedback message: decreased motivation, depression and a lack of self-efficacy. But what evidence is there that Bill, or any other member of the group, was responsible for the failure of the project? Clearly, the external environment—the recession and supplier problems—was the primary cause. Yet, the relatively small bonuses may have sent a failure message to group members, including Bill.

Bill's organization could have provided bonuses similar to those given in earlier years, despite the poor outcome of the project. There are situations when it may be appropriate to tie rewards to effort rather than actual performance. By doing so, organizations and managers avoid giving negative feedback to employees for performance outcomes that were beyond individual control.

In the second case, Julie Kandel also behaves in ways consistent with low self-esteem; she lacks motivation and direction, and is performing poorly. But Julie is a victim not only of her own low self-esteem but also of inconsistent feedback messages and budget constraints on pay decisions. Julie's manager, first, should have communicated clearly to Julie that her raise was more a function of the budget than of her performance. This would have helped Julie understand the pay decision and avoided the inconsistency. Second, Julie's manager could have offered other "goods", besides a higher salary, to reward her for her performance—days off, upgrades of equipment or office space, public recognition among her peers are examples. Non-monetary rewards would have provided a more consistent feedback message.

Managing Employee Reactions

Employees may respond in a variety of ways to negative feedback from pay decisions, but there are some steps that managers can take to lessen the possibility of negative outcomes.

- Take notice of the signs of low self-esteem—high needs for direction from superiors and approval from others, unwillingness to take risks or responsibilities, pointed criticism of others' behaviours and/or performance. Be particularly sensitive to the content and process of feedback messages when dealing with these employees. If possible, put your money where your mouth is.
- Phrases such as "great work", "super job", "outstanding" will be undercut by an average pay increase, because the pay message is likely to be interpreted as the most important one. Verbal strokes are important and valuable; most employees appreciate such feedback, but the two messages should be consistent. If an employee has done a really outstanding job for an extended period of time, and has been told so, raise his or her pay.
- If pay messages are not consistent with other feedback, explain why? In many cases, there are legitimate reasons why merit pay or bonuses cannot match what an employee deserves. A simple way to deal with the inconsistency is to be honest. Tell employees through memos, one-to-one conversations, or group meetings about the constraints on pay. And tell them as soon as the problem becomes known, not during an appraisal session. If employees know beforehand that raises will be limited, they

can evaluate pay feedback messages in terms of current conditions rather than those of previous years.

- Be aware of external constraints on performance. By acknowledging the many legitimate external reasons for failure, managers can help employees maintain their self-esteem.
- When pay is limited by budget constraints, consider alternative rewards—days off, increases in discretionary time or budgets to allow individuals to work on pet projects, upgrades in equipment or office space, and educational or personal development opportunities. Meaningful alternative rewards may require some thought and sacrifice by management. The reward must be something that employees will truly value and view as an acknowledgment of their performance. Otherwise, the reward may be regarded as just a ploy to buy their loyalty.
- Provide a legitimate process by which employees can challenge pay decisions. Managers are not always right and perfectly just. Mechanisms that allow employees to challenge pay decisions can give them the feedback they truly deserve.
- Remember that negative feedback is often unintended. Be aware that the same message may be interpreted differently by different employees. Consider the individual to whom the feedback is directed and pay attention to the way the feedback is communicated.

Richard C. Ringer is a doctoral candidate at the University of Colorado, Boulder.

Talent Retention and Inculcating Loyalty

Some Facts

- Nearly 70 per cent of organizations report that staff turnover has a negative impact.

- Approximately, retention of 50 per cent of organizations experience regular problems with employee.
- Over 50 per cent of the people recruited into an organization will leave within 2 years.
- 1 in 4 people recruited will leave within 6 months.
- Over 70 per cent of all employees respond to competitors' job offers during work hours?
- Voluntary resignations are at the highest level in over 20 years?
- Nearly 50 per cent of all middle managers are either currently looking for another job or plan to do so?

Why is retention becoming one of the top issues in HR?

- The enormous cost associated with staff turnover.
- The difficulties experienced in replacing people.
- Each new recruit represents risk.
- Costs associated with training.
- The overall impact on the organizations ability to meet the needs of its customers.

Types of Talent Retention

Research Initiative

- To develop an objective understanding of issues relating to employee retention.
- Accurately diagnose the problem areas.
- Evaluate the effectiveness of retention interventions.

Issue of Retention

- Each new recruit represents risk.
- The enormous cost associated with staff turnover.
- The difficulties experienced in replacing people.
- Costs associated with training.
- The overall impact on the organizations ability to meet the needs of its customers.

Rewarding Talent

- Be careful here. While rewarding good performance, once should ensure that it nourishes healthy competition.
- A manager should try to create balance while encouraging people to perform better.
- An employee's performance should be appreciated and rewarded, but in such a manner that is motivates his peers.
- It often happens that an employee is rewarded and it becomes a bone of contention between another employee and the organization.
- So don't go overboard, but also try not to be parsimonious.

Top Ten Talent Retention Tips

1. What do employees really wants?
2. Work environment.
3. Challenging work.
4. Recognition and rewards.
5. ***Grow competencies, situationally.*** Look for opportunities to put people into challenging situations where their skills and competencies will grow.
6. ***Meet one-on-one, routinely.*** Conduct regular, but brief one-on-one meetings between manager/leaders and direct reports. Begin by asking, "What's on your mind?"—then listen and act.
7. ***Make retention everyone's responsibility.*** Encourage all members of the work group to feel responsible for the retention of their peers and to be alert to problems that can be fixed.
8. ***Be a career builder.*** Talk to people about their long-term career aspirations and help them use or build the skills and competencies they need for the future.
9. ***Help people get an*** "A". Give the gift of being clear about what an "A" level performance looks like.

10. ***Walk your talk.*** Be aware that people are always watching and assessing you and your actions as a leader.

Employee Retention Analysis

Retaining employees are crucial but uncontrollable job if you are planned and ready with pros and cons. Retention manager should discuss things in advance with employer to handle the situation confidently. The discussion stuff includes Name of employees, Date of joining, Designation, Gross Salary, Under paid/Over paid/balanced, Required level of skills, Any special skills, Punctuality, Personality, Attitude and behaviour, Decision making ability, Negotiation skills, problem solving techniques, Motivation ability, etc. you can put grade under each head like excellent, average or below average.

First collect above said data with the consent of employer and prepare a list. Put your final grade to each of them like excellent, average or below average. For example, your employer is out of the country and on the moment he/she is not reachable and one of your excellent rank employees is going to resign or resigned but there is probability to retain him/her. This is really a crucial time for any retention manager. If you had discussed with your employer about all three segments of employees in advance then probably you could perform your job without any tension.

There discuss with employer about all three types of employees. He/she might suggest you let them go to below average employees and he/she will give you some extra package to deal with the rest two segments and he may give the range to retain them in case they try to switch over.

You should redesign every time the package and compensation and benefits of excellent employees so that you won't give them chance to look beyond otherwise there is a probability of loosing excellent employees.

Turnover Benefits

Turnover can bring both costs and benefits to the call centre. Costs are often broadly categorized as follows:

- Recruiting and hiring costs, which may include the cost of advertising for new positions, the cost and time involved in interviews and background checks, any costs associated with search firms or placement agencies, and, potentially, relocation costs.
- Training and orientation costs, which include the direct cost of training, the cost of overall lower productivity from newer employees, and the cost of overtime if current employees must help cover hours.
- In commercial organizations the most severe costs can be those associated with poor customer service—lost sales, reduced loyalty and outright defections to competitors.

Turnover can also yield benefits. For example, if employees leave for other positions within the organization, the call center gains experienced advocates in other departments. Turnover may also reduce structural costs (assuming new employees are brought in at lower pay scales) and create the means for the call centre to bring in new employees with needed skills and fresh insights.

The causes and costs/benefits will vary by type of turnover. For example, voluntary external turnover is more of a detriment to the organization than planned internal turnover. Do enough analysis to be able to estimate the relative impact of each type of turnover.

Identifying the Causes of Turnover

To manage turnover, you must understand what causes it. Common ways to identify causes include:

- Conduct a job and salary analysis vis-a-vis market conditions.
- Conduct group meetings with agents to discuss environmental factors, such as stress, management style, workload, etc.
- Review the orientation program to ensure jobs are being accurately represented to new employees.
- Analyze exit interviews.
- Conduct regular employee satisfaction surveys.

Specific causes can vary widely, and identifying the top five to seven things driving turnover will be a huge step towards creating an appropriate prevention strategy.

In any attempt to define our times, words and phrases such as 'accelerating pace of change', 'discontinuity' and 'complexity' figure often. Everything, however, somehow boils down to change and speed, mixed with a generous dose of confusion and chaos. Conventional truths and guideposts are now meeting their nemesis.

In such conditions, business survival and prosperity are clearly not a function of capital resources alone. Nor are they as dependent critically on scale or technology or labour, in the conventional sense of the word.

Even the newer strategic models do not give us sufficiently clear bearings on how to run our business. The point is, that when everyone in a Grand Prix drives a Ferrari, it is clearly the driver—and his skills, attitude, temperament and sense of purpose—that make the difference.

The one, single dominant force that has then emerged is talent. Management means attracting talented people, nurturing them, developing them, and giving them space.

People no longer want to just work, but are equally engaged in a search for their own identity and for a holistic meaning to their life.

The sharp focus on talent today stands out clearly. Microsoft employs around 200 full-time recruiters. A recent survey by a leading international consulting firm (Amrop) revealed that 40 per cent of top management's time is spent on HR or talent related issues.

Another survey by the Harvard Business School identified the ability to spot talent and develop it as being the third most sought after attribute for a successful CEO.

Customers, yes. Shareholders, yes. But businesses will also have to embrace this stakeholder just as well—the employee, the talent pool, the intellectual capital, the resource that is the most fungible, the one that can easily walk out the door.

Every organization has to create a sense of ownership among people who will not be owned. A business of any worth today has to grapple with this compulsion. Talent is, in fact, central in the new paradigm. Without 'people power' even the best of operational and strategic thinking will come to naught.

Talent Issues in Indian Organizations

At this point, I would like to share my thoughts on some of the critical talent related issues that we in Indian organizations need to address. No doubt, many readers are already working to tackle similar issues, and you would be having your own unique perspectives.

In my own organization, although we have been putting in a lot of effort, in these and related areas, we are some distance away from having all the right answers. Perhaps, many of these are fuzzy issues and there are no definitive answers. Each organization must chart out its own approach and course, given the specific context in which it operates.

Adrenaline: The first major issue is how to keep the adrenaline flowing in talented people. The game does not stop at identifying talent or inducting it. Talented people get bored easily and so they have to be kept constantly challenged.

In our organization, we address this issue by fast tracking deserving talent, offering definite career paths, providing cross functional exposure across different businesses, and secondments to our operations abroad.

The objective is to offer a high quality of exposure, faster, thus enabling the manager to increase his overall intrinsic worth and to take on higher responsibilities, much earlier in his career.

Integration: A second issue concerns how best one can integrate talented people into the organization, in a way that there is no undue disruption. I bring this point up because, quite often, mediocrity tends to drive out talent or make it ineffective.

Integrating talented people into the organization involves handling a host of sensitive issues and this is a task that will fully test the leadership abilities of senior management.

At the same time, as we move about with the process of integrating talent, we do need to subject ourselves—and talented people—to some kind of a reality check, every now and then. The best of talent has to operate, ultimately, within the boundaries of organizational objectives, and talent, no matter how highly regarded, cannot become dysfunctional.

Creating an ivory tower is not desirable. In the same vein, we have to keep in mind that talent means much more than 'white collar'. We cannot glorify a certain kind of talent, at the cost of talent in other areas. As always, maintaining the right balance is the challenge.

Compensation: The third issue I would like to touch upon is one very much in the spotlight today: the growing divergence in compensation and reward levels between the talented and those less so. This differential is widening by the day—in absolute and relative terms.

How we handle this divergence is again absolutely critical to an organization's health. Today, the clamour for stock options runs high. Incorporating a significant performance-based component in the compensation package is almost mandatory. Again, there are no clear cut solutions. It goes much beyond the criteria of affordability.

We have to look at larger and fundamental issues such as equity, value systems and organizational morale.

Until we find an answer to this dilemma, let me read out this very interesting text of an advertisement, which appeared in the London newspapers in the year 1900. Ernest Shackleton, the famous explorer, inserted this advertisement when recruiting team members for the National Antarctic Expedition.

The advertisement read as follows: ***Men Wanted for Hazardous Journey***. *Small wages, bitter cold, long months of complete darkness, constant danger, safe return doubtful. Honour and recognition in case of success.*

Shackleton later said of the call for volunteers that, 'It seemed as though all the men in Great Britain were determined to accompany me, the response was so overwhelming.' Perhaps, taking the cue from this, the real challenge lies in striking the right balance between material rewards and the larger sense of mission.

What Per Cent?

In conclusion, I believe that making India talent-friendly will require actions at the macro level also. Nurturing talent and keeping it here and putting it to good use requires resolving some tough quality of life issues.

For instance, India ranks low in any human development or quality of life index. Talent cannot flourish if the enabling social and physical infrastructure is not in place. Only then can we reverse the brain drain decisively. This is a task that needs the involvement of all of us—in business, in government, in our educational institutions, in our professional bodies.

Attracting brains is a lot more difficult than attracting FDI or portfolio investments. But then that is also what will make us really competitive.

At the end of it all, we have to ask ourselves not only whether we have talented people, but also whether we have enough of them; and whether we are doing everything we can to nurture them in greater numbers.

We are a billion Indians, about one-sixth of humanity. Do Indians constitute the universe of talented people, in equal proportion?

What Retards Talent in India?

On the flip side, we need to recognize and deal with some of the powerful attitudes and forces that not only retard talent, but also are hostile to it.

For one, there is the fear of failure. There is an almost indelible stigma attached to failure, much more than in the West. The family, the peer group, the society, the banker—all still frown on failure—of any sort, no matter how heroic and daring the effort that preceded it.

This attitude thwarts experimentation and stifles innovation. Better to be 'mediocrely' right than 'stunningly' wrong. The possibility of getting a second chance is rare.

It is difficult to think of the exploits of a Thomas Alva Edison happening here: the daring experiments, the failures, the bankruptcy, and then the success, the most well-known of which is the electric bulb.

A second obstacle to talent is conformity. There is less acceptance of the offbeat. Dissidence is not looked upon too favourably: it's the nail that sticks out that invariably gets hammered down. Conformity is all around us: in the dress code, in the jargon of our times, in our patterns of strategic thinking, at a point in time.

The herd instinct is evident even in the way we invest, with everyone running after the same scrips, in the same industries, at a particular moment. Being different is difficult. Where are the contrarians?

Finally, I believe that our educational system contributes, in substantial measure, to our inability to draw out the store of talent latent in us. Students at the school level are overburdened with rote learning. Listening and being talked to is the norm.

Questioning, discourse, the spirit of discovery, curiosity and inquiry are rare. The curriculum is narrow and outdated and, to a large extent, 'memory-centric'. Unlike in the West, the options offered are few.

What is Talent?

Let's reflect a bit about what exactly 'talent' means. I believe the term has become too complex to define. Instead, let me quote from the book *Excellence*, written by John W. Gardner, the American social reformer. According to him, 'There are those who perform great deeds and those that make it possible for others to perform great deeds. There are pathfinders and path preservers. There are those who nurture and those who inspire. There are those whose excellence involves doing something well and those whose excellence lies in being the kind of people they are, lies in their kindness or honesty or courage.'

Going a step further, the term 'talent' has developed some broader connotations. Earlier, 'talented' might have referred to a person with expertise in a given functional area or a given business, or even a person who had achieved a pre-determined objective.

Today, these 'talents' are almost taken for granted. We now take stock of a person's managerial and leadership potential, the ability to straddle different functional areas, businesses, cultures and geographic boundaries—all in a seamless manner. We need to assess not only intellectual skills, but also softer skills such as emotional intelligence, values, creativity, the ability to work in teams, to think out of the box, entrepreneurial abilities, and also, importantly, the willingness to learn and share.

A recent study by Janice McCormack, Professor at Harvard Business School, aptly describes topnotch talent today as someone 'having the vision of an architect, the theoretical mindset of a physicist, the attention to detail of an engineer and the financial acumen of an investment banker.

In short, the ability to not get cowed down by 'competing imperatives'.

Why Now?

People have always been important, so one may legitimately ask, why all this commotion now? Let us try to answer this question.

First, there is no doubt that the supply-demand imbalance in the talent area has become acute, not only in India, but also globally, and is getting more so. In India, a host of new industries —information technology, financial services, media and entertainment—are vying for the best people.

A flood of multinational companies is out to attract the best brains, not just for their operations in India, but for their overseas needs. The outstanding success of India's leading educational institutions, especially the IITs and IIMs, has drawn them to take a pick from our brains and capabilities. India has, in effect, become the world's scouting ground for talent.

Second, the desire to 'be one's own boss' is more common. More and more talented people want to strike out on their own, or work in a company which offers a significant entrepreneurial environment. So the pool of people from which to select is contracting, relative to the demand for them.

There is a third factor behind the scarcity of talent. Until recently, our pre-occupation with talent was confined largely to the higher levels of an organization. Today, every level of a company's operations requires talented people. In the wake of intense competition, and the consequent need for speed, the top-down approach to managing is increasingly proving ineffective.

Dispersal of decision-making is also being driven by complexity—the sheer geographic spread of companies, the diversity of product lines and the need to be close to the customer. Decisions need to be made at every level and decisions need to be quick. So, we have to spot, incubate and groom talent at every level of the organization, because more people need to be making high quality decisions.

And finally, much higher degrees of business complexity result in a much larger premium on talent. Complexity calls for an integrated approach, the ability to look at a problem from different perspectives, and a high degree of creative and non-linear thinking.

Coupled with that, there is the need for heightened cultural sensitivity as national boundaries are becoming hazy and business is becoming truly global.

India Well Placed to Nurture Talent

I have tried to identify some of the key factors driving the demand for talent, which has now come to be the strategic resource. However, despite the scarcity, we are fortunate that India has many of the right ingredients that help to nurture talent.

We just have to look at our present times to realise the considerable advantages we possess as regards talented people. I am sure we all must have been taken aback with the surge in the globalization of Indian talent. We all knew it was there—but today the entire world recognises it, and how.

As the joke in Silicon Valley runs, if a person's name is Shreedhar, don't bother checking his IT skills! Across a range of areas—engineering, computer programming and financial services—the Indian brain has begun to command the highest brand equity.

Indians are breaking the glass ceiling and staking their claim at the upper levels of global firms, in increasing numbers.

How did this happen? Unlikely as this may seem, India does seem to have some of the prerequisites that can be leveraged to nurture talent. We have the much sought after facility with today's Lingua Franca, the English language, as also a relatively high degree of numerical aptitude.

And, we have an innate capacity to adapt, without which it would not have been possible for Indians to strike roots overseas and become among the more successful of the immigrant communities, in a number of countries.

Of course, competition also does much to nurture talent. And we in India, work in a very competitive environment, pretty much from childhood. We even have interviews to get admitted to a nursery school.

Even leaving aside this extreme, we are constantly being graded, scored, evaluated and ranked. The admissions-to-applicants ratio at our premier educational institutes is more demanding than that of even the most elite universities abroad. The same is true of our Civil Service.

Retention Strategies

While there is no single formula for agent retention that is appropriate for all call centres, there are plenty of tried and true strategies that will greatly enhance the chances of retaining your agents and ensuring they perform at their best. Some of the most common areas of focus include:

Improve hiring and job fit. Hiring candidates based on the right job qualifications and behavioural competencies will improve your chances for a better job fit. If turnover rates are high, revisiting the hiring process should be the first step in improving retention.

Improve competitive pay and benefits. Ensure that jobs in the call center are internally and externally equitable. Even if you're budgets are tight, don't count this strategy out—it might be more practical and less expensive than meets the eye if you've really analyzed and identified the true costs of turnover.

Ensure that agents receive timely coaching and feedback. Encouraging the positive aspects of the agent's performance, modeling desired actions/behaviours and working with them to create feasible action plans that will enable them to achieve objectives are essential steps.

Provide opportunities for ongoing skill and career development. Agents who see their position as dynamic and evolving are more likely to remain committed to the call centre. Create a skills-based pay program and, if possible, a compelling career path in the call center to encourage agents to continually expand their knowledge and capabilities.

Provide as much flexibility in work schedules as possible. Call centre scheduling takes creativity and communication since both workload requirements and agent requirements must be accommodated as much as possible.

Improve supervisor training. It's often said that agents don't leave companies—they leave their supervisors. Taking steps to ensure that your supervisors have the skills and knowledge necessary to be the best managers possible can improve retention dramatically.

Provide recognition. According to much of the research on turnover, just saying thanks for a job well done goes a longway towards job satisfaction. This can be formal, e.g. through newsletters and announcements, and informal through everyday conversations.

These suggestions represent the proverbial tip of the iceberg. Other strategies can range from implementing a telecommuting program, to establishing a mentoring program, designing better incentive plans and improving facilities design.

Finding the Right Balance

A certain amount of turnover is inevitable and acceptable—your challenge is to determine just what that acceptable level is. To do so, it's important to understand the full cost of turnover and compare it to the costs associated with staff retention programs. The key is to find the right balance: you don't want to spend more money retaining staff than it costs to replace them, but you also don't want to spend more money replacing staff than it costs to keep them.

Among the practical criteria to consider when seeking the right balance are:

- The maximum amount the company is willing to pay for these positions.
- Availability of a skilled labour pool to fill agent vacancies.
- The cost (money and time) of effectively training new-hires.
- The relative costs of lower quality and productivity when turnover increases.
- Organizational values and culture. In sum, there is much that can be done to address turnover and improve retention. Don't leave it to chance.

Attrition rate = (Employee left the organization/Total number of employees) × 100

A simple formula is (Total number of Resignations in a month/ Total number of Employees in a month) × 100 will give you a monthly attrition rate.

Summary

Today, more and more organizations are changing the way they view and pay their employees. The move is away from the traditional "cost-of-doing-business" concept. Successful businesses are developing creative programs to guide employees to focus on improving business performance and rewarding them for their contributions. Unfortunately, many businesses and employees are still not ready to make the change.

In today's business environment, clearly the long-term winners will be companies that provide a flexible and challenging work environment, along with employee recognition and rewards. Organizations have to be willing to share their successes. If employees are asked to share the risks, then they have to share the rewards. If you want outstanding results, you need to be prepared to pay outstanding rewards. Implementation of a "total compensation" plan will motivate employees to improve not only their own performance but the performance of the firm as well.

Chapter nine

ABSENTEEISM MANAGEMENT

Absenteeism is the failure of employees to report for work when they are scheduled to work. Employees who are away from work on recognized holidays, vacations, approved leaves of absence, or approved leaves of absence would not be included.

Broadly speaking absenteeism means absent (excluding entitled leaves + OD)—should be counted as absenteeism. If individual remains absent beyond 3 times in period of 12 months without intimation, then he called as habitual absent case. Normally, 6-8 per cent absenteeism found in all industry. If it beyond consecutively, then the matter is serious.

There are many kinds of absence. Some, such as annual vacation, are generally considered beneficial for both the organization and the employee. Since they are usually scheduled, their effect on the organization can be fairly easily absorbed; the same can be said of statutory holidays. Other absences, such as those caused by illness and family-related demands, are generally unavoidable, as are those due to inclement weather.

Frequent absence from the workplace may be indicative of poor morale or of sick building syndrome. However, many employers have implemented absence policies which make no distinction between absences for genuine illness and absence for inappropriate reasons. One of these policies is the calculation of the Bradford factor, which only takes the total number and frequency of absences into account, not the kind of absence. As a result, many employees feel obliged to come to work while ill, and transmit communicable diseases to their co-workers. This leads to even greater absenteeism and reduced productivity among other workers who try to work while ill. Workforces often do excuse absenteeism caused by medical reasons if the worker supplies a doctor's note or other form of documentation. Sometimes, however, in the workforce, people choose not to show up for work and do not call in advance, which most businesses find to be unprofessional and inconsiderate. This is called a no call, no show.

Absent does not only mean not being at work. Absent also means:

Arriving late (or poor timekeeping, if you like. It is still absent as long as the employee is not at work.)

Leaving early (again, if you like, poor timekeeping. It is still absent if he is not at work.)

Extended tea or lunch breaks—the employee is not at the workstation, and therefore absent.

Attending to private business during working hours—the employee is at work, but is not attending to his/her duties in terms of the employment contract—and is therefore absent.

Extended toilet breaks—same as extended lunch or tea breaks.

Feigned illness—thus giving rise to unnecessary visits to the on-site clinic, or take time off to "visit the doctor"—which they never do, because they don't need a medical certificate for less than 2 days off.

Undue length of time in fetching or carrying (tools from the tool room, for example, or drawings from the drawing office, etc.)

Other unexplained absences from the workstation or from the premises.

There are a number of remedies—a large number, in fact—that can be used to combat this scourge.

Causes of Absenteeism

The causes of absenteeism are many and include:

- Serious accidents and illness
- Low morale
- Poor working conditions

- Boredom on the job
- Lack of job satisfaction
- Inadequate leadership and poor supervision
- Personal problems (financial, marital, substance abuse, childcare eldercare etc.)
- Poor physical fitness
- Inadequate nutrition
- Transportation problems
- The availability of income protection plans
- Stress
- Excessive workload
- Employee discontent

Cost of Absenteeism to the Employer

There are many cost associated wit absenteeism that employees would not expect.

Decrease in Productivity

- employees may be carrying an extra workload, or supporting new or replacement staff
- employees may be required to train and orientate new or replacement workers
- staff morale and employee service may suffer

Financial Costs

- overtime or agency cost for replacement workers
- cost of self-insured income protection plans
- premium costs may rise for insured plans

Administrative Costs

- staff time is required to secure replacement employees or to re-assign the remaining employees
- staff time is required to maintain and control absenteeism

The management of workplace attendance is an important aspect of supervision in the workplace. The cost of absenteeism is greater than the direct payment of wages and benefits paid durance the absence. Organizations must also consider the **indirect** costs of staffing, scheduling, re-training, lost productivity, diminished moral, turnover, and opportunity cost. The indirect costs often exceed the direct cost of absenteeism.

Each occurrence of absence costs the employer an average of $2,500 in both direct and indirect costs (based on 9 days absent out of 250 working days and an average payroll of $35,000). Effective supervisory efforts to manage attendance will affect a relatively small percentage of employees, but will result in substantial savings, increased productivity and morale.

Do You have an Absenteeism Problem?

Many organizations allocate 3 per cent of their labour budget for absenteeism based on an average of eight (8) working days missed per employee annually. Since the rate of absenteeism varies by industry, division and department it is best to compare to the most relevant benchmark available.

Trends in Absenteeism

Surveys indicate the following generalities in absenteeism:

- The higher the rate of pay and the greater the length of service of the employee, the fewer the absences.
- As an organization grows, there is a tendency towards higher rates of absenteeism.
- Women are absent more frequently than men.
- Single employees are absent more frequently than married employees.
- Younger employees are absent more frequently than older employees.
- Older employees are absent for longer periods of time than younger employees.
- Unionized organizations have higher absenteeism rates than non-unionized organizations.

Understanding Absenteeism

The definition, causes, affects on productivity, and costs of absenteeism are quite clear. The challenge is to develop methods that support attendance and control absenteeism, in such a way as not to create mistrust, costly administrative procedures and systems avoidance. Traditional methods of absenteeism control exclusively utilizing disciplinary procedures have proven to be ineffective. It is almost impossible to create a fair disciplinary procedure, because even well run disciplinary systems, which treat similar actions with consistent repercussions, are usually seen as unfair. This perception is common, because discipline alone neither identifies nor addresses the root causes of absenteeism. Every employee who takes time off in defiance of company regulations has reasons, which they believe justifies their actions. Unless a management attendance program identifies and addresses the causes of employee absenteeism, it will be ineffective and viewed as unfair. Traditional disciplinary programs alone can, at best, give the illusion of control. It is no secret that there are ways to beat even the best systems. The fear of discipline often only increases the desire to avoid management systems.

If absenteeism is to be controlled, the physical and emotional needs of employees must be addressed. In a 1985 study on "Rates of Absence among Nurses", it was found that 50 per cent of absenteeism could be controlled through attending to employees' physical and emotional needs.

Purpose of Attendance Management

The purpose of attendance management is to develop a willingness on the part of all employees to attend work regularly, and to assist them in motivating their co-workers to attend work regularly. This can be done through:

1. Addressing the physical and emotional needs of employees.
2. Communicating the attendance goals of the organization so employees can understand and identify with them.
3. Dealing with cases of excessive absenteeism effectively and fairly to produce deterrence.

Successful administration of an attendance management program requires managers and supervisors to be aware of, and to create work environments in which the following can be actualized:

1. The greater the extent to which individuals identify with the goals of the organization and care what happens to it, the greater their motivation to be regular in attendance.
2. The more the people find their jobs meaningful to them, the greater their motivation to be regular in attendance.
3. As employees' workloads increase due to the absence of a co-worker, peer pressure is exerted on the absent co-worker to attend work on a regular basis.
4. The more people like working for the organization, the higher their motivation to attend regularly. Recognition of good employee attendance helps improve attendance.
5. Employees will have a lower absence ratio if they feel free to discuss their on-the-job problems with their immediate supervisor.
6. Employees with a low absence ratio feel confidence and have supportive relationships in their workplace. Low absence ratio employees are found to be more satisfied with their opportunity for promotion and upgrading.

Commitment to Attendance

This paper provides the information necessary to begin an effective attendance management program, which will yield long-term results. This paper is intended to be a guide rather than an instruction manual or policy. To make an attendance management program truly successful, it will require insight into the special dynamics present in your work place. It will require two-way communication, as both the needs of the employees and of management must be met if good attendance is to be achieved. Attendance is the responsibility of everyone, especially those who directly manage the human resources of your organization.

Attendance is not only an expectation; employers have the right to receive good attendance. Each and every employee has a contractual obligation to attend work regularly. All levels of management must believe in, be committed to, and communicate their expectations of good attendance. If a specific number of sick days are considered acceptable per employee, at best that will be the result. Employees will live up to the expectations that you set for them. Expectations must be clear to both management and employees in order for an attendance management program to get maximum results. Goals must be tangible. Attendance expectations must be clearly communicated and followed.

Income Protection

A common misconception about income protection plans is that there are entitlements, like vacation benefit, and as such, should be fully utilized. The reality is that income protection plans are a form of insurance. The sole and only purpose of pay for sick leave is to assist in protecting employees against loss of income in the event of an unavoidable absence due to sickness or a non-work related injury. Use of income protection plans for any other purpose negates their intent and, therefore, is inappropriate. Communicating the true intent of income protection plans and our commitment to maintaining this original intent is an essential aspect of attendance management.

Deal with Absenteeism

A policy that provides guidance within an organization about how to manage the state of chronic absence from work. Absenteeism is usually addressed through progressively stricter disciplinary measures that can result in the termination of the individual's employment. This is generally governed by the organization's attendance policy. Absenteeism is a minor problem that can snowball into a much larger problem. However, there are ways to deal with it.

(1) **Keep track of absences.** Take note when an employee doesn't show up, and see if there is a pattern, i.e. if an employee calls out sick on Fridays or days with good weather.

(2) **Establish a firm policy, and make sure that employees are aware of it.** Make employees call and speak to someone when they call out sick, not just leave a message. Ask employees to bring doctors' certification if the level of absenteeism becomes excessive.

(3) **Always give employees a "return-to-work" interview.** The interview should make the employee feel that his or her work is valuable and that consequently, his or her presence was missed in the office. The supervisor should use the interview as an opportunity to explore reasons for the employee's absence and to express any doubts or concerns about the employee's attendance.

Attendance Management Program

An attendance management program can be split into three basic parts:

1. Development of information/communication systems.
2. Information Testing.
3. Taking appropriate group action.

1. *Information Communication Systems*

The first step of an effective attendance management program is to identify specific areas which are affecting attendance. Some general causes of absenteeism are listed at the beginning of this paper. The best way to find which specific areas are affecting absenteeism in a specific work environment is to develop open communication between managers, supervisors and employees. The reason for this is that it is not really the physical realities of the work place that influence employees willingness to work but rather their perceptions of these realities. For example, workload is only a problem if it is thought to be one. It is important that employees are encouraged to voice their concerns so their perceptions of the work place are clear and can be dealt with. This type of communication is especially important in unionized environments as employees often tend to communicate only with their union representatives. The result is that, vital feed back necessary for effective management is lost. Cooperation with union representatives can be very helpful in attendance management and should be encouraged if possible.

Formal communication networks such as regularly scheduled department meetings are an excellent way not only to hear employee perceptions and concerns but also to communicate organizational goals. When employees are encouraged to make a difference they are less likely to withdraw their participation through absenteeism. Employees must not only be heard, they must be answered in such ways as to assure them their input is worthwhile. Staff development meetings are important in moulding company ideals with employee needs. They are also important in developing a sense of team spirit among co-workers. Full participation in such meetings is to be encouraged if they are to be effective.

Informal communications are also very effective in identifying and dealing with employee needs and perceptions. Informal communication involves all levels of managers and supervisors. Supervisors are especially important because of their hands-on approach and contact with employees. An employee's relationship with their supervisor can greatly influence their feelings about their work, their co-workers and thus their attendance at work.

Insight, intuition, creative thinking and listening are all powerful ways of finding areas which affect attendance. Ideas and information should be encouraged from all sources. The establishment of varied communication channels is useful in gathering information and to an extent, in confirming it. Effective communication in itself can effectively reduce absenteeism.

2. *Information Testing*

Once communication networks are established, information on perceived problems from employees will be bountiful. Before taking action on any issue, no matter what the source of information, it should be confirmed.

A simple and effective way to check whether a specific issue truly affects absenteeism is by finding correlations through using attendance records. If it is suggested, for instance, that absenteeism is increasing due to employee dissatisfaction with their workload, all one need do is match the attendance records during a period of "high" workload to a period of "normal" workload. If absenteeism is found to be significantly higher during increased workload periods, then it has been confirmed that actual workload "is related to" absenteeism levels. If no correlation exists, it may be that employee perception of workload affects absenteeism. In this case the importance of the employee perception could be confirmed through staff development meetings. In any case, two different problems have been distinguished which require different types of attention.

Attendance records also should be used to monitor attendance trends. Are long-term or short-term absences more common? What percentage of employees have excessive absences? The answers to these questions trigger attention to individual employees when their absences become excessive as will be discussed in the Guidelines for Absenteeism Control section. Attendance record forms are designed to facilitate the determination of whether or not absenteeism patterns exist.

3. *Taking Appropriate Group Action*

The best way to handle any given situation is to handle it on its own merits and within the guidelines of the goals one is trying to achieve. This paper does not attempt to give all the answers to every possible situation but rather, offers suggestions and guidelines on which answers can be built.

In summary, to run an effective attendance management program it is important to:

1. develop ways for each and every employee to feel free to contribute ideas and suggestions even though these may be outside the scope of their job responsibilities,
2. make each employee aware that they are a valued member of the "team", that they play an important role in your organization and that their attendance is critical,
3. hold regular meetings, keep your staff informed and involved,
4. know your employees; without prying show an interest in their personal lives,

5. be aware of problems that may effect employee attendance or performance,
6. familiarize yourself with community programs which you can recommend to an employee if he/she has a need for assistance (i.e. marital or financial counselling), and
7. awareness, commitment and involvement by all levels of staff.

Positive motivation should be the main body of any attendance management program because it produces the best results. If an employee's experiences in the work place are pleasant, if he/she feels valued and appreciated, if supervision is fair but firm, that employee will be more motivated to attend work regularly.

Guidelines for Bonafide Absence

Reporting Absences

Employees must personally notify, either by telephone, or in person, their immediate supervisor or designated person-in-charge before the start of their shift if they anticipate being absent from work. Employees should be encouraged to give as much notice as possible for anticipated absences. Employees should give a minimum (1) hour notice or the minimum notice if stated in their collective agreement.

Contact with Employees

Absent employees should be requested to keep contact with their employer. The employer should be informed of any changes in the employee's health status. Employees should be called if they are not keeping contact with the employer. The purpose is to show concern and desire for the employee to regain a healthy status and return to work. It is important that the employee does not feel imposed on. Refer to collective agreement provisions regarding sick leave reporting.

Reporting Back to Work

In order to avoid duplicate coverage of a scheduled shift, an employee who has been absent from work must give as much notice as possible of their intention to return to work. Before returning to work employees should be notified of the amount of notice which is necessary to re-schedule them back to work. If they must produce a physician's certificate it should be handed in upon their return to work. Most collective agreements have provisions for return to work notification.

The Role of the Supervisor in Managing Absenteeism

Addressing Unscheduled Absences

According to the most recent CCH Unscheduled Absence Survey, employers are losing ground when it comes to keeping workers on the job. Unscheduled absenteeism rates have risen to their highest level since 1999. What continues to be of most concern is that almost two out of three employees who don't show up for work, aren't physically ill.

For most companies, the responsibility for managing absenteeism has fallen primarily on immediate supervisors. These supervisors are often the only people who are aware that a certain employee is absent. They are in the best position to understand the circumstances surrounding an individual's absence and to notice a problem at an early stage. Therefore, their active involvement in the company's absence procedures is pivotal to the overall effectiveness and future success of an absence policy or program.

Sadly, however, most supervisors have not received any guidance or training in managing absenteeism. They have been left on their own to carry out the often unpopular task of identifying, confronting and resolving absence abuse.

To ensure that supervisors are comfortable and competent in their role of managing absenteeism, they need to have the full support of senior management. All parties must be aware of the aim of absence policies and procedures. Should there be discrepancies between departments; a policy can lose its effectiveness. To provide more consistency, supervisors should be trained in their responsibilities about managing absenteeism, advised how to conduct effective return-to-work interviews, and educated in the use of disciplinary procedures when necessary.

The Responsibilities of the Supervisor

In addition to ensuring that work is appropriately covered during the employee's absence, there are a number of other critical actions that supervisors need to take to manage absenteeism. They should:

- ensure that all employees are fully aware of the organization's policies and procedures for dealing with absence,
- be the first point of contact when an employee phones in sick,
- maintain appropriately detailed, accurate, and up-to-date absence records for their staff, (e.g. date, nature of illness/reason for absence, expected return to work date, doctor's certification if necessary),
- identify any patterns or trends of absence which cause concern,
- conduct return-to-work interviews, and
- implement disciplinary procedures where necessary.

The Return-to-Work Interview

The training of supervisors in how to best manage absenteeism should include instructions on how to conduct effective and fair return-to-work interviews. Recent national surveys indicate that these interviews are regarded as one of the most effective tools for managing short-term absenteeism.

The return-to-work discussion will enable the supervisor to welcome the employee back to work, in addition to demonstrating management's strong commitment to controlling and managing absenteeism in the workplace. The interview will enable a check to be made that the employee is well enough to return to work.

The necessary paperwork can be completed, so that the absence and its conclusion are properly recorded. The fact that an established procedure is in place to investigate and discuss absence with an employee may, on its own, act as a deterrent for non-attendance for disingenuous reasons.

Interviews need to be carried out as promptly as possible following the absentee's return to work (no later than one day after his or her return). The employee should be given ample opportunity to outline the reasons for his or her absence. The supervisor should use the interview as a time to explore any issues that the employee may have which are leading to absence.

The goal is to foster an open and supportive culture. The procedures are in place to make sure that help and advice is offered when needed and to ensure that the employee is fit to return to work. Employees will usually appreciate the opportunity to explain genuine reasons for absence within a formalized structure. Should the supervisor doubt the authenticity of the reasons given for absence, he/she should use this opportunity to express any doubts or concerns.

At all times, the employee must be aware that the interview is not merely part of company procedures, but a significant meeting during which the absence has been noted and may have implications for future employment. The company's disciplinary procedure, in the event of unacceptable levels of absence, should be explained to the employee.

The manager may choose to outline how the absence affected the department. The message should be that the employee was missed and that productivity suffered. The manner in which the department was required to re-organize staffing arrangements might also be explained. This would demonstrate that the efficiency of the work unit was adversely affected by the absence.

The supervisor should then brief the returning employee about the current situation (i.e. what tasks are now priorities, what work has already been carried out and where the employee should now focus his/her efforts).

At no point during the meeting should the interview become a form of "punishment", but should be seen as an occasion to highlight and explain the repercussions of absence within the department. The vast majority of employees derive a sense of pride and achievement from their work and management should be encouraged to treat these individuals as responsible adults.

Most employees understand reasonable rules and do not want to be threatened into compliance. The small percentage of employees who indeed have an absence problem will require close supervision and possibly even punitive measures for excessive absenteeism. These few employees who are irresponsible should be handled individually and firmly. The following guidelines outline the recommended steps to be taken in cases where short-term absence is considered to be above an acceptable level in a particular period of time.

Stage 1: *Counseling Interview*

- The immediate supervisor should advise the employee of his concern over the absences, try to establish the reasons for the sickness and determine what needs to be done to improve attendance.
- If any medical condition is identified at this stage, and is likely to have an effect on job suitability, the supervisor should arrange an appointment with a company-approved doctor. This should be confirmed to the employee in writing within five working days.
- If, from the discussion, the problem does not appear to be due to an underlying unfitness for work, the supervisor should advise the employee that, while the recorded ailments may be genuine, a sustained improvement in attendance is expected or the next stage in the procedure will be taken.
- A review of the attendance will automatically be made each month for the next six months.

Stage 2: *First Formal Review (Verbal Warning Stage)*

- If the employee's absences continue to worsen following analysis and regular monitoring, he should be invited to attend a formal review meeting with the supervisor.
- The absence record should be detailed in a letter inviting the employee for this interview. The employee should be advised that she is entitled to be represented by a union representative or a colleague as appropriate.

- The purpose of this meeting will be to:
  - — continue to discuss the underlying reasons for the absences,
  - — advise the employee of the service and cost implications of her absence, and
  - — warn the employee (except when deciding to seek medical advice) that if there is not a substantial and sustained improvement, her employment may be terminated because of her inability to maintain an acceptable attendance level. This constitutes the verbal warning.
- Where medical attention is warranted, action must be taken immediately. The meeting is therefore only adjourned to allow this part of the process to be completed. Within five working days, the employee must receive medical advice. The meeting is then re-convened with HR and the doctor's opinion is discussed.
- If the doctor confirms fitness for work, the employee should be warned about the consequences of continued absence.

Stage 3: *Second Formal Review (Written Warning Stage)*

- Where regular monitoring indicates that no improvement in the absence pattern has occurred, a second formal meeting will be arranged with HR.
- The letter inviting the employee to the meeting will include the absence record and, again, advice on representation.
- Any new information given at the meeting regarding ill health or a change in the nature of sickness may need to be assessed by a company-approved doctor.
- The employee should be given the opportunity to explain his or her absence record. If appropriate, the supervisor should inform the employee that a formal written warning is being issued and that this warning will remain in the employee's file for a

specified period. A copy of the warning should be issued to the employee and to his/her representative.

- The employee should be informed that failure to comply with the company's attendance expectations, and to improve on the present unacceptable record of absence, will result in the termination of the employee's employment.
- Where fitness for work is in doubt, proceed with redeployment options according to the guidance received by the doctor. Consult with the employee's union representative (if applicable) on the re-deployment process and options.

Stage 4: *Temporary Suspension from Work*

- If, following the implementation of the previous stages of the disciplinary process, no improvement in attendance occurs, management may proceed with a temporary suspension without pay. The intention to suspend should be confirmed in writing with details of start and end dates. A copy of the letter of suspension should be sent to the employee's representative (if applicable).

Stage 5: *Termination of Employment*

- This is the final stage in the disciplinary process whereby the employee is dismissed for inability to comply with the company's requirements for attendance at work. Dismissal can only take place with the written authorization of a senior manager and HR.
- The letter calling the employee in, will again, include advice on representation and will outline the absence record. The employee should be advised that, as a result of the interview, he or she may be dismissed for incapability to perform work duties.
- Again, the company doctor may have to be consulted if any new information is forthcoming in regard to the employee's health or capacity for work.

- Where re-deployment is not possible, or appropriate, consider proceeding with dismissal for reasons of capability. Eligibility for disability benefit will depend on the circumstances of each case.
- If a decision is made to dismiss on the basis of capability, a copy of the letter of dismissal should be sent to the employee's representative (if appropriate).
- The employee may have the right to appeal against dismissal. The appeal should be in line with the company's disciplinary procedures.

Challenges in Managing Absenteeism

Be aware that supervisors are often uncomfortable or unwilling to report on those who have exceeded acceptable levels of absenteeism. Because of the many pressures already on supervisors, the consistent implementation of absenteeism policies is not always their top priority.

It is important to try to take the subjectivity out of managing absenteeism and to ensure that all employees are treated the same. It is essential to be consistent, persistent, and fair to all. When absence is not addressed or addressed in an inconsistent manner, lower morale can result. Employees can feel they have been treated unfairly when they perceive other absent employees are "getting away with it".

The majority of employees will appreciate policies and programs that are facilitative, rather than punitive. Stringent or punitive measures that force employees to come to work can result in employees that then become, "absent while at work".

They do as little as possible and resist any effort to get them to do more. Other programs should be implemented that help employees be present at work, such as flexible work, such as flexible work scheduling, job sharing, attendance awards and wellness programs.

Preventing Absenteeism Through Employee Motivation

Motivated employees overcome obstacles to make it to work. The key to reducing employee absenteeism is to create a culture where employees want to come to work.

Many employers attempt to crack down on excessive absenteeism through tighter control. They require employees to attend a meeting with their supervisor immediately upon their return to work, they demand a note from a doctor or use some other punitive mechanism that targets the symptoms of absenteeism rather than its underlying causes. But the problem will not go away unless the root causes are removed.

Indirect Costs of Absenteeism

Many employers focus only on the direct costs of absenteeism because they are measurable, such as productivity loss, benefits and wages paid out. But the indirect costs could be greater. The most significant such cost is the impact on the morale of employees who have to pick up the slack. Their productivity suffers due to the increased workload and their feeling that a colleague has an undeserved day off while they are stuck at work. They also resent the fact that management does not appear to be doing anything about it—they perceive a lack of fairness that can destroy their morale and loyalty to the employer.

Causes of Absenteeism

To understand the causes of absenteeism, we need to look beneath the surface. Superficial factors such as sickness, stress, car breakdown, lack of daycare keep only those people away from work who are not very motivated to be there in the first place. It is well known that highly motivated managerial and professional workers have a lower rate of absenteeism than bored or demotivated hourly and non-professional employees. Punitive measures fail because there's always a way around them. Employees coerced to come to work are absent in spirit. Either way, it is a lose-lose strategy to rely on punitive approaches to reduce absenteeism. Frequently absent employees feel little commitment to the organization's success, have little interest in their jobs and feel they can't communicate openly with their immediate supervisor.

Preventing Absenteeism

Managerial and professional employees generally have the most interesting jobs and the greatest amount of responsibility. They feel valued and committed. Their job is a career, not just a way of earning a living. Tackling this issue strategically means focusing efforts where there is the greatest likelihood of a good return on time, effort and money. The first step, therefore, is to assign employees to 3 categories—those with legitimate reasons to be absent, chronic problem employees and those most responsive to efforts to turn them around. This is not a matter of guesswork. All employees should be given an equal chance to improve their level of commitment. Being strategic means that the most responsive employees, after some initial effort, should be given more attention. Those who do not respond at all may not justify further investment.

The Role of the Supervisor in Managing Absenteeism

The second step is to train supervisors on how to build supportive, trusting relationships with employees to foster open, two-way communication. Then it is a matter of holding regular individual meetings to build trust and to gain an understanding of how employees feel about their jobs and what is important to them. Such attention alone will foster a good degree of loyalty. Finally, as far as possible, the supervisor needs to find ways to make employees feel more committed. These include giving more responsibility, adding interesting tasks, asking them for their input and praising them regularly for desirable actions. All such engagement must take place in regular individual and team meetings. Ad hoc attention too easily drifts into never.

Dealing with Chronic Absenteeism

Punitive measures are unlikely to be successful with employees who persistently fail to show up for work. In any case, such measures create a negative atmosphere which can make an organizational culture seem like a prison, thus even further motivating employees to seek ways of escaping. Unless specific employees are essential or very hard to replace, there may be no alternative but to find replacements who are more interested in making a commitment.

Combating Absenteeism

For Supervisors/Managers: Recently, I was asked by a manager how he should deal with the fact that on any given day 10 per cent of his employees are absent from work. I informed the manager that the problem of employee absenteeism is a problem best resolved by taking the following four positive interventions versus taking a negative or punitive approach.

Change Management Style: We are all aware of the fact that when employees call in ill, it does not mean they are truly too physically ill to work. One reason, outside of illness, that employees are absent is stress, and the number one reason employees are stressed has to do with their relationship with their manager/supervisor. Management styles that are too authoritarian tend to promote high levels of absenteeism among employees. Authoritarian managers are managers who have poor listening skills, set unreachable goals, have poor communication skills, and are inflexible. In other words, they yell too much, blame others for problems, and make others feel that it must be their way or the "highway." Authoritarian managers tend to produce high absenteeism rates. By identifying managers who use an authoritarian style, and providing them with management training, you will be taking a positive step not only toward reducing absenteeism, but also reducing turnover, job burnout, and employee health problems such as backaches and headaches.

Change Working Conditions: The employees in your company probably work in a well-lighted climate controlled building. The working conditions I am referring to relate to co-worker relationships. Not only does relationship stress occur between the employee and manager, but it also exists between employees. Frequently I hear employees say they did not go to work because they are fearful of or angry with another employee. These employees usually report they just could not deal with "so and so" today, so they called in ill. Companies that adopted policies and values that promote employee respect and professionalism, and promote an internal conflict resolution procedure, are companies that reduce employee stress. A reduction in employee stress reduces employee absenteeism.

Provide Incentives: Giving employees incentives for reduced absenteeism is not the same as rewarding or giving employees bonuses for reduced absenteeism. An incentive provides an employee with a boost to their motivation to avoid unnecessary absenteeism. It simply helps the employee decide to go to work versus staying home and watching Jerry Springer. The types of incentive programs used by companies are numerous. Some companies allow employees to cash-in unused sick days at the end of every quarter, others give an employee two hours of bonus pay for every month of perfect attendance; and still others provide employees with a buffet lunch, a certificate of achievement, or even a scratch-off card concealing prizes. The type of incentive program that your company uses should be one created especially for your company. You can create an incentive program tailored to your unique company by allowing employees to help you develop the incentive program. For example, your employees may not care about receiving a Rs.100/- saving bond for perfect attendance, but they might respond very well to being able to leave one hour early on Friday if they have perfect attendance all week. The duration of the incentive program is also very important. Once again, allow your employees to help guide you to determine the length of time between incentives. Some companies find that they can simply reward employees with perfect attendance once a year, while others decide once a month is best, and still others decide once a week works best. The general rule of thumb is to reward workers more frequently the younger they are and the more difficult the work is to perform. Also, it is best to start with small incentives and work up to larger ones if necessary.

Develop an Attendance Policy: Every company should have an attendance policy. An attendance policy allows a manager to intervene with an employee who is frequently absent. Besides stress as a primary reason for employee absenteeism, other causes relate to alcoholism, domestic violence, and family problems. If you confront an employee about his or her frequent absenteeism, and they inform you it is due to personal problems, consider referring the employee to an Employee Assistance Program (EAP). If the employee's absenteeism relates to a medical problem or a family member with a medical problem, you may have to consider allowing the employee to use the benefits allowed to them under the Americans with Disability Act (ADA) or the Family and Medical Leave Act (FMLA). Early identification of these employees will get them back to work as fast as possible. Lastly, make sure that you have an attorney review your attendance policy to make sure it does not violate any State or Federal labour laws. By incorporating the above four strategies into your company you will not only reduce absenteeism you will reduce employee burnout, turnover, poor morale, and workplace negativism.

Absenteeism and Turnover in Healthcare Industry

Nowadays, healthcare industries are trying their level best to acquire most talented staff from different stream of skill sets for efficient operations. This is a labour and capital intensive industry. Highly skilled manpower is what sets a hospital exclusive from other service providers in market and provides an USP (unique selling point) in market area to build a long lasting growth oriented brand equity and brand loyalty.

Within a decade, Indian global players have entered into healthcare business with global quality standard. On the other hand, cost of recruiting potential employees is also increasing day by day as methodology of recruitment has also changed due to augmentation of media vehicles such as news papers, magazines and web-based search for employment. Obviously, after recruitment, hospitals like any other industry prefer to have optimum input from employees for continuous delivery. Hindrances are absenteeism and turnover. Due to increase in number of service providers, hospitals are focusing more on cost containment and quality services and therefore it becomes more important that absenteeism and turnover are dealt with continuous monitoring to reduce cost of manpower to hospital.

"Absenteeism and turnover are types of withdrawal behaviour that an employee exhibits when he encounters personal and professional problems and the relative importance of a particular problem is more then the other job factors in his life."

It is observed that:

- Female workers have more absolute absenteeism rate then males whereas turnover rate is more in males as compared to females.
- Absenteeism is high in males of age group between 18-25 years and less in age group of 40-65.
- Unmarried females and males have lesser rate of absenteeism as compare to married employees.
- Individuals who are more skilled then job requirements show higher turn over rates.
- Absenteeism and turnover of employees is generally due to one of the following reasons:

Psychological factors

Every individual comes across one or the other psychological problem ranging from personal problem i.e. ego, complex and family problem i.e. problem in married life, over burdened with family responsibilities. In such cases, it is seen that due to mental trauma an employee shows withdrawal from his job responsibilities. The solution to these problem is continuous counselling so that employee understands that coming on job will provide him different social and work environment helping in reducing tension as his attention diverts and mentally he is more occupied.

Physiological problems

Physiological problems like acute sickness-common cough, cold and fever and chronic illness like cancer and TB are the causes that prevent an employee from attending duties. Hospital's Medical Benefit Policy can be utilized for continuous monitoring of these employees.

Job related problems

Job description does not match the employee's skill set, either he is over-skilled or under-skilled leading to job dissatisfaction and in long range frustration of the employees. In some cases, employee may not be satisfied with salary structure as it may not be on par with salary structure of other hospitals. Due to increase in number of hospitals better job opportunities are available where an employee has opportunity for vertical growth in designation, job responsibilities and better salary. These entire factors taken together are amply responsible for turnover of the employees.

Supervisory style like pointing out even slightest deviation from set standards of discharging duties lead to frustration in employees and so a employee refrains from his work during the work hours of such a supervisor. This tendency is more observed in menial staff.

Immediately before the peak of job responsibilities, employee show a tendency of absenteeism. In case of nurses, it is generally observed that immediately after completion of night duty for a fixed number of days, many of nurses do not report on day succeeding the day of completion of night duty.

Compulsory retirement and voluntary retirement schemes are also responsible for employee turnover in organisation but these are uncontrollable factors and beyond control of any organisation.

Cost of Absenteeism and Turnover

In case of absenteeism, it is generally observed that employee try to regularise attendance by applying for sick leave and as an employee can avail fixed number of paid sick leave therefore hospital has to pay an employee even for his absenteeism. Apart from that whenever an employee is absent, his work has to be attended by other employee and he has to be paid overtime if alternative manpower cannot be arranged from available manpower. Overtime rate varies from hospital to hospital but general practice is it is paid at twice of daily Basic and HRA resulting in increase in the cost of manpower.

In case of turnover, cost is associated with recruitment, on the job training, and termination. In case of recruitment cost is associated in terms of time spent in screening applications, organizing and conducting interviews, selection and joining formalities and induction. Apart from that time is also spent in Exit Interview of employee who leaves the organization. In all this activities cost can be measured in terms of man hours utilized. To the cost of administrative activities, cost for medical examination to determine fitness for joining Hospital and cost for training of new employee is also added.

Overall calculation suggests that there is a very heavy cost associated with absenteeism and turnover of the employee and it has a direct bearing on the cost of manpower to hospital. It is not only the cost factor that escalates due to absenteeism and turnover continuity and quality of service delivery is also affected resulting in irreparable loss to Brand equity of the hospital.

Control of Job Turnover

Hospitals may use the formula of Bureau of Labour statistics USA for controlling turnover.

Separation rate: The number of employees who left due to any reason including resignation, dismissal and lay off during the month is divided by total number of employees on the pay roll in the mid i.e. 15th of the month.

S (Number of separations)/M (Mid-month employment) × 100 = S (Separation Rate)

Quit Rate: The number of resignations in the month is divided by the mid-month employee strength during the same month.

R (Number of resignation)/M (Mid-month employment) × 100 = Q (Resignation rate)

The major steps that can help in controlling turnover can be:

- Providing job responsibilities according to qualification and skill sets of the candidates.
- Developing salary structures at par with other hospitals and if possible other industries.
- Developing employee benefit schemes like educational loan, housing loan and vehicle loan.
- Developing career progression plan.
- Training and development for higher job responsibilities for job enrichment.

Control of Absenteeism

The model program that a hospital can adopt to reduce absenteeism is depicted: For any hospital, continuity of service delivery is important, so it becomes mandatory at times to provide requisite manpower in a shift by allowing overtime due to absenteeism and turnover. But for cost containment, it is very important that unnecessary utilization of overtime policy is strictly monitored.

Formula for Absenteeism Rate

A = B / C

Where:

A = Absenteeism rate for the period

B = Total number of mandays lost due to absenteeism in the period

C = Total number of working mandays available in the period

And where:

C = D × E

D = Total employees planned to work in the period

E = Number of available working days in the period

Measures to Control Absenteeism

Everybody misses a day of work now and then. But it's a problem when an employee misses too many days of work. Not showing up for work can cause serious problems when other employees have to cover for the missing worker or, worse, the work simply doesn't get done. Here are keys to controlling absenteeism in your growing company:

Find out whether the absent employee missed work voluntarily or involuntarily. Involuntarily means illness or another unavoidable reason—this is the kind of absenteeism you shouldn't concern yourself with as a manager, unless some kind of counseling or assistance could help the employee regain his or her health. Voluntary absenteeism is the kind you need to worry about. This occurs when an employee is absent without good reason. Get documentation—for example, a doctor's note—to ascertain whether an absence was involuntary or voluntary.

Decide whether the absenteeism is excessive. Compare the employee's attendance record with other employees' records. If one employee's record is way out of line, unless there are extenuating circumstances, that's probably excessive absenteeism.

Meet with the employee to explore the absences. Keep your discussion friendly and oriented toward understanding and solving the problem, not placing blame and dispensing discipline.

If things don't get better, explain the problem to the employee and request improved performance. Employees may not know their absences are affecting others unless you tell them and ask them to improve.

Put the problem in writing. Make sure you give the employee a copy of the written notice. In addition, you should also put one in his or her personnel file.

Most employees will straighten up and start coming to work regularly during this process. If they don't, however, you'll be prepared to terminate them, if necessary, if you follow these guidelines.

Absenteeism—Causes and Cures

But before we begin any analysis, a definition of "absence" must be established. For the purpose of this column, an absence refers to time an employee is not on the job during scheduled working hours, except for a granted leave of absence, holiday or vacation time. Using the standard U.S. Department of Labour formula, the rate of absenteeism is calculated by dividing the number of working days lost through absence in any given period by the total number of available working days in that same period, as follows:

Absenteeism Rate = Number of lost working days due to absence /(Number of employees) × (Number of workdays) × 100

For Example:

(a) Average number of employees in work force	100
(b) Number of available workdays during period	20
(c) Total number of available workdays (a × b) = 100 × 20	2,000

(d) Total number of lost days due to absences during the period 93

(e) Absenteeism per cent = (d) [divided by] (c) × 100

$$= \frac{93 \times 100}{2000} = 4.65\%$$

I like to think of absenteeism as a disease that appears whenever a company fails to inoculate itself through the use of sound management practices. To cure excessive absenteeism, one has to know the exact causes and then examine the available, workable and proven solutions to apply against those causes.

Establishing the Basic Facts

To embark upon a successful absenteeism reduction program, you need to make sure you have some basic information and facts about absenteeism in your company. Consider the following questions, and as you begin to dig for the answers, you likely will become aware of many ways to address your problems.

Getting to the Root of the Problem

Once you have completed the above checklists, your responses should give you food for thought and direction for combating absenteeism. If you have not made it a policy to keep track of the items above, your first step now should be clearly mapped out for you. As a next step, consider the following four questions, which should help you further focus your ideas and put a plan into action.

1. Why is your present absenteeism policy ineffective?

Absenteeism policies vary in effectiveness. Most ineffective policies I have reviewed have a common denominator. They allow "excused" absences, whereas those that do work are "no fault" policies.

2. Where and when is excessive absenteeism occurring?

Numerous studies have concluded that under trained supervisors are one of the main causes of absenteeism. Therefore, any company experiencing absenteeism of greater than 3 per cent should consider supervisors as a potential contributor to the problem.

Given that this may be the case, you first should check the percentage of employee absenteeism by supervisor to see if it is concentrated around one or two supervisors. If it is, you've begun to uncover the obvious—undertrained supervisors. If, however, your research reveals that the rate of absenteeism is almost equally distributed throughout your factory, you will need to investigate other possible causes.

3. What are the real causes for absences?

People-oriented companies are very sensitive to employee opinions. They often engage in formal mini-studies to solicit anonymous employee opinions on topics of mutual interest. These confidential worker surveys commonly ask for employee opinion regarding higher-than-normal absenteeism. The responses have revealed rather surprising results: low pay, poor benefits and high workloads were not major causes, nor was actual sickness. Instead, absenteeism generally was found to be a symptom of low job satisfaction, sub-standard working conditions and consistent negative and unfair treatment received by first-line supervisors.

In other words, employees revealed that repetitive, boring jobs coupled with uncaring supervisors and/or physically unpleasant workplaces led them to make up excuses for not coming to work, such as claiming to be sick. If your employees perceive that your company is indifferent to their needs, they are less likely to be motivated, or even to clock in at all.

One way to determine the causes of absenteeism is to question your supervisors about their employees' excessive absenteeism, including what causes it and how to reduce it. Of course, if your supervisors have made no efforts to get to know the employees in their respective departments, they may not be able to provide reasons. However, just the act of questioning may get the ball rolling and signal to your supervisors that their involvement is important.

4. How much formal training have your supervisors received on absenteeism containment and reduction?

If you find that your supervisors hesitate to provide meaningful answers to your questions, then you're on the right track towards a solution. Ask yourself, "How much formal training have I given my supervisors in the areas of absenteeism reduction and human resources skills?" If your answer is none or very little, your solution can't be far behind. The fact of the matter is, you cannot ask a person to do a job he or she has never been trained to do.

If you have an absenteeism problem, it should now be clear that the place to begin the cure is with its main causes: undertrained supervision and unsatisfactory working conditions. Without improvement in these areas, you can expect your high rate of absenteeism to continue.

Attendance Policy and Absenteeism Policy Samples and Examples

An effective attendance policy or absenteeism policy helps your business ensure employee attendance to accomplish work. Depending on the type of work, the attendance policy or absenteeism policy may designate the number of days on which employees can be absent from work. A fair and consistently administered attendance policy or absenteeism policy is critical for business success.

The Role of the Supervisor in Managing Absenteeism

Almost two out of three employees who are absent, are not ill. For most companies, the responsibility for managing absenteeism has fallen primarily on immediate supervisors. These supervisors are often the only people who are aware that a certain employee is absent. They are in the best position to understand the circumstances surrounding an individual's absence and to notice a problem at an early stage. Their active involvement in managing absenteeism is critical.

Sample Hourly Employee Attendance Policy

Excellent attendance is an expectation of all employees of Your Company, Inc. Daily attendance is especially important for hourly employees whose customers and co-workers have the expectation of on-time product shipping and delivery. Emergency personal time is made available to employees for such unscheduled events as personal illness, immediate family member illness, and doctor appointments. See a sample attendance policy.

New Approaches to Cutting Staff Absence

Developing positive workplace practices and new ways of working:

- Organizations with the worst records have twice the absence rates of the best ones—there may be factors relating to the work involved, but it indicates that many firms have scope for improvement.
- Men under 40 have half the absence rate of women of the same age.
- Public sector employees report sick more often than those in the private sector.
- Trade unionists report sick more often than non-union employees.

There is scope to draw some contentious conclusions from these findings—for example, is greater job security in the public sector a reason for not being so motivated to struggle in to work? Whatever the reasons, these differences highlight areas where, at least to some extent, individual's criteria for considering themselves unfit for work vary.

The Industrial Society report *Maximising Attendance* also highlights a divergence of opinion between what managers think are the top five causes of absence and what employees say themselves:

How Employees Report Absence	In Manager's Own Opinion
1. Cold/Flue	1. Cold/Flue
2. Stomach Upset/Food Poisoning	2. Stress/Emotional Problems/ Personal Problems
3. Headaches/Migraines	3. Monday Morning Blues/ Extending The Weekend
4. Back Problems	4. Low Morale/Boring Job
5. Stress/Emotional Problems/ Personal Problems	5. Childcare Problems/Family Sickness

If managers are correct as seeing the reason in the left hand column as often being "code" for some of the reasons they list, it pinpoints areas where employers could take positive action to reduce absenteeism. Leaving aside surveillance, interrogation and other more draconian approaches, which no doubt some employers might favour, there are preventative measures which employers could take. For example:

- Family friendly policies, from flexible hours to workplace crèches to help employees cope with childcare problems.
- Providing more varied/interesting/responsible work to combat "low morale/boring- job" syndrome.
- Compressed working week options to cater positively for those who may need longer weekends.
- Mentoring, counselling, fitness programs, on-site massage etc. to help people through stress, emotional problems or personal problems, plus careful monitoring of workloads.

The Industrial Society suggests other steps, organizations could take:

- Having a clear policy on absence monitoring.
- Training managers to manage attendance.
- Training employees to recognize and manage signs of stress.
- Improving employee motivation through training and development opportunities.
- Using return-to-work interviews after illness and informal procedures to keep individuals informed and to resolve problems by consensus.

These approaches tackle absenteeism by seeking to reduce the number of absences. An alternative approach is to alter the nature of absences, so that absence from the workplace does not mean that no work is done at all. When people are absent—unless for an agreed appointment with the doctor or dentist—it is usually for a whole day at a time. But people who may not feel up to the commute journey and 8 hours of continuous work may non-etheless feel able and willing to put in a few hours of work. This is particularly the case where the reported illness really belongs to the employee's child, rather than the employee.

Looked at this way, it can be said that traditional and inflexible work practices require people to be absent from work for longer than they need to be. All across the country parents (usually it is mothers) call in sick when they are not, so that they can look after a sick child. They then crawl into work when they really are sick by way of compensating, or if they feel they can't be sick "again" so soon after the last absence. Unhealthy patterns emerge amongst parents: they routinely work when they should be recuperating, and share their diseases in the workplace.

Much simpler, more honest and more productive are work environments where employees feel free to tell their line managers and colleagues that their child is ill, and then work from home. (And it helps to be properly set up for this, with remote access, etc.)

A similar process could apply to people who are well enough to work intermittently at home, but for whom, a day in the office could be very debilitating. This is especially helpful for people with chronic or intermittent conditions. A work regime which requires nine-to-five seven days a week can be intrinsically disabling for some people with chronic conditions or long-term illnesses, or who are recuperating from serious illness or injury. Flexible hours and home based working can allow people in this position to maximize their contribution, and to increase their wage-earning potential.

In the end, the solutions should be about focusing on what people can do, rather than on their non-attendance on the workplace.

Management Strategies to Curb Absenteeism

Absenteeism in Indian Industries

Absenteeism in Indian industries is not a new phenomenon. It is the manifestation of a decision by employees not to present themselves at their place of work, at a time when it is planned by the management that they should be in attendance. Many research reports reveal that there has been a phenomenal increase in absenteeism in some industrial sectors. The absenteeism becomes a problem to organizational management particularly when employees absent from their work environment without giving sufficient notice and by justifying their stand by furnishing fake reasons.

The reasons for absenteeism are many. The factors contributing to absenteeism from work includes individual and environmental factors. These consists of sickness, accidents, occupational diseases, poor production planning (flow of work), bad working conditions and inadequate welfare conditions, lack of trained labourers, insecurity in employment, collective bargaining process, rigid control system, lack of supervisory support, lack of interest, lack of cohesive and cordial culture and so on. The individual reasons may vary from organization to organization depending upon the organizational climate, employee's attitude and influence of external organizational factors (market forces, social activities that influence the industrial culture prevailing in geographical zone etc.).

The Problem

High rate of absenteeism is neither desirable to employers nor good for the employees. In majority of organizations, high rate of absenteeism has an adverse effect on quality and quantity of production, efficiency of workers and organization, organizational discipline and more importantly on the organization's intention to fulfill the new market demands. The absenteeism develops a considerable loss to organization because work schedules gets upset and delayed and management has to provide overtime wages to meet the delivery dates.

The causes of absenteeism, its effect on productivity and cost in terms of finance and administrative effectiveness are quite clear, but what is unclear is how to take affirmative action to control absenteeism. This should be done in such a way as not to develop mistrust, costly administration and system avoidance. Traditional methods of absenteeism control based on disciplinary procedure have proven to be ineffective and have failed to motivate the work force to meet organizational demands to compete at a global level. Unless management identifies and addresses the actual factors that influence employees to remain absent from work, it will be difficult for the organization to remain competitive at national and international levels. It is therefore imperative to probe into micro and macro aspects of organizational absenteeism to meet organizations long-term cherished goals.

The levels of absenteeism and reasons for its occurrence are dependent on many variables in an organizational environment. This particular research identifies seven key factors that affect the absence rate for employees. These seven factors can be detailed as follows:

1. Family circumstances;
2. The physical health of the worker;
3. The work environment;
4. The degree of job stress;
5. Employer-employee relations;
6. Union coverage; and
7. Work schedules.

Absenteeism has the potential to cause numerous impacts upon an organization; these include lost productivity, poorer quality of product/service, decreased customer satisfaction, and a negative effect on the performance/morale of other employees. Other operational consequences of absenteeism include greater financial costs to the employer, as well as a greater employee workload. Each of these impacts has the potential to cripple an organization's operational ability, and seriously undermine its efforts to stay competitive or viable. Hence, it is necessary to develop effective strategies to curb the absenteeism in Indian organizations.

Strategies to Curb the Absenteeism

1. High collaborative culture.
2. Be aware of problems that may effect employee attendance or performance.
3. Develop open communication between managers, supervisors and employees.

4. Employees are encouraged to voice their concerns so their perceptions of the work place are clear and can be dealt with.
5. Cooperation with union representatives can be very helpful in attendance management and should be encouraged.
6. Regularly scheduled department meetings are an excellent way not only to hear employee perceptions and concerns but also to communicate organizational goals.
7. An employee's relationship with their supervisor can greatly influence their feelings about their work, their co-workers and thus their attendance at work.
8. More openness and transparency on the part of management.
9. Encourage risk taking and experimentation among members.
10. Make each employee aware that they are a valued member of the "team", that they play an important role in your organization and that their attendance is critical.
11. Hold regular meetings, keep your staff informed and involved. Know your employees; without prying, show an interest in their personal lives.
12. Familiarize with community programs which you can recommend to an employee if he/she has a need for assistance (i.e. marital or financial counseling).
13. Awareness, commitment and involvement by all levels of staff.
14. Match the attendance records during a period of "high" workload to a period of "normal" workload.
15. Bonus for unused sick leave.
16. Official warnings.

17. Develop a comprehensive and collaborative continuous improvement program throughout the department.
18. Counsel individual employees. Discuss with all employees problems of unjustifiable time off.
19. Bonus work (e.g. Saturday) should not be available to any worker who has been absent during the week.
20. Introduce an incentive scheme to reward those who don't have an absent day. This is measured quarterly and annually.
21. Greater attention by supervisors and more accountability of operations management and other management has improved sick leave.
22. Front line management will be held accountable for attendance management performance.
23. A management structure be engineered to identify and execute objectives relating to absence prevention, disability management and attendance control.
24. Effective training and development program.
25. Effective career planning and development program.
26. Each worksite should develop and maintain an attendance management policy.
27. Employers should track attendance and assign costs based on reliable data.
28. The Attendance Management Team should be given the ability to develop complex case management strategies and aggressively intervene where appropriate.
29. Employees should be encouraged to give as much notice as possible for anticipated absences. Absent employees should be requested to keep contact with their employer.
30. The employer should be informed of any changes in the employee's health status.
31. Employees should be called if they are not keeping contact with the employer. The purpose is to show

concern and desire for the employee to regain a healthy status and return to work.

32. In addition to individual counseling make use of family counseling methods.

Guidelines for Absenteeism Control

There are two types of absenteeism, each of which requires a different type of approach.

Innocent Absenteeism

Innocent absenteeism refers to employees who are absent for reasons beyond their control; like sickness and injury. Innocent absenteeism is not culpable which means that it is blameless. In a labour relations context this means that it cannot be remedied or treated by disciplinary measures.

Culpable Absenteeism

Culpable absenteeism refers to employees who are absent without authorization for reasons which are within their control. For instance, an employee who is on sick leave even though he/she is not sick, and it can be proven that the employee was not sick, is guilty of culpable absenteeism. To be culpable is to be blameworthy. In a labour relations context this means that progressive discipline can be applied.

For the large majority of employees, absenteeism is legitimate, but innocent absenteeism occurs infrequently. Procedures for disciplinary action apply only to culpable absenteeism. Many organizations take the view that through the process of individual absentee counselling and treatment, the majority of employees will overcome their problems and return to an acceptable level of regular attendance.

Identifying Excessive Absenteeism

Attendance records should be reviewed regularly to be sure that an employee's sick leave days are excessive compared to other employees. If a supervisor suspects that an employee is excessively absent, this can be confirmed through reviewing the attendance records.

If all indications show that an employee is excessively absent, the next step is to gather as much information as possible in order to get a clearer picture of the situation. The employees' files should be reviewed and the employees immediate supervisor should document all available information on the particular employee's history.

Individual Communication

After all available information has been gathered, the administrator or supervisor should individually meet with each employee whom has been identified as having higher than average or questionable (or pattern) absences. This first meeting should be used to bring concerns regarding attendance to the employee's attention. It is also an opportunity to discuss with the employee, in some depth, the causes of his or her attendance problem and possible steps he or she can take to remedy or control the absences. Listen carefully to the employee's responses.

The tone of the meeting should not be adversarial, but a major purpose of the interview is to let the employee know that management treats attendance as a very important component of overall work performance. Keep your comments non-threatening and work-oriented. Stick to the facts (i.e. patters, profiles, rates etc.). The employee should be given a copy of there attendance report with absences highlighted for discussion.

This interview will give you the opportunity to explore in-depth with the employee, the reasons for his or her absence. Gather facts, do not make any assumptions. Provide support and counselling and offer guidance as the occasion demands to assist the employee to deal with the specific cause of the absence.

Often, after the initial meeting employees reduce their absenteeism. The meeting shows that you are concerned and that absenteeism is taken seriously. The employee's attendance should be closely monitored until it has been reduced to acceptable levels. Appropriate counselling should take place as is thought necessary. If a marked improvement has been shown, commend the employee. The meeting should be documented and a copy placed in the employee's file.

Proof of Illness

Sometimes, it is helpful in counselling employees with excessive innocent or culpable absenteeism to inquire or verify the nature and reasons of their absence.

The extent to which an employer may inquire into the nature of and reasons for an employee's absence from the workplace is a delicate issue. The concepts of an employee's privacy and an employer's need for information affecting the workplace often come into conflict. Seldom is the conflict more difficult to resolve than where personal medical information is involved.

Unions will often strongly object to any efforts by management to inquire more deeply into the nature of an employee's illness. You will need to consider the restraints of any language in collective agreements in relation to this issue. Generally speaking, however, the following "rules of thumb" can be derived from the existing jurisprudence:

1. There is a prevailing right to privacy on the part of an employee, unless the employer can demonstrate that, its legitimate business interests necessitate some intrusion into the employee's personal affairs.
2. When such intrusion is justified, it should be strictly limited to the degree of intrusion necessitated by the employer's interests.
3. An employee has a duty to notify his employer of an intended absence, the cause of the absence and its expected duration. This information is required by the employer to meet its legitimate concerns to have at its disposal facts which will enable it to schedule work and organize its operation.
4. An absent employee has an obligation to provide his employer with information regarding any change to his condition or circumstances relating to it which may affect the employer's needs as described in point no. 3 above. As such, the interests of the employer in having this information outweighs the individual employee's right to privacy.

5. An employer rule requiring proof for every absence is unreasonable if an absenteeism problem does not exist.
6. A mere assertion by the person claiming to be sick is not satisfactory proof.
7. The obligation to prove sickness, where the employer requires proof, rests with the employee.
8. An employer is entitled upon reasonable and probable grounds to refuse to accept a physician's certificate until it contains sufficient information to satisfy the employer's reservations. (i.e. seen by physician, some indication of return to work, etc.). Non-production of a required medical certificate could result in loss of pay until the certificate is produced.
9. Where a medical certificate is rejected by an employer (as in point no. 8 above) the employer must state the grounds for rejection and must point out to the employee what it requires to satisfy the onus of proof.
10. An employer may require an employee to prove fitness for work where it has reasonable grounds to do so. In a health care setting the nature of the employer's business gives it a reasonably irresistible interest in this personal information for the purpose of assessing fitness.
11. Where any unusual circumstances raise reasonable suspicion that an employee might have committed an abuse of an income protection program, an employer may require an employee to explain such circumstances. For example, an employer may require responses as to whether the illness confined an employee to his/her bed or home; whether an employee engaged in any outside activity and the reasons for the activity.

In summary then, any intrusion into the employee's privacy must be shown to be reasonable, based on the individual circumstances and in relation to the operation of the employer's business. If income protection abuse is suspected the extent to which such intrusion is "reasonable" would be far greater than in the case where it is not. If you are not clear on whether an inquiry is legally justified it is advisable to consult your superior.

After the Initial Interview

If after the initial interview, enough time and counseling efforts, as appropriate, have passed and the employee's absenteeism has not improved, it may be necessary to take further action. Further action must be handled with extreme caution—a mistake in approach, timing or severity can be crippling from both an administration and labour relation's point of view.

Determining whether counseling or disciplinary action is appropriate, depends on whether the employee's absences are innocent or culpable. If the employee's absenteeism is made up of both innocent and culpable absences, then each type must be dealt with as a separate issue. In a labour relation's context innocent absenteeism and culpable absenteeism are mutually exclusive. One in no way affects the other.

Counseling Innocent Absenteeism

Innocent absenteeism is not blameworthy and therefore disciplinary action is not justified. It is obviously unfair to punish someone for conduct which is beyond his/her control. Absenteeism, no matter what the cause, imposes losses on the employer who is also not at fault. The damage suffered by the employer must be weighed against the employee's right to be sick. There is a point at which the employer's right to expect the employee to attend regularly and fulfill the employment contract will outweigh the employee's right to be sick. At such a point the termination of the employee may be justified, as will be discussed. The procedure an employer may take for innocent absenteeism is as follows:

1. Initial counseling(s)
2. Written counseling(s)
3. Reduction(s) of hours and/or job reclassification
4. Discharge

Initial Counseling

Presuming you have communicated attendance expectations generally and have already identified an employee as a problem, you will have met with him or her as part of your attendance program and you should now continue to monitor the effect of these efforts on his or her attendance.

If the absences are intermittent, meet with the employee each time he/she returns to work. If absence is prolonged, keep in touch with the employee regularly and stay updated on the status of his/her condition. (Indicate your willingness to assist.)

You may require the employee to provide you with regular medical assessments. This will enable you to judge whether or not there is any likelihood of the employee providing regular attendance in future. Regular medical assessments will also give you an idea of what steps the employee is taking to seek medical or other assistance. Formal meetings in which verbal warnings are given should be given as appropriate and documented. If no improvement occurs written warning may be necessary.

Written Counseling

If the absences persist, you should meet with the employee formally and provide him/her with a letter of concern. If the absenteeism still continues to persist then the employee should be given a second letter of concern during another formal meeting. This letter would be stronger worded in that it would warn the employee that unless attendance improves, termination may be necessary.

Reduction(s) of Hours and/or Job Reclassification

In between the first and second letters, the employee may be given the option to reduce his/her hours to better fit his/her personal circumstances. This option must be voluntarily accepted by the employee and cannot be offered as an ultimatum, as a reduction in hours is a reduction in pay and therefore can be looked upon as discipline.

If the nature of the illness or injury is such that the employee is unable to fulfill the requirements of his/her job, but could for example benefit from modified work, counsel the employee to bid on jobs of such type if they become available. (*N.B.* It is inadvisable to "build" a job around an employee's incapacitates particularly in a unionized environment. The onus should be on the employee to apply for an existing position within his/her capabilities.)

Discharge

Only when all the previously noted needs and conditions have been met and everything has been done to accommodate the employee can termination be considered. An Arbitrator would consider the following in ruling on an innocent absenteeism dismissal case:

1. Has the employee done everything possible to regain their health and return to work?
2. Has the employer provided every assistance possible? (i.e. counseling, support, time off.)
3. Has the employer informed the employee of the unworkable situation resulting from their sickness?
4. Has the employer attempted to accommodate the employee by offering a more suitable position (if available) or a reduction of hours?
5. Has enough time elapsed to allow for every possible chance of recovery?
6. Has the employer treated the employee prejudicially in any way?

As is evident, a great deal of time and effort must elapse before dismissal can take place. These points would be used to substantiate or disprove the following two fold test:

1. The absences must be shown to be clearly excessive.
2. It must be proven that the employee will be unable to attend work on a regular basis in the future.

Corrective Action for Culpable Absenteeism

As already indicated, culpable absenteeism consists of absences where it can be demonstrated that the employee is not actually ill and is able to improve his/her attendance.

Presuming you have communicated attendance expectations generally, have identified the employee as a problem, have met with him/her as part of your attendance program, made your concerns on his specific absenteeism known and have offered counselling as appropriate, with no improvement despite your positive efforts, disciplinary procedures may be appropriate.

The procedures for corrective/progressive discipline for culpable absenteeism are generally the same as for other progressive discipline problems. The discipline should not be prejudicial in any way. The general procedure is as follows: [Utilizing counselling memorandum]

1. Verbal Warning(s)
2. Written Warning(s)
3. Suspension(s)
4. Discharge

Verbal Warning

Formally, meet with the employee and explain that income protection is to be used only when an employee is legitimately ill. Advise the employee that his/her attendance record must improve and be maintained at an improved level or further disciplinary action will result. Offer any counselling or guidance as is appropriate. Give further verbal warnings as required. Review the employee's income protection records at regular intervals. Where a marked improvement has been shown, commend the employee. Where there is no improvement a written warning should be issued.

Written Warning

Interview the employee again. Show him/her the statistics and point out that there has been no noticeable (or sufficient) improvement. Listen to the employee to see if there is a valid reason and offer any assistance you can. If no satisfactory explanation is given, advise the employee that he/she will be given a written warning. Be specific in your discussion with him/her and in the counseling memorandum as to the type of action to be taken and when it will be taken if the record does not improve.

As soon as possible after this meeting provide the employee personally with the written warning and place a copy of his/her file. The written warning should identify any noticeable pattern.

If the amount and/or pattern continue, the next step in progressive discipline may be a second, stronger written warning. Your decision to provide a second written warning as an alternative to proceeding to a higher level of discipline (i.e. suspension) will depend on a number of factors. Such factors are, the severity of the problem, the credibility of the employee's explanations, the employee's general work performance and length of service.

Suspension (only after consultation with the appropriate superiors)

If the problem of culpable absenteeism persists, following the next interview period and immediately following an absence, the employee should be interviewed and advised that he/she is to be suspended. The length of the suspension will depend again on the severity of the problem, the credibility of the employee's explanation, the employee's general work performance and length of service. Subsequent suspensions are optional depending on the above condition.

Dismissal (only after consultation with the appropriate superiors)

Dismissals should only be considered when all of the above conditions and procedures have been met. The employee, upon displaying no satisfactory improvement, would be dismissed on the grounds of his/her unwillingness to correct his/her absence record.

Summary

It is reported that absenteeism management strategies got effective feed back from the employees and employer's part in order to curb the absenteeism. It is reported that the rate of absenteeism reduced from 34 per cent to 20 per cent within a period of 6-10 months. The requirement here is the committed management force with single task to carry forward this strategic function with fidelity and accuracy. Many strategies like community intervention programs and industrial counseling strategies have major impact on the behaviour of absented employees. It is envisaged that a culture of open communication and collaboration can reduce the level of absenteeism through strategic interventions.

Attendance improvement programs can work. What the employees require is commitment and support from all levels of management, an effective attendance record-keeping system, consultation and open communication on the reasons for the attendance program.

Implementing and maintaining a work environment where open communication and team spirit can thrive will at first sometimes seem a mammoth and somewhat unrealistic task. If you need encouragement just consider some of the benefits; reduced absenteeism, open communication, team spirit, reduced grievances and greater employee satisfaction.

Only when the positive approach is unsuccessful, does the employer need to use the remedial approach to deal with habitual abusers or with excessive absentee cases. In all cases the employer's actions must be fair and reasonable and consistently applied. With a well communicated, implemented, and administered program, the majority of the employees should agree with the attendance management program and cooperation should follow.

The best and finest way to control absenteeism is to show them his or her career design, his or her career plan and motivate them to work on that with full dedication. On regular basis we should try to develop desire and derive towards promotion and increment. These desire and derive will create fire with full energy to achieve the personal and organization goal. The loyal and natural behaviour to achieve objective is the crux of professional success.

Chapter ten

HIRING & FIRING TECHNIQUE

Hiring an employee is a very responsible activity of the organization because company has to invest a lot till probation on product training, management training and induction program. Therefore, when you hire people you must try to assess or guess how long he or she will stay with the organization after finishing probation. It is reality most of the new hire starts contributing after finishing probation period.

Firing an employee is a challenging, emotional experience and a pathway to possible lawsuits. The decision to employ or terminate someone will influence you, that individual, his or her family, your team, your customers, and your stakeholders. It is normal to experience strong emotions when making these decisions, emotions that may hinder your ability to make effective decisions and perhaps edge you inadvertently into saying or doing somethings that are illegal.

Impact of Hiring and Firing

The ultimate and true success of any business enterprise is solely dependent upon an effective head and competent employees. If you ever own your business and it becomes successful, be sure if you start expanding that you keep a controlling interest. Be careful when you start to hire new employees as many businesses fail because of unqualified associates. Slick, silken-tongued, prospective employees are easy to find and abundant and could easily cause you ruin. With careful observation, using your own intuition and judgment, you can pick employees with superior qualities. But check their references and be very observant and open-minded with keen vision.

When interviewing a prospective employee, the intuitive way of reading character is through the eyes. The contents of a man are reflected in their eyes because they are the direct index of the mind. Be careful of revengeful, crafty, sarcastic, untrustworthy, shifting, or cruel eyes. Any lack of straight-forwardness or hate-projecting eyes along with a sinking feeling in your stomach, beware of that person.

Feeling the vibrations in people can help you determine accurate results. How do you sense good or bad vibrations in relation to people? Certain people will vibrate with cruelty, some with temper, and some with nervousness. Other people are spineless and vibrate no will at all. The ones that vibrate kindness you like them at once.

The surest way to read the good or bad vibrations people radiate is by watching your feelings so you can sense the vibratory rate of their mind, body and soul. A sick or ailing person has inharmonious and negative body vibrations and should be rejected. Free yourself from any feelings or attraction for the opposite sex as you must be in a neutral state of mind. Keep a kind, unprejudiced feeling in your heart and the microphone of pure feeling will judge superior than any intelligence in the land.

The transcendental way of interviewing a prospective employee if you are somewhat advanced spiritually is when meditating; in meditation, visualize the eyes of that person and examine the feeling that materializes in your heart. If you sense any fear or hesitation, don't hire that person. Keep this in mind, if you are receptive and calm during the interview and you penetrate their eyes and study that person, your first impression will be correct. If you awaken your creative ability any difficulty can be overcome. The success of your business lies within yourself.

How do you attract intelligent employees who are honest and will remain loyal? Seek out creative ability and most of all trustworthiness with those who will make your business and your ambition their business and their ambition. Make sure you test any new employees as to their honesty with money, as you should never take for granted the integrity of any employee. Make sure you subject your employees who are handling money to temptation to see their reaction. You never know what a dishonest person can do to your business. Try to confidentially find out about the honesty, character and ability of a prospective employee when you check their references.

On the other side, and if you are an employee and you hear something detrimental or harmful, stay away from that employer altogether and look for another position.

Never forgive a treacherous employee, but forgive minor mistakes twice or thrice. Remember, treachery in an employee will be repeated when you least expect it. Find out through mutual friends, if any of your business associates talk against you and if they do, find out their intentions. Discharge any employees who drink too much and dissipates, that show no signs of reform. Never hire anyone who is mentally or physically, a lazy person. Taking a friend as a business associate can mean trouble as he would be inclined to be too familiar as he would not take orders from you and would try to capitalize on that friendship. Remember, business is business and for warned is for armed.

Worldly people never consider who their real employer is, God. It is He who has employed you under someone else. It is He who promotes you to carry out His work. Therefore, by perfoŕming your job duties with the right attitude to please your real employer no matter how important or unimportant your job is, you will never fail, no matter what direction you choose.

The majorities of people want significant or privileged positions, but is unrealistic in their expectations on how to achieve them. The first step to increase the bottom line for your company is to develop the proper qualities by loyal unselfish actions for the betterment of the employer. These unselfish initiatives will automatically propel you to a better position by activating the laws of cause and effect. The biggest to the smallest companies the world over are looking for this type of worker because there is no type of business that can succeed by going it alone. So be full of enthusiasm, honesty, dependability, loyalty, creativity and be ready to swing into action.

All commercial businesses should be spiritualized. If your business does not conform to divine laws it will never last. If your business caters just to human lavishness, and the mighty dollar, unethical or false pretenses, it will certainly be ruined by the execution of the spiritual law of the survival of the virtuous. Any business that hurts the true spiritual well-being of the individual does no real good, and is certain to meet with devastation by the very same nature of its actions. Money-making alone should not be the goal of business. Service should be the true spiritual goal of business.

By spiritualizing service in your work rather than having money-making your entire goal, you will change the plan for your life and never will you be left out. Profiteering should not be synonymous with business. Eradicate this idea completely from your mind. Businesses blunder into periodic inflation and depressions by operating at the expense of others well-being with their own self-interest. This metaphysical blunder will cause selfish enterprises to fail.

Remember, hiring process should always be slow and you must be smiling during interaction. Apart from this, you talk less and listen more of candidate so that you understand him/her accurately. But when you are firing some one, don't let them explain, talk more, don't listen and try to change your face with aggression so that candidate can understand, there is no way out, but to resign. Taking resignation is a wise step rather than termination because in this case, you can save notice period amount. If you terminate, then you have to pay his salary and notice period amount as well.

You should be ready for the aggressive repercussion of firing people specially where employee union is strong. In India, few states are having violent and ill-mannered employee union where you have to take an extra precaution such as Punjab, Haryana, Uttar Pradesh, and Delhi. I remember the initial employment days when one General Manager of Pharmaceutical Company was brutally beaten up and the union people forced him to get out from the office in underwear. The reason was, one medical representative was sacked within his probation period without prior intimation and without giving any valid reason. It happens when you are away from the head office. If you have planned to fire someone and you are away from the office, then fire the targeted person at the last moment of meeting and try to get resignation at any cost. If you take resignation then legally union can't help him out and one more important thing that you have to come to the same area for working or meeting.

Hiring and Firing of Employees

Hiring and firing strategies varies from country to country. In India, both employee and employer has liberty to make decision on the basis of personal benefits. If you will find some good opportunity, you will not take second thought in switching over. Good employees always first inform to the employer at least one month in advance before leaving the organization and this attitude not only shows your professionalism, but also gives you right to come back in future. On the other hand, employer sometime fires non-performer without informing the employee and this is not the ethical. At least, one month notice should be given to the employee so that he/she can find any good job within this duration.

Couple of days back, I read in newspaper, TCS fired some 500 employees and IBM fired around 700 freshers. In the month of September, 2008 twenty lakhs employees had lost their jobs in United States due to global recession. We might hear more bad news in the coming days. But in India, it is not so even when world is facing recession all around. Recently, Jet Air Ways fired more than one thousand employees to cut wages after the merger with King Fisher Airlines but ultimately, Jet had taken back its decision and rejoined all of them.

Why do employers hire in large scale and then fire later. Even though they say poor performers, how far is it justified given the fact that many employees in IT firms are in bench (idle, do not have projects, they are just stand alone). Is it only because of rupee appreciation or the so-called poor performance. If it is poor performance, why does HR hire such people first and fire later. Why can't an organization fire top management for "poor performance", i.e. inability to bring more projects, lack of counter measures for rupee appreciation etc. Is poor performance only attributed to employees in lower ranks? Can there not be poor performers in top management who recruit employees in large scale without assessing their skills, without proper planning and resource utilization of resources?

Situation for Hiring and Firing

There are four main situations that will indicate when you need to hire an employee or additional employees:

- When you don't have the skills and expertise to do a job.
- When it will cost you more to do the job yourself than to hire someone else to do it.
- When one person can't do the job.
- When you hate doing a task that must be done.

You must then determine if the person you need will be needed to work on a full-time or part-time basis as an employee or as an independent contractor. Before you begin the interview process, it's best to have a job description designed as well as a basic compensation package developed for the prospective employee.

Finding the right people for your organization is usually a matter of looking carefully at past experience and present capabilities. Getting referrals from a previous employer or acquaintance is probably the best way. When that isn't possible, get and check references, look at samples of past work or track record, or provide a pre-employment test to determine actual skill level. Don't be surprised when previous employers will do little more than confirm employment dates. They may be doing so only as a matter of company policy to reduce the potential for lawsuits. What is your policy about providing referrals? You do have one, don't you?

During the interview process, raise the problems and concerns you have in relation to the work you are hiring for. If you are under a tight deadline or the workday is pressure filled, express your concern that the job can be done right and on time. Explain any special circumstances that the individual may be involved in, such as regular overtime, weekend work, fieldwork, driving to and from jobsites, etc. Then listen and watch the person respond. Do they appear to have solutions? Are they confident about handling the situations you present?

The success of your organization is largely based on the work performance of the employees you hire. Why hire someone you may eventually fire? What a waste of your time in interviewing, training, trying to solve their problems and making them adapt to company policies if you're not convinced from the beginning that this is the kind of employee you want in order to build a successful organization. When selecting an employee, make sure they understand the kind of performance you expect from them. Feel confident and be sure to check their references.

Establish a company policy that new employees are to be evaluated over a probation period before regular employment is offered. Print this policy on an application form and explain it to the applicant so that no doubt exists. Have a written contract outlining mutual responsibilities and obligations.

If a valued employee wants to terminate on his/her own volition, find out why. Should your efforts to keep them be unsuccessful, leave the door open for them to return at a later date under amicable conditions? Phone them after a period of several months to tell them how much their work was appreciated, and invite them to return. They may have decided they were better off with you as an employer, but were reluctant to make the first call.

But the time does come when you find that the attitude or production of an employee is below your acceptable standards. Have the employee in for an interview held in confidentiality and privacy (it's a good idea to have a quiet observer to these interviews), giving enough time and limiting outside interruptions. Tell them what you like about them and specify where their performance is satisfactory. Try to find out the source of their problem and offer your help. Opening the lines of communication may uncover a situation or personal or work problems that can be resolved.

If there is no alternative to firing, do so without animosity. If there is a temporary problem that can be worked out, decide whether the employee is valuable enough for you to exercise patience. If you keep an employee, follow up with periodic checkups. Don't retain an employee who is unwilling to compromise or who sets a poor example for other employees within the organization. A firing is an admission by both parties that one or the other, or both, failed to prevent the termination.

Points to Consider When Hiring

Remember that ability problems can be solved. Attitude problems are more difficult to deal with.

- Consider employees' potential for upgrade to positions of greater performance.
- Realistically consider the high cost of turnover in personnel.
- Develop a list of questions for applicants that provide the information you need to make a qualified employment decision.
- Determine the actual reason why an applicant left a former position.
- Check on references and verify past experience listed.
- Identify his/her short-range and long-range personal and professional objectives.

Points to Consider When Firing

- Conduct corrective interviews.
- Determine, if there is an ability problem or an attitude problem.
- Have a personal interview and prepare a written report signed by either management or the supervisor, and the employee. Date the report and maintain a copy in the personnel folder.
- Correct poor communication.
- You have a right to know what your employees are doing.
- Employees have a right to know what the consequences of their actions are.

Keep Hiring Legal

If you think common sense is a good enough rule of thumb for keeping hiring legal, think again. All hiring managers need to have a basic understanding of the legalities of hiring. And some of the legal issues are probably not as straightforward as you may think. This applies not just to those making a final hiring decision, but to every single person interviewing a job candidate. Although this section addresses the legalities of hiring in general in India, remember that every hiring situation has its own unique legal concerns. Furthermore, employment law changes quickly with new court decisions. When in doubt, don't be penny wise and pound foolish—consult with an expert employment attorney before you get into trouble.

In India, labour law prohibits employers from discriminating against job candidates on the basis of race, colour, national origin, religion, sex, physical handicap, or age. In some states or localities, additional characteristics, such as sexual orientation, may also be prohibited from entering into the hiring equation. Although the actual law seems straightforward, court interpretations have more narrowly defined what constitutes discriminatory hiring practices. Even questions that negatively affect a protected class of applicants may be, and often have been, deemed illegal.

As a rule of thumb, job interview questions should focus specifically on the applicant's ability to successfully perform the duties inherent to the position being applied for. These questions are examples of the most commonly asked illegal questions. Other questions of the same type may also have been deemed illegal, but because of the broad interpretations of the courts, it would be impossible to list all questions that might be considered illegal.

Are you Married?

Many questions that relate to the sex of the applicant are illegal, including any question about marital status.

Do You have Children?

It is illegal to ask an applicant any questions about children, primarily, because such questions can lead to discrimination against women.

How Old are You?

It is illegal to ask an applicant, his or her age. This law is designed to protect applicants over the age of forty. You may ask the applicant if he or she is over the age of eighteen—if the applicant is not, you may need to know the applicant's age to ascertain the applicability of federal, state, and local child labour laws.

Did You Graduate from High School or College?

An educational degree should not be a job requirement and should not be asked about in an interview unless the employer can demonstrate that successful performance on this job requires a specific level of education. Otherwise, this requirement and line of questioning can be construed as discriminatory because some minorities have less educational background than non-minorities.

Have You ever been Arrested?

You should not ask an applicant if he or she has been arrested. You are generally well advised not even to ask about felony convictions, unless such a conviction would be unusually relevant to the position being sought. These questions can be discriminatory, because some minority groups have, on average, higher records of arrest and convictions than non-minorities.

How Much do You Weigh?

All questions about physical appearance are illegal because they tend to discriminate against women and some minorities.

What Country are You from?

This question is clearly illegal because it discriminates on the basis of national origin.

What is Your Native Language?

This question discriminates on the basis of national origin.

Are You Handicapped?

You cannot ask about an individual's possible handicaps. Furthermore, employers are generally required to make special accommodations for physically challenged applicants.

Tips of Hiring Good Employee

1. Never hire your relatives in your organization.
2. Reference check is mandatory before hiring.
3. Hire needy one.
4. Must know the total family members.
5. Don't allow your wife or husband to work with the same organization.

Tips of Firing Non-performer

1. Fire demotivated employee.
2. Don't drag to reason master.
3. Don't hire girl friend or boy friend.
4. Don't indulge into affair with office colleague otherwise you will be fired.

Strategies of Hiring and Firing

Hiring or firing an employee is a challenging, emotional experience and a pathway to possible lawsuits. The decision to employ or terminate someone will influence you, that individual, his or her family, your team, your customers, and your stakeholders. It is normal to experience strong emotions when making these decisions, emotions that may hinder your ability to make effective decisions and perhaps edge you inadvertently into saying or doing some things that are illegal. To reduce the emotional trauma and to be more effective in hiring and firing people, try these time-tested strategies.

Involve Human Resources

The people in your Human Resources (HR) department are your best friends in these situations. Talk with them before doing anything. Invite them to review your ideas before you take action. And have them with you in the room when you do act. If you do not have an HR department, then involve your attorney. Either one will provide a calming and rational influence. No matter how experienced you are, your HR professional or attorney has seen more and stranger things than you have and is trained to deal with them. In my experience, these professionals would love to be more involved, if only to see that the interests of all parties—the employer and the employee—are protected. In addition, they can add value in ways that you may never have imagined, such as helping you avoid legal pitfalls. Let them help you.

Standardize Procedures

Handle each hiring the same way. For current and potential employees, have a job description in place for each position in your organization. Have a list of standard interview questions for each job in your organization. Send copies of those questions to HR for review before starting to use them, and ask HR to have your legal department review them as well. Have standard procedures drawn up for how each candidate is interviewed, including the interview starting time and who will attend.

Document in writing each step of the hiring process for every candidate. But be certain, you do not inadvertently put anything into your notes that might cause legal problems later, such as "looks pregnant". Send copies of the documentation to HR. Remember, the palest ink is better than the most retentive memory. You must also handle each firing the same, unless emergency circumstances require extraordinary action. Document every behaviour leading to disciplinary or corrective action. Document every attempt on management's part to coach, counsel, retrain, or otherwise help the employee improve the quality or quantity of her or his work. Send copies of that documentation to HR, and discuss with HR all options before making a final decision to terminate an employee.

Focus on Goals

Your decisions about hiring or firing should focus on several interrelated goals important to the company and to you. These goals are higher productivity, stronger employee loyalty, better team morale, reaching a fair decision, correct behavior within the law, good public relations, and a decision that allows you to sleep at night.

In hiring or terminating someone, you need to focus on positive goals. Before you begin your meeting, take a few minutes to review these objectives and share them later with the job candidate or the person being fired. This helps the potential employee understand the hiring process and what you expect from your team. For an employee being let go, this review will explain the reasons for termination, and when you outline the company's severance package, many employees will accept the decision more readily.

Physical Environment

A surprising number of managers, particularly new ones, acknowledge being nervous during a hiring or firing session. Your nervous mental state affects your body in a negative way. Your mouth gets dry, your hands sweat, and your bladder shrinks. But if you can overcome these physical effects, you can also calm your mental state. What to do? Prior to the meeting, rehearse what you will say. Have water available for everyone attending; a dry mouth makes for awkward conversation. Take time to wash your hands, which helps reduce tension. Take a series of deep breaths just before the person enters the room.

Hiring. As soon as a job candidate arrives at your office, have the receptionist offer him or her drink of water or a beverage and use of the rest room. They may have spent 30 to 60 minutes traveling to your office, and then time waiting somewhere if they got there early. By acknowledging their physical needs and offering to hélp satisfy them, you are going a longway toward building a positive emotional relationship with this potential employee. During the interview, focus on the person's job-related qualifications, and avoid such matters as marital status, age, religion, or physical handicaps. They are lawsuit landmines.

Firing. Before the employee being terminated arrives, have a box of tissues ready. Under the unusual emotional stress of being fired, many people cry, just as they do at weddings and funerals. The people you are sure will not weep, will; the ones you think will, might not. If the person cries, offer a tissue and wait until he or she regains composure. If it seems appropriate, you could offer a drink of water or a brief break. Be compassionate and helpful. By doing so, you are going a longway toward providing dignity to another human being in an otherwise awkward and painful circumstance.

Reciprocity

How you treat your candidates during the hiring process, and how you treat them during termination, is how your team will treat your customers. Treat your employees with courtesy, respect, dignity, and compassion, and they will treat you and your customers likewise. It is not the people you fire who come back to haunt you. It is the ones you don't fire who come back to your facility everyday to damage the work environment and your business.

So hire wisely. Then train, empower, and motivate your team members. If necessary, provide discipline and corrective action. But if nothing works, move the offending employee out the door.

Precautions Before Firing an Employee

1. Avoid personal statements which might degrade or humiliate the individual, or vague statements which might suggest that the situation is reversible.
2. Be honest and completely clear about the reasons for discharge.
3. It is sometimes helpful to have another individual, such as a professional from human resources, present as a witness and a support for the employee, particularly if emotional reactions are anticipated.
4. Present a precise explanation of severance pay procedures, benefits continuation forms, pension or profit-sharing payouts and other available assistance, such as outplacement counseling. In larger corporations, the human resources department handles the filling out of the necessary forms and documents.
5. Prematurely, early notification may significantly affect production and possibly invite undesirable reactions.
6. Plan the interview carefully to anticipate responses and diffuse reactions.
7. Consider the possibility of an irrational response by a dismissed employee.

8. Take the necessary precautions to change security codes, access codes to computers and entry to the corporate premises.
9. Fire at the last moment of your meeting if you are outside the head office, because this strategy will help you to protect yourself with union people and local people.
10. Take written resignation by hook or crook and use termination as a last resort.
11. Termination is a loss-making step for company with both the aspects, economically and legally.
12. Allow the individual to remove personal belongings at a low-visibility time, after hours or on a weekend. Prepare a checklist of company property that should be accounted for, including keys, credit cards, ID cards, computer disks, detailing bag etc.
13. Must confirm with the colleagues, subordinates, boss and distributors about any loan, pending bills etc.
14. Must inform all his colleagues and distributors about his resignation if he is working in the field.
15. Respond to all questions and discuss the cover story to be presented when future employers inquire about the individual. Be prepared with a version that is supportive of the employee but does not threaten the company's credibility.

After Firing an Employee

1. Document the termination in writing immediately, detailing conversation, reactions and emotional tone of both parties. This is essential for response to any future challenge to the termination.
2. Inform the staff or co-workers of the termination by word of mouth or by memo. In the case of for-cause termination, the incident should be mentioned only briefly, in a non-defamatory manner. If performance is the reason, experts suggest that simply stating that the employee and the organization have agreed to part company should suffice.

3. In the case of staff reduction or layoffs, the remaining staff should be assured that downsizing was warranted and that no additional layoffs are anticipated at this time. (If additional reductions are expected, employees should be informed that such an action may be required, and that they will be informed on or before a specific date.)
4. Invite employees who have additional questions and concerns to meet with specified representatives of the company privately.
5. Inform clients or customers who deal with the discharged individual that the company will continue to serve their needs. When necessary, name a specific individual who will replace the terminated employee.

Hiring and Firing, Fast and Slow

I'm generally a proponent of the "hire slow, fire fast" school of thought. It can be extremely painful to hire slow, but typically, not quite as painful as the destruction. A bad hire can wreak on a company or team. I recently read Dick Costolo's (of Feedburner) *post on hiring fast vs. slow* and I really like what he has to say. He notes that positions where it's tougher to measure success are the good candidates for hiring slow and firing fast, but that positions where success is (relatively) easier to quantify (i.e., sales roles), he's a proponent of hiring fast and firing fast. Basically because it can be tough to dial in the right person for the product/channel/environment mix before you see their actual results.

What's interesting is that there's no "fire slow" school of thought. It's either hire slow or hire fast, but always fire fast. A bad hire, regardless of how fast you filled the requisition, is always a bad hire and can ruin a culture, company or team. Hire the experience and/or the "best available athlete" that you need, but don't walk away. Monitor, evaluate and communicate progress and levels of satisfaction. And fire fast when needed.

Hiring executives has always been a daunting task—and today's economy makes it tougher than ever. The global scope and breakneck pace of business, the shrinking supply of job candidates, and the constant shift of organizational structures have increased the stakes exponentially; one wrong hire can quickly derail a company. Yet, recent studies indicate that between 30 per cent and 50 per cent of executive-level hires end in firings or resignations. What makes hiring go wrong so often? And how can executives substantially improve the outcome of the process? This article provides some surprising answers to those questions. Fernandez-Araoz presents ten common hiring traps and many real-world examples of how those traps have scuttled business plans in a variety of industries worldwide. A large consumer goods company, for instance, slipped into the delegation gaffe trap when it handed over the screening and interviewing process to a mismatched team of managers that had an agenda different from the CEO's. And the ignoring emotional intelligence trap tripped up a U.S. telecommunications company that hired a CEO with a great track record—only to fire him less than a year later when his lack of cross-cultural social skills was discovered. Hiring well is a strategy—perhaps an organization's most important one, the author says. To sidestep the hiring traps, he suggests ways to systematically assess the company's needs and to determine how those needs mesh with the open job description—before candidates walk through the door. Fernandez-Araoz's search strategy incites managers with hiring responsibilities to be creative, determined, and courageous when embarking on a candidate search.

Hiring/Managing/Firing Employees—A Guide For Small Business Owners:

This section isn't designed to give you detailed information about legal requirements involved in hiring/managing/firing employees (that advice is best found by consulting a good employment law attorney). Rather it is designed to give you some simple advice.

Hire your people carefully. Screen resumes and check resources. Consult your state business resources to find out what questions you can and cannot ask in an interview, the acceptable limits of background checks, etc. Always get signed waivers from a potential employee allowing you to conduct a background check. Take the time to hire carefully and institute a regular process for deciding upon selecting new hires. Select the best people you can find.

If you find you've made a hiring error and the employee isn't working out, then it's probably wise to fire the employee as soon as possible. Be sure to give performance feedback so that the employee knows what is expected of him and what improvements must be made. Document firing decisions. Business owners tend to say it is the employees they should have fired, but didn't, who cause them the most grief.

Management of employees is a personal skill. In fact, as Daniel Goleman discusses in *Working With Emotional Intelligence* personal skills are by far the largest determinant of managerial success.

Employees need meaningful feedback. Some need more guidance than others to do a good job. Always let an employee know when they have done a job well, and let them know what is expected of them. Encourage questions. Establish company rules, and be sure all employees understand these rules, and why they exist.

Hiring Steps

1. *Advertising*—Beforing putting advertising is now mandatory to take advantage of multiple medium which is more economical with maximum reach. For example if you need executive level employee, you go for English or Hindi but for higher level you can go for English only.
2. *Interview process*—Firstly, employer should be on time with a proper dressing sense. We should start with professional career plan and experience required and then to move toward personal objective of the employee. We must cross-check standard of qualification and experience. It is important that the employment agreement contains warranties from the employee.
3. *References and qualifications*—Usually, they are matters which are discussed at the selection interview, rather than being incorporated in the employment

agreement itself. Where references are required it will usually be highly advisable under the Privacy Act for the employer to obtain a form of consent from their prospective employee. Where qualifications etc. are necessary to enable the employee to carry out the job legally, this should be included in the employment agreement.

4. ***Questions asked at the interview***—We cannot breach the Human Rights Act. We should ask question in a cool and cooperative mood and try to avoid question related to religion or region, colour or creed.
5. ***Job descriptions***—We should be ready with the prescribed job description so that recruiter can ask relevant question during recruitment and can assess perfectly according to the need of the organization for future growth. If you want to recruit an area sales manager then you must try to know how many subordinates are working under him. Is he capable in handling super distributor in terms of closing sales and taking payments on time?
6. ***Legal requirements***—Legal requirement before entering into an employment agreement is mandatory. New hired employee should submit resignation and no objection certificates from previous employees then and there, so that no legal technicality can't waste time of both the parties in any case.
7. ***The employment agreement***—Minimum requirements of employment agreement include probation period (minimum six months and can be extended to one year in case of non-performance). Any new employment agreement entered into must be in writing. *The minimum written requirements for an employment agreement are:* names of the parties, description of work, where work is to be performed, the times the employee is to do the work, the wages or salary payable, services available for the resolution of employment relationship problems, acknowledgement

regarding holidays and notice period from both the parties with remuneration detail failing to inform from either side about advance notice.

8. *Staff handbook*—The Company Policy—This allows employers a degree of flexibility by incorporating this into the agreement by reference to a revisable staff handbook or policy. The Employer will need to make sure that this is given to the employee, along with other agreement documents before the agreement is entered into.
9. ***Probationary or trial periods***—The probationary period must be specified in writing in the agreement. Does not circumvent the requirements relating to unjustified dismissal. But sets platform, time frame and standard for performance review.
10. ***Employee & employer's benefits***—Plain language should be used in regards to agreement. From the employers perspective important topics include:
    (a) Probationary period.
    (b) Accuracy of representations about qualifications.
    (c) Mobility.
    (d) Grounds of termination.
    (e) Restraint of trade.

From the employees perspective, important topics include:

(a) Salary.
(b) Salary reviews.
(c) Relocation costs.
(d) Annual leave.
(e) Training.
(f) Redundancy provisions.
(g) Restraint of trade.

Firing Steps

Before terminating any employment you must have a good reason (the "WHY") as well as follow the correct procedure (the

"HOW"). So even if you have the best of reasons but you don't follow the correct procedure then you could end up paying twice.

1. *Dismissals (the "why")*—Number of reasons, which may lead to termination of the employment agreement by the employer. These include:
   (a) Attitude.
   (b) Performance.
   (c) Frustration of contract.
   (d) Misrepresentation.
   (e) Abandonment of Employment.
   (f) Serious misconduct.
   (g) Redundancies.
2. ***Procedure for dismissal (procedural fairness) (the "how")***—The procedure used will be a final decider as to whether the matter is heard as a personal grievance. It will include substantive matters ("the why") and procedural Fairness ("the how"). The minimum requirements for procedural fairness include:
   - Notice
   - Opportunity
   - Unbiased consideration

Knowledge of rules and penalty—It is not sufficient for the employer to rely on the fact that rules in a disciplinary procedure are in place. There should be full investigation, promptness, consistency, free from biased and predetermination.

Warnings—Generally held expectation that there will be a series of progressive warnings. No statutory requirements regarding warnings. Duration of Progressive Warnings – No fixed rules – reasonableness. Duration of Serious Warnings – suggested timeframe for a serious warning to remain in place is usually for a one year period. Duration of Permanent Warning – remains in place for the duration of employment. Witness – the onus is on the employer to ensure that they have the opportunity to have a witness present.

3. *Disciplinary process—advantages of staff disciplinary code*—The staff disciplinary code should cover the following:
    - Coverage.
    - Administration of policy.
    - Levels of disciplinary action.
    - Examples of types of serious misconduct.

For new employees—a declaration should be signed by the employee and for *existing employees,* the rules, the mean and how they are to apply should be fully explained to employees at a series of briefing sessions. Names of that employee's attending such meetings should be recorded. Employees should receive a copy and have the opportunity to ask questions.

4. *Examples of levels of disciplinary action*—It includes progressive, serious permanent warning, instant dismissal and suspension. Progressive Warnings apply to behaviour considered to be misconduct. Warnings remain live for a specified period of time. *Serious warning* applies to behaviour which falls somewhere between misconduct and serious misconduct. A warning issued at this level remains live for a period specified. Any further warning or misconduct within this period will result in dismissal. *Permanent* warnings at this level are permanent. A repetition of the same type of behaviour will result in instant dismissal. This would apply to instances of serious misconduct. *Instant or Summary dismissal*—The penalty if instant dismissal applies to behaviour called serious misconduct. Suspension of Employment is not itself disciplinary action. Employee must be told the reason and likely duration. Wages/salary are payable.

    Reasons for suspending employment—Inappropriate to allow the worker to continue to attend work until the allegation is either rebutted or established. Investigations may be better served if the worker is not at work. Provides time for employee.

5. ***Format for all levels of disciplinary action***—First we go for preliminary action which includes Informal interviews and the objective of such interviews is to remedy any problems. The employee should be advised that for performance and attitude problems, if there is no improvement within a specified period the formal disciplinary procedure will be invoked.

Prior to formal interview:

(a) Advise employee of allegation and penalty where allegation is established.

(b) Advise employee to discuss matter with the person who may serve as a witness.

(c) Issue a notice or warning of dismissal.

(d) Penalty for repetition and/or any other breach of code.

Apart from this, it is the right to have a witness present at the formal interview. In the formal interview, name of witness should be noted. Employee should be advised of the formal interview process and the roles of the parties. Alleged misconduct and penalty where allegation is established should be advised. Employee should be given opportunity to explain. The written agreement should provide a right to summarily dismiss an employee for serious misconduct.

Summary

Between hiring and firing by far, the greater liability exists in the firing process. However, bad hiring practices can contribute greatly to the need to fire. Consequently, great care needs to be taken to undertake both hires and fires in a proper manner. Prior to making a termination decision, review file and frequently, file reflects satisfactory performance. Maintain accurate and up to date records of employee discipline and counseling will show that the employee was aware of the problem. Don't be emotional during firing. Try to be talkative and not a listener. Be bold enough and reject all his or her arguments. Try to be loud and make your face as you are very angry. Meet in private, with a witness present and prepare a statement prior to this. It is not required to give the employee a reason for termination. If a reason is given, offer only legitimate reasons. Decide in advance whether the employee will be asked to leave immediately or will be allowed to remain during a transition period.

Chapter eleven

HAPPINESS QUOTIENT

Have you thought? Why can't I just be happy? If so, the answer may be staring you right in that mirror. We all have it within us to be happy, but often, we get so caught up in everyday life that we neglect important parts of ourselves that bring us contentment and even joy.

Happiness begins with understanding that we are multi-dimensional creatures operating on four distinct levels: physical, intellectual, emotional and spiritual. When all four dimensions are working in harmony, it is much easier to achieve a state of inner peace.

The Four Dimensions

The 4 Dimensions are equal in importance but impact our lives in very different ways. Learning the purpose and qualities of each helps you understand yourself and others more clearly and gives you insight into, how you can improve your happiness quotient.

Physical Dimension—Health? Play? Pleasure. Tune into how your body feels, when you're happy.

This dimension helps us experience life through our senses, body and the energy around us. Our health, appearance and ability to enjoy play, exhilaration and pleasure reside here. When we nurture our physical being, we are better able to deal with health issues, body image, stress and various stages of life like child-rearing, career building, midlife and retirement. It's also possible to build Happiness memory, just as you build muscle memory by being aware of how your body feels, when you're content, and then making a conscious effort to recapture that feeling.

Intellectual Dimension—Reason- Logic-Performance. Practice quieting your mind each day, focusing on the moment.

This dimension rules our minds and allows us to reason, apply logic, appreciate precision, quality and performance. It also allows us to learn, accumulate knowledge, make rational decisions and bring order to our lives. All of this is good, but many of us spend too much time in our intellectual being. Thinking about work, planning or thinking about the past and the future can overwhelm us. When this happens, it's hard to appreciate the moment and we miss many opportunities to experience happiness through our other dimensions.

Emotional Dimension—Relationships, Self Image. Notice how you feel when you focus on the positive?

Probably, the most challenging of the dimensions, this heartland governs our relationship with ourselves and others. A healthy emotional dimension allows us to be self-assured, confident and understanding of others' Emotions. It also helps us establish and maintain fulfilling relationships. Too often, we dwell on negative emotions and this causes us to block out all the good we can receive from the other dimensions.

Spiritual Dimension—Beliefs-Concepts-Creativity. Allow nature, beauty and creativity to be an everyday part of your life.

While most people think of spiritual as meaning religious, in dimensional terms, it refers to our conceptual selves. It governs our belief systems and inspires creativity and passion. When our spiritual dimension is given its due, we see the world outside ourselves more clearly, open up to creative expression and access the positive characteristics of the other dimensions more easily.

When you allow yourself to play and enjoy the sensory side of life, engage and disengage your mind at the right times, connect with yourself and others and find meaning through beliefs or creativity you will experience a life of greater harmony—a life that is truly priceless.

Positive Attitude

Who is great, a leader or a manager? obviously, a leader because a leader manages emotion of human capital but a manager manages the process designed by the employer to achieve the target. A leader achieves his vision through targeting both heart and brain but a manager achieves target by creating pressure that force subordinate to achieve their target. Remember, a politician and a manager or leader has only one difference. Politician creates problems and a manager or leader is a problem solver. As a manager, your duty is not only to solve problems, but also to reduce the chances of entry that causes problems. We should look first towards the solution of problem. Remember, no one will manufacture a lock without key. Similarly, God won't give problems without solutions.

Without leaps of imagination or dreaming, we lose the excitement of possibilities. Dreaming after all, is a form of planning. Dreams are more valuable than money, because dreams find opportunities. By changing our environment or attitude we will change the way we think. By changing the way we think we will discover new opportunities. Opportunities will allow us to rise in the crowd. Bollywood king Amitabh Bachchan was very much disappointed when his voice got no place in Doordarshan program but he never stopped hammering the opportunity. Now there is no need to explain his success story. World knows him for his positive attititude and putting positive efforts to achieve the dream.

Impact of Negative Thinking

Once upon a time in India, an honest and brave-hearted king was having one successful businessman friend. Friendship of businessman and the king was very famous because of their honesty and diehard friendship. They were so good friends that they were ready to sacrifice life for each other. Businessman always tried to contribute money as gift to the kingdom of his friend to strengthen financial health quite frequently. Similarly, the king always tried to provide more and more facilities to businessman friend so that he can augment his profitability in a greater quantity.

When both the friends were at their pinnacle of success and booming globally, the king thought if my friend dies naturally or through conspiracy, then the kingdom can get more funds to maintain a global image. The businessman also started thinking if the king dies naturally through conspiracy, then the image global business leader can be maintained fearlessly. Both of them met next day and planned to give poison to each other during dinner. Both the friends died unnaturally on the dinner table leaving kingdom and business empire alone for others.

They were very good friends when they were having positive thinking and boomed in their field equally but the moment their negative thinking started, the negative force created the negative impact and finally ruined both of them with bad note forever. Therefore, if you think negative for your friend, automatically your friend will think accordingly. In the mobile era, when we give miss call to any one, similarly the other person can return back miss call simultaneously. In short, negative force and negative thinking always returns back negative force and negative thinking.

Global Survey on Happiness Quotient

It has been proven in global survey of http://www.JewishWorldReview.com that Citizens of Denmark are the happiest people in the world. Puerto Ricans are second, followed by people in Colombia. Residents of the United States rank 16th.

These are the conclusions of the World Values Survey (WVS), published this past July in the journal *Perspectives on Psychological Science*. "Researchers measured happiness [in 97 nations] by simply asking people how happy they were, and how satisfied they were with their lives as a whole."

Based upon survey results, researchers concluded that happiness derives from increased personal freedom, prosperity, and social tolerance. Evidently, it is the acquisition of wealth and the opportunity to use it as one wants without social criticism that makes us happy.

Upon reading these results, Anton Kaiser wondered if something was not rotten in the state of Denmark. The retired career army officer did some research and reported his findings in the *Dakota Voice*: "Denmark, Puerto Rico, and Coloumbia are highly literate democracies (98%, 94%, and 93% literacy, respectively), whose people speak primarily one language (Danish, Spanish, and Spanish, respectively), and who are overwhelmingly

Christian (Lutheran 90%, Catholic 85%, and Catholic 85%, respectively)."

Kaiser wondered why these statistics did not lead researchers to conclude that opportunity, education, common culture, and religious commitment might have been the relevant criteria for producing happiness. But he didn't wonder for very long.

The City of Happiness is Found in the State of Mind

Denmark has topped the WVS list of happiest countries for years. The salient characteristics of Danish culture include legalized abortion, legalized prostitution, legalized drug use, legalized same-sex unions. The majority of Scandinavian countries—namely Norway, Sweden, and Iceland—have similarly "relaxed" social moves, and all rank high on the happiness scale. Of course, it may be mere coincidence that the WVS Association has its headquarters in Stockholm, Sweden.

Kaiser began searching for other factors common to the three highest-ranking countries. He also wondered why Puerto Rico —a province of the United States—had been ranked as a country at all.

"I discovered that Colombia began legalizing abortion in 2006, and in 2007 extended social security and health insurance benefits to same-sex couples, and on April 17, 2008, extended pension benefits to same-sex partners. I then analyzed Puerto Rico and, sure enough, its legislature had just rejected a gay marriage ban in June 2008." It may simply be another coincidence that the WVS rankings came out the following month.

Then again, it may be that the WVS Association is pushing an aggressive social agenda by asserting that happiness is proportional to social permissiveness and inversely proportional to traditional values. One might easily imagine that any addict visiting a den of drugs and prostitution with no fear of legal, social, or economic consequences would rate his own happiness quotient off the charts.

Debunking the Myth of Satisfaction

The sages of the Talmud address the question of happiness with pithy insightfulness: *Who is wealthy? The one who is happy with his portion*. In contrast to the researchers who concluded that wealth produces happiness, the sages observe that happiness is the source of true wealth. One need not look far to discover that many wealthy people endure miserable lives, where many who barely scrape by enjoy lives of joy and fulfillment.

Furthermore, the sages consider a person wealthy because he is *happy* with his portion—not because he is *satisfied*. Satisfaction results from the attainment of a goal and is usually fleeting; often, we experience sharp pangs of melancholy after the initial rush that accompanies success. Conversely, happiness results from striving toward a goal that is both attainable and worthwhile. It is this struggle that makes us truly happy, and a life spent striving for goals of intrinsic value is a life of immeasurable happiness.

Indulging every whim and impulse may prove pleasurable, but such pleasure-seeking will merely distract one from the lack of purpose that would otherwise make life intolerable. One who anesthetizes himself with chemical substances and sensory stimulation may deaden his receptors to the paralyzing pain of futility, but he knows nothing of real happiness.

The Pursuit of Happiness

The holiday of Sukkos, which follows Rosh HaShonah and Yom Kippur, has been described by the sages as *zman simchaseinu*—the season of our happiness. A curious appellation for a holiday characterized by exposure to the cool winds of approaching winter beneath a roof of palm branches and bamboo, without either the comforts of the living room or the amusement of electronic entertainment.

Strictly speaking, there is no prohibition against DVDs, video games, or web-surfing in the *sukkah*, but the spirit of the holiday clearly discourages such distractions. The *sukkah*—even when elaborately decorated—is essentially a structure of austerity, evoking the distant collective memory of our ancestors wandering through the desert with only simple huts for shelter.

Even by the standards of way back then, the thatched roofs of those Jewish dwellings provided little security. Rather, it was the Clouds of Glory, the manifestation of the Divine Presence, that protected the Jews in that foreboding wilderness and kept them safe from the inimical creatures and hostile elements that threatened them on every side. In the absence of material comfort, with only the manna from heaven to sustain them, the Jews experienced the most profound spiritual joy of divine intimacy with their Creator.

For what purpose did the Almighty engineer, the miraculous exodus from Egyptian, hand down His law at Sinai, and lead the Jews toward the land He had promised their forefathers? For this purpose, for them to light up the world with God's glory, to radiate divine wisdom and justice from one end of the earth to the other, to inspire all the nations of the earth to accept the yoke of morality and virtue.

The *sukkah* is a microcosm of the world—unfinished and incomplete. It is here, sitting in his humble *sukkah*, that a Jew today can experience true happiness by rediscovering the unique sense of meaning that comes from being a partner in Creation. After the judgement of Rosh HaShonah and the atonement of Yom Kippur, after struggling to touch the heights of true spiritual awareness, the holiday of Sukkos brings us back down to earth, reminding us that freedom and wealth become the source of genuine happiness when we see them not as ends in themselves but as tools to use in pursuit of a higher purpose.

The Happiness Quotient of Professionals

Five professionals from five different industries share their passion for their work. *Gulf News* Report by Latha Krishnan, Published: April 14, 2008.

Five individuals of different nationalities pursuing five different careers. Living and working in Dubai has been rewarding to them, and they continue to be successful in their chosen fields.

Mustafa Mohammad Hormozi, a UAE national, is Manager of the Al Rumoul branch of Emirates Bank International (EBI). He chose to work in a bank because he believes banking in the UAE is very organized.

"Whatever may be your nationality, you can succeed in a bank and reach the topmost position if you work hard. This is one place where we are appreciated for the work we do. Moreover, banking is internationally relevant, as it is basically the same anywhere in the world and is the most important of all financial concerns," he says.

Hormozi joined EBI 15 years ago as a young retail officer and has grown step by step to become the branch manager. He works in the retail lending section of the bank and enjoys interacting with different kinds of people.

"Working here has enhanced my people skills and has also taught me to live a good life. I have cultivated long-term relationships with some of my clients."

"My work is my passion and I continue to enjoy working here. It is my firm belief that all young UAE nationals should study well and aim to succeed in the profession they choose."

Dr. Philip John, Consultant Psychiatrist at Child Guidance Medical Centre (CGMC) in Sharjah, has 27 years of experience in child and adult psychiatry.

"To me, psychiatry is the most intellectually stimulating of all specialities in medicine. I have always had this fascination to find out what is happening in people's heads.

"I also took it up because I like getting involved in people's problems, and that is what keeps me going even today. One has to be temperamentally suited to become a psychiatrist and I think I have that temperament.

"I like to help people know themselves better and at the same time educate the rest of the world about why some of us are a little different and need understanding," he says.

Psychiatry is undergoing great changes, and Dr. John, who deals with both adult and paediatric psychiatric problems, has kept up-to-date with the advances in the field.

He has special interest in learning, developmental and behavioural disorders in children and has authored numerous papers and articles on the subject.

From time to time, Dr. John conducts workshops and seminars for parents and teachers to make them more aware of the learning problems in children and deal with them in the right manner. He heads a multidisciplinary team at CGMC, which works for the cause of children with learning disorders.

Magda Mohammad is from Egypt and has been teaching at Al Diyafah High School in Dubai for 25 years.

Currently, she is Adviser on Education and Ministry Matters at Al Diyafah, but she started her career teaching Arabic in the same school in September 1982. She has grown into her current position and heads a team of 15 Arabic teachers.

Mohammad says, "Even though I don't actively teach now, I help with the methods of teaching Arabic by reading, researching and drawing ideas from my teachers."

Co-workers and the management of Al Diyafah attest to the sincerity that Mohammad has shown to her job. "I believe in being innovative and using new methods of teaching in class and I encourage teachers to make their classes interesting to students of all ages. We need to make an impact on the lives of the students, and when they come out of school they should at least be able to form a few sentences in Arabic. I like my work so much that it has become second nature to me. The school is now part of me just as I'm part of it and I cannot be away from it for long."

Metin Sayer is a personal trainer and holds a second band black belt in martial arts such as Taekwondo and Hapkido. He is from Australia and was an English teacher till 2004. Always interested in martial arts and fitness, he decided to take it up as a profession to have a more flexible career and give time to his family.

Sayer took a course in personal training from the International Sports Science Association (ISSA) based in the US and also did a fitness trainer course as well as specialist martial arts conditioning course. "In the beginning it was a bit lonely working freelance, but my English teaching skills came in handy in communicating to my clients as to how to keep fit and eat right. Now I enjoy working with them and feel happy and rewarded when I can motivate them to take up proper exercise as a way of life. I have informal chats with my clients during and after the exercises. I'm very glad with the way life has turned out for me as a personal trainer. It also keeps me in shape, as I like to practise what I preach," says Sayer.

Placida Maria Corazon O Contreras came from Philippines to Abu Dhabi in 1990 and started working in Gulf Scientific Corporation (GSC). When the office moved to Jebel Ali in 1993, Contreras also moved, taking up the position of Executive Secretary to the General Manager Nadia Abu Hijleh.

As years passed, she took on more responsibilities as personnel assistant and administration support in different sections of the office. She rose to the position of Office Administrator dealing with administration and human resources at GSC in 1999 and continues to be a loyal and significant part of the company.

"Our Managing Director Dr Wahib Afyouni and Nadia Abu Hijleh trained me to work in different capacities, and that gave me the experience to do my job well. I can summarize my role in the office as a support to the employees as well as the management. I enjoy my job even though I face many challenges dealing with so many people from so many different cultures. Everyday is a challenge with new problems cropping up, but I like finding solutions and love working here," says Contreras.

What is Your Happiness Quotient?

When my son still lived at home, I would ask him, "What's your hunger quotient?". I didn't ask him if he was hungry because it wasn't really a yes or no question. If he was fine I could go on with whatever I was doing. If he was feeling a little peckish, I could finish what I was doing but I needed to start moving towards producing a meal. If he was starving, I needed to stop what I was doing and cook. There was also the question of how much food he needed. Would a snack do? Or a sandwich? Or would only a full meal satisfy?

Happiness is sort of like that. Am I happy? It's a simple question without a simple answer. Ask yourself this question every hour throughout the day and you may come up with a different answer every time you ask. Although most of us are not happy all the time, we seem to feel we deserve to be. Our inability to realize this impossible expectation can lead to unhappiness with our reality. What does it mean to be happy? If you ask one hundred different people what happiness means, you will probably get one hundred different answers. Instead of asking yourself, "Am I happy?", ask, "What's my happiness quotient?". Am I content? Am I feeling productive and purposeful? Am I relieved about a choice I have made or a problem I have solved? Am I slightly down but mostly okay? All of these answers represent different levels of happiness. We need to stop chasing whatever myth of perfect happiness we have created in our minds and find it all around ourselves.

Feeling gratitude for where we are and what we have is the first step on the road towards real true happiness. If you've just lost your home or your job or your mate or you are drowning in debt, feeling happy may seem like an impossible mission. "Fake it till you make it" is an expression frequently used in twelve step programs. While you don't want to "fake it", you should not expect gratitude and ultimately happiness to come without effort. Make a choice in the midst of your sadness or depression to be grateful for something. You may have to work at it, but you will be able to find a target. Perhaps, you just looked out the window and saw some kid playing outside. Instead of allowing your thoughts to segue into how unfair it is that you don't have a child, just enjoy that boy out there laughing. Don't allow yourself to think of anything else for the few minutes he's in your line of sight. Now be grateful for that few minutes. Try this exercise for a few minutes out of every hour. At the end of the day, you'll have several small positive experiences you can reflect on. Perhaps, the day will not look quite so grim.

This gratitude exercise is just exactly that; an exercise. Think of it as an assignment. As you search for a way to complete it each hour, you will become more aware of the good things around you. You only have to *choose* to see them. Life is full of these little moments of happiness. Next try smiling at the people around you. Most of them will smile back. It may seem trite but you'll find it's true; smiling makes you happy. Smile at the woman behind you in the checkout line at the end of an exhausting day. You'll both feel better. Smile and thank the kid who loads your groceries into your car. Smile at the dry cleaner, smile at your neighbour. If someone grimaces in return, smile at someone else. All that smiling and gratitude throughout the day represents more little pockets of happiness.

While smiling and being grateful will not magically find you a new love, make you thinner or reduce your credit card debt, it will make you feel more positive. Positive people have an amazing ability to attract other positive people. Feeling more positive will help you see solutions to your problems. Actively working on your problems will build your self-confidence and allow you to see the temporary nature of whatever is getting you down. Seeing your problems as temporary will decrease their ability to make you unhappy. Into that void will rush…happiness. That happiness might not take the form of Prince Charming whisking you away to his mortgage-free castle but that's okay. Dreams are just dreams. In this moment, if you let it, reality can make you happy. Right now, what is your happiness quotient? What can you do to increase it?

What is Your Blueprint?

Do you wake up everyday bright-eyed and bushy-tailed, ready to take on the world and enjoy the next challenge? Does your level of happiness stay constant regardless of whether you are headed into a hectic work-week or if you are loading up the car for a very much anticipated vacation? Do you remain cheerful, upbeat, and positive regardless of what is going on at any given point in your life?

Most people—if answering honestly would have to say "no" to at least some of those questions. Very few people are able to truly stay in touch with a high level of happiness as they travel down the often bumpy road of life. As much as that point of view can be understood, it still begs the question: What blueprint are you creating for the rest of your life?

- When a very young child does not get their way, and they throw a temper tantrum, do we simply concede and then give that child what they want so that they will stop crying?

- When a spoiled teenager gets into trouble at school or with their friends, do we continue to give them special treatment, thus adding fuel to that fire?
- When a troublesome employee or co-worker makes waves at work, do we bow to their will so that they will stop causing trouble?

The answer to each of those questions is, of course, No. Why, then, do we allow our lives to follow the same self-destructive pattern that we do not encourage in others?

By allowing our level of happiness to be dictated by the circumstances that are going on in our life at any given time, all we are doing is sending ourself, the message that our happiness depends on the circumstances.

Sure, it would seem easier to be happy when you just won a million dollars than when you can't even afford to pay your rent. However, by conceding that fact, you are saying that a certain level of financial abundance is needed in order for you to be happy.

In another example, most people would agree that whenever they are involved in a successful relationship that their relationship status is part of their level of happiness.

Again, that makes sense. However, by saying that your happiness is due—even in part—to your relationship status means that you are also saying that you will always need to be involved in a successful relationship in order to be completely happy.

What about your career status? Does your job or chosen career bring you great joy and satisfaction? If so, then good for you, and keep doing whatever you are doing.

However, what would happen if it all went away? What if your job was eliminated, your company went out of business, or you became physically incapable of doing the work any more? If you need your career status in order to be happy, then what will happen when you retire? A lot of retirees suffer from depression for this very reason.

In each of these examples, the point is not to say that your finances, your relationships, your career, or the other circumstances of your life should not be valued. They absolutely should, and they should help you to experience a wonderful life.

You should take pride in and experience happiness as a result of everything in the world that brings you joy or a feeling of satisfaction. However, true happiness is completely internal, and is something that you should be able to experience regardless of your outer circumstances.

You are a magnificent human being who is incredibly adaptive to the myriad of different circumstances that life will throw at you. Don't sell yourself short by only being happy if your life goes a certain way. Instead, use your power to find great happiness in life.

Globalization has Boosted India's Happiness Quotient: Netizens

22 Sep. 2007, 1445 hrs. IST, Pallavi Shahi, Indiatimes News Network

Someone rightly said, happiness lies in the mind. It is the one thing that is the final destination, no matter what path we tend to take. For centuries, people have wondered what brings happiness and how one can achieve perpetual happiness. So when a survey revealed that Indian youths are the happiest in the world, there was mixed reactions. Letters poured in to ask if young India was, actually, a happy lot?

At the TimesofIndia.com, we decided not to take Young India's happiness for granted. We asked if young Indians are happier because their expectations are fewer, and a strong 58 per cent begged to differ. People were of the opinion that although young Indians were happy, it had little to do with fewer expectations. With the world coming closer, barriers and boundaries have disappeared and it was easier to strike friendships, leading to happiness in some form. Many agreed that with a liberalised economy, the material benefits that young India shares has gone up, considerably, giving them happiness, albeit for a day. But most agreed that happiness had practically nothing to do with fewer expectations.

Amita Jain, writing in from Pune, said, "Nowadays, expectations are high. Material luxuries are easily available and one wants to have more. The world is becoming smaller and more interaction is making people greedier and less satisfied with their lives." Sheela from IT city Bangalore agrees with Amita that "the expectations are growing without limit, day by day, especially the young want to achieve their goal and expectation very early and really faster than ever."

Navneet from Delhi went to the extent of saying that, "If young people have little expectations, then who has high expectations?"

No individual can operate in a vacuum and live in a private utopia, circumstances prevalent in the society do affect the individual either positively or negatively. So, it is but obvious that the present government, the policies, the malpractices all go a long way in either making the youth a happy or a sad lot.

Reiterating this chain of thought, Krishna from Hyderabad, says that, "Majority of young Indians are unhappy because their dreams are not taking proper structure because of poverty and the system of reservations. Students mainly in rural background can't even express their problems." Aanchal from Gurgaon opines that, "neither the young Indian nor the grown-ups are happy in India. Youngsters are busy on a 24×7 schedule and elders are sad seeing their plight".

Sunita Jindal from New Delhi said, "In fact, the situation is just the opposite it. Young Indians' expectations are not met by their parents and society. They are always in a worry and feel insecure due to unfulfilment of their expectations." Tarun Khurana from Bangalore said, "First of all, young Indians are not happy and even if some of them are, it is because they are not ambitious at all."

The lobby that believes that due to a good number of reasons the happiness quotient has actually gone up is packed up with a lot of zeal. Better quality of life, greater opportunities, the globalization effect which has brought in the best of the entire world right into our homes are reasons that have gone a long way in making life a happy experience for scores of young people in India today.

Anjali, writing in all the way from London, said, "Compared to the youth world over, Indian children are brought up to be achievement-oriented. The Indian youth is ambitious and hard working." Sunil from Fiji agrees, "Young Indians are happy because they have the chance to achieve their dreams and fulfil expectations," he says.

S.P. Singal from USA said, "they are happier because they have resources to meet their expectations which per se are higher than the earlier generation's. They earn more and have will and the capacity to spend more. They have done the country proud and are putting our cunning politicians to shame."

For Mumbaikar B.P. Dixit, Indian youth "have started realising their worth and cherishing it. They feel secure and are hence, a happy lot". Ankur from Gurgaon added, "Young Indians believe in enjoying their lives with whatever they have. Their expectations are not limited, they are ambitious and at the same time, they are satisfied, they enjoy whatever they have at present and dream for the future."

Some people also believed that the amount of freedom enjoyed by the youth today is far more than their predecessors and with fewer restrictions the youth have been privileged enough to see their dreams take shape. They have also been able to strive hard to achieve them. Whatever said and done, happiness for the Indian youth has been a mixed bag.

The Happiness Quotient All About

I believe that one of the most important aspects of deliberately using the Law of Attraction and deliberately creating the life that you want is to be happy and joyful, to really feel good. When you are full of happiness and joy and your heart is full, you are open to the inspirations and the gentle nudging of the Universe. You hear the call.

But when you are stressed out or complaining and unhappy, it's almost like you have turned off your cell phone in a packed sports arena, either the call doesn't ring or when the call comes in you can't hear it but for the jangle of the noise in your own heart and mind.

My husband has always said to just "Be Happy". No matter what happens life is precious and you should just "Be Happy". He's easy going and even-tempered and he is a happy man. We have a great life.

A few years ago we watched a Barbara Walters Special where she interviewed major religious leaders throughout the world. As Barbara interviewed the Dalai Lama, he said "Be Happy just Be Happy". I have to say that of all of the religious leaders from all over the world that she interviewed that night, the Dalai Lama impressed me the most. He absolutely radiated joy. It was palpable even through the T.V.

Now there will be people who will say that he's happy because of all kinds of reasons that they just don't have but the fact of the matter is that anyone can be happy. Happy is an inside job. It never comes from material things or a lack of challenges or because the Sun was shining on the day you were born. You decide how happy you are going to be. In fact, you are a wise man if you are familiar with the following words:

"Most folks are about as happy as they make their minds up to be."

Abraham Lincoln

A while back, I wrote an article about *Happiness*. I gave some tangible tips on how to use the emotions and feelings of Gratitude, Love and Awe to help you find the happiness inside of you. All three of those emotions can assist you in finding your own happiness. All three of those emotions can feel so wonderful and so exhilarating and so intoxicating and when you focus on that wonderful feeling, happy is a side effect.

But you really need to feel it. Deep in your heart and soul nothing feels as good as being totally Grateful, totally Loving, and totally in Awe. Gratitude, Love and Awe are the most magnificent gifts you can give to yourself.

Be thankful and be grateful. Be loving and be joyful. Find the Awe of Life.

Practice these things and you will not have to pursue happiness because you will have found it within yourself.

Be Happy and Make Others Happy

Life laughs at you when you are unhappy
Life smiles at you when you are happy
Life salutes you when you make others happy
So be happy and make others happy.

Don't compare yourself with any one in this world
If you compare, you are insulting yourself.

Every successful person has a painful story
Every painful story has a successful ending
Accept the pain and get ready for success
Then you will be happy and make others happy.

If you miss an opportunity don't fill the eyes with tears
It will hide another better opportunity in front of you.

Easy is to judge the mistakes of others
Difficult is to recognize our own mistakes
It is easier to protect your feet with slippers
Than to cover the earth with carpet.

No one can go back and change a bad beginning
But anyone can start now and create a successful ending.

Be bold when you loose and be calm when you win
Heated gold becomes ornament
Beaten copper becomes wires
Depleted stone becomes statue
So the more pain you get in life you become more valuable.

Mistakes are painful when they happen
But year's later collection of mistakes is called experience
Which leads to success.

D.C. Jain

Founder of AKUMS Drugs &
Pharmaceuticals Ltd.

Divine Blessings

When I asked God for strength
He gave me different situations to face.

When I asked God for brain and brawn
He gave me puzzles in life to solve.

When I asked God for happiness
He showed me some unhappy people.

When I asked God for wealth
He showed me how to work hard.

When I asked God to favours
He showed me opportunities to work hard.

When I asked God for peace
He showed me how to help others.

God gave me nothing I wanted
He gave me everything I needed.

Swami Vivekanand

Summary

In the fastest moving world, every person is busy and it is very hard to spare sometime even for family event celebration. Professionals want to invest more of their time in the office for better career growth. But on the other hand, family members want more time with the family. Working executives are always sandwiched and remain tense. What to do and what not to do is a common question for working executive nowadays. If you will make wife happy then boss gets angry and vise versa. Surely stress will decrease your talent and efficiency level day by day. Forgetfulness and mood irritation will be common symptoms with you. If you won't save yourself with this menace, then it will hard to accomplish your vision, mission, objective and target. This situational mismanagement sometime leads to suicidal tendency mostly in the case of entrepreneurs and managerial level.

Make a trend of morning walk or evening whatever suit you but do something for your good health. You can do *yoga* morning and evening as it is telecast everyday on *Aastha* channel globally. Work while you are working and enjoy when you are with family. Receive professional calls in the office timing and receive less personal calls while you are in the office.

Listen to your wife and kids everyday or at least once in week. Funda of time management is not to managing time but to managing schedule according to time. No one can manage time because there are 24 hours in one day. Hence, our schedule should be well planned in advance for better management.

Listen to your subordinate about his personal and professional rift which is common everywhere and try to solve them. You devote sometime in solving others problems and be problem solver. The moment you face challenge or problem, try to listen and understand the problem. You feel fortunate enough and take up problems as an opportunity. Now onwards, don't say problem, say problem, an opportunity.

Chapter twelve

METAMORPHOSIS IN HRM

Human resource management is undergoing a massive transformation that will change career paths in as yet uncertain ways. Employers are placing greater emphasis on business acumen and are automating and outsourcing many administrative functions, which will force many HR professionals to demonstrate new skills and compete for new, sometimes unfamiliar roles.

Job titles and functions will likely remain in flux for some time but the standard niches—such as HR generalist and benefits specialist—will become less common and less important, giving way over time to new ones such as HR financial analyst.

In the fastest moving world of internet, mobile, laptop and palmtop, it is really very hard to spare time for skills upgradation. But Human resource practitioners who master the business skills need for demanding new roles will take flight as HR trend goes under future metamorphosis.

Now we are living in global village and the positive impact of globalization can be seen in every country. Every businessman wants to expand wings globally and therefore they follow the global trend and not the stereotyped traditional trend. If you are a profit center for the organization then no matter what do you demand salary and compensation, you will be honoured and obliged. Today's businessman is ready to invest on those who has capability of entrepreneurship. Through the development of entrepreneurship, businessman can get desired profit without getting busy and taking less tension.

D.C. Jain, CMD of Akums Drugs & Pharmaceuticals Limited gave two division of generic marketing across India to Mr. Bhatia as test marketing on profit sharing basis without making any investment and apart from this Mr. Jain has promised to pay full salary till six months. Mr. Bhatia earned profit from second months, 10 times of his monthly salary package. Mr. Jain has given similar type of opportunity to one more known sales manager on profit sharing basis without a single penny investment. This is how one businessman has developed competent employees into entrepreneur. Similarly, those who aspire to leadership roles within the profession will have to become more strategic, more proactive, more involved in the overall business of their employer.

But there is an upside to this upheaval. HR people who develop business competencies and embrace the new roles—in the process redefining themselves and their profession—can aspire to greater and much more rewarding careers than were possible for HR people a generation ago.

Human resource management is purely a knowledge based industry and it is the most vital nerve centre of any company. Now, most of the companies have its own full-fledged HR department and offering very lucrative package, but earlier this department was taking care by marketing people only. This domain has really taken a paradigm shift in recent few years in India and globe. Lot new terminologies, concepts and theories have been introduced to augment profitability of the organization by improving efficiency of the employees.

HR professionals who put the business first and foremost are really going to get the desired pay package and compensation. The most successful HR people will be those who think from the outside in, "When we talk about being strategic, we mean thinking from the customer back to the organization." In this new HR era, professionals are expected to know the business well enough to align human capital with business needs, either developing the needed talent or going outside the organization to get it. HR is proactive. HR goes looking for problems to solve. HR doesn't just have a seat at the table; HR helps set the agenda.

There are lots of challenges in HR profession. Do you think whatever you have studies in the college is more than sufficient to tackle the practical HR queries? Exactly not, the amount of skills and knowledge you have will help you but you should be vibrant and proactive to learn new thing perfectly. What exactly will be the desirable HR jobs in the next decade and beyond? How does HR get there from here? And how can HR people obtain the education and training they need to secure and keep those jobs?

HR as a Career

Like every profession, HR profession has got tremendous face lift and in present scenario there are lots of job with lucrative salary package. Second points which obviously comes to every professional that HR duty is very flexible and it requires only 8 hours. Most of the companies offer 5 days working. There is no target sort of things linked to this profession and this is totally an office job. Most of the females join this profession because they want to work and this is the only "decent job" in corporate world which, gives them respect and dignity. They don't want to join "field jobs" (Marketing). This is the only profession where time suits them…as per the family needs and restrictions. What more you need, you are getting good salary; flexible office timing and you are taking care of your family as per your plan and desire.

HR Challenges

Old days and bad days for HR personnel have gone and now HR people have got a paradigm shift in terms of job responsibility, job opening, salary package and profit generation for the organization. Now retention of employee is one of the bigger problems for small and medium size companies. It is directly linked with the globalization and boom in jobs market especially due to lots of job opening into banking sectors, life insurance sectors, call centers, telecommunication sectors and many more sectors.

HR Practice in Past

Those who are not working they still have so many myths about this profession. They think that this is a very easy going job and doesn't require MBA qualification. Even a graduate can do this job. "Oh! ho! HR job is that Na…which involves filling and maintaining so many forms, and settling the claims". These days HR is a Synonym of recruitment. Tell anybody that you are in HR and they will reply, "Oh, ok so you are a recruiter". But they have underrated HR job? It is because HR responsibility was taken by simply marketing people and accounting people. Marketing people was also involved in conducting interview, manpower planning and recruitment and preparation of salary was covered by accounts fellow.

HR Practice Today

Only five years back from now specialization in HR was not so demanding because every company was used to appoint one or two HR people or marketing manager was taking extra HR responsibility. The human resource marketplace is a highly competitive and fragmented industry that is poised for enormous growth in the next 10 years as companies and countries around the world invest in their human resources infrastructure.

Image of HR Profession in the public or in the corporate world is very good and we are really doing much to improve the same. Frankly speaking, HR professionals have the top corporate secrets and much more associated with the organization in comparision with the other employees. I feel sad when people ask queries like: What is the difference between HRM & HRD? What is the concept of CTC? What is the difference between Offer-Letter and Appointment-Letter? How much amount should be deducted for P.F. & E.S.I. from salary? How many leaves we should give to our employees? How to calculate attrition rate or rate per hire? What components of salary are taxable? And many more questions that play a pivotal role and that are directly linked with image of HR professionals.

It is not necessary that you should have third eyes like "Chankaya"; clever like "Birbal" and visionary like Lord Krishna (A mythological character), but you should have a sharp eye for recognizing the talent, talent identification, talent management and talent development. You should be an excellent motivator and can motivate any person to get best out of him in a stipulated time period. You should have a talent to motivate and inspire a non-performer in such a way that over a period of time that person gets counted in the high-performers in your organization and starts getting rewards for his performance.

You are great in crisis management. If there is any incident or accident in the organization; if there is any rumour in the organization or any crisis, you can ensure that a minimum possible damage is caused, keeping in mind the interests of the organization and its people but remember one thing decision should always be in favour of the organization. You have to rule on emotion of the employees and always try to show them achievable dream plan.

You should design career map linked with performance, attitude, skills and knowledge. You don't think from your heart and understand the way people think. You are a problem solver and solve both personal and professional problem of employee so that they can concentrate more on assigned job. It is important to note that when you are hiring people be smiling, talk less and listen more but when you are firing don't let them explain, talk more, don't listen and try to change your face with more aggression. Be caring, smiling but don't be sharing.

Future of Outsourcing Explosion

With outsourcing becoming such a huge business, should early-career HR professionals consider going to work for an HR outsourcing firm? "It's an attractive career proposition for many people." It allows a worker to become familiar with several businesses that the outsourcing firm services, not just one. At an outsourcing organization, "you're providing services to real paying customers. A lot of people have seen tremendous boosts in their careers."

These changes will take place in different ways, and at different rates, in various organizations. However, they are being accelerated by the furious phenomenon of HR outsourcing, which was a roughly $60 billion business in 2001 and could soon top $100 billion per year. Simply put, the economies of scale allow an outside firm to do most transactional HR functions more cheaply than the organization itself. What started with a trickle in payroll outsourcing during the 1980s and 1990s has become a flood, with some large corporations moving toward "total HR outsourcing" to vendors such as Exult Inc. Exult has signed billions of dollars worth of long-term HR contracts with large multinational corporations and is being challenged by other aggressive outsourcing firms.

"The market is huge. And the market has not been fully understood". Business outsourcing "is where the Internet was five years ago." Outsourcers, and many of their clients, say that the big upside of outsourcing routine HR functions is that it frees HR to do more strategic work within the organization. But taking advantage of that opportunity requires the right background. A master's degree in business administration is ideal, but an undergraduate business degree or community college courses can help.

While business knowledge is a significant way to advance the profession and the careers of individual professionals, certification programs can help as well. Many HR professionals, organizations and academics note that current HR professionals and young entrants can gain a competitive edge through certification. "In a good economy or a bad economy, people look for ways to differentiate themselves" and one of the best is professional certification.

Inculcating Talent in HR Managers

In many cases, HR professionals will need to start small in their efforts to demonstrate hands-on competency in business matters. "Do this at several levels—front-line supervisors; midlevel supervisors; senior management—even if you're a fly on the wall. Then get a mentor at that higher level," suggests Herman. "Find out what they see as the challenges in five years."

This internal consultant role could be the trickiest. Technology will enable line managers to lessen their dependence on HR departments by handling recruitment, salary reviews, succession planning and other functions at their computers. But working with line managers who welcome regular collaboration with seasoned HR professionals can be one of the most effective roles for HR in the coming decades, say the experts. That will be particularly true for HR professionals who can master the numbers, the holy grail of HR statistics demonstrating which practices generate profits.

"We are on the cusp of measuring things in human capital and human resources that have never been measured before". "People with a strong sense of empirical methods will distinguish themselves." "Top executives are going to be turning to HR" to set financial baselines for recruitment, training, turnover and the like-not content to accept benchmarks or best practices from other organizations that might not apply equally in theirs.

In many organizations, there will be a struggle to update the image of the HR profession and the practitioner. "To change your image, don't be afraid to take on a challenge". Eventually, "you'll be invited to the table", he says, "and you can demonstrate your value to management once you're there".

"HR people need to be very savvy in terms of the relationships they strike up". "Build internal relationships" not only to learn the business but also to improve your image. "If you can push interviewing and hiring out to the line managers, that's great", says Ford. "Where the glory goes is not an issue," she says, because the line people you help will know the value of your contributions. HR's image has been worse than it should be because "some HR people have continued to be bogged down in administration, preventing them from demonstrating the value they can provide."

Career Path

Salary depends strongly on the type of organization as well as the HR specialty. The range of salary package mentioned below is not restricted to any particular management college. Actually it is an average of all management colleges. The highest paid salary in India is IIM (Indian Institute of Management) graduate. The highest paying HR specialty, according to Bureau of Labour Statistics, is training and development, and the lowest paying is employment and recruiting. It is noteworthy salary package also depends on your involvement and performance. Up to entry level you behave like an employee but from midlevel you start behave like an employer and finally, at senior level you thinking will match with employer and your thinking, behavior and attitude will be similar to your employer. If you gradually change positively like this, then you will decide your salary package without any hesitation. Wipro has recently fired one of his executive who was getting IR-8,00,00,000 and he was highest paid executive in India. In senior level you should perform with six sigma quality (Error free) and organizational benefits should be above all things in this world.

Entry Level: Roles entail Benefits specialist, placement specialist, negotiations specialist. Qualification required is degree or diploma in MBA with HR and experience should be 0-4 years. Course work should tie in to speciality: statistics and economics for benefits, social and behavioral sciences for negotiations. Salary varies according to speciality and the present salary package in India is IR-20,000-50,000 and in international market it ranges in between $31,000-$45,000.

Mid Level: Roles include Compensation manager, hiring manager, labour relations manager, training supervisor. Qualification required is HR or general business masters or MBA, with associated post-graduate speciality in training, excellent people skills and excellent communication skills. Rest all entry-level requirements along with 5-10 years. Current salary package in India is IR-50,000-1,00,000 and in international market it ranges in between $49,000-$90,000.

Senior Level: Major roles or designations are director of employee benefits, employee relations director, director of human resources development. All mid-level requirements with post-graduate speciality course work, multi-faceted, creative problem solving skills and confident decision-maker. Current salary package in India is IR-1,00,000-2,00,000 and in international market it ranges in between $90,000-$120,000.

Future Prospects of HR Practice

Great leaders and practitioners think about what HR professionals must learn to fulfill the demanding new roles that will await them in the future. Employees and employers would be more and more impatient and tensed in day-to-day life due to advancement in living style. We are more or less living in a nuclear family but in days to come we would follow pure nuclear living pattern. Therefore, managing human emotion will be a challenging assignment and that will require lots of patience and skills.

"HR professionals have to examine their own background and what they are comfortable doing." Regardless of whether they aspire to be on the cutting edge of human capital management or to remain in their current niche, "if they don't execute the basics of HR flawlessly, they won't succeed". HR professionals need to motivate themselves to keep up with changes in the profession, not waiting for their HR colleagues to join them: "Most of your peers will not do this. You are driving your own career. Do not depend on anyone else to drive your career."

We are living in global village and in time to come, we should be a perfect mix of multilingual, multicultural and multiskilled to tackle the situation aggressively without an error. Talent is honoured in every industry today and so will in the future. Talent manager would be responsible for finding, developing and keeping the best and the brightest workers to meet the needs of the organization. He or she will manage learning and succession planning, moving people through the talent pipeline. We would be more competent in controlling cost to the company of every employees and functions or programs which do not add value should be eliminated.

Future Demanding HR Specialist

For sometime now, HR has been a profession in transition—and the evolution is far from over. Having been exhorted to be "strategic" and learn the business, do you know how to get there from where you are now? To put a finer point on what being strategic means for your career. Leaders and practitioners think about what human resource professionals must learn to fulfill the demanding new roles that will await them in the future.

The talent manager—Talent is honoured in every industry. Talent manager is responsible for finding, developing and keeping the best and the brightest workers to meet the needs of the organization. He or she will manage learning and succession planning, moving people through the talent pipeline.

The internal consultant—This person helps spread HR competencies through the organization, empowering line managers to recruit, interview, hire and retain the talent that they need while counseling the managers on crucial legal and ethical matters such as disability and age discrimination laws.

The CFO for HR—This number cruncher can apply the metrics to demonstrate the inherent economic value of HR and to analyze the cost-effectiveness of various practices HR proposes or implements: How much do certain employees contribute to the bottom line? How much does the right training help the business? Which functions or programs do not add value and should be eliminated?

The vendor manager—He or she determines which functions can be handled better and less expensively outside the organization. This professional monitors quality and costs, stays on top of trends in this business, and maintains a close working relationship with outsourcing firms and other vendors.

The self-service leader—This person works with internal and outside information technology specialists to establish and run web-based portals for many automated functions, such as benefits and pension administration that employees can access from their desktop computers.

In these and other possible HR jobs of the future, HR leaders "have got to create a product at the right price and with certain characteristics that the buyer needs." The product is the contribution of the workforce to specific business goals.

Future Demanding HR Skills for Survival

In a global arena, HR professionals should be multilingual, multicultural and multiskilled. If you want to practice in United Arab Emirates, Arabic lingual will be preferred and if you want to work in India, it is better you should know Hindi or Urdu. "People are finally realizing that, to be successful in HR, you need more than HR knowledge." The primary missing link is knowing business and its language. "There's a technical skill set and a strategic skill set that you're going to need to survive," "You've got to be able to put forward a business case as strong as any other put before management". For HR to make a breakthrough, it has to focus on cost," and if you can impact labour cost, you've made a real bottom-line impact.

Guideline for Future HR Manager

It is noteworthy "HR people have to be true believers" that the business comes ahead of advocacy for employees. "You have to be recognized first as a contributor to the business. The business mindset 'is not something that is just needed to win. It's needed to play' in the new world of HR. There are all kinds of ways you can have a direct cause-and-effect impact, and you can go from there to a bigger, strategic role."

The ultimate goal of this transformation of HR is "the integration of HR becoming good business people and business people becoming good HR people." If you want to be business associate, "You've got to bring something to the table. You will be welcomed by the employer." Remember to earn money—two things are required innovation and marketing. If you have some business project or plan, then you should have guts to convince your employer.

Go out to lunch with other people in the organization—not just HR people. "Everybody in the organization should have a line of sight between their goals and those of the business." It is very good if "You know finance, sales strategy, market strategy, technology, staffing and training needs, managing change, managing culture. You have to develop credibility".

In some organizations, "it's going to be very difficult" persuading top management that you've up your skills through business education and can take on new responsibilities. "The process will take some time, some dedication."

"There's going to be a lot of HR people feeling like victims," because "The world is changing around them." HR professionals need to motivate themselves to keep up with changes in the profession, not waiting for their HR colleagues to join them: "Most of your peers will not do this. You are driving your own career. Do not depend on anyone else to drive your career".

Jobs will still be available for many who want to stay roughly where they are today. "HR professionals have to examine their own background and what they are comfortable doing". Regardless of whether they aspire to be on the cutting edge of human capital management or to remain in their current niche, "if they don't execute the basics of HR flawlessly, they won't succeed".

Summary

Respect, power, authority and autonomy of HR people always remains top in the employee group and they are treated just next to employer. Human resource department is the most vital nerve centre of any company and keeps all corporate secrets. HR professional should have very good amount of patience and farsightedness to keep up balance in all fronts. Major HR challenges are turnover cost and inculcating loyalty in employees. HR as a profession is very exciting and this professional provides an opportunity to keep abreast with what happens in HR fraternity. Sometimes, from now marketing managers were used to involve in HR practices as well but now trend has totally changed. Now HR professional has taken a paradigm shift in terms of image, responsibilities, offerings and job security. In most of the organizations, HR hierarchy is very flat and it starts from entry level or executive level, middle level or manager level and finally senior level or vice president. Pay package is very lucrative and you can get if you have better talent, patience, experience and confidence. The crux of success is based on good career mapping and well in advance.

Chapter thirteen

HR CALCULATION

Human resource personnel have got a paradigm shift in terms of job responsibility, job opening, salary package and profit generation for the organization. It is directly linked with the globalization and boom in jobs market especially due to lots of job opening into banking sectors, life insurance sectors, call centers, telecommunication sectors and many more sectors. Therefore, retention of employee has now become one of the biggest problems for small and medium size companies.

Undoubtedly, Human resource personnel have the top corporate secrets and much more associated with the organization incomparision with the other employees. It is very good when people ask queries with human resource executives like: What is the difference between HRM & HRD? What is the concept of CTC? What is the difference between Offer-Letter and Appointment-Letter? How much amount should be deducted for P.F., P.P.F., gratuity and E.S.I.? How many leaves we should give to our employees? How to calculate attrition rate or rate per hire? What components of salary are taxable? And many more questions that play a pivotal role and that are directly linked with image of Human resource personnel.

Measuring ESI

ESI is Employee State Insurance and it is used for the benefit of the employee and if the gross salary of the employee is <= 10K, than it is applicable on the employee and 1.75 per cent amount will be deducted from the gross salary. One can get the medical benefit from the ESIC.

ESI = (1.75% of employee's share and 4.75% of employer's share on total salary)

In addition to necessities of food, clothing, housing, etc., man needs security in times of physical and economic distress consequent upon sickness, disablement etc. The Employees' State Insurance Scheme is an integrated measure of Social Insurance embodied in the Employees' State Insurance Act and is designed to accomplish the task of protecting 'employees' as defined in the Employees' State Insurance Act against the hazards of sickness, maternity, disablement and death due to employment injury and to provide medical care to insured persons and their families. The Scheme covers employees of non-seasonal power-using factories employing 10 or more persons. There is, however, a built-in provision for its extension to other establishments or classes of establishments, industrial, commercial, agricultural or otherwise. The Scheme has been progressively extended to cover employees in non-power using factories employing 20 or more persons and to commercial establishments.

How does the Employees' State Insurance Scheme Assist You?

The dependence of an individual on cash income is a characteristic feature of modern economy. An interruption of money income even for a small period is, therefore, a hardship; a prolonged loss of income is indeed a catastrophe. By coming forward to provide health protection and income maintenance in a series of oft-experienced contingencies like sickness, maternity, disablement and death due to employment injury, the Employees' State Insurance Scheme tends to ameliorate your economic anxiety and to be a friend in need and distress.

Why is it Called a Health Insurance Scheme?

The Employees' State Insurance Scheme performs a dual role; by providing assistance in kind (medical care) it tries to restore your health and working capacity and by assistance in cash (cash benefit) it tries to sustain you when your income is interrupted. With a better and facile health protection, greater vitality, and assurance of income-maintenance in times of need, it makes you every inch a better, a healthier, secure worker and therefore, a happier man. The assistance comes to you not as an act of benevolence but in virtue of an acquired right.

Who Administers the Employees' State Insurance Scheme?

The Employees' State Insurance Scheme is administered by a corporate body called the Employees' State Insurance Corporation (ESIC), which has members representing Employees, Employers, the Central Government, State Governments, Medical Profession and the Parliament. The Director General is the Chief Executive Officer of the Corporation and is also an ex-officio member of the Corporation. The other bodies at the national level are the Standing Committee (a representative body of the Corporation) and the Medical Benefit Council, a specialized body which advises the Corporation on administration of Medical Benefit. At the Regional and Local levels, the Regional Boards and Local Committees have been constituted. There is, thus, an association of interests and interest groups at all levels.

ESIC is the trustee of the interests of the insured persons. It discharges its obligations and duties through a net-work of Regional Offices and Local Offices, Hospitals and Dispensaries spread over the entire country.

Whom does the Scheme Protect?

The Scheme protects all "employees" engaged on a monthly remuneration not exceeding Rs. 6500 in a factory/establishment to which the Act applies. Persons employed for wages on any work connected with the administration of the factory or establishment or any part, department or branch thereof or purchase of raw materials, or distribution or sale of the product of a factory or establishment are also covered. Mines, Railway Running Sheds, Naval, Military and Air Force Workshops and specified seasonal factories are excluded. The scheme also provides full medical cover to the dependants of insured persons. In the event of death of an insured person due to employment injury dependants become eligible to cash benefit.

Where do Employees' State Insurance Funds come from?

The Employees' State Insurance Funds are primarily built out of employer's contribution and employees contribution payable monthly as a fixed percentage of wages.

Measuring EPF

The Employee Provident Fund, or provident fund as it is normally referred to, is a retirement benefit scheme that is available to salaried employees. PF is applicable if the basic salary of the employee is up to Rs. 6500 and above Rs. 6500 basic salary it is optional for the employee, 12 per cent amount deducted towards PF from the basic+DA and this amount goes to PF authority.

Under this scheme, a stipulated amount (currently 12%) is deducted from the employee's salary and contributed towards the fund. This amount is decided by the government. The employer also contributes an equal amount to the fund.

However, an employee can contribute more than the stipulated amount if the scheme allows for it. So, let's say the employee decides 15 per cent must be deducted towards the EPF. In this case, the employer is not obligated to pay any contribution over and above the amount as stipulated, which is 12 per cent.

PF = (12% of employee's share and 13.61% of employer's share on basic)

The Employees' Provident Funds and Miscellaneous Provisions Act, provides for compulsory contributory fund for the future of an employee after his retirement or for his dependents in case of his early death. It extends to the whole of India except the State of Jammu and Kashmir.

Who are Covered Under it?

Every factory engaged in any industry specified in Schedule 1 in which 20 or more persons are employed, every other establishment employing 20 or more persons or class of such establishments which the Central Government may notify, any other establishment so notified by the Central Government even if employing less than 20 persons.

Who are the Contributors Towards the Fund?

As per amendment dated 22.9.1997, both the employee and the employer contribute to the fund at the rate of 12 per cent of the basic wages, dearness allowance and retaining allowance, if any, payable to employees per month. The rate of contribution is

10 per cent in the case of some establishments which are mentioned in the Act. What is the interest rate?

The rate of interest is fixed by the Central Government in consultation with the Central Board of trustees, Employees' Provident Fund every year during March/April, so it can vary from year to year. The rate is yet to be finalised for this year with the EPF Board toying with an 8 per cent and the Unions demanding a 9.5 per cent. Can you withdraw from the Provident Fund?

The entire amount of the PF along with the accumulated interest can be withdrawn by an employee on retirement after attaining the age of 55 years. However, in cases of termination, retirement on account of permanent disablement, on migration from India for a permanent settlement abroad and in cases of retrenchment, the amount can be withdrawn before the completion of 55 years. A person can also withdraw 90 per cent of the amount a year before his or her retirement.

What are the Special Cases Where You can Withdraw from PF?

In case a person is going for a job change, his Provident Fund account can be transferred for further continuation in the next office. For this, the concerned person has to fill the Transfer Application in Form 13 and submit it to the concerned Provident Fund office. If a person is switching to an organization which does not come under this act, he can receive all the accumulated money which is in his PF account till now. In cases of untimely death of the person, his nominees receive the same.

Measuring PPF

The Public Provident Fund has been established by the central government. You can voluntarily decide to open one. You need not be a salaried individual; you could be a consultant, a freelancer or even working on a contract basis. You can also open this account if you are not earning.

Any individual can open a PPF account in any nationalized bank or its branches that handle PPF accounts. You can also open it at the head post office or certain select post offices.

The minimum amount to be deposited in this account is Rs. 500 per year. The maximum amount you can deposit every year is Rs. 70,000. The return on investment in EPF is 8.5 per cent per annum and in PPF is 8 per cent per annum.

How Long is the Money Blocked in EPF & PPF?

The amount accumulated in the PF is paid at the time of retirement or resignation. Or, it can be transferred from one company to the other if one changes jobs. In case of the death of the employee, the accumulated balance is paid to the legal heir.

The accumulated sum in PPF is repayable after 15 years. The entire balance can be withdrawn on maturity, that is, after 15 years of the close of the financial year in which you opened the account. It can be extended for a period of five years after that. During these five years, you earn the rate of interest and can also make fresh deposits.

What is the Tax Impact?

The amount you invest in EPF is eligible for deduction under the Rs. 1,00,000 limit of Section 80C. If you have worked continuously for a period of five years, the withdrawal of PF is not taxed. If you have not worked for at least five years, but the PF has been transferred to the new employer, then too it is not taxed. The tenure of employment with the new employer is included in computing the total of five years. If you withdraw it before completion of five years, it is taxed. But if your employment is terminated due to ill-health, the PF withdrawal is not taxed.

The amount you invest in PPF is eligible for deduction under the Rs. 1,00,000 limit of Section 80C. On maturity, you pay absolutely no tax.

What if You Need the Money?

If you urgently need the money, you can take a loan on your PF. You can also make a premature withdrawal on the condition that you are withdrawing the money for your daughter's wedding (not son or not even yours) or you are buying a home. To find out the details, you will have to talk to your employer and then get in touch with the EPF office (your employer will help you out with this).

You can take a loan on the PPF from the third year of opening your account. So, if the account is opened during the financial year 1997-98, the first loan can be taken during financial year 1999-2000 (the financial year is from April 1 to March 31).

The loan amount will be up to a maximum of 25 per cent of the balance in your account at the end of the first financial year. In this case, it will be March 31, 1998. You can make withdrawals during any one year from the sixth year. You are allowed to withdraw 50 per cent of the balance at the end of the fourth year, preceding the year in which the amount is withdrawn or the end of the preceding year whichever is lower. For example, if the account was opened in 1993-94 and the first withdrawal was made during 1999-2000, the amount you can withdraw is limited to 50 per cent of the balance as on March 31, 1996, or March 31, 1999, whichever is lower. If the account extended beyond 15 years, partial withdrawal up to 60 per cent of the balance you have at the end of the 15 year period is allowed.

The Better Option?

In both cases, contributions get a deduction under Section 80C and the interest earned is tax free. Having said that, PF scores over PPF in two aspects. In the case of PF, the employer also contributes to the fund. There is no such contribution in case of PPF. The rate of interest on PF is also marginally higher (currently 8.50%) than interest on PPF (8%).

Measuring Pension

What is Pension Fund?

The Employees' Provident Fund and Miscellaneous Provisions Act, 1952 was amended in 1971 and was renamed as the "The Employees' Provident Fund and Family Pension Act, 1952". It was felt that in case of premature death of the worker or a permanent disablement the Provident Fund was too less an amount to support him and his family. This led to an introduction of another social security benefit in the name of pension.

After the last amendment in 1995, Employees' Pension Scheme-95 came into effect from 16.11.95. The assets and liabilities of the erstwhile Pension Fund were transferred and merged with the new Pension Fund. The benefits and entitlements to the members under the old scheme remain protected and continued under the new Employees' Pension Scheme-95. The existing members (as on 16.11.95) of the Provident Fund who did not opt for joining the erstwhile Employees' Family Pension Scheme-1971 and the beneficiaries under the erstwhile Employees' Family Pension Scheme-1971 in case of death/exit occurring between 1.4.93 and 15.11.95 have option to join the new scheme.

Who are Covered Under the Pension Scheme?

All the members of the ceased Family Pension Scheme and anyone who joins a covered establishment (it has 20 or more than 20 people working) on or after 16.11.95 has to compulsorily join this scheme. But his salary range should be higher than Rs. 6500 per month at the date of appointment.

How do You Contribute Towards Pension Fund?

An employer contributes to the pension at the rate of 8.33 per cent of the employees' salary. The Government's contribution is 1.16 per cent. It is calculated on the basis of the wages at the end of the year. The employee does not make any contribution. The calculation of pension is done on the basis of last salary drawn and the number of years of services rendered by the employee. Actual amount accumulated in the Pension fund is not taken into consideration.

When are You Entitled to get Pension?

A person is entitled to receive pension after the completion of 10 years of service and on attaining the age of 58 years. On ceasing employment earlier than 58 years, pension may be availed of by a member at his option, before attaining the age of 58 years but not below 50 years. Such early pension will be subject to discounting factor. These eligibilities are not counted in cases of permanent disability or death of person.

In case of death, the spouse is entitled to receive (ceases in case of remarriage) or children (should be below 25 years of age). In case the person has died and has not got any eligible family members, the parents; are entitled to receive it. If absence of any family member the nominee of the deceased person can get it.

Measuring Gratuity

A gratuity (means 'gift') usually means a tip. Gratuity is a lump sum amount that your employer pays you when you retire or resign from the organization. An Employee does not contribute any portion of his salary towards this amount.

The Act provides for the payment of gratuity to workers employed in every factory, shop and establishments or educational institution employing 10 or more persons on any day of the proceeding 12 months. A shop or establishment to which the Act has become applicable shall continue to be governed by the Act even if the number of persons employed falls below 10 at any subsequent stage.

Gratuity is paid out at the time of superannuation (if you retire at the age of 58), when you retire (at any other age) or resignation, and in the event of your death or being rendered disable because of an accident or illness. You need to have at least five full years of service with an employer to qualify for gratuity. This rule is relaxed in the last instance. In the event of your death, the gratuity will be paid to your nominee.

Gratuity = Last drawn salary × 15/26 × No. of years of service

Your last drawn salary will comprise your basic + DA. For computation of gratuity, your service period will be rounded off to the nearest full year.

Who all are Covered Under it?

Previously, there was a wage ceiling above which employees were liable to the benefits. After the 34th amendment to this act in 1994 no such ceiling exists. All employees irrespective of their salary amount are now covered under this Act.

Who Contributes to this Fund and What is the Maximum Amount Payable?

The employer has to contribute to this fund. The amount of gratuity payable is computed at rate of 17 days wages based on the rate of wages last drawn, for every completed year of service. The maximum amount of Gratuity payable was Rs. one lakh earlier but after the 11th amendment to the Act in 1998 the amount payable under the scheme has been raised to Rs. 3.5 lakh. Companies have a choice of opting for a higher benefit of gratuity that is—a higher total amount to be paid.

When can You Expect Gratuity?

Completion of at least five years of continuous services is necessary to receive this amount. However, it does not apply in cases where a person has stopped working due to death or disablement. In the natural course an employee can receive it on his superannuation, retirement or resignation.

Measuring Absenteeism

You can calculate any organization's annual cost of absenteeism..... Calculation about Annual Cost of Absenteeism per year in May & Baker

_________ × _________ = _________

(# work days lost per year) × (cost per work day) = (Annual cost)

There are 180 employees working in May & Baker Pharmaceuticals Ltd. on an average one employee remain 3 time absent in a year. Employee's average salary is 170 per day.

Total employees = 180

Average work days lost per year = 180 (employees) × 3 (days in year) = 540 days

Average salary per employee = 170

Annual cost of absenteeism per year = 540 days × 170 (salary per day) = Rs. 91,800

Measuring CTC

Cost to Company (CTC) is a term used to describe an investment without return. Travel expenditures, interviewing, spending time with potential customers can all be interpreted as CTC's.

Cost to Company can also be used to refer to the total cost that an organization is spending towards their employee including the Salary, Perks, Cost related to benefits, Cost related to hiring, Training, Retrials, Statutory Contributions etc.

Cost to Company is a buzz word to describe how the company can slowly pay you less and less, and remove all your benefits, until you are "self funded"—in other words you pay for all your "benefits" yourself, while the company receives the tax benefits for these payments. This improves their profit ratio, and if this system is extrapolated, you will eventually pay the company to work there. So you'll need a second job to fund this.

Cost to company is a trick of a company and HR department, to show we are paying a big salary, but unfortunately it is just bubble. They overload total expenses of human resources on salary, and show that they are paying this much salary to the staff, but actually they pay less and show more. For example—your salary is Rs. 6.00 Lakh p.a. Means—you are getting Rs. 50,000 per month. But actuly person gets only Rs. 25,000 per month—all other money is deducted for facilities. Means we are paying for getting facilities, but company shows they are giving us good facilities in the organization. In short, we pay from our salary for getting facilities, but company says they are giving good facilities to there staff. So you are paying for even unwanted facilities which you don't need. Before deciding CTC, ask for breakup of facilities.

How to Calculate Your Compensation?

Total compensation includes the value of all the perks and benefits one gets from the Company in addition to ones salary. Calculating Annual Cost to the Company is important while changing jobs as it more often than not determines what your compensation will be in the new Company. At the same time all the components are not always apparent. In order to arrive at a comprehensive figure one has to carefully add the value of all components or their cash equivalent. Given below is a format which may be downloaded and filled up to arrive at the Annual Cost to the Company.

Gross Compensation

Components	Applicability	Amount
1. *Salary Details:*		
Basic Salary	Yes/No	
House Rent Allowance	Yes/No	
Company Leased Accomodation	Yes/No	
Daily Allowance	Yes/No	
City Compensatory Allowance	Yes/No	
Special Allowance	Yes/No	
Conveyance Allowance	Yes/No	
Lunch Allowance	Yes/No	
Entertainment Allowance	Yes/No	
Books/Periodicals Allowance	Yes/No	
Education Allowance	Yes/No	
House Maintenance Allowance	Yes/No	
Furnishing Allowance	Yes/No	
Dress/Uniform Allowance	Yes/No	
Other Allowances	Yes/No	
2. *Benefits/Perks/Reimbursements*		
Value of Company Car	Yes/No	
Car Subsidy (or equivalent tax savings)	Yes/No	
Driver's Salary	Yes/No	
Maintenance and Petrol Expenses	Yes/No	
Leave Travel Allowance	Yes/No	
Canteen Subsidy	Yes/No	
Telephone Expenses	Yes/No	
Mobile Phone	Yes/No	
Club Membership	Yes/No	
Electricity/Gas	Yes/No	
Servant/Gardener	Yes/No	
Credit Cards	Yes/No	
Furnishings/Durables	Yes/No	
Holiday Facilities	Yes/No	
Medical Reimbursements	Yes/No	
Medical Insurance	Yes/No	
Personal Accident Scheme	Yes/No	
Others Benefits	Yes/No	

3. ***Retirals***

Provident Fund	Yes/No
Superannuation Fund	Yes/No
Gratuity	Yes/No

4. ***Bonus***

Fixed Bonus	Yes/No
Productivity Linked Variable Bonus(*)	Yes/No
Any Other Performance Oriented Incentive including Stock Option Plan(*)	Yes/No

5. ***Soft Loans***

Interest Subsidy	Yes/No

(*) Please take the average value of the amounts received by you in the present grade, to reach at a fair estimate.

However, the exact formula for its computation varies from one company to the other depending on what employee costing model the company has adapted.

CTC = Gross (Basic + HRA + Spl Allow + Conv + Etc)

Measuring Cost of Attrition

To ignore why people are leaving the organization is to ignore the organization's greatest assets – its people. The attrition rate varies from country to country. The maximum attrition rate is in US 42%, Australia 29%, Europe 24%, Global Average 24% and India 18%. The average employee turnover rate is 14.4 per cent annually, according to the Bureau of National Affairs.

The 'rule of thumb' appears to be very inaccurate indeed and, while it depends upon the category of staff, it is probably better to estimate around 80 per cent of salary as a truer rule of thumb—and this will be on the conservative side. What does this mean? Well, it means that if a company has 100 people doing a certain job paid 25,000 and that turnover or attrition is running at 10 per cent,

The cost of attrition is: (Total staff × attrition rate %) × (annual salary × 80%)

- 100 staff at 10 per cent attrition means 10 people leave and are replaced each year.

- A replacement cost of 80 per cent of a salary of 25,000 means the cost of each replacement is 20,000.
- The cost of turnover is therefore 10 × 20,000 or 200,000 a year.
- The on cost to the overall salary bill is 8 per cent.

There are various reasons behind leaving an organization and any attempt to find one comprehensive explanation for this phenomenon would be futile. It has been proved in a study conducted by Hewitt that one of the top reasons for talent attrition is, "external inequity in compensation". They also show that 27 per cent of the employees in their EXIT interview mentioned compensation as the primary reason. It comes no surprise to many that money is an important factor but what besides this, there are several factors that influence an employee's decision to leave. According to a survey, there are four main reasons that are followed by other common reasons:

1. In equity in compensation
2. Limited career opportunities
3. Role stagnation
4. Less challenging job profile.

In order to know the cause of excessive employee turnover, the causes of dysfunctional and avoidable turnover should be known. Few reasons for dysfunctional turnover may be:

- Compensation package differences.
- Job and employee skill mismatch: the job may be less or more satisfying and challenging according o the employee.
- Inferior facilities, tools, etc.
- Less recognition.
- Less or no appreciation for work done.
- Less growth opportunities.
- Poor training.
- Poor supervision.
- Less work and life balance practices.

The list can be endless but the reason why employees leave the organization is varied according to the nature of the business and nature of management. Therefore, it's very challenging task for an HR expert to cope up with this situation and retain talent with an organization. We are concerned about the associated cost with high Attrition and it simply includes talent loss, recruitment cost, training cost, motivation cost, low productivity cost, cost due to a person leaving, new hire cost, lost sales cost etc.

Measuring Employee Turnover

Most organizations simply track their crude turnover rates on a month by month or year by year basis. The formula is simply:

$$\frac{\text{Total number of leavers over period}}{\text{Average total number employed over period}} \times 100$$

The total figure includes all leavers, even people who left involuntarily due to dismissal, redundancy or retirement.

When does Employee Turnover become Problematic?

There is no set level of employee turnover that determines at what point, turnover starts to have a negative impact on an employing organization's performance. Everything depends on the type of labour markets in which you compete. Where it is relatively easy to find and train new employees quickly and at relatively little cost (that is where the labour market is loose), it is possible to sustain high quality levels of service provision despite having a high turnover rate.

By contrast, where skills are relatively scarce, where recruitment is costly or where it takes several weeks to fill a vacancy, turnover is likely to be problematic for the organization. This is especially true of situations in which you are losing staff to direct competitors or where customers have developed relationships with individual employees.

Some employees turnover positively benefits organizations. This happens when a poor performer is replaced by a more productive employee, and can happen when a senior retirement allows the promotion or acquisition of welcome 'fresh blood'. The more valuable the employees in question the more damaging the resignation, particularly when they move on to work for competitors.

Moderate levels of staff turnover can also help to reduce staff costs in organizations where business levels are unpredictable month on month. When business is slack it is straightforward to hold off filling recently created vacancies for some weeks.

Measuring Employee Retention

A good principle to follow is that if you want outstanding results, you need to be prepared to pay outstanding rewards. Implementation of a "total compensation" plan will motivate employees to improve not only their own performance but the performance of the firm as well. These training resources will help your organization to hire and retain the quality people needed for organizational success. Hiring the right person for the job can be easy—if you know how. Effective interviewing takes skill and knowledge. Selection decisions shouldn't be left to a hunch or a gut feeling. A variety of interviewing training programs are included in this recruitment and retention directory.

Retaining employees, especially high-performing employees, can be challenging in this fast-paced employment world. Help your organization retain seasoned employees through communicating support and appreciation with the help of these training programs and resources.

When your new employee starts the job, it takes him/her a while to adjust to new surroundings, new rules and new expectations. Begin your successful retention efforts with a proper orientation. New employee orientation efforts can help new team members feel more at home and let them know what others expect of them.

What do Employees Really Want?

In our work as consultants, we often discuss what owners and employees think are the key motivating factors. Most business owners initially think, money is the key issue. However, many employees state that they are looking for challenges, recognition, and empowerment.

Despite the current softness in the economy and the rise in the unemployment rate, the shortage of skilled insurance workers is still restraining growth for many agencies. Given this environment, what can a firm do to retain and attract the best and brightest employees, while challenging them to achieve the business' goals?

First, recognize that money, by itself, will not do it. High performing employees are searching for something more than just a high salary. The typical employee compensation plan should include a total package of rewards, recognition and environment. Some of the elements are "satisfiers" that allow a firm to attract and retain employees such as benefits, flex-time and training. Other elements of compensation are "motivators" such as bonuses, incentives, challenge and opportunity. A well-designed plan will have long-term and short-term compensation components.

The key to attracting and retaining the best people to the firm is the use of a "total compensation" approach. A firm that takes the time to carefully customize a "total compensation" package will transform individual employees into high performing, and committed employees.

There are ten basic ingredients to the total compensation package that every agency must have:

(1) **Challenging work**—The old system of directing and monitoring every task that an employee performs is out. Employees with multiple skills and authority are in. For example, a major retailer has a one-paragraph employee handbook that states: "Rule #1: Use your judgement in all situations. There will be no additional rules." To truly perform at this level requires enormous trust in the employees. However, if a business is able to perform at this level, it will reach incredible heights.

Provide additional opportunities for learning and skill development to spice work up. Encourage the staff to take classes to get licensed and for courses to earn the necessary CEUs. But, an expansion of training could provide more flexibility through a higher skilled workforce. Send the employees to Dale Carnegie, Microsoft software training, business skills seminars, team building sessions or a sales class (such as Dynamics of Sales sponsored by CIC).

(2) **Work environment**—Today's workforce is looking for flexibility on the job and balance in their life. Management needs to evaluate ways to realistically provide this sought after flexibility in work. For example, tradition has it that the employees' work in an office with established work hours. Could the firm allow for variations, such as 4-day workweeks, working at home two days a week or job sharing? Flexible work hours are becoming a common tool to attract and retain good employees.

(3) **Recognition and rewards**—Non-cash recognition awards are a very effective way to reinforce the agency's values. They can be a low-cost, high-impact element of the total compensation package. For example, employees who provide outstanding or innovative customer service receive special awards. One way is for employees to be nominated by customers or their peers.

Management needs to think about the types of awards that make sense for employees. Here are some examples:

- Provide a day off with pay.
- Provide tickets to sports, music or cultural events.
- Take out an advertisement in the local newspaper thanking your employees for their contributions.
- Provide a donation in an employee's name to the charity of his or her choice.
- Pay for tutoring for the winner's child.
- Have the winner's car detailed during work.
- Pay for the winner's house to be cleaned.
- Pay for an evening out for the winner and their spouse—dinner and babysitting.

Once the basic ingredients are established, the firm can then look into advanced tools to attract and retain employees. The following are some of the approaches that owners should also consider:

(4) **Profit sharing**—Although money is not always king, it still has a lot of clout. Firms that establish a bonus plan based on the business profitability will have employees that strive to increase sales and cut expenses. Profit sharing can be based on the profitability of the overall business or by profit centers such as commercial lines versus personal lines versus life and health. The pool of bonus money can then be distributed to the staff based on management's discretion.

A variation of profit sharing is to reduce the employees' base compensation while providing quarterly bonuses based on a department's performance. A plan that tracks employee performance will then allow them to see a direct correlation between their effort and their compensation.

(5/6) **Phantom stock and stock appreciation rights**—Stock appreciation rights (SARs) and phantom stock are both specialized deferred compensation techniques designed to provide an employee with the economic benefits of stock ownership without the employee actually owning any company stock. When an owner cannot or will not change the existing ownership structure, SARs and phantom stock are often used, to provide an employee with some sort of incentive compensation based on the actual business performance.

A SAR is simply a grant to an employee which gives that person a right, at some specific time in the future, to receive a cash award equal to the appreciation in value of a certain number of shares of company stock. In concept, SARs are similar to stock options, but different in several points. Stock options require the employee to purchase the company's stock at the grant price. However, SARs do not require a cash outlay from the employee. The employee only receives the appreciation in value of the stock.

Phantom stock on the other hand can be viewed as units of value, which directly corresponds to an equivalent number of shares of company stock. These phantom stock units are then granted to an employee for a specific period of time. When the maturity period is reached, the employee is then compensated directly in cash, based on the value of the phantom stock. Unlike SARs, the amount of compensation with phantom stock usually includes the underlying value of the stock as well as any appreciation above the grant price. Another difference is that SARs are typically paid out when the employee chooses to exercise the SAR, while phantom stock typically has a fixed award date.

(7) **Deferred compensation**—Deferred compensation is a method for producers to build long-term value for their efforts directly related to their books of business. We recommend using deferred compensation instead of ownership in the producer's book of business. The plan is often phased in overtime until the producer is fully vested in the plan.

The agency benefits by having a system that encourages the producers to build their books as well as remain with the firm. It must be noted that a deferred compensation plan (as well as SARs and phantom stock) creates a contingent liability for the firm, which does negatively affect agency value. However, deferred comp is also "consideration," which helps uphold the covenant not-to-compete in a producer contract.

(8) **Split-dollar life policies**—A split-dollar plan is a way to provide life insurance for an employee or their spouse at a reduced cost to that individual. The premium for the insurance is shared by the employee and his or her employer (thus the name "split-dollar").

It is an effective way to retain key employees while the business is reimbursed for every dollar it advances. From the employer's perspective, split-dollar is an inexpensive method of buying life insurance for any personal or business needs of select employees. It enhances employee loyalty by providing substantial insurance benefits. Some split dollar policies can provide funds which may be used for additional employee benefits in the future (deferred compensation, salary continuation, stock redemption, or retirement income).

From the employee's perspective, split-dollar can help replace needed family income that would be lost at the employee's death or help pay any estate taxes. If the employee owns the policy and collaterally assigns the policy to the employer, the employer can borrow against the cash value to the extent allowed by the collateral assignment form.

(9) **ESOPs**—Employee Stock Ownership Plans (ESOPs) are a way for business owners to sell shares in the company or to provide an additional benefit to all qualified company employees. These plans were initially created as a win-win for business owners and employees. ESOP contributions are tax deductible as are dividends if they are paid to employees directly, on their behalf to the ESOP or applied to the loan payments of a leveraged plan. Because the ESOP is funded with pre-tax dollars, the company's tax savings may increase even further.

The selling shareholder can also defer the capital gains on stock sold to an ESOP as long as the ESOP owns 30 per cent or more of the company's stock and the seller rolls over the sale proceeds into qualified replacement property (stocks or bonds of domestic companies). Employees pay no tax on the contributions until they are entitled to receive the stock when they leave the company or retire. At this point, the company generally buys back the stock through a buyback provision in the ESOP.

ESOPs are expensive to set up and maintain. Businesses need to be a certain size before it makes financial sense. We recommend that agency owners do their homework before seriously considering this option.

(10) **Stock equity**—Stock ownership usually conjures up visions of importance and respect. Producers and employees feel that having the word "Owner" on their business card will improve sales and stature. Often the employees only understand the benefits of stock ownership and the drawbacks are ignored or not understood.

Agency owners are often unclear themselves whether or not they should offer stock to an employee. They usually first think about it either when a current employee is about to walk out the door and may not come back. Owners might often feel that they are forced to offer stock in order to entice a new producer to join the firm or to retain the employee, such as a producer with a book of business.

We recommend that owners think long and hard before offering stock to an employee. The decision whether or not to make an employee an owner needs to be based on a review of many factors. The right decision can propel the agency forward for many years to come. The wrong decision can mire the firm in unimportant muck.

Ten Ways to Attract and Retain Great Employees

Today, more and more organizations are changing the way they view and pay their employees. The move is away from the traditional "cost-of-doing-business" concept. Successful businesses are developing creative programs to guide employees to focus on improving business performance and rewarding them for their contributions. Unfortunately, many businesses and employees are still not ready to make the change.

In today's business environment, clearly the long-term winners will be companies that provide a flexible and challenging work environment, along with employee recognition and rewards. Organizations have to be willing to share their successes. If employees are asked to share the risks, then they have to share the rewards.

Attracting and Retaining Talent

We have observed a rapidly-growing trend by leadership in every industry to attract and retain good people, who are capable of creating and maintaining a very competitive, creative, and cutting-edge culture. After two decades of corporate downsizing, middle-management layoffs, merger-mania, and hostile take-overs, companies in every industry are waking up to the reality that they must make the management and motivation of their employees their number one strategic priority—or risk falling behind the competition.

Organizations are investing more time, energy, talent and dollars in this area than ever before and with good cause. Obviously, without a responsive, top-notch workforce, it is impossible for management to fully execute and sustain a strategic plan. Without your people enthusiastically supporting your goals, your plan is likely to remain just that: a plan, and not a reality. Those who decline to invest in those areas mentioned above are certainly destined to pay even higher costs in the future.

Today's workers are an entirely new breed: more demanding, more diverse, more technically astute, and less likely than workers of a generation ago to believe that the employer has their best interests at heart. They obviously want fair compensation. They know what they're worth and they're going to get it somewhere. However, that isn't all they want. Today's employees expect more than a job and a pay cheque.

How to Retain Good Employees

1. Determine what motivates your individual employees. For most employees, money is not the key issue; relationships, fulfillment and recognition are.
2. Notice how much recognition an employee needs. Some employees can go years without praise, whereas others will leave after six months.
3. Understand that many employees are motivated by their social network at work. Encourage activities that make your employees feel like valued members of a team.
4. Realize that incentives don't have to be huge. A surprise gift certificate for the local ice cream parlor in the weekly pay cheque will generate positive feelings.
5. Make benefits more accessible. If your company reimburses tuition for college courses, have a college administrator come to your company, so employees can find out about classes and programs.
6. Consider telecommuting, job sharing and other flexible working arrangements.

7. Offer profit sharing incentives to encourage longevity.
8. Create clear career paths at the company.

A stability index indicates the retention rate of experienced employees. Like turnover rates, this can be used across an organization as a whole or for a particular part of it. The usual calculation for the stability index is:

$$\frac{\text{Number of leavers with more than one years service}}{\text{Total number of staff in post one year ago}} \times 100$$

Summary

Human resource executive responsibility is to manage the individual once they are hired as an employee—appraisal, evaluation, recognition, promotion, retention, and succession planning services. They are also responsibly related to managing the various aspects of labour laws, labour relations, legislation, litigation, alternative dispute services. In addition to these specific human resources categories, it is also important to highlight services that are cross-functional in nature and relate to one or all the HR pillars.

Frankly speaking, Human resource personnel must know the basic calculation to take care the benefits of both employee and employer. Human resource personnel should be expertise in understanding what is the concept of CTC calculation? How much amount should be deducted for P.F., P.P.F., gratuity and E.S.I.? How many leaves we should give to our employees? How to calculate attrition rate or rate per hire? What components of salary are taxable? And many more questions that play a pivotal role and that are directly linked with image of Human resource personnel.

Chapter fourteen

SOCIAL SECURITY BENEFITS

Social security benefits are the right of every employee and it has to be provided by the employer at any cost. It is a matter of fact that we really don't know how to get social security benefits. In this topic, lots of questions and answers are designed to clarify it beautifully. It is a matter of discussion with the employer prior to joining any organization or even in the initial days of joining. For example, you are a fresher and you join your first job, then you should know the initial 6 months will be your probation period. Leaves are not allowed during probation except emergency leave. In emergency, you take leave of Saturday and Monday because Sunday is allowed weekly off but mind it, Sunday will also be treated as leave because this leave is in a continuous fashion. Therefore, it is mandatory to all these things in advance to cope up with the situation. It is prevailing in one internationally acclaimed organization if you take leave of continuous three days, then you will be marked as four days on leave because they have their own reason. They say, Sunday is a gift for those who work for six days and if you won't work up to six days, then you are not eligible for Sunday as a gift. One more question arises why one day is deducted and why not half day, then in this case they say this is the company policy. We are bound to accept rules and regulations of the company but we should be aware. In a big organization, it is a common trend that they provide employee HR policy manual to go through and we should take advantage of this at the time of joining. We should be well aware about the major social security benefits of organization well in advance and not when we need social security benefits.

Sickness Benefit

What does 'Sickness Benefit' Mean?

Sickness signifies a state of health necessitating medical treatment and attendance and abstention from work on medical grounds. Financial support extended by the Corporation as a contingency is called Sickness Benefit.

What are the Contributory Conditions?

The contribution conditions required to be fulfilled for admissibility of sickness benefit during any benefit period is that contributions should have been paid in respect of an insured person in the corresponding contribution period for not less than 78 days.

How much is the Standard Benefit Rate?

The daily rate of Sickness Benefit during any benefit period is the "standard benefit rate". This rate corresponds to the average daily wage of an insured person during the corresponding contribution period and is roughly half of the daily wage rate. Benefit is paid for Sundays also. 28 wage groups have been evolved for working out the daily rate of Standard Sickness Benefit. Standard Benefit rates for 28 wage groups are shown in Annexure 'A'.

What is the Duration of Sickness Benefit?

Sickness benefit is payable for a maximum period of 91 days in any two consecutive benefit periods. Benefit is not paid for an initial waiting period of 2 days unless the insured person is certified sick within 15 days of the last spell in which Sickness Benefit was paid.

Extended Sickness Benefit

What is Extended Sickness Benefit?

Extended Sickness Benefit is a Cash Benefit paid for prolonged illness due to any of the 34 specified diseases as mentioned below.

Diseases

1. Tuberculosis
2. Leprosy

3. Chronic Empyema
4. Bronchitis
5. Interstitial Lung disease
6. AIDS
7. Malignant Diseases
8. Diabetes Mellitus with proliferative retinopathy/ diabetic foot/nephropathy.
9. Monoplegia
10. Hemiplegia
11. Paraplegia
12. Hemiparesis
13. Intracranial space occupying lesion
14. Spinal Cord Compression
15. Parkinson's disease
16. Myasthenia Gravis/Neuromuscular Dystrophies
17. Immature Cataract with vision 6/60 or less
18. Detachment of Retina
19. Glaucoma
20. Coronary Artery Diseases
21. Congestive Heart Failure-Left, Right
22. Cardiac valvular Diseases with failure/complications
23. Cardiomyopathies
24. Heart disease with surgical intervention alongwith complications
25. Chronic Obstructive Lung diseases (COPD) with congestive heart failure (Cor Pulmonale)
26. Cirrhosis of liver with ascitis/chronic active hepatitis ("CAH")
27. Dislocation of vertebra/prolapse of intervertebral disc
28. Non-union or delayed union of fracture
29. Post Traumatic surgical amputation of lower extremity
30. Compound fracture with chronic osteomyelitis
31. (a) Schizophrenia
    (b) Endogenous depression

(c) Maniac Depressive Psychosis (MDP)
(d) Dementia

32. More than 20% Burns with infection/complication
33. Chronic Renal Failure
34. Reynaud's disease/Burger's disease.

In addition, extended sickness benefit may also be sanctioned by the prescribed authority, in case of any rare disease or special circumstances on the recommendation of the specified authority.

What are the Contributory Conditions?

Except in case of disability from administration of drugs/ injections, the insured person should have been in continuous employment for a period of 2 years and should have contributed for atleast 156 days in 4 preceding contribution periods.

How Much is the Benefit Rate?

The daily rate of Extended Sickness Benefit is 40 per cent more than the Standard Sickness Benefit rate admissible.

How Long is the Benefit Available?

After exhausting Sickness Benefit payable for 91 days, the ESB is payable upto a further period of 124/309 days that can be extended upto 2 years in special circumstances. Thus, together with the Sickness Benefit for 91 days, it puts a claimant on benefit for an aggregate period 400 days for all specified diseases and 2 years in chronic suitable cases on recommendation of competent authority.

Enhanced Sickness Benefit

What is Enhanced Sickness Benefit?

Enhanced Sickness Benefit is cash benefit for the insured persons undergoing sterlisation operation of vasectomy/tubectomy for family planning.

What are the Contributory Conditions?

The contributory conditions are the same as for claiming sickness benefit.

How Much is the Benefit Rate?

The daily rate of this benefit is double the standard benefit rate. Say, not less than the daily wage.

How Long is the Benefit Available?

The benefit is available upto 7 days for vasectomy and upto 14 days for tubectomy operations. This period can however be extended in cases of post operative complications or sickness arising out of these sterilisation operations. Its duration is not counted towards the total number of 91 days for which the sickness benefit is available during any two consecutive benefit periods.

How to Claim Sickness Benefit?

A claim for Sickness Benefit should be supported by a Medical Certificate issued by an Insurance Medical Officer/Insurance Medical Practitioner in the appropriate Form. Medical Certificates are issued at intervals of not more than seven days, except in cases of prolonged sickness, where Special Intermediate Certificates may be issued at longer intervals not exceeding 4 weeks. On the back of each certificate, except the Special Intermediate Certificate, a Claim Form is printed. The Claim Form is essentially a declaration in regard to abstention of the claimant from work during the period of claim. Separate Claim Forms are also available.

The Claim Form should bear signatures/thumb impression of the claimant and should be submitted to the Local Office personally, by post, through a messenger or by deposit in certificate boxes, wherever provided. All claims should preferably to submitted to the Local Office within three days. The Receptionist at the Local Office renders all assistance in filling in the claim on your behalf.

Disablement Benefit

What is 'Disablement'?

Disablement is a condition resulting from employment injury which may be:

(a) **temporary** i.e. rendering an insured person incapable of work temporarily and necessitating medical treatment;

(b) **permanent partial** i.e. reducing the earning capacity of the insured person generally for every employment;

(c) **permanent total** i.e. totally depriving the insured person of the power to do all work.

What Constitutes an "Employment Injury"?

Employment injury means a personal injury caused to an employee by an accident or occupational disease arising out of and in course of his employment in a factory or establishment covered under the Employees' State Insurance Act.

The law relating to Employment injury has been liberalised. Now, an accident arising in the course of employment is presumed also to have arisen out of his employment if there is no evidence to the contrary. Further, an accident brought about by wilful disobedience, negligence or breach of regulations etc. or an accident happening while travelling in a transport provided by the employer or while meeting an emergency is accepted subject to certain conditions, to have arisen in the course of and out of employment. Injuries suffered while under the influence of drinks and drugs take away the right of the employee to this benefit.

Roadside accident caused while commuting between place of residence and workplace is also treated as notional extension of employment for purpose of death or disablement benefit.

What are 'Occupational Diseases'?

Occupational Diseases are such diseases as are susceptible of being traced back to their occupational origin. These are specified under Schedule III of the Employees' State Insurance Act, which enumerates the compensable Occupational Diseases and the corresponding industrial processes involving exposure to the diseases are thus recognised without any further evidence.

What are the Benefits Granted?

Temporary Disablement Benefit is paid periodically in arrears as the evidence of incapacity (medical certificate) is produced.

Permanent total disablement and permanent partial disablement benefits are paid in the form of pensions. Current employment for wages or engagement in any gainful activities is no bar to payment of permanent disablement benefits. An insured person suffering from an occupationd disease is also entitled to full medical care.

How Much is the Benefit Rate?

The daily benefit rate for permanent total disablement and temporary disablement is 40 per cent more than the Standard Sickness Benefit rate and is roughly equivalent to about 70 per cent of the wage rate. For permanent partial disablement, the rate of benefit is proportionate to the percentage of loss of earning capacity. The benefit is paid for Sundays also.

What are the Contributory Conditions?

There are no qualifying conditions as to the length of employment or the number of contributions paid. Protection accrues from the very moment of entry into insurable employment.

What is the Duration of Benefit?

Temporary Disablement Benefit is paid as long as disablement lasts. There is a waiting period of 3 days (excluding the day of accident), but if incapacity exceeds this period, benefit is paid from the very first day. The permanent disablement benefit is paid for the life-time of the beneficiary.

How is Permanent Disablement Assessed?

There is indeed no way of adequately compensating a permanently disabled employee. Yet some method of determining whether an employment injury has resulted in permanent disablement and of assessing the extent of permanent damage caused by that employment injury has to be adopted for the purpose of determining the scale of compensation for the loss of earnings. This is done by evaluating loss of earning capacity with reference to general disability for all work. The evaluation is done by a Medical Board whose decision can be appealed against to a Medical Appeal Tribunal presided over by a judicial officer, with a further right of appeal to Employees' Insurance Court or directly to Employees' Insurance Court. Pending an appeal, payment for permanent loss of earning capacity as recommended by the Medical Board is made, subject to adjustment later. Loss of wages and expenditure on conveyance occasioned by attendance before the Medical Board are compensated by the Corporation in accordance with rates framed for the purpose.

Where the assessment of loss of earning capacity by the Medical Board is not of a final character, the beneficiary is required to appear again before the Medical Board for a review of the assessment.

Can the Decisions of Medical Board or of Medical Appeal Tribunal be Reviewed?

Yes. If the Medical Board or the Medical Appeal Tribunal is satisfied by fresh evidence that a decision was given because of non-disclosure or mis-representation of a material fact, it can review its earlier decision at any time. A Medical Board can also review its earlier assessment of extent of disablement, if it is satisfied that there has been substantial and unforeseen aggravation of the results of the relevant injury and substantial injustice would be done by not reviewing it. Such review, however, cannot be made earlier than 5 years or in the case of the provisional assessment, earlier than 6 months of the date of assessment to be reviewed.

Is Lumpsum Benefit Allowed in Place of Pension?

Yes. At the option of the beneficiary, permanent disablement pension, where the daily rate payable is not significant, can be commuted for a lumpsum payment subject to the fulfilment of the following two conditions:

(i) that the permanent disablement has been assessed as final, and

(ii) the daily rate of permanent disablement does not exceed Rs. 5/- and the total commuted value does not exceed Rs. 30,000/- (effective from April 2003).

How to Claim 'Disablement Benefit'?

(a) *Temporary Disablement:*

(i) Notice of the injury should be given either orally or in writing personally or through an agent, to the employer/foreman/duty supervisor or particulars of the injury should be entered in the Accident Book kept in the factory, personally or through an agent.

(ii) A medical certificate of incapacity should be obtained from the Insurance Medical Officer/ Insurance Medical Practitioner.

(iii) The claim form printed on the back of the medical certificate should be filled in and submitted promptly to Local Office along with the medical certificate.

(iv) A final certificate should be obtained from the Insurance Medical Officer/Insurance Medical Practitioner and submitted to the Local Office before resumption of duty.

(b) *Permanent Disablement:*

(i) If suffering from permanent effects of employment injury, the insured person should make an application to the Regional Office of the Corporation for reference of his case to the Medical Board (reference to the Medical Board is made otherwise also by the Regional Office).

(ii) Where loss of earning capacity has been assessed and communicated to the insured person, he should submit a claim in the appropriate form to the Local Office.

(iii) After the claim has been admitted, the beneficiary should submit at six-monthly intervals (with the claim for June and December every year) a life certificate in appropriate form duly attested by the prescribed authority.

Is There Any Provision for Physical Rehabilitation?

Yes. Insured Persons who suffer physical disablement due to employment injury are provided artificial appliances or other physical aids such as wheel chairs, crutches, dentures and spectacles etc.

What about Vocational Rehabilitation?

The Corporation at its cost arranges for the vocational rehabilitation of disabled insured persons provided the disability has been assessed at above 40 per cent and the beneficiary is not over 45 years of age. The training is provided at vacational rehabilitation centres run by the Govt. of India etc. The fee, travelling expenses etc are borne by the Corporation.

Dependents' Benefit

What is 'Dependents' Benefit'?

Dependents Benefit is a monthly pension payable to the eligible dependents of an insured person who dies as a result of an Employment Injury or occupational disease.

Who are the Beneficiaries and How Long is the Benefit Available?

Dependants entitled to the benefit could be:

(a) Widow/Widower during life or until remarriage.

(b) Legitimate or adopted son until age 18 or if legitimate son is infirm, till infirmity lasts;

(c) Legitimate or adopted unmarried daughter until age 18 or until marriage, whichever is earlier, or if infirm, till infirmity lasts and she continues to be unmarried.

In the absence of any widow or legitimate child, the benefit is payable to a parent or grandparent for life, to any other male dependant until age 18 or to an unmarried or widowed female dependant until age 18.

How Much is the Benefit for Each Beneficiary?

The total divisible benefit is equivalent to the temporary disablement benefit rate (roughly 70% of the wage rate). The widow/widows share 3/5th of the benefit and the legitimate or adopted son and daughter 2/5th each of the benefit. If the total benefit so divided exceeds the full rate, there is a proportionate reduction in the respective shares of the beneficiaries.

How to Claim 'Dependants' Benefit'?

To establish title to Dependant' Benefit, the following documents should be submitted at the Local Office:

(a) Claim in the appropriate form;
(b) Evidence of death being due to employment injury;
(c) Proof of relationship to the deceased supporting eligibility of the claimant as a "dependant";
(d) Evidence of age of the claimant(s) (certified copy of official record of birth, Baptismal register, school records, original horoscope etc.);
(e) Certificate of infirmity from Medical Referee or any other prescribed authority in case of legitimate infirm son or legitimate or adopted unmarried infirm daughter.

After the claim to Dependant's Benefit has been admitted, the beneficiary should submit at six-monthly intervals (with the claim for June and December), a declaration that he/she is alive and has not married/remarried, attained the prescribed age/ continues to be infirm, as the case may be duly attested by the prescribed authority.

Can Dependant's Benefit be Reviewed?

Yes. Dependant's Benefit once awarded can be reviewed by the Corporation at any time if it is satisfied on fresh evidence that the earlier decision was due to non-disclosure or misrepresentation of material facts. It can also be reviewed on birth, death, marriage, re-marriage and attainment of age 18, by a claimant. The benefit can be continued, increased, reduced or discontinued.

Maternity Benefit

What is Maternity Benefit?

Maternity Benefit is cash payable to an insured woman for the specified period of abstention from work for confinement or miscarriage or for sickness arising out of pregnancy, confinement, premature birth of child or miscarriage. "Confinement" connotes labour resulting in the delivery of a living child or labour after 26 weeks of pregnancy whether the resultant issue is alive or dead. "Miscarriage" means expulsion of the contents of a pregnant uterus at any period prior to or during 26th week of pregnancy. Criminal abortion or miscarriage does not, however, entitle to benefit.

What are the Contributory Conditions?

The contribution condition is the same as for Sickness Benefit.

How Much is the Benefit?

The daily benefit rate is double the Sickness Benefit rate and is thus roughly equivalent to the full wages. Benefit is paid for Sundays also.

What is the Duration of the Benefit?

The Benefit is paid as follows:

(a) ***For confinement:***

For a total period or 12 weeks beginning not more than 6 weeks before the expected date of child birth. If the insured woman dies during confinement or within 6 weeks thereafter, leaving behind the living child, the benefit continues to be payable for the whole of the period. But if the child also die during that period, the benefit will be paid upto and including the day of death of the child.

(b) ***For miscarriage:***

For a period of 6 weeks following the date of miscarriage.

(c) ***For sickness arising out of pregnancy, confinement, premature birth of child or miscarriage:***

For an additional period of upto four week.

In all the cases, the benefit is paid only if the insured woman does not work for remuneration during the period for which benefit is claimed. There is no waiting period.

How to Claim Maternity Benefit?

Where an insured woman wishes to claim Maternity Benefit after confinement or for miscarriage, she should obtain from the Insurance Medical Officer/Insurance Medical Practitioner, a certificate of confinement or miscarriage and submit it to her Local Office personally or by post alongwith a claim for Maternity Benefit. The claim form also contains a declaration of abstention from work.

If Benefit is desired before confinement, a Notice and Certificate of Pregnancy and a Certificate of Expected Confinement obtained from the Insurance Medical Officer/ Insurance Medical Practitioner are also required to be submitted.

For claiming Benefit in the event of death of an insured woman leaving behind a child, her nominee and if there is no such nominee, her legal representative should submit personally or by post to the Local Office of the deceased insured woman, a claim for the Benefit together with a certificate of death of the insured woman.

An insured woman claiming Maternity Benefit for Sickness arising out of pregnancy, confinement, premature birth of child or miscarriage should submit her claim in the manner as for sickness benefit.

Where a claim to Maternity Benefit is not submitted alongwith prescribed certificates referred to above, the Corporation has the discretion to accept other evidence in lieu thereof.

What is Medical Bonus?

Medical Bonus is lumpsum payment made to an insured woman or the wife of an insured person in case she does not avail medical facility from an ESI hospital at the time of delivery of a child. This bonus of Rs. 250 has been increased to Rs. 1000 from 1st April 2003.

Medical Benefit

What is Medical Benefit?

Medical Benefit means medical care of insured persons and their families, wherever covered for medical benefit.

What does Medical Benefit Consist of?

The standard medical care consists of out-door treatment, in-patient treatment, all necessary drugs and dressings, pathological and radiological specialist consultation and care, ante-natal and post natal care, emergency treatment etc.

Where are 'Out-patient' Services Provided?

Out-door medical care is provided at State Insurance Dispensaries or Mobile Dispensaries manned by full-time doctors ('Service' system) or at the private clinics of Insurance Medical Practitioners ('Panel' system). The scope of medical services also includes simple ante-natal and post-natal care for women, family welfare planning services and immunisation against the common infectious diseases.

The Scheme provides at the sole cost of the Corporation, artificial limbs to insured persons who lose their limbs due to employment injury or in certain circumstances otherwise also, dentures, spectacles and hearing-aids where the loss of teeth, impairment of eye-sight or hearing respectively is due to employment injury.

How and where are 'In-patient' Services Provided?

ESIC has a network of 141 hospitals countrywide. Majority of these hospitals are administered by the State Govts. In-patient and diagnostic services in basic specialities are available at these hospitals. State schemes have also tie-up arrangements with a number of Medical colleges, major state hospitals, as well as, private hospitals for advanced treatment for malignant diseases and complicated surgical interventions.

What about Preventive Health Care Services?

ESI Scheme provides preventive health care services through the network of its dispensaries and hospitals. These include immunization against some killer diseases, pulse polio vaccination and family welfare services etc. The scheme also participates in all major national preventive health service campaigns.

How Long is Medical Benefit Available?

Insured worker and the members of his family are eligible for medical care from the very first day of the worker coming under ESI Scheme. The medical care includes primary medical care, diagnostic services, specialist consultations and indoor medical care. Whenever the patient is not able to travel by himself/herself, ambulance services are also provided. The I.P. or his family members are not required to pay for any of the services.

A worker who is covered under the Scheme for the first time is eligible for medical care for a period of three months. If he/she continues in insurable employment for three months or more the medical care is available to him/her till the start of the first benefit period. If he/she contributes atleast for 78 days in a contribution period the eligibility is there upto the end of the corresponding benefit period.

A worker is also eligible for extended sickness benefit when he/she is suffering from any one of the long-term 34 diseases listed in the Act. This is admissible after the worker has been under ESI coverage for atleast 2 years during which he/she should have contributed atleast for 156 days. When these conditions are satisfied medical benefit is admissible for a maximum period of 730 days for the I.P. and his/her family.

Funeral Expenses

What are Funeral Expenses?

This component consists of a lump sum payment towards the expenditure on the funeral of the deceased insured person.

What is the Amount Payable?

The lump sum amount of this benefit is equal to the actual expenditure, not exceeding Rs. 2500 towards the funeral of the deceased insured person.

Are There any Contribution Conditions?

No contribution condition is required for this Benefit. The only condition for admissibility of this Benefit is that the deceased person should have been an insured person at the time of his death. The Funeral expenses are thus payable in respect of an insured person in receipt of Permanent Disablement Benefit even if he may not be employed at the time of his death in a factory or establishment covered under the ESI Act.

To Whom are the Funeral Expenses Payable?

The expenses are payable to the eldest surviving member of the family of the deceased insured person. If the insured person did not have a family or if he was not living with his family at the time of his death, the benefit is payable to the person who actually incurs the expenditure on the funeral of the deceased insured person.

How to Claim the Funeral Expenses?

To claim the expenses, the claimant should submit his/her claim personally or by post to the Local Office of the deceased insured person within three months, together with the following documents:

(a) Death certificate as proof of death of the insured person issued by the Insurance Medical Officer/ Insurance Medical Practitioner or such other Medical Officer of a hospital or other institution who attended the insured person at the time of death or examined the body after the death; (Death certificate issued by cremation/burial ground or by Municipal authorities or certified copy of death records provided by village panchayat, municipality, etc. may also be accepted as evidence of death);

(b) A declaration of the claimant, either

  (i) that he is the eldest surviving member of the family of the deceased insured person and incurred expenditure on the funeral of the deceased, or

  (ii) in case the claimant is other than the eldest surviving member of the family, that the deceased insured person did not have a family or was not living with his family at the time of his death and that the claimant actually incurred expenditure on the funeral of the deceased insured person. The declaration should be countersigned by a competent authority.

Allied Provisions

How are the Employees Registered Under the Scheme?

Simultaneously, with his/her entry into employment in a covered factory or establishment, an employee is required to fill in a Declaration Form. The employee is then allotted a Registration Number, which distinguishes and identifies the person for the purposes of the Scheme. A person is registered once and once only upon his entry in insurable employment.

What is an Identity Card?

On registration, every insured person is provided with a "Temporary Identification Certificate" which is valid ordinarily for a period of 3 months but may be extended, if necessary, for a further period of 3 months. Within this period, the Insured Person is given a permanent "family photo Identity Card" in exchange for the Certificate. The Identity Card serves as a means of identification and has to be produced at the time of claiming medical care at the dispensary/clinic and cash benefit at the Local Office of the Corporation. In the event of change of employment, it should be produced before the new employer as evidence of registration under the Scheme to prevent any duplicate registration. The Identity Card bears the signatures/thumb impression of the insured person.

Since medical benefit is also available to the families of insured persons, the particulars of family members entitled to Medical Benefit are also given in the Identity Card affixed with a postcard size family photo.

If you lose your Identity Card before it has run its normal life, a duplicate card is issued on payment as prescribed.

What are the Rates of Contribution?

Contributions payable in respect of an employee comprise of employer's contribution and employee's contribution prescribed in Schedule I of the Act.

An employee covered under the scheme has to contribute 1.75 per cent of the wages whereas, an employer contributes 4.75 per cent of the wages payable to an employee. The total contribution in respect of an employee thus works out to 6.50 per cent of the wages payable.

Who is Exempted from Payment of Contribution?

Employees earning less than Rs. 40 a day are exempted from payment of contribution. The employers share of contribution is, however, payable.

How are the Contributions Collected?

The Contribution is deposited by the Employer in cash or by cheque at the designated branches of some nationalised banks. The responsibility for payment of all contributions is that of the employer with a right to deduct the Employees' share of contributions from employees' wages relating to the period in respect of which the Contribution is payable.

What are 'Contribution Periods' and 'Benefit Periods'?

Workers, covered under the ESI Act, are required to pay contribution towards the scheme on a monthly basis. A contribution period means a six-month time span from 1st April to 30th September and 1st October to 31st March. Thus, in a financial year there are two contribution periods of six months duration.

Cash benefits under the scheme are generally linked with contributions paid. The benefit period starts three months after the closure of a contribution period. The two types of periods are illucidated below:

Contribution Period	Corresponding Benefit period
1st April to 30th September	1st January to 30th June of the following year
1st October to 31st March	1st July to 31st December

What is a Local Office?

A net-work of Local Offices has been established by the Corporation in all implemented areas to disburse all claims for sickness, maternity, disablement and dependents' benefit. The Local Office also answers all doubts and enquiries and assists otherwise in filling in claim forms and completing other action necessary in connection with the settlement of claims. These offices also interact with the employers of the area. The Local Offices are managed by a Manager and work under the direction and control of the Regional Offices.

Some Miscellaneous Provisions

- **Disqualification for benefits in certain cases:**

  A person who works and receives wages on any day is not entitled to sickness benefit or maternity benefit or temporary disablement benefit in respect of that day.

  A recipient of sickness benefit or temporary disablement benefit must remain under medical treatment and obey the instruction given by his Insurance Medical Officer. He should not leave the area of treatment without the permission of his medical officer and should present himself for examination by the medical officer or any other person authorised by the Corporation.

- **Safeguarding the right to Benefit:**

  Cash benefits payable under the Employees' State Insurance Act are not liable to attachment or sale in execution of any court decree or order. Also, the right to receive any benefit is not transferable or assignable.

- **Protection from Dismissal, discharge or other Punishments:**

  An employee is protected against dismissal, discharge, or other punishments during the following periods:

  (1) a period of 6 months in case of a recipient of disablement benefit;

  (2) a period of 6 months in case an employee is under medical treatment for sickness or certified illness due to pregnancy or confinement;

(3) a period of 12 months in case an employee is under medical treatment for T.B. Leprosy, Mental, Malignant or any of the 34 specified diseases.

- **Remittance of Cash Benefit at the cost of the Corporation:**

  At the option of the beneficiary, cash benefits under the Employees' State Insurance Act are remitted by Money Orders at the cost of the Corporation, irrespective of the amount involved.

- **Adjudication Machinery:**

  To make the right of claimants effective, every claimant has a right of raising a dispute in the Employees' Insurance Court. It consists of a judicial officer appointed by the State Government. The jurisdiction of a Civil Court is barred in all such cases.

- **Repayment and recovery of Benefit payments:**

  If a person receives any benefit to which he is not legally entitled, he is liable to repay the value of any such benefit to the Corporation.

- **Punishment for false statement etc.**
- Any false statement or false representation made or caused to be made for the purpose of obtaining benefit wrongfully etc. constitutes an offence under the Employees' State Insurance Act, punishable with imprisonment upto three months or with fine upto five hundred rupees or both.
- **Treatment at outstation**

  In case an insured worker leaves his station on duty or otherwise, he/she is eligible for treatment at any ESI medical unit, subject to production of identity card and a certificate from Employer in Form 105.

Do You Know About Paternity Leave?

Paternity leave is given to the would be father if his wife is pregnant. It is a great social security benefit if some organization offer this leave. In India, Wipro has been practising and giving paid paternity leave. Offering paternity leave is just like emotional marketing with the employee and through this, you can strengthen your retention strategy in a better way. Why paternity leave is so important for both employee and employer. Employee is the first customer of the employer and if this service is being offered by the employer then this is one the best gift for the employee. Paternity leave is important for employee because this is the expansion family plan and this plan should be successful by hook or crook. Therefore, the company who are not offering paternity leave they should must offer it without any further discussion because now we are leaving in a nuclear family and we have to take care of family. For us family and the company are prime customer and we cannot ignore.

Summary

In the nook and corner of the world, human resource policy is becoming more and more human friendly and not employer or employee friendly because of globalization and economic reform. Now, we are a citizen of global village and we are bound to change accordingly otherwise survival is going to be more and tougher day by day. Employer should have very lucrative social security offer for the employee so that they can feel friendly and homely. In nutshell if first customer (employee) is happy and satisfied with the employer then all direct and indirect customer will automatically follow the trend. Therefore, we should remember, "employee is the face of any organization and beautiful face is always luring for everyone". Employer should take care his employee as a doctor, as a mother, as a father, as a brother, as a son and as a friend.

Chapter fifteen

FACE READING

Face Reading has been practised for more than five thousand years. Face reading is known as Physiognomy (fizzy-OG-nuh-me), Personology, which means interpreting the face to learn about the inner person. Face reading gives you the facts you need to make important decisions, and alerts your perceptions to develop a deeper understanding of every person you will ever interact with

Face is a mirror of our behaviour, character, present, past and future. Our face is a visual metamorph of our life. A face can be read like a map. The most unforgettable and unique feature of a human is his/her face. A trained face reader can read each facial feature and line on a face to develop an accurate profile of its owner. Each face reflects in its structures and lines its owner's personal history, mental attitudes, intimacy needs, ethics, emotional style, and verbal communication. Almost anything you want to know about a person is literally as plain as the nose on their face.

Characteristics like honesty, intelligence and reliability are major attributes that we all seek in friendship or romantic partnerships. It's one thing looking for those characteristics in others, but finding them is not always that easy. A person who seemingly appears reliable at first may soon exhibit quite the opposite personality traits. How could you have known at the outset?

Face reading will immediately offer you valuable information about human beings. You can begin practising face reading by observing friends, family members and work colleagues. Naturally, very few people fall into "pure" type categories, but more often than not, the predominant shape will be recognizable.

Experiment with "the face" and see whether you recognize any of the character traits in yourself or others.

Since childhood, all of us have learned how to give a desired impression. Physiognomy shows things about faces that can't be faked or manipulated, so face reading will be far more reliable as a way to learn about character. Expression shows mood, which is a passing thing. Afterwards, reality sets in. How many times have you heard a friend's sad story begin with these words: "I trusted him because he looked so nice?"

"Nice", on a date or job interview, reveals precious little about a man's long-term behavior. How about his personal style with power or intimacy or work? How about his character, for crying out loud. To read information like that, you need Face Reading. Unlike expression, face data can't be faked, which makes for a more accurate kind of information.

What are the Benefits of Face Reading?

If you're a people watcher, you'll find the insights fascinating. With face reading, you can learn more in 10 minutes than many non-face readers learn in months. Think that might help you at work? How about socially?

Regarding practical benefits, they include better communication, because this system of face reading shows you very clearly that other people have talents unlike yours. I like to say that I help my face reading students to "Open up the heart of compassion."

Personal empowerment, self-confidence, and self-esteem grow, with face reading. You learn to appreciate the talents that show in your face, viewing changes to your face over time as part of your personal evolution.

Whether you do face reading on yourself now, your old pictures from the family photo album; whether you're reading faces on a new neighbor, an old relative who has always annoyed you, some exciting new business prospect—through face reading, I can improve your ability to see individuals rather than stereotypes.

Sales people love face reading. One super-successful sales manager called to thank me for helping him earn his first million. Another student of mine travels the world, giving sales workshops featuring what she has learned from me. It is my delight to bring more success and honesty to all walks of life by teaching face reading and related skills.

For many people, face reading is the perfect first step for exploring all the forms of Deeper Perception: Aura reading, empath empowerment, learning to cut cords of attachment and do other skills of Energy Spirituality.

Myth and Meaning of Face Reading

Is it fair to read faces considering that our looks are based on heredity? Genetics is part of the truth about life. It's not the entire truth. It may not even be a particularly useful kind of truth in the context of face reading. Truth has many levels, you know. After all, a cell from your hand, when seen under a microscope, seems entirely different from the hand you hold out to greet a friend.

Yet both these perspectives of your hand are true because of life's many interlocking levels. One of our privileges as human beings is the freedom to put our attention, at any one time, on whichever level of life we choose. We can make a mountain out of a molehill or a molehill out of a mountain.

Similarly, with face reading you can emphasize the individual or you can look for stereotypes. Okay, that latter choice isn't face reading at all. It's what people do before they really learn to do authentic face reading. This approach will become clear if you study face reading with me. Here's how I recommend handling heredity.

When you're being a scientist, sure, consider face traits pure genetics. Roll out the gene study for genealogy or physical anthropology. Otherwise, don't concern yourself with heredity. Show your interest in learning by learning about people, one face at a time. That's face reading.

I believe your soul chooses from what's available in the gene pool. And sometimes it's a pretty long reach in that pool to find the trait that's needed. For instance, one face reading student of mine pointed out that, in his family, there are four brothers. All of them look alike except "the rebel," whose face looks completely different from all the others.

Coincidence? Not When You do Face Reading

Here's another face reading example. Think of any couple you know who have been happily married for at least ten years. Haven't their faces started to look alike? Well, who did they inherit that from, their kids?

Face Reading Secrets is *not* a pretext for judging people as good or bad. It is an opportunity to learn, not to judge. Also, face reading system is *not* deterministic, because your face changes during your lifetime, and your face comes to reflect these changes.

Furthermore, face reading is *not* about putting people into racial categories. Face reading has you notice the shapes and angles and proportions within a face. It is not about color or texture of hair, color of eyes, or color of skin—the ethnic tip-offs.

Surely You can't Deny that Certain Features Go with Particular Ethnic Groups, can You?

Stereotyping does set us to expect certain features to go with particular groups. But face reading is the opposite of stereotyping. With face reading, you look, really look, you see individuals. That's the fascinating part. And, of course, face reading requires that a person does really look. Once, when I was interviewed on national television, the host asked this question: "How can you read faces of black people when they all look alike?"

Shock waves ran through the studio audience. Interestingly, this talk show host had coffee-colored skin and blue eyes, coloring like the more famous biracial celebrity James Earl Jones. Probably she, herself, was a mixture of black and white. So she really knew better than to ask such an insulting question. But she wanted to stir things up.

Publicly, few people today would come out and say "All black people look alike" or "All people from East Asia look alike." We don't say it, but frequently we think it. Face reading is an opportunity to stop thinking in stereotypes and start seeing individuals. When you do this, your example helps to reduce racial tensions. This is one of my dreams as a teacher of face reading.

If We do Want to See the Real Person, Instead of a Stereotype, How can Your Face Reading Help Us?

You look at one face part at a time, and within that face part you keep on looking. Each face part has plenty of items of face data to choose from. So if you've been raised to believe that certain face parts, like noses, always go with one ethnic group, you're going to be in for a big shock.

Take the example of the nose trait I call the nose bonus. Some people have an extra chunk of nose that hangs down below the nose tip, between the nostrils. (Cosmetic surgeons call it a "hanging columella" and it's one of many facial non-deformities they will very happy to remove, even if the inner consequence is to remove the associated talent.)

In *The Power of Face Reading*, I give examples of great people who have had this face data. The list includes: Martin Luther King, Jr., Albert Schweitzer, Anwar Sadat, Leo Esaki, Henri Bergson, Jacinto Benavente Martinez, Odysseus Elytis, Yuan T. Lee, Har Gobind Khorana, Camillo Golgi, Ivan Pavolv, Tiger Woods.

What is the inner meaning of a nose bonus? With face reading, it's not an excuse to cut people's faces open and remove their most distinctive characteristics. With face reading, that data represents both a talent, and need, for your work to truly help people. Service keeps such nose owners motivated more than profit, fame, or other motivations. Whatever the characteristics of your particular nose, face reading can help you to appreciate it. With face reading, you appreciate that the physical face is a sacred spiritual alphabet. Read those letters and you can fall in love with just about any face.

How Much is There to Really See When You do Face Reading?

Although I can't speak for every system of face reading, here's what happens with Face Reading Secrets. You discover new things about your own face you never noticed before, like ear position and the degree of sculpting on your philtrum. What, never heard of your philtrum? That's just the part of your face loaded with information about sex. Think you might find that interesting?

How could this be? Before these people were well educated, even sophisticated. Yet they didn't pay close attention. Why should they? They weren't doing face reading yet. Therefore, most face parts weren't meaningful. In fact, faces have so much information that a full face reading session for one person can take an hour or longer.

What if, after You Learn Face Reading, You can't Stop Yourself? Could Face Reading Turn me into Some Kind of a Weirdo, Where I Drive Myself and other People Crazy?

Not to worry, when you learn face reading, you're not headed for The Twilight Zone. You won't obsessively go for the deep stuff every time you see a couple of ears or a chin. This is a skill. You can turn it off or on at will.

Think of face reading knowledge like having a TV set. When you choose to know more about people, zap!, you can turn it on. When you're more interested in something else, say sex, use your inner "remote." (This station clicker isn't really that far away.) One simple choice does it. Automatically the part of you that does face reading will turn off so you're back to being a normal person...whatever that is.

Where does Face Reading Come From?

Here's an excerpt from the foreword to my how-to book, *The Power of Face Reading*, by physiognomist Dr. Narayan Singh Khalsa: "Systematic study of faces started with the shamans. Generally it has remained an esoteric understanding for the rare specialist. For instance, the Chinese system involves an apprenticeship training process sometimes lasting 40 years. Therefore, systematic forms of Face Reading have not been readily available.

"In the West, during the Middle Ages, this began to change. A man by the name of Lavater began seriously studying and drawing faces, starting an unusual tradition of seeking to make

Face Reading public domain. Historically, however, we humans have been effectively paranoid (that is, intensely judgmental). Due to this pattern, Face Reading literature has been harsh in the extreme. Once I read this: "A concave nose is one step away from animality and bestiality." Now who has concave noses? Most children, for starters.

"No wonder only the most dedicated students of physiognomy attempt to survey the full range of literature in this field, 60 titles since Lavater that I, personally, have encountered. As I was reviewing this literature for my first book on the meaning of facial features, I ran across a little gem of a book called, *I Can Read Your Face*." Now, nine years later, Rose has written what I consider to be another breakthrough book, applying Face Reading to everyday situations with lots of examples of events and people to concretize what she is talking about. She makes Face Reading understandable, easy to learn, and memorable.

"Her communication style is refreshingly upbeat, zestful, enthusiastic, and passionately involved (like her lifestyle, to judge from her anecdotes and my personal experience of her). Beneath the surface you'll find a depth of understanding about people and the meaning of faces that doesn't exist elsewhere in the literature."

What will Your Face Reveal?

All About Faces. Here you will find everything you need to succeed and it can all be done because of what your face reveals. Your Face reveals your personality, character, background, destiny. Your face tells a story. Your face is a gift that will show you the way to health, wealth, happiness.

Achieve Success With Face Reading—Discover how you can —Communicate Better, Improve Your Relationships, Find A Compatible Partner, Improve Your Health, Find Your "Right" Career, Improve Your Interview Skills, Increase Sales, Make More Money, Predict & Prevent Violence.

You will have **The Advantage, The Edge**. Your face will lead the way. Discover how to read faces and you will succeed.

Your Face Reveals Your Personality

Your face is a road map of your mind. What you think about most of the time shows up on your face. All faces reveal personality and destiny. If you frown all the time, or are happy, the lines become permanent, which can be interpreted.

What does Your Face Reveal?

Your Forehead shows your thinking style.

Your Eyebrows indicate your thought process.

Your Eyes indicate your outlook—attitude.

Your Nose shows your work style and how you manage money.

Your Mouth shows how you express yourself.

Your Ears indicate your learning style.

Face Reading (Physiognomy) goes back to Hippocrates. It is also known as Siang Mien, Face Language, Personology. Aristotle, Caucer, Darwin, Johann Lavatar, Robert Whiteside, Mac Fulfer, Lailan Young, are just a few who have published their research.

What can be seen in a face? Your strengths, weaknesses, your past, your personality, your destiny. Your personality is not positive, negative, good or bad. It is how you choose to use your personality—to your advantage or disadvantage.

Nationally Recognized Face Profiler, Kathy Thompson will Help You Change Your Life Forever.

Your Face and Your Relationships

Couples who have their faces profiled are more likely to succeed in their relationships. If you are not compatible, and have don't have 5 specific traits in common, you will tend to drift apart. Couples can put you both on the right track. Now you have everything you need to have long lasting relationships. Save your relationships now—will help you improve your relationships with your partner, family, children, friends, everyone you meet.

Your Face and Your Health

By looking at the face, you can tell the health status of several organs in the body. If there is any discoloration or something not right on the face part, that indicates a problem in the specific organ. The nose displays the condition of the lungs. The mouth is connected to the spleen. The eyes show the condition of the liver. The ears are connected to the kidneys. And yes, if there is a crease on the ear lobe, it can denote heart problems. And the groove under the nose displays sexual organ problems. Improve Your Health Now.

Your Face and Your Career

Many of us go through life looking for the "right" career. Your abilities, aptitudes, interests, (personality), point to what you were born to do—"Doin' What Comes Naturally". Certain personality traits do well in specific careers. **Teachers** should be tactful, optimistic, self-confident. **Managers** should be possessive, domineering, analytical, impersonal, self-confident. **Service Fields** need people who are generous, helpful, considerate, friendly, magnetic. **Sales** reps need to be friendly, physical, tactful, domineering, objective. **Entrepreneurs** should be risk takers, innovative, domineering, ambitious, impersonal, analytical self-confident. **Are You Doing What Comes Naturally?** You Can Get Your Own "Your Path Profile".

Your Face and Selling—By knowing the personality behind the face, you can adjust your sales presentations according to each individual's unique personality. You can approach anyone and immediately successfully communicate, persuade, and sell them. To help you improve your sales, the following products are available; "29 Secrets Tips To Increase Sales", "How To Read Faces and Profit," Check them out Here.

Areas That Can Make Use Of Face Reading—Human Resources, Schools, Law Enforcement, Security, Employment Agencies, Attorneys, Sales Professionals, Counselors, Detective Agencies, Teachers.

The Face Unmasked

In introducing the general overview of the face, a couple more important points are noteworthy. They relate to the height and width of the head and face. A person with a developed backhead is more emotional, family and socially orientated. The narrower the backhead—the less so. The height of the crown indicates the idealism but more so the authority of the person. When the crown is low the person lacks in confidence to the degree that the crown is underdeveloped.

Obviously, an overdeveloped crown produce a tyrannical, authoritarian nature. Next time you're in the office you'll be inspecting a few crowns on superiors heads I suspect. An ambitious nature is also revealed by a well developed crown. The upper portion of the top of the head relates to imagination in proportion to its development and the dominance

Passivity can be detected by the width or narrowness of the head when viewed front on. The length of the head reveals foresight. A short head, when viewed side on indicates lack of forethought and a more live-in-the-moment attitude.

The Hair

Your hair is a measure of physical insulation, endurance and overall strength. If your hair is fine, delicate and silky, you are sensitive and also likely to be fragile physically especially if you are of a slender build. Thick wiry hair is an indication of your physical prowess and your resilience in life. You have great recuperative powers and may like a challenge in life.

The Face is a Living Personality Profile

The Forehead

The Forehead can be broadly categorized as follows—A wide forehead expresses your cleverness and practicality—being someone capable of executing duty diligently. This gives you high idealism and a wealth of ideas. A high rounded and deep forehead depicts your idealism, but with a focus on strong friendship. A narrow forehead is considered an obstacle to fulfilment, especially in social situations. Constraints in family life. Need to think things through.

Shallow forehead with a low hairline may cause many obstacles to your career success and parental troubles between the ages of 15 and 30.

Flat forehead gives you a more pragmatic nature, given to factual expression.

Exaggerated forehead reveals you are certainly a dreamer—one who needs to anchor your ideas firmly to a plan of achievement.

The receding or "flying" forehead betrays your impatient and spontaneous manner in life. Possessing an indented forehead is not a good omen for your employment or business prospects. Plan and work carefully. Indented with powerful eyebrow ridge means you are quick tempered, impulsive and ambitious.

A pointed forehead shows your high intelligence if your hairline is set back and not too narrow.

The Eyes

Most importantly, look to the eyes. Prominent eyes with bright sparkle or glitter are pe referable to small, squinty or shifty eyes which reveal an introverted and secretive nature. In fact the eyes are the most important feature in your close encounters of the business kind. In your search for that employee or partner, look for eyes that sit firmly whilst gazing steadily. This reflects a solid and persevering nature and a person of stability and forthright disposition. In contrast, a wandering or shifty eye portends a nature given to unsettled and inconsistent habits. Restlessness will be evident and other features supporting your observation and gut feeling, a tendency to dishonesty and unreliability will be marked in this type. In short, this is a person of meagre commitment.

Unevenly set eyes convey an unique meaning. Firstly, the person is capable of seeing things from a different perspective and applying lateral thought processes to resolving problems. These people will analyse your comments and observations with a "left-of-field" mentality. Often you will be amazed at the impromptu insights that they offer. If you are looking for someone with a flair for shifting paradigms—then here's your man or woman. These people become invaluable assets to a company looking for ingenuity in it's approach.

If the eyes slant upwards the person is an opportunist—more so if the brows also slant in that direction (cats eyes look). Many models like Elle McPherson and Claudia Schiffer possess these eyes. They know how to get what they want. If the eyes are of the opposite slant i.e. slanting downwards, the person may be a little self deprecating and at the mercy of others. They are hardly able to say "no".

The late Princess Dianna and Michael Jackson share a feature of the eyes. They possess floating irises also known as sampaku. The whites are visible under the iris. This indicates an inner turbulence—a person at odds with the world. Though spiritual in nature, they are hard to please or understand and have very high expectations of others. Martin Luther King and Abraham Lincoln also shared these traits.

The whites visible above the irises may indicate some dangerous elements within the personality. An explosive temper may be latent in this type and the nature very forceful. Caution is the operative word in this case. Charles Manson exhibited these eyes. Chinese face readers call them wolves eyes.

Look at how close or widest the eyes are. Ideally, there should be at least one eye width between both eyes. That being the case, you can assume your subject has a balanced judgement and clear view of the world. The closer set the eyes the narrower the opinion and view of the world at large. It may also reflect an overdependence on parental and family structures. These people may need a nudge to develop their own independent lifestyles. Their willpower should be strengthened in the search for their own self assurance. Employees and workers displaying eyes of this type certainly need continual encouragement to grow in self confidence. You will find these types possess little forbearance or tolerance and may crack under stress. Trivial matters can be blown out of all proportion.

In contrast, the wideset eyed character is far more tolerant and broadminded in perspective. People of this class may present a flagrant disregard for authority and advice. A delicate blend of firmness and understanding will iron out the initial stresses between you and this type. Offer them alternative choices in their decision-making processes. In respect of career, these types need room to breathe. Give them plenty of space to explore their creative potential. At times these types possess too broad and superficial an opinion. Pauline Hanson is a case in point.

Deepset eyes betoken an intense, possessive, yet observant nature. When you look into the deepset eyed person you can be sure that the mind motivating them is idealistic and inspirational. Often writers and creatively driven personalities possess deepset eyes. They are romantic to the core. Omar Shariff's or Val Kilmer's eyes represent this class. This idealism is tempered after the age of 35 and surprisingly, reveals a more than capable ability in financial matters. They are of sound judgement, compassionate and serious minded. A philosopher's face may often also display a deepset "soul window". You will need to carefully analyse and balance the other facial features to see whether this type is scattered and impractical. The square or round chin will anchor this type to a more empirical lifestyle. In this case, from a commercial point of view, the middle aged with deepset eyes may be a positive asset to you.

Besides, a roving and unsteady eye, one incapable of looking at you directly, is an attempt to mask inner intentions. Sometimes though, the shy and discouraged will also reflect a similar eye. The look in these cases is an important factor in discriminating between one or the other. Through practice the "look" can be ascertained quite easily and can reveal amazingly accurate character snapshots of your subjects.

What does the look entail? Some looks are cold, others endearing, angry, weak or strong. It is the look which can override an otherwise attractive face. Soft, enticing features will be neutralised by a stern and unfeeling eye or a look which is hard and cruel. Always balance your judgement of character by the look in the eyes that present themselves before you.

Be watchful of people who look drunk even when they haven't had a single beer. Their eyelids sit very heavily over the eyes. Remember, don't jump to conclusions in any of your assessments. For example, the heavy lidded one may have had little sleep the night before. A sleepy or drunken look is one that is seen in both men and women. It offers a preview of a personality given to strong sexual desire, more so if the lips are excessively thick and slightly opened. Here is a libidinous nature, but one which may be lazy too. Periods of misfortune and despondency are also revealed in this look. Unless you prefer a casual and uncommitted worker or relationship—next please. Cold and unflinching eyes with small pupils and sharp eyelight may appear cruel. If the person possesses other features such as a pointed and downward turning nose, sharp angular shaped face and tightly pursed thin lips, be certain that the individual is indeed cruel—both mentally and even perhaps physically. This is a combo for ruthlessness. Accentuated jowels add more weight to your testimony.

The "look" of the eye and its internal expression is something that cannot be taught in words but doesn't necessarily require years of experience to learn. In fact we more or less instinctively do it when we meet people in various situations.

The colour of the iris is also an important determinant in your appraisal of character. A deep blue colour means that you are in the company of a highly sexed yet gentle and sensitive being. Light blue eyes suppose an individual who is likely to enjoy flirting with the opposite sex.

Deep green eyes are not only highly energised like their blue eyed cousins but very inventive too—both in practical and personal affairs. You will need a lot of time to understand the spontaneous and sometimes wilful mind of a green eyed person. Men and women of genius often possess this coloured eye. You'll need to sharpen your intellectual skills with green eyed people.

Grey eyes reveal a high degree of intelligence and imagination but passion may be less pronounced in this type as reasoning may subdue a part of their initiative. They are a refined class of people with a fastidious streak.

Black eyes are very rare and when encountered are extremely striking. They are somewhat strong natured individuals and don't always present their case with what you'd call, finesse. You'd need to toughen up your skin to live or work with a black eyed character. A tumultuous road lay ahead if you opt for a life of black eyed fun.

The Eyebrows

The eyebrow speaks of reputation, fame and temperament too. In many cases I have found a developed brow line also shows a high degree of dexterity or ability with the hands (engineers, electronics, civil engineers, drafts persons and architects). Individuals who are observant and who have to combine refined measurements with dexterity will have the brow line well developed.

The highly arched or ideal brow often seen in the faces of film stars is described as a dramatic brow.

The low set brow reveals an impulsive temperament whilst a higher brow signals a more cautious attitude to decision-making.

A single thick brow over the nose bridge is a sign of intensity and possessive or jealous nature.

A straight brow is the sign of an aesthetic and sensitive temperament.

The Nose

The intensity of physical action is related to oxygen intake, and the external instruments of the body responsible for that function is the nose. A good sized nose is certainly an indication of wealth too and the capacity to earn money. It shows the attitude a person has to the issue of finances. Ideally the nostrils should be well concealed for the best financial prospects. The ages of 40 to 50 are ruled by the nose.

The Ideal nose has a high, straight, full and fleshy tip with gently flared but protected nostrils.

The fleshy tip indicates cordiality and warmth of personality. Deep empathy with others. Set high standards for themselves and are good mannered (Lailin). Oversized nose tip results in violent tendencies. The larger—the more prone to an act of violence.

An Aquiline nose portrays strong will, independence and enterprise with successful mid years.

An upturned nose betokens a luck in social circumstances and a love of mixing with people.

Other noses may include:

- **High bridge and pointed:** High degree of energy and very curious mind.
- **Large:** High energy levels but may be more materially concerned than spiritual.
- **Small:** Reserved, shy type.
- **Thin:** Highly strung, on edge and somewhat irritable with trifles.
- **Wide:** Expressive but may develop a devil may care attitude.
- **Long:** Prudent but anxious.
- **Short:** Happy, natural.
- **Short Snub:** Friendly but also secretive. Slow meticulous approach to life.
- **Straight:** Disciplined nature which is methodical.

The Philtrum

The groove on the upper lip, below the nose is worth mentioning. It is called the philtrum. If it is clearly marked, deep and long, it augurs well for a strong and healthy energy levels and vitality. Flat, weak and unpronounced philtrums are a mark of reduced life force and drive.

The Mouth

The mouth is related to communication, speech and the sensual appetites like eating and sex. The lips relate to our ability to nurture others in loving relationships. If the upper lip is considerably thinner than the lower lip, it reveals an inability to reciprocate in relationships. Conversely, a thinner lower lip indicates an overly giving nature.

Lips which are full, round and even convey to you that the person is caring and sensitive. The upper and lower lips in equal distribution reveal a well meaning and communicative personality.

If the lips are large, it means an expensive and somewhat luxurious taste, but an expressive and generous temperament nonetheless. Often the large mouthed person can be very vocal under pressure, needing to verbalise, sometimes excessively, their dissatisfaction and frustration.

Small lips which are also tightly pursed warn of a self centred and mean character. The downward curvature of the lips is an marking pointing to discontent in most matters. You may find it hard to please these types irrespective of what you do or say. Look for upward curved lips which indicate the opposite—someone cordial and optimistic with a sunny disposition. Ex Prime Minister Bob Hawke exhibited the thin downward turned lips.

Narrow lips reveal an unemotional character who lives more or less an internalised life, never able to enjoy the pleasure of sharing deeper feelings.

As well:-

Large lips mean a rich and luxurious taste. Expressive and generous temperament.

- **Small:** Selfish, miserly.
- **Curving down:** Discontented.
- **Large lips:** Hedonistic.
- **Curving up:** Cheerful.
- **Curved lips:** Changeable.
- **Straight lips:** Self-controlled.
- **Narrow lips:** Unemotional.

The Chin

This relates to the stamina of the individual. The stronger the jaw line, the greater the degree of stamina and endurance. People with very strong jaw lines can sometimes be considered stubborn. If the jaw line exceeds the balance of other features in the face, don't be too hasty in your judgement as this may simply mean a person who has strong convictions and who is not easily swayed by the opinions of others.

The chin should be rounded or square in shape with a gentle fullness. If this is the case, the latter part of life, during the 60's and 70's will be satisfying and lucky.

A protruding chin displays a strongly independent, determined individual.

Weak or receding chin reveals a weaker willed personality.

Jawline extending beyond earline betokens an individual who doesn't like losing and who may brook no opposition.

The Ears

The ears fall in the mid-section of the head but represent the early, formative years of life between birth and 15. As such, look to the ears to determine the foundation of life and the potential for achievement especially during the mid life ages 40-50.

The ears should exhibit good, fleshy inner and outer helixes. Thin and poorly shaped outer helixes may reveal diminishing health.

Some other general types of ears are as follows:

- Set Close to Head: Plans ahead and is thrifty. Doesn't like to leave too much to chance.
- Protruding: An original thinker. Lonely. Non-conformist.
- Ears with small lobes: Not easy to achieve sexual fulfilment Dependant and may lack initiative.
- Ears with large lobes: Independent, strong minded.
- Large ears: Intellectual.
- Longer than wider ears: Keen, impractical.
- Small ears: Instinctive.
- Ears with no lobes: Unresponsive and lacks purpose.

The Cheeks

If status and position mean anything at all to you, you'll begin paying a lot more attention to this part of your own and others' faces. Cheeks tell the story of industriousness, power and authority in a person's life. Although as westerners we have a preference for a prominent and bonier style of cheek, the eastern (especially Chinese face readers) have a different perception.

Ideally, your cheeks should be prominent, fleshy and high set with full body, colour and a warm glow. These attributes must be balanced against the position and strength of your nose. Both these features should harmonise with each other. The cheeks should stand somewhat apart from the nose not crowding it, nor too distant. The height of both should not detract from each other. If you do indeed possess fine cheeks of this description you will have very good chances of all round happiness.

In describing the ideal cheeks, Santa Clause may spring to mind with his rosy and shiny set of chubby cheeks. But according to eastern opinion, the excessively shiny cheek is indicative of digestive trouble. The cheeks are a pretty good barometer of health changes from time to time. Keep a close watch on your own biological gauge your cheeks. Other cheek colours to take note of in yourself and others are...

- **Overly red cheek:** lung and bronchial imbalance
- **Shiny and red:** gallbladder and/or heart problems
- **Red and rashy:** trouble in the intestinal region

And in the sphere of personal relationships the colour of the cheeks may also herald some very important changes. For example,

- Blue or greenish tinge—turbulence or difficulty in love life.
- Dark or grey tinge—inner dissatisfaction and poor circumstances generally.
- Any moles or marks which appear suddenly are indicators of danger or trouble through deception.

The stronger the cheeks, the more authoritative you are. Those in positions of control, executive power and leadership will often be seen to possess very strong, prominent cheeks. In romance and marriage, the partner with the more powerful cheeks is said to control the other. When meeting others of the opposite sex take note of the strength of the cheeks. Compare your own and study the play of energies between you. Who is the dominant partner? Do you or the other person own the stronger cheeks? In this way you should foster the spirit of understanding and insight into your relationships—both for business and pleasure.

If your cheeks are prominent yet not fleshy, it shows your frugal and economical disposition. You have a natural thrift not only where money matters are concerned, but in virtually every department of life. You hate waste. You may be the one in the family who must eat the last vegetables left on your child's plate for fear that they may end up in the bin. Or, if you have a pet, you take pleasure in seeing that no scraps have been discarded by being offered at the door of the kennel for the next morning's breakfast.

In the case of undeveloped cheeks means, you or not that forceful in your communication style and tend to be a little laid back but usually quite happy with what providence brings along. You must be a little wary that this doesn't deteriorate into an apathetic stance, which may cause lost opportunities for you.

Sometimes, the cheeks appear to be strong in their presentation and are pronounced but lacking at the base. This means you are a forceful individual who is combative by nature. You are reactive to the circumstances and people around you and are learning the lessons of graciously living and letting live.

If your cheeks are narrow but strong, you have a very stubborn streak in your nature. You are not easily changed in opinion or swayed from the course of action you set your mind upon. You are also extremely forceful in the way you present your opinions and ideas to others. This may not serve you as well as you think—especially if you require the support of your peers and superiors in your professional arena.

The Nature of Physiognomy

The term "physiognomy" refers to features of the face, especially so when, in the narrow sense, these features are used to infer the relatively enduring character or temperament of an individual. On this site, physiognomy connotes a broader meaning, i.e. it refers to relatively unchanging facial features that might convey messages about any inner or hidden aspect of the person. Most of these facial features have as their basis the bony structure of the skull, on which the soft tissues lie. These features include the shapes and positions of major areas and landmarks of the face, such as the forehead, eyebrows, nose, cheeks, and mouth. The important facial features can be fairly accurately reconstructed by experts from the skull alone. A diagram of the human cranium shows the major features of the skull, from which much of the visible appearances of the face can be extrapolated. Other physiognomic features are not directly linked to the bony skull, such as skin texture and coloration, hair placement and texture, and detailed shapes of fleshy features. All of these features change slowly and relatively little over time, and they are the sign vehicles for physiognomic messages. Proposing an association between these facial features and other aspects of the person, including personality, character, outcomes of medical treatment, romantic compatibility, or the destiny of the person, is a physiognomic approach. The validity of the association or inference based on physiognomy is a separate issue that can be established or discredited by empirical evidence. Accurately face reading these signs depends upon knowing which relations are valid and which are spurious.

Types of Messages

What might such physiognomic messages be about? Well, logically, as the signs of physiognomy change little or slowly, they can only be about characteristics that are relatively enduring and that change little or not at all. Such messages might include a person's genetic background (e.g. race, ethnicity, and family membership), genetic diseases (e.g. Down's syndrome), and more fuzzy concepts such as personality, character, and temperament. These facial features are unlikely to convey messages about characteristics that change rapidly or often, such as a transient emotions, because they cannot capture such rapid changes in their time scale of change. However, the possibility remains that repeated transient experiences, such as an often elicited emotion, might cumulate an effect on such slowly changing features. Also, observers often confuse some of these permanent signs with transient signs that actually do convey information about rapidly changing characteristics.

Topics related to physiognomy have a very long history in human cultures. In China and other Asian cultures, formal systems of face reading techniques developed sometime in the first millennia b.c.e., integrated with religious beliefs such as

Confucianism. Substantial confidence in such methods developed in these cultures, and physiognomic inferences included descriptions of character, suitability for certain positions, and predictions about life and death. In Western cultures, the association of facial features with a person's characteristics also has a history, first noted in the writings of the ancient Greeks. Much later, several pseudo-scientific and cultish movements exploited the inference of character from physiognomic features. The physiognomy movement proper (which cultivated the narrow connotation for this term) was Phrenology, popularized by the 18th century Swiss philosopher Lavater. Some other applications of physiognomy are discussed further on the Physiognomy Applications page.

The face, despite recent advances in assessing identity such as biometrics and DNA testing, remains paramount in ordinary experience for identifying a individual person. The relatively permanent features of the face convey most of the information about identity, although styles in the production of more transient signals and other body shapes and sizes may also contribute to identity information. The signs of identity can be preserved in representations as schematic as the monochromatic drawing at the right, which Americans can easily identify as George Washington. Such permanent features of the face also convey information about the genetic background of the individual, including ancestry and ethnicity.

Tools for Studying Physiognomy

Visage is a project that attempts to represent the features that are used to describe the face and the characteristics that are associated with such facial features. A relational database stores the feature names, the characteristics, and the relations among them. You can get an idea of what this database contains from the Visage applet. It shows illustrations of a limited set of facial features that you can use to describe a face, then retrieves some of the descriptions that have been associated with these features.

Applications of the Physiognomic Approach

The practice of attributing ability, character, and other traits to people based on the physical appearance of their faces goes back millenia. The applications of physiognomy range from ancient methods for understanding people and predicting their futures to relatively modern employment practices. Physiognomy has historically played important, if circumscribed, roles in social transactions, not merely grist for chats over coffee. Besides the formal systems discussed below, people have a seemingly irresistible urge to make informal judgments about people based on their facial features. It is important to note that none of these applications has any scientific evidence to support it and none uses any of the scientific evidence and theory discussed on the Science page as a basis for its practice.

Phrenology

A pseudo-science related to physiognomy is Phrenology. The phrenologist claims that specific areas of the cranium reflect certain personality and character traits. By examining these areas of the head for features such as size and shape, an expert can infer hidden attributes of individuals. This approach developed in the early 19th century, based on the discovery that areas of the cerebral cortex under the skull were specialized and related to specific kinds of activities. Thus, the skull area over each area takes on certain forms matching the abilities of the brain underneath it. Unfortunately for this theory, the early ideas of specialization of the brain are seriously flawed, and the assumption that specialized areas have anything to do with shapes of the cranium is false. Nevertheless, this idea of phrenology became very popular, and many experts on phrenology published volumes describing the applications of this technique. Numerous followers promoted the fad and supplied their services to an eager public, usually for a fee. None of their claimed expertise have any basis in fact, and the subject seems little more than a humorous relict today. Most people looking back can shrug off this phenomenon as an obsolete fad, but it is a good example of how a bogus program wrapped in an appropriate jargon and presented elegantly by authoritative promoter not only can defraud the unwary but also can mask a pervasive ignorance. Some phrenology examples are presented on the phrenology pages.

Chinese Face Reading

Physiognomy associates any feature of the face and head with personal characteristics, and as a practice, it has a long history in Western and Eastern cultures. European physiognomists prospered from the Middle Ages until the critiques of empirical science blunted its unsubstantiated claims. It still attracts attention as a curiosity and books and popular articles retain an interest. Examples of these physiognomic techniques are presented on the physiognomy practice pages. Some traditional physiognomists, such as the Chinese face readers, insist on a much stronger relation between facial appearance and character than do scientists or western physiognomists. They posit a virtual identity between facial and psychological characters, such that if one is changed, a change in the other will follow. Thus, the life of a person is not determined by the original natural facial appearance, because changing the face will change the destiny. The Chinese approach to face reading was popularized in the United States by such proponents as David Marr, a student of a Chinese master. The method he describes uses rather more complex ideas about facial features than that of the Western physiognomist. For example, Marr describes the relationship between a number of facial features, their sizes and positions, and certain personality traits.

Merton Method for Employers

Holmes W. Merton invented the Merton Method in the late 19th and early 20th century to match a person's character to a suitable job. Merton specialized in matching personal characteristics to vocations, and he invented a unique set of traits that he claimed are relevant to job performance and satisfaction. He divided the face into dozens of different areas, each area reflecting one or more of his traits, thus matching a face to a job. Many large corporations used this method in the first half of the 20th century to make employment and job assignment decisions. The notion of vocational apptitude persists in job counselling professionals, and although few subscribe to the detailed relationships described in the Merton Method, the use of more generic facial characteristics (such as the babyface verses the square-jawed, tough-guy face) is probably still applied, though perhaps less formally. Another name associated with this method is Margaret Waring Buck, a student of Merton's and popularize of his method in the second half of the 20th century. Some practitioners of this bogus technique may still today apply this approach to unsuspecting victims in certain human resources departments.

Stereotypes of Police

Analysis of physiognomic characteristics has been employed in the criminal justice system. Some paid legal consultants offer advice to trial lawyers about their clients, prospective jurors, and witnesses based on their facial characteristics. They know that jurors respond to the faces of the defendant and the witnesses, so they try to optimize the favorableness of the impressions jurors are likely to form (such consultants are most often used by the defense). As an example of the effect that the face has on juror deliberations, consider that research shows that a babyfaced person is less likely to be convicted of an intentional crime and more likely to be convicted of a negligent crime. Some consultants also claim to have insight into the proclivities and characteristics of prospective jurors based on their faces (and other sources). An old face reading tradition in law enforcement circles that persists today is that you can tell a criminal from his or her face. Surveys of policemen indicate that even today, many believe they can detect the criminal by examining their face. The practice of using formal training methods for associating particular facial characteristics with criminal personality has, it is believed, died out in the United States but may still be encouraged elsewhere.

Acting

Another area in which physiognomy is used, though typically in an informal way, is the selection of actors to fill roles. For example, pedantic women, evil or virtuous men, and incompetent or stupid characters are often portrayed by actors who "look the part" though makeup can often compensate for discrepancies between actual and desired appearance. Character actors often spend their professional lives performing only limited roles that match their facial appearance.

Our beauty is a reflection of our health, both physical as well as mental. According to face reading experts, you can correct some aspects of your skin by treating the organs that are affecting it. There are a few versions of the face reading technique. The following pages explore the interpretation of face reading by Dr. Haushka and traditional Oriental medicine.

The Forehead

Represents the nervous system functions. The lines and wrinkles in this area indicate that the person spends a lot of time thinking, instead of acting on instinct. Thinking is from the mind, instinct is from the heart.

Pimples in this area also indicate excessive thinking that takes a lot of energy from the digestive system. In Oriental medicine, the forehead is related to the following organs: the gall bladder, liver and stomach. If there is no proper elimination of toxins by the gall bladder and intestines, this will produce pimples.

Lines between the eyebrows correspond to the liver. According to Jon Sandifer in his book "Oriental Face Reading", if this area is prone to develop pimples or is oily, or has deep lines, it indicates liver imbalance. To correct the imbalance, Sandifer recommends reducing consumption of animal products, alcohol and spices, eat more vegetables as well as to do *yoga* or Tai chi. In order to have a healthy forehead, the most important thing is to stop obsessing over your thoughts and be more joyful; this will strengthen the organs.

Food is also important to strengthen the organs. Dr. Hauschka recommends eating more whole grains, green/root vegetables, drinking enough water, avoiding processed foods, decreasing caffeine and engaging in some artistic expression.

The Mid Face

This is the area from the eyebrows to the bottom of the nose. The organs that dominate this region are the heart and the lungs. Kidneys, stomach and liver reflect in areas around the eyes. If the lungs are healthy, this reflects in healthy, clear, rosy cheeks. Shallow skin in this area indicates lung's congestion or poor oxygen levels. According to Dr. Hauschka, pimples in this area indicate an excess of fat and sugar in the lungs. In order to improve the skin in this area, according to face reading experts, you may:

- Stop smoking, reduce or eliminate greasy and fatty foods, and eliminate trans fats or hydrogenated oils found in a lot of baked products.
- Eat more green vegetables, especially cruciferous such as broccoli and cauliflower.
- Exercise or walk daily to eliminate toxins from your body.

Puffiness, redness, rashes and broken capillaries on the cheeks also indicate lung's imbalance. The eye bags are related to the kidneys. Swelling occurs when the kidneys are weak. To improve the kidney function, it is recommended to reduce or eliminate alcohol, coffee and sodas, and drink more water. The kidneys are also taxed with high consumption of animal products and high levels of salt.

The nose is associated with the heart. If the bulb of the nose is red and swollen, this indicates that the heart is overworked. To have a healthy heart, eat less saturated fats found in dairy and meats, eliminate trans fats (often found in plenty in fast food and processed foods) and eat more vegetables and whole grains. Exercise daily and reduce stress.

The Lower Region

This is the area from the nose down to the chin. It is related to the digestive tract. The chin is related to the functioning of the kidneys and gall bladder and reproductive organs.

If there are pimples or blemishes in the chin region, this indicates accumulation of fat and hormonal imbalance in the reproductive organs. The lips are related to the intestines; swollen lips indicate congestion in the digestive tract.

A healthy lifestyle including diet, stress reduction, soul nurturing through art or a hobby help to balance the organs and to have a healthy, glowing face according to this theory.

Face reading also includes many other aspects such as personality and there are many books on the topic.

What is Energy Spirituality?

Energy Spirituality explores the human energy field, or aura, as a point of entry for healing the body-mind-spirit-system. Just as mathematics is the language of science, aura reading is the language of energy spirituality. Practically speaking, Energy Spirituality relates to Healing, Deeper Perception and Self-Aware Consciousness—all explored on this website.

Self-Aware Consciousness Sounds Like Fun. What is it?

Self-Aware Consciousness means being awake inside. Energy Spirituality helps this to shift, bringing mystical experience, a higher state of awareness or simply becoming more effective at daily life. You need it to become a skilled empath, for aura reading, for growing as a person.

Energy Spirituality brings clarity to the search for self-aware consciousness. For example, **Empaths** are my largest group of clients who benefit from developing self-aware consciousness, since 1 in 20 people is born as an empath. Empaths can directly experience what it is like to be other people. Until an empath is skilled, not "merely" talented with one or more inborn gifts as an empath, suffering results.

An unskilled empath constantly picks up other people's pain, whether physical, emotional, intellectual or spiritual. It is immensely important for empaths to wake up to their gifts and then learn how to use them consciously. Unfortunately, the advice from pop culture for empaths comes from the last millennium, not this one. It is socially oriented advice, not advice that makes use of the most important factor in the everyday life of every born empath.

Every empath flies in spirit due to gifts of spiritual consciousness. Harnessing that consciousness is needed to become a skilled empath, not shielding or armoring. Trying to "strengthen your boundaries" or "center yourself" is not going to make a natural empath into a skilled empath. Instead, guess what? After a lot of hard work, there will be a natural empath with walls, big enough walls to show in an aura reading incidentally.

But for all the efforts to put up an invisible shield or firm set of boundaries, that unskilled empath still will constantly pick up STUFF from other people's auras. Only now the empath has a wall that makes it harder for other people to get to know who that individual authentically is.

Sound Like a Great Solution to You?

I love to help empaths who do better. I've personally helped thousands of empaths become truly skilled empaths, using their own inner power of consciousness to wake up from inside.

In addition to teaching skills for empaths, the emotional and spiritual healing from Energy Spirituality helps anyone—empath or not—to become more stable, with a clearer aura. Another limiting form of advice to empaths and others is to avoid psychic vampires, narcissists, and psychic attack. Blaming other people is not the surest way to grow, personally. Cut cords of attachment, rather than simply identifying "bad guys."

Energy Spirituality also includes removing types of astral debris, like psychic coercion, and using Energy Release Regression Therapy to move out STUFF from a person's aura. Your destiny is to carry your aura, with its many distinctive gifts, without also carrying STUFF that locks fear, pain, guilt, depression, etc. into an aura.

Most of my techniques of Energy Spirituality can be learned from my books. They also can be done for you, one on one, through personal sessions, making use of my experience working as a teacher of personal development since 1970.

What Kind of Healing can Result from Energy Spirituality?

Any effective technique for holistic healing enhances the full body-mind-spirit. Although the whole self is affected, there must be an entry point. For instance, Donna Eden's **Energy Medicine** starts with the physical body and its energy meridians. A client might have the intention, "Cure my chronic fatigue". Gary Craig's EFT and David Feinstein's **Energy Psychology** begin psychologically. A client might have the intention, "Fix my fear of heights". By contrast, the point of entry for **Energy Spirituality** is spiritual, the client's aura itself.

What is the goal of using Deeper Perception for Energy Spirituality?

Direct perception enriches the quest for Spiritual Source, be that called God or Self, a sacred name of any kind, or simply an experience of reading life deeper. The goal may be to **co-create with God**, or some other form of self-actualization.

Whatever the goal, Energy Spirituality aims to make it happen with direct experience rather than mere theory. How can a seeker —or consumer—tell the difference? Aura reading to the rescue. Face reading to the rescue. Empath empowerment to the rescue. By teaching techniques for Deeper Perception as part of Energy Spirituality, this website aims to transform transpersonal questing into everyday experience. Join our community as we grow with Energy Spirituality.

Spiritual Healings with Deeper Perception

What are Spiritual Healings?

Did you ever try to protect (or strengthen) yourself energetically? If not, why not? To understand how much you can benefit from Spiritual Healings, let's start by defining auras.

Okay, What is My Aura?

Your aura, or field, or energy field is a set of overlapping bodies around your physical body. Think of the layers of an onion. Only, of course, you smell better. Auras are important because they contain bits and bytes of information about you. This information is clustered in chakras, and I now read 50 different databanks in any chakra worth reading. (I can teach you to do the same, incidentally.)

Any databank within an aura contains information about gifts of your soul, ways you are put together as an individual, magnificent talent, how you are unique. Auras also contain "STUFF" basically dirt that clouds those gifts of the soul. STUFF can always, and I mean always, be healed.

Much of the STUFF in an aura has to do with your personal story. To heal that, there are techniques of **Energy Spirituality**, Energy Psychology and Energy Medicine. (As a spiritual and emotional healer, my contribution lies in the first of these three specialties. All of them can work.) Typically, when I do Personal Sessions of Energy Spirituality, I facilitate **Cutting Cords of Attachment** as well as Aura Reading to validate gifts of the soul. Depending on the blockage, I may recommend **Regression Therapy** as the most efficient way to pull STUFF out of an aura.

But a great deal of STUFF in an aura can come from outside. It has no significant connection to your personal story. It is, basically, astral debris. You know how dust can accumulate in your house unless you do the occasional cleaning. Astral debris is similar. To heal it, do Spiritual Healings. And, if you're wise, you will use highly efficient and quick techniques for doing so. This is what I can teach you. (Or I can simply do them for you during a personal session, if you prefer.)

What are Some Examples Where Someone would Need Spiritual Healings?

As I go into this list, be prepared. All of the following problems are extremely common. They can be healed easily, though. That is the good news. So here come the Top Five types of astral debris: Ghosts, Negative thought forms, Psychic coercion, Outdated personality projections, Psychic ties.

How did You Learn about Spiritual Healings, Rose?

In 1985, I studied a great system called "Inner Sensitivity" (from *Teaching of the Inner Christ*). This system includes the most effective techniques for Spiritual Healings that I have ever encountered.

First, I studied with the late, great Rev. Rich Bell. Then I sponsored and studied with **Rev. AlixSandra Parness**. She surprised me by making me a lay minister for this system, asking me to teach in the greater Washington area. Later I wrote to the founder of this system, Rev. Ann Makeever Meyer and she gave me permission to teach and write about what I had learned.

Do You Teach Exactly the Same Techniques as the Inner Sensitivity Group?

No, I have adapted these techniques and added some additional ones. Also, this group teaches things I do not, especially emphasizing channeling. I have the utmost respect for Inner Sensitivity (and T.I.C.), and for Rev. Parness, and invite you to explore their offerings.

How can I Learn These Techniques from You?

Weekend Intensives are recommended, but I can also teach you through Mentoring Sessions by phone.

Aren't Techniques Like These Taught Whenever People Study Reiki or Angelic Healing or Other Holistic Techniques?

Not in my experience. Wonderful things are taught by holistic professionals, including plenty of things that I do not teach. However, Inner Sensitivity offers a valuable perspective on astral debris because, unlike most systems that are popular today in the holistic community, the practitioner's awareness goes beyond the astral level where problems reside. Therefore, this system exposes problems that otherwise go unnoticed (or else are noticed but can't be removed as efficiently).

You will note that I said "in my experience." Since 1986, I have done personal sessions with clients, many of whom are practitioners of various holistic techniques, some of whom are really talented teachers of those techniques. Yet their auras were full of astral debris, and so Spiritual Healings made a big difference for them.

How can Spiritual Healings Help with Ghosts?

Removal—that's the quick answer. Did you know that most people who work with angels or Reiki healing inadvertently pick up astral entities? Empaths and spiritual seekers are also especially at risk. Talk about energy drains! Some psychics take hours or weeks to move out one spirit, but the healing I use and teach is just as effective. It helps the entity move on to its next place of development, while cleaning your own aura or home.

How can Spiritual Healings Help to Clean up Negative Thought Forms?

I can't overstate how important it is to remove this kind of astral debris. What happens when you have a bad day? One consequence is having negative thought forms dumped into your aura. What else can let in these subconscious poisons? Arguments, bullies, and many other situations in everyday life.

Negative thought forms are real energy structures that can clutter up your aura, your car, everything you own. Many times, affirmations are designed to replace negative thought forms. Much as I love (and personally use) affirmations, they can work much more effectively after the negative thought forms are gone.

How can Spiritual Healings Help with Psychic Coercion?

Psychic coercion is the most common energy drain on the planet, yet few people even know what it is: "Shoulds" that are stuck in your aura. Psychic coercion can be deposited unintentionally by family members, friends, people who pray for you, and more. You may be carrying truckloads in your aura right now, limiting the use of your free will, unbeknownst to your conscious mind. Free yourself up completely. When I facilitate this type of healing, I include finding and removing the subconscious vulnerability pattern that has caused you to be susceptible to this kind of pressure.

Can Spiritual Healings Help with Outdated Personality Projections?

Fortunately, yes. Many people carry around personality patterns from teenage years, or before. Unless you can update these, you are doing the equivalent of wearing the same clothes from back in the day. Spiritual Healings are a super-effective way to align all of your personality projections for every type of relationship, and help you move forward as the unique and magnificent soul you have come here to be.

How can Spiritual Healings Help with Psychic Ties?

Psychic ties are **tiny energy drains** from people you meet on the road or gossip about. Little things can add up into a big chunk of blockage, making it hard to know what you really want in life. Spiritual Healings clear them all up very quickly. I can also teach you how to keep yourself clear—one of the very easiest type of Spiritual Healings to master.

Summary

Everyday, meeting a number of people and judging all of them is not an easy task. Those who meet with full warm and loud are generally dangerous and one those remain at very low speech and cool are also dangerous. Again, it is very challenging with whom you should deal your business or whom you should delay negotiations.

Girls or guys who share his or her family affairs with you in a very short meeting is a dangerous person because he or she is trying to give you personal touch and making you feel part of family. These type of people are sometimes very emotional with you and can explain about past untoward mishappening of family to make you emotional and close. The moment you get convinced, you will loose your financial health and relation both.

Mother says, if you are in a fix in your judgement then listen your heart and make a bold decision. Some will agree and some won't agree on this argument, because heart gives mixed feeling decision. Sometimes it guides to do it and then in a fraction of second, it misguides not to do it. It is a fact that we cannot listen to our heart because heart gets message from angel and Saturn both and human being cannot distinguish the difference between angels and Saturn's feeling. Then what to do?

Spiritualists say the place of our soul is towards left arm. Soul is a part of God and it gives right message and guideline time to time.

Face Reading is easy and a simple method of understanding yourself and others. After knowing the personality behind the face, you can approach each individual according to their personality. Understanding, accepting, and relating to basic differences in personality is the key to better communications and relationships for everyone in your life.

Chapter sixteen

CHANAKYA NITI

Chanakya was a great mentor and king maker (350-283 BC) of Magadh dynasty. He was running a very big educational institute and was renowned for his talent and extraordinary skills. He was disgraced at the courtyard of king Mahanand of Magadh dynasty. He vowed to dethrone the haughty king who was harassing the people of the land. After fulfilling that vow, he made Chandragupta, the Emperor.

Chanakya became an adviser and a prime minister to the first Maurya Emperor Chandragupta (340-293 BC), and architect of his rise to power. **Kautilya** and **Vishnugupta**, the names by which the ancient Indian political treatise called the *Arthashastra* identifies its author, are traditionally identified with Chanakya. Some scholars consider Chanakya to be "the pioneer economist of the world". He is known as "The Indian Machiavelli" in the Western world. Chanakya was a professor at Takshashila University and is widely believed to be responsible for the creation of Mauryan empire, the first of its kind on the Indian sub-continent.

He is generally called Chanakya but, in his capacity as author of the *Arthashastra*, is generally referred to as Kautilya. The *Arthashastra* identifies its author by the name Kautilya, except for one verse which refers to him by the name Vishnugupta. One of the earliest Sanskrit literature to explicitly identify Chanakya with Vishnugupta was Vishnu Sarma's *Panchatantra* in the 3rd century BC.

Editorial of Chanakya

Two books are attributed to Chanakya: *Arthashastra* and *Nitishastra* which is also known as Chanakya *Niti*. The

Arthashastra discusses monetary and fiscal policies, welfare, international relations, and war strategies in detail. *Nitishastra* is a treatise on the ideal way of life, and shows Chanakya's in depth study of the Indian way of life.

Chanakya was a Great Legend

Thomas R. Trautmann lists the following elements as common to different forms of the Chanakya legend:

- Chanakya was born with a complete set of teeth, a sign that he would become king, which is inappropriate for a Brahmin like Chanakya. Chanakya's teeth were therefore broken and it was prophesied that he will rule through another.
- The Nanda King throws Chanakya out of his court, prompting Chanakya to swear revenge.
- Chanakya searches for one worthy for him to rule through. Chanakya encounters a young Chandragupta Maurya who is a born leader even as a child.
- Chanakya's initial attempt to overthrow Nanda fails, whereupon he comes across a mother scolding her child for burning himself by eating from the middle of a bun or bowl of porridge rather than the cooler edge. Chanakya realizes his initial strategic error and, instead of attacking the heart of Nanda territory, slowly chips away at its edges.
- Chanakya changed his alliance with the mountain king Parvata due to his obstinacy and non-adherence to the principles of the treaty as agreed.
- Chanakya enlists the services of a fanatical weaver to rid the kingdom of rebels.
- Chanakya adds poison to the food eaten by Chandragupta Maurya, now king, in order to make him immune. Unaware, Chandragupta feeds some of his food to his queen, who is in her ninth month of pregnancy. In order to save the heir to the throne, Chanakya cuts the queen open and extracts the fetus, who is named Bindusara because he was touched by a drop (*bindu*) of blood of poison.

- Chanakya's political rivalry with Subandhu leads to his death.

Chanakya was an intelligent saint. Once, it is said that Mauryan forces had to hide in a cave. There was no food. Soldiers were starving. They could not come out of the cave either, as their was a threat to their lives. Chanakya saw an ant taking a grain of rice, whereas, there was no sign of food or grain anywhere. Moreover, the rice grain was cooked. He ordered the soldiers to search and they found that their enemies had been dining under the cave. Somewhat like, at the ground floor. As soon as they saw this, they escaped and thus were saved.

The Grass Uprooted

In his hurried walk, he stumbled on a stump of grass and was about to fall. He became very angry. The roots of that type of grass go deep into the earth. But he was undeterred. He wrath would brook no opposition. He sat down right there in that burning sun, removed that grass to its root from the earth, and then resumed his journey.

His name was Chanakya. Seeing all this stood another man, at the door of the choultry. He was young but looked bright. He was Chandragupta, and was the officer in charge of the choultry. And he thought, "What a determined man! Such a person's help is worth having." He went to Chanakya, addressed him very respectfully, and took him into the choultry with all courtesy. Chanakya made inquiries about him and asked, "Who are you? You seem to be worried".

"The Kingdom is Yours"

The officer with great reverence said, "Sir, my name is Chandragupta." "You look as if you have gone through a lot of sufferings and have great worries. You can tell me why." "I am in dire trouble, Sir," said Chandragupta. "But should I worry you with my troubles?"

"Still you can tell me. I shall see if I help you," said Chanakya, with a degree of assurance. "I am the grandson of king Sarvarthasiddhi," Chandragupta, began his tale of woe. "He had two wives, Sunandadevi and Muradevi. Sunanda got nine sons called the Navanandas. Mura had only one called Maurya and he was my father. We were a hundred brothers. The Nandas, out of jealousy, tried to kill all of us. All others were killed and somehow I have survived. I am really disgusted with all that has happened. This is my painful story. I have suffered much because of the Nandas. Would you help me to come out of my agony?"

Chanakya was greatly moved by this tale of woe. He thought that somehow he must help Chandragupta. "I will get you the Kingship Chandragupta," he consoled him. "But look, these Nandas have not directly, offended me in any way. With some ruse, I will first see that they ill-treat me. And then, you may feel sure, your work is done."

"Till I Destroy Your Family"

It was a hot and sultry afternoon. It was lunchtime in the choultry. Banana leaves had been spread in many rows. Hundreds of persons were sitting there for their lunch.

Just nearby was also a throne. Chanakya had his bath and going straight to the throne, sat on it. Just then the Navanandas also came there. They were very angry that on the throne where-kings should be seated, an ordinary man was sitting. They had Chanakya pushed out. Chanakya's tuft became untied and the hairs were loosened. He was in a fury. Hissing like a cobra he said, "You wicked fellows, I will not tie up my hair until I destroy your whole family. This is my oath. Remember it." Thundering like that, he walked off with resounding steps. The Nandas were not afraid. "What nonsense from a begging Brahmin! It is prattle to be ignored," they said contemptuously, and went back to the palace.

The Nandas had a very intelligent minister. He was Amatya Rakshasa. He was brave and capable. In statecraft he was highly experienced. He protected the Nandas as eyelids do an eye. But Chanakya was not discouraged. He singly stood opposed to the might of the Nandas and the brain of Amatya Rakshasa. He dethroned the Nandas, put Chandragupta on the throne, and also installed Amatya Rakshasa, who was trying his utmost to destroy Chandragupta, as the minister. This is the story about

Chanakya, popular in our country for hundreds of years. However, according to historians, this is not completely true.

Whether all the events that took place as this story mentions them are true or not, the one thing that has to be accepted is that, it truly reflects the nature of Chanakya.

Extraordinary Person

Chanakya was a very brilliant person. He was full of determination in achieving any objective. He was well versed in all 'Shastras' or branches of knowledge, an expert economist; a statesman par excellence. He was a master in the four methods—persuasion, enticement, sowing dissension, and punishment or war. He was mature in the strategy of war, and very intelligent. None could makeup what was going on his mind. So secretive was he in his method, and far-sighted. In any endeavour, his calculations never went wrong and he never missed his aim. He was at the same time very religious and given to strict renunciation. Apparently of a harsh nature, he could employ various methods carefully at the right time to destroy enemies. There was no branch of knowledge, which he had not mastered. He was widely experienced in the world. There seemed to be nothing, which he did not know. He was, in other words, a conglomeration of all things that make a genius. Considered in any way, persons equal to Chanakya are very rare in the world. An expression "like the strategy of Chanakya" has become proverbial. He is the memorable man who destroyed the despotic Nanda kings, put Chandragupta on the throne and brought into being the great Maurya dynasty of rules.

Chanakya had the other name of Kautilya also. Some say that he got the name Chanakya because he was born in China. A great book which clearly shows his genius is still extant. It is called the "Arthashastra." It has been translated into many other languages including English, French and German.

Unfortunately, what is authentically known about him is not much. We can only add various points and scattered material available in several books and present what could perhaps be his biography.

Student at Takshashila

Chanakya had his education at a famous school in a city well known in those days as Takshashila (corrupted later into 'Taxila'). The teachers at Takshashila were great scholars known all over the world. Students from different parts of Bharat went there for their education. Even kings sent their sons for education there. It is said that a certain teacher there had one hundred and one students and all of them were princes.

Generally, a student entered the University of Takshashila at the age of sixteen. The four Vedas, archery, hunting, elephant-lore, and eighteen arts were being taught there. The faculties there, which taught law, medicine and warfare, were famous not only in Bharat but also abroad. Such was the centre where Chanakya had his education. With this education, his inherent brilliance became like a polished diamond.

"I will Dethrone You"

Chanakya went from Takshashila to Pataliputra, which was famous as a centre of learning and was known to honour scholars. Pataliputra sheltered scholars who were intellectual giants in different branches of knowledge. There to get recognition for his scholarship. One of the Nandas by name Dhanananda was the king there at that time. He was very avaricious. He was never satisfied with the amounts of money he received, never content with the number of taxes to collect money. People were complaining that there was tax on hides, tax on wood and tax even on stone. No one knew how much wealth Dhanananda himself had amassed. It was believed that he had buried all his wealth under a boulder in the bed of the river Ganga.

By the time Chanakya came to Pataliputra, there was a change even in Dhanananda. He was giving gifts also. He had formed a trust or committee to administer his gift and charities. A great scholar would be the president of the trust. Even the other members of the trust would be well-known scholars. It is said that the president had powers to make gifts up to ten million gold coins. The juniormost member of the trust would make gifts up to one-lakh gold coins.

Chanakya possessed an extraordinary scholarship. The scholars of Pataliputra recognized his genius and honoured him. Chanakya became the president of the 'Sangha' (Trust). The work of the Sangha was to administer the king's grants and charities. Therefore, the president of the Sangha had to meet the king often.

When the president of the Sangha met the king for the first time, the king felt disgusted at the ugliness of Chanakya. He developed contempt towards Chanakya. There was no refinement in the words and conduct of Chanakya. He always spoke bluntly and straight. He was, besides, filled with intense egotism.

The king had been receiving only praise and obedience from all. So he did not like the ways of the new president. He removed Chanakya from the presidentship. Chanakya was very angry. He had not committed any mistake. All other scholars had accepted that his scholarship was extraordinary. In his anger, Chanakya erupted like volcano and told the king:

"Your position has made you arrogant. You have removed me from presidentship for no fault of mine. You think that there is none to question you, whatever injustice you commit and however you behave. You have removed me from my rightful place, and I shall also dethrone you." The king of course would not keep quiet hearing such words. He was also very angry. He ordered that Chanakya be arrested. Chanakya disguised himself as a sanyasi—a monk—and fled from the capital.

This is The Man

Later, Chanakya met Chandragupta. Even of Chandragupta, very little is known. Several things are said about his family. Probably he belonged to the Mourya community. (He got the name of Chandragupta Maurya afterwards and his royal lineage came to be known as the Maurya dynasty). His mother was perhaps the daughter of a village headman. His father, king of a forest area called Pippatavana, died in a war. The mother came to Pataliputra with her son.

The boy grew up as a village lad among other village boys. But he was a leader by birth. Even as a boy, he was accepted as a leader by all other boys. His word was law to them. Chandragupta and other boys used to play in a field. There was a tall boulder. The boy Chandragupta would be seated on the rock. In there games, he was always the king.

The other boys were all his. They would bring up their quarrels and disputes before him. He would hear the arguments on both sides and pronounce his degree. Once, Chanakya was passing that way. He was attracted by the dignity with which the boy was seated and the radiance of his face. He stood watching the play.

Chanakya was astonished by the sharp intellect and the style of the boy's speaking while judging the disputes. 'If king Nanda were dethroned, the realm would need an able king. Chanakya thought this boy would make a good king.

He stood there until game was over. Then he talked to the boy. Chanakya's physical features were ugly. That was why king Nanda had treated him with contempt. But the boy Chandragupta became aware of the intellect behind that face, and developed great respect for Chanakya.

Chanakya talked to him affectionately. He came to know who he was and his circumstances. He went with the boy to his house and spoke to his mother and other elders. He said, "Send the boy with me. He will have his education at Takshashila." Chandragupta's mother was at first unwilling to send the boy with a stranger. But what future did the boy have in a village? And how to educate this fatherless boy?

Schooling in Takshashila would be a boon, a divine gift. This chance might not come again. She was highly impressed by the brilliance of the stranger's face and also by his good words. Chandragupta left for Takshashila with Chanakya. For seven or eight years, Chandragupta had his education there, and that, with teachers selected by Chanakya. The art of warfare and the art of government were mastered by him equally well.

The Greek Invader

By then, significant events in the history of Bharat were taking place under the very eyes of Chanakya and Chandragupta. A young prince came from Greece with a big army. He had already conquered many realms. He was Alexander.

Even as Chanakya and Chandragupta were looking on, the soil of Bharat was going under foreign yoke. The people of Bharat did fight bravely. It looks as if even women took part in the fight. But not being united, they were defeated. In Chanakya's eyes, foreign rule was poison. It was his belief that alien rulers would exploit, loot and impoverish the country.

It is said that Chandragupta met Alexander. As he talked boldly and defiantly Alexander was enraged and ordered his arrest. But Chandragupta somehow escaped. Chandragupta's education was over, and Chanakya thought that their first task should be to drive out the Greeks.

Troops are Amassed

Details are not available as to how exactly Chanakya and Chandragupta fought against the Greeks. Chandragupta was not a king, nor had he any position. It would by no means be easy for such as one to gather a big army. But even this seemingly impossible work was made possible because of Chanakya's expertise. Both of them toured in different areas. They gathered soldiers mainly from the mercenary communities.

Chanakya felt that this was not enough. He befriended a king by name Parvataka, or Parvetesha of the Himalayan region and secured his help for Chandragupta. Thus Chandragupta could get the support of the strong Himalayan soldiers.

Alexander had settled some Greeks wherever he went. But they did not wish to stay there and wanted to return to Greece. Alexander had divided the realms he conquered in India into some regions and had appointed 'Satraps' to rule them. Some of them were Greeks and some were Indians. The Greeks always lived in the fear of mutinies and murders. As soon as Alexander left a Satrap incharge of a province, there would be rebellion and sometimes the Satraps would be murdered. Philip, who was very able and experienced, was thus killed. Alexander who was at a distant place could not do anything. Satraps who were Indians were burning with frustration. They were only waiting for the proper time to rebel and become free. After Alexander went out of India and died suddenly in distant Babylon in 323 B.C., all his Satraps declared themselves independent.

Freedom from the Greeks

By now, Chanakya had made the rustic boy playing the role of kings in boyish games into a great leader educated at Takshashila. He had made him a military commander too.

The source of strength for Chandragupta and his army was the power of mind and the towering personality of Chanakya. In that war of independence for Northern India, Chandragupta was the physical instrument, while its thinking brain was Chanakya.

In the primary task of eliminating the Satraps, one Satrap by name Nicossar was killed even when Alexander was alive, and another, Philip, was killed after his death. After Alexander's death in Babylon, all his Satraps were either killed or dislodged, one by one. Alexander's lieutenants divided his empire among themselves in 321 B.C. No realm east of the Indus—the river Sindhu—was mentioned in that settlement. It meant that the Greeks themselves had accepted that this region had gone out of their rule.

Chanakya Niti

Sri Chanakya Niti-Sastra

The Political Ethics of Chanakya Pandit

Chapter One

1. Humbly bowing down before the almighty Lord Sri Vishnu, the Lord of the three worlds, I recite maxims of the science of political ethics (*niti*) selected from the various *satras* (scriptures).
2. That man who by the study of these maxims from the *satras* acquires a knowledge of the most celebrated principles of duty, and understands what ought and what ought not to be followed, and what is good and what is bad, is most excellent.
3. Therefore, with an eye to the public good, I shall speak that which, when understood, will lead to an understanding of things in their proper perspective.
4. Even a *pandit* comes to grief by giving instruction to a foolish disciple, by maintaining a wicked wife, and by excessive familiarity with the miserable.

5. A wicked wife, a false friend, a saucy servant and living in a house with a serpent in it are nothing but death.
6. One should save his money against hard times, save his wife at the sacrifice of his riches, but invariably one should save his soul even at the sacrifice of his wife and riches.
7. Save your wealth against future calamity. Do not say, "What fear has a rich man, of calamity?" When riches begin to forsake one, even the accumulated stock dwindles away.
8. Do not inhabit a country where you are not respected, cannot earn your livelihood, have no friends, or cannot acquire knowledge.
9. Do not stay for a single day where there are not these five persons: a wealthy man, a *brahmin* well versed in *Vedic* lore, a king, a river and a physician.
10. Wise men should never go into a country where there are no means of earning one's livelihood, where the people have no dread of anybody, have no sense of shame, no intelligence, or a charitable disposition.
11. Test a servant while in the discharge of his duty, a relative in difficulty, a friend in adversity, and a wife in misfortune.
12. He is a true friend who does not forsake us in time of need, misfortune, famine, or war, in a king's court, or at the crematorium (*smasana*).
13. He who gives up what is imperishable for that which is perishable, loses that which is imperishable; and doubtlessly loses that which is perishable also.
14. A wise man should marry a virgin of a respectable family even if she is deformed. He should not marry one of a low-class family, through beauty. Marriage in a family of equal status is preferable.
15. Do not put your trust in rivers, men who carry weapons, beasts with claws or horns, women, and members of a royal family.

16. Even from poison extract nectar, wash and take back gold if it has fallen in filth, receive the highest knowledge (Krsna consciousness) from a low born person; so also a girl possessing virtuous qualities (*stri-ratna*) even if she were born in a disreputable family.
17. Women have hunger two-fold, shyness four-fold, daring six-fold, and lust eight-fold as compared to men.

Chapter Two

1. Untruthfulness, rashness, guile, stupidity, avarice, uncleanliness and cruelty are a woman's seven natural flaws.
2. To have ability for eating when dishes are ready at hand, to be robust and virile in the company of one's religiously wedded wife, and to have a mind for making charity when one is prosperous are the fruits of no ordinary austerities.
3. He whose son is obedient to him, whose wife's conduct is in accordance with his wishes, and who is content with his riches, has his heaven here on earth.
4. They alone are sons who are devoted to their father. He is a father who supports his sons. He is a friend in whom we can confide, and she only is a wife in whose company, the husband feels contented and peaceful.
5. Avoid him who talks sweetly before you but tries to ruin you behind your back, for he is like a pitcher of poison with milk on top.
6. Do not put your trust in a bad companion nor even trust an ordinary friend, for if he should get angry with you, he may bring all your secrets to light.
7. Do not reveal what you have thought upon doing, but by wise counsel keep it secret, being determined to carry it into execution.

8. Foolishness is indeed painful, and verily so is youth, but more painful by far than either is being obliged in another person's house.
9. There does not exist a pearl in every mountain, nor a pearl in the head of every elephant; neither are the *sadhus* to be found everywhere, nor *sandal* trees in every forest. [Note: Only elephants in royal palaces are seen decorated with pearls (precious stones) on their heads].
10. Wise men should always bring up their sons in various moral ways, for children who have knowledge of *niti-sastra* and are well behaved become a glory to their family.
11. Those parents who do not educate their sons are their enemies; for as is a crane among swans, so are ignorant sons in a public assembly.
12. Many a bad habit is developed through over indulgence, and many a good one by chastisement, therefore beat your son as well as your pupil; never indulge them. ("Spare the rod and spoil the child.")
13. Let not a single day pass without your learning a verse, half a verse, or a fourth of it, or even one letter of it; nor without attending to charity, study and other pious activity.
14. Separation from the wife, disgrace from one's own people, an enemy saved in battle, service to a wicked king, poverty, and a mismanaged assembly: these six kinds of evils, if afflicting a person, burn him even without fire.
15. Trees on a riverbank, a woman in another man's house, and kings without counsellors go without doubt to swift destruction.
16. A *brahmin's* strength is in his learning, a king's strength is in his army, a *vaishya's* strength is in his wealth and a *shudra's* strength is in his attitude of service.

17. The prostitute has to forsake a man who has no money, the subject, a king that cannot defend him, the birds, a tree that bears no fruit, and the guests, a house after they have finished their meals.
18. *Brahmins* quit their patrons after receiving alms from them, scholars leave their teachers after receiving education from them, and animals desert a forest that has been burnt down.
19. He who befriends a man whose conduct is vicious, whose vision impure, and who is notoriously crooked, is rapidly ruined.
20. Friendship between equals flourishes, service under a king is respectable, it is good to be business-minded in public dealings, and a handsome lady is safe in her own home.

Chapter Three

1. In this world, whose family is there without blemish? Who is free from sickness and grief? Who is forever happy?
2. A man's descent may be discerned by his conduct, his country by his pronunciation of language, his friendship by his warmth and glow, and his capacity to eat by his body.
3. Give your daughter in marriage to a good family, engage your son in learning, see that your enemy comes to grief, and engage your friends in *dharma*. (Krsna consciousness).
4. Of a rascal and a serpent, the serpent is the better of the two, for he strikes only at the time he is destined to kill, while the former at every step.
5. Therefore, kings gather round themselves, men of good families, for they never forsake them either at the beginning, the middle, or the end.
6. At the time of the *pralaya* (universal destruction), the oceans are to exceed their limits and seek to change, but a saintly man never changes.

7. Do not keep company with a fool, for as we can see, he is a two-legged beast. Like an unseen thorn, he pierces the heart with his sharp words.
8. Though men be endowed with beauty and youth and born in noble families, yet without education, they are like the palasa flower, which is void of sweet fragrance.
9. The beauty of a cuckoo is in its notes, that of a woman in her unalloyed devotion to her husband, that of an ugly person in his scholarship, and that of an ascetic in his forgiveness.
10. Give up a member to save a family, a family to save a village, a village to save a country, and the country to save yourself.
11. There is no poverty for the industrious. Sin does not attach itself to the person practising *japa* (chanting of the holy names of the Lord). Those who are absorbed in *maunam* (silent contemplation of the Lord) have no quarrel with others. They are fearless who remain always alert.

12-13. What is too heavy for the strong and what place is too distant for those who put forth effort? What country is foreign to a man of true learning? Who can be inimical to one who speaks pleasingly?

14. As a whole forest becomes fragrant by the existence of a single tree with sweet-smelling blossoms in it, so a family becomes famous by the birth of a virtuous son.
15. As a single withered tree, if set aflame, causes a whole forest to burn, so does a rascal son destroy a whole family.
16. As night looks delightful when the moon shines, so is a family gladdened by even one learned and virtuous son.
17. What is the use of having many sons if they cause grief and vexation? It is better to have only one

son from whom the whole family can derive support and peacefulness.

18. Fondle a son until he is five years of age, and use the stick for another ten years, but when he has attained his sixteenth year, treat him as a friend.
19. He who runs away from a fearful calamity, a foreign invasion, a terrible famine, and the companionship of wicked men is safe.
20. He who has not acquired one of the following: religious merit (*dharma*), wealth (*artha*), satisfaction of desires (*kama*), or liberation (*moksa*) is repeatedly born to die.
21. Lakshmi, the Goddess of wealth, comes of Her own accord where fools are not respected, grain is well stored up, and the husband and wife do not quarrel.

Chapter Four

1. These five: the life span, the type of work, wealth, learning and the time of one's death are determined while one is in the womb.
2. Offspring, friends and relatives flee from a devotee of the Lord: yet those who follow him bring merit to their families through their devotion.
3. Fish, tortoises, and birds bring up their young by means of sight, attention and touch; so do saintly men afford protection to their associates by the same means.
4. As long as your body is healthy and under control and death is distant, try to save your soul; when death is imminent, what can you do?
5. Learning is like a cow of desire. It, like her, yields in all seasons. Like a mother, it feeds you on your journey. Therefore, learning is a hidden treasure.
6. A single son endowed with good qualities is far better than a hundred devoid of them. For the moon, though one, dispels the darkness, which the stars, though numerous, cannot.

7. A stillborn son is superior to a foolish son endowed with a long life. The first causes grief for but a moment, while the latter like a blazing fire consumes his parents in grief for life.
8. Residing in a small village devoid of proper living facilities, serving a person born of a low family, unwholesome food, a frowning wife, a foolish son, and a widowed daughter burn the body without fire.
9. What good is a cow that neither gives milk nor conceives? Similarly, what is the value of the birth of a son if he becomes neither learned nor a pure devotee of the Lord?
10. When one is consumed by the sorrows of life, three things give him relief: offspring, a wife, and the company of the Lord's devotees.
11. Kings speak for once, men of learning once, and the daughter is given in marriage once. All these things happen once and only once.
12. Religious austerities should be practiced alone, study by two, and singing by three. A journey should be undertaken by four, agriculture by five, and war by many together.
13. She is a true wife who is clean (*suci*), expert, chaste, pleasing to the husband, and truthful.
14. The house of a childless person is a void, all directions are void to one who has no relatives, the heart of a fool is also void, but to a poverty-stricken man all is void.
15. Scriptural lessons not put into practice are poison; a meal is poison to him who suffers from indigestion; a social gathering is poison to a poverty-stricken person; and a young wife is poison to an aged man.
16. That man who is without religion and mercy should be rejected. A *guru* without spiritual knowledge should be rejected. The wife with an offensive face

should be given up, and so should relatives who are without affection.

17. Constant travel brings old age upon a man; a horse becomes old by being constantly tied up; lack of sexual contact with her husband brings old age upon a woman; and garments become old through being left in the Sun.
18. Consider again and again the following: the right time, the right friends, the right place, the right means of income, the right ways of spending, and from whom you derive your power.
19. For the twice born the fire (*Agni*) is a representative of God. The Supreme Lord resides in the heart of His devotees. Those of average intelligence (*alpa-buddhi* or *kanista-adhikari*) see God only in His *sri-murti*, but those of broad vision see the Supreme Lord everywhere.

Chapter Five

1. *Agni* is the worshipable person for the twice born; the *brahmana* for the other castes; the husband for the wife; and the guest who comes for food at the midday meal for all.
2. As gold is tested in four ways by rubbing, cutting, heating and beating—so a man should be tested by these four things: his renunciation, his conduct, his qualities and his actions.
3. A thing may be dreaded as long as it has not overtaken you, but once it has come upon you, try to get rid of it without hesitation.
4. Though persons be born from the same womb and under the same stars, they do not become alike in disposition as the thousand fruits of the *badari* tree.
5. He whose hands are clean does not like to hold an office; he who desires nothing cares not for bodily decorations; he who is only partially educated cannot speak agreeably; and he who speaks out plainly cannot be a deceiver.

6. The learned are envied by the foolish; rich men by the poor; chaste women by adulteresses; and beautiful ladies by ugly ones.
7. Indolent application ruins study; money is lost when entrusted to others; a farmer who sows his seed sparsely is ruined; and an army is lost for want of a commander.
8. Learning is retained through putting into practice; family prestige is maintained through good behaviour; a respectable person is recognized by his excellent qualities; and anger is seen in the eyes.
9. Religion is preserved by wealth; knowledge by diligent practice; a king by conciliatory words; and a home by a dutiful housewife.
10. Those who blaspheme *Vedic* wisdom, who ridicule the life style recommended in the *satras*, and who deride men of peaceful temperament, come to grief unnecessarily.
11. Charity puts and end to poverty; righteous conduct to misery; discretion to ignorance; and scrutiny to fear.
12. There is no disease (so destructive) as lust; no enemy like infatuation; no fire like wrath; and no happiness like spiritual knowledge.
13. A man is born alone and dies alone; and he experiences the good and bad consequences of his *karma* alone; and he goes alone to hell or the Supreme abode.
14. Heaven is but a straw to him who knows spiritual life (Krsna consciousness); so is life to a valiant man; a woman to him who has subdued his senses; and the universe to him who is without attachment for the world.
15. Learning is a friend on the journey; a wife in the house; medicine in sickness; and religious merit is the only friend after death.

16. Rain which falls upon the sea is useless; so is food for one who is satiated; in vain is a gift for one who is wealthy; and a burning lamp during the daytime is useless.
17. There is no water like rainwater; no strength like one's own; no light like that of the eyes; and no wealth more dear than food grain.
18. The poor wish for wealth; animals for the faculty of speech; men wish for heaven; and godly persons for liberation.
19. The earth is supported by the power of truth; it is the power of truth that makes the sunshine and the winds blow; indeed all things rest upon truth.
20. The Goddess of wealth is unsteady (*chanchala*), and so is the life breath. The duration of life is uncertain, and the place of habitation is uncertain; but in all this inconsistent world religious merit alone is immovable.
21. Among men, the barber is cunning; among birds the crow; among beasts the jackal; and among women, the malin (flower girl).
22. These five are your fathers; he who gave you birth, girdled you with sacred thread, teaches you, provides you with food, and protects you from fearful situations.
23. These five should be considered as mothers; the king's wife, the preceptor's wife, the friend's wife, your wife's mother, and your own mother.

Chapter Six

1. By means of hearing, one understands *dharma*, malignity vanishes, knowledge is acquired, and liberation from material bondage is gained.
2. Among birds, the crow is vile; among beasts, the dog; the ascetic, whose sins is abominable, but he who blasphemes others, is the worst *chandala*.

3. Brass is polished by ashes; copper is cleaned by tamarind; a woman, by her menses; and a river by its flow.
4. The king, the *brahmana*, and the ascetic *yogi* who go abroad are respected; but the woman who wanders is utterly ruined.
5. He who has wealth has friends. He who is wealthy has relatives. The rich one alone is called a man, and the affluent alone are respected as *pandits*.
6. As is the desire of Providence, so functions one's intellect; one's activities are also controlled by Providence; and by the will of Providence, one is surrounded by helpers.
7. Time perfects all living beings as well as kills them; it alone is awake when all others are asleep. Time is insurmountable.
8. Those born blind cannot see; similarly, blind are those in the grip of lust. Proud men have no perception of evil; and those bent on acquiring riches see no sin in their actions.
9. The spirit soul goes through his own course of *karma* and he himself suffers the good and bad results thereby accrued. By his own actions, he entangles himself in *samsara*, and by his own efforts, he extricates himself.
10. The king is obliged to accept the sins of his subjects; the *purohit* (priest) suffers for those of the king; a husband suffers for those of his wife; and the *guru* suffers for those of his pupils.
11. A father who is a chronic debtor, an adulterous mother, a beautiful wife, and an unlearned son are enemies (in one's own home).
12. Conciliate a covetous man by means of a gift, an obstinate man with folded hands in salutation, a fool by humouring him, and a learned man by truthful words.

13. It is better to be without a kingdom than to rule over a petty one; better to be without a friend than to befriend a rascal; better to be without a disciple than to have a stupid one; and better to be without a wife than to have a bad one.
14. How can people be made happy in a petty kingdom? What peace can we expect from a rascal friend? What happiness can we have at home in the company of a bad wife? How can renown be gained by instructing an unworthy disciple?
15. Learn one thing from a lion; one from a crane; four from a cock; five from a crow; six from a dog; and three from an ass.
16. The one excellent thing that can be learned from a lion is that whatever a man intends doing, should be done by him with a whole-hearted and strenuous effort.
17. The wise man should restrain his senses like the crane and accomplish his purpose with due knowledge of his place, time and ability.
18. To wake at the proper time; to take a bold stand and fight; to make a fair division (of property) among relations; and to earn one's own bread by personal exertion are the four excellent things to be learned from a cock.
19. Union in privacy (with one's wife); boldness; storing away useful items; watchfulness; and not easily trusting others; these five things are to be learned from a crow.
20. Contentment with little or nothing to eat although one may have a great appetite; to awaken instantly although one may be in a deep slumber; unflinching devotion to the master; and bravery; these six qualities should be learned from the dog.
21. Although an ass is tired, he continues to carry his burden; he is unmindful of cold and heat; and he

is always contented; these three things should be learned from the ass.

22. He who shall practice these twenty virtues shall become invincible in all his undertakings.

Chapter Seven

1. A wise man should not reveal his loss of wealth, the vexation of his mind, the misconduct of his own wife, base words spoken by others, and disgrace that has befallen him.
2. He who gives up shyness in monetary dealings, in acquiring knowledge, in eating and in business, becomes happy.
3. The happiness and peace attained by those satisfied by the nectar of spiritual tranquillity is not attained by greedy persons restlessly moving here and there.
4. One should feel satisfied with the following three things; his own wife, food given by Providence and wealth acquired by honest effort; but one should never feel satisfied with the following three; study, chanting the holy names of the Lord (*japa*) and charity.
5. Do not pass between two *brahmanas*, between a *brahmana* and his sacrificial fire, between a wife and her husband, a master and his servant, and a plough and an ox.
6. Do not let your foot touch fire, the spiritual master or a *brahmana*; it must never touch a cow, a virgin, an old person or a child.
7. Keep one thousand cubits away from an elephant, a hundred from a horse, ten from a horned beast, but keep away from the wicked by leaving the country.
8. An elephant is controlled by a goad (*ankusha*), a horse by a slap of the hand, a horned animal with the show of a stick, and a rascal with a sword.

9. *Brahmanas* find satisfaction in a good meal, peacocks in the peal of thunder, a sadhu in seeing the prosperity of others, and the wicked in the misery of others.
10. Conciliate a strong man by submission, a wicked man by opposition, and the one whose power is equal to yours by politeness or force.
11. The power of a king lies in his mighty arms; that of a brahmana in his spiritual knowledge; and that of a woman in her beauty youth and sweet words.
12. Do not be very upright in your dealings for you would see by going to the forest that straight trees are cut down while crooked ones are left standing.
13. Swans live wherever there is water, and leave the place where water dries up; let not a man act so—and comes and goes as he pleases.
14. Accumulated wealth is saved by spending just as incoming fresh water is saved by letting out stagnant water.
15. He who has wealth has friends and relations; he alone survives and is respected as a man.
16. The following four characteristics of the denizens of heaven may be seen in the residents of this earth planet; charity, sweet words, worship of the Supreme Personality of Godhead, and satisfying the needs of *brahmanas*.
17. The following qualities of the denizens of hell may characterise men on earth; extreme wrath, harsh speech, enmity with one's relations, the company with the base, and service to men of low extraction.
18. By going to the den of a lion pearls from the head of an elephant may be obtained; but by visiting the hole of a jackal nothing but the tail of a calf or a bit of the hide of an ass may be found.
19. The life of an uneducated man is as useless as the tail of a dog, which neither covers its rear end, nor protects it from the bites of insects.

20. Purity of speech, of the mind, of the senses, and a compassionate heart are needed by one who desires to rise to the divine platform.
21. As you seek fragrance in a flower, oil in the sesamum seed, fire in wood, ghee (butter) in milk, and jaggery (guda) in sugarcane; so seek the spirit, that is in the body by means of discrimination.

Chapter Eight

1. Low class men desire wealth; middle class men both wealth and respect; but the noble, honour only; hence, honour is the noble man's true wealth.
2. ...
3. The lamp eats up the darkness and therefore, it produces blackened lamp; in the same way, according to the nature of our diet (sattva, rajas, or tamas), we produce offspring in similar quality.
4. O wise man! Give your wealth only to the worthy and never to others. The water of the sea received by the clouds is always sweet. The rainwater enlivens all living beings of the earth both movable (insects, animals, humans, etc.) and immovable (plants, trees, etc.), and then returns to the ocean where its value is multiplied a million fold.
5. The wise who discern the essence of things have declared that the yavana (meat eater) is equal in baseness to a thousand chandalas (the lowest class), and hence a yavana is the basest of men; indeed there is no one more base.
6. After having rubbed oil on the body, after encountering the smoke from a funeral pyre, after sexual intercourse, and after being shaved, one remains a chandala until he bathes.
7. Water is the medicine for indigestion; it is invigorating, when the food that is eaten is well digested; it is like nectar, when drunk in the middle of a dinner; and it is like poison, when taken at the end of a meal.

8. Knowledge is lost without putting it into practice; a man is lost due to ignorance; an army is lost without a commander; and a woman is lost without a husband.
9. A man who encounters the following three is unfortunate; the death of his wife in his old age, the entrusting of money into the hands of relatives, and depending upon others for food.
10. Chanting of the *Vedas* without making ritualistic sacrifices to the Supreme Lord through the medium of *Agni*, and sacrifices not followed by bountiful gifts are futile. Perfection can be achieved only through devotion (to the Supreme Lord) for devotion is the basis of all success.
11. ...
12. ...
13. There is no austerity equal to a balanced mind, and there is no happiness equal to contentment; there is no disease like covetousness, and no virtue like mercy.
14. Anger is a personification of *Yama* (the demigod of death); thirst is like the hellish river *Vaitarani*; knowledge is like a *kamadhenu* (the cow of plenty); and contentment is like *Nandanavana* (the garden of Indra).
15. Moral excellence is an ornament for personal beauty; righteous conduct, for high birth; success for learning; and proper spending for wealth.
16. Beauty is spoiled by an immoral nature; noble birth by bad conduct; learning, without being perfected; and wealth by not being properly utilised.
17. Water seeping into the earth is pure; and a devoted wife is pure; the king who is the benefactor of his people is pure; and pure is the *brahmana* who is contented.
18. Discontented *brahmanas*, contented kings, shy prostitutes, and immodest housewives are ruined.

19. Of what avail is a high birth if a person is destitute of scholarship? A man who is of low extraction is honoured even by the demigods if he is learned.
20. A learned man is honoured by the people. A learned man commands respect everywhere for his learning. Indeed, learning is honoured everywhere.
21. Those who are endowed with beauty and youth and who are born of noble families are worthless if they have no learning. They are just like the kimshuka blossoms (flowers of the palasa tree) which, though beautiful, have no fragrance.
22. The earth is encumbered with the weight of the flesh-eaters, wine-bibblers, dolts (dull and stupid) and blockheads, who are beasts in the form of men.
23. There is no enemy like a *yajna* (sacrifice) which consumes the kingdom when not attended by feeding on a large scale; consumes the priest, when the chanting is not done properly; and consumes the yajaman (the responsible person), when the gifts are not made.

Chapter Nine

1. My dear child, if you desire to be free from the cycle of birth and death, then abandon the objects of sense gratification as poison. Drink instead, the nectar of forbearance, upright conduct, mercy, cleanliness and truth.
2. Those base men who speak of the secret faults of others destroy themselves like serpents that stray onto anthills.
3. Perhaps nobody has advised Lord *Brahma*, the creator, to impart perfume to gold; fruit to the sugarcane; flowers to the sandalwood tree; wealth to the learned; and long life to the king.
4. Nectar (*amrita*) is the best among medicines; eating good food is the best of all types of material happiness; the eye is the chief among all organs;

and the head occupies the chief position among all parts of the body.

5. No messenger can travel about in the sky and no tidings come from there. The voice of its inhabitants is never heard, nor can any contact be established with them. Therefore, the *brahmana* who predicts the eclipse of the sun and moon, which occur in the sky, must be considered as a vidwan (man of great learning).
6. The student, the servant, the traveller, the hungry person, the frightened man, the treasury guard, and the steward: these seven ought to be awakened if they fall asleep.
7. The serpent, the king, the tiger, the stinging wasp, the small child, the dog owned by other people, and the fool: these seven ought not to be awakened from sleep.
8. Of those who have studied the *Vedas* for material rewards, and those who accept foodstuffs offered by *shudras*, what potency have they? They are just like serpents without fangs.
9. He who neither rouses fear by his anger, nor confers a favour when he is pleased, can neither control nor protect. What can he do?
10. The serpent may, without being poisonous, raise high its hood, but the show of terror is enough to frighten people—whether he be venomous or not.
11. Wise men spend their mornings in discussing gambling, the afternoon discussing the activities of women, and the night hearing about the activities of theft. (The first item above refers to the gambling of King Yudhisthira, the great devotee of Krisna. The second item refers to the glorious deeds of mother Sita, the consort of Lord Ramachandra. The third item hints at the adorable childhood pastimes of Sri Krisna who stole butter from the elderly cowherd ladies of Gokula. Hence Chanakya Pandita advises

wise persons to spend the morning absorbed in Mahabharata, the afternoon studying *Ramayana*, and the evening devotedly hearing the *Srimad-Bhagvatam*.)

12. By preparing a garland for a Deity with one's own hand; by grinding *sandal* paste for the Lord with one's own hand; and by writing sacred texts with one's own hand—one becomes blessed with opulence equal to that of Indra.
13. ...
14. Poverty is set off by fortitude; shabby garments by keeping them clean; bad food by warming it; and ugliness by good behaviour.

Chapter Ten

1. One destitute of wealth is not destitute, he is indeed rich (if he is learned); but the man devoid of learning is destitute in every way.
2. We should carefully scrutinise that place upon which we step (having it ascertained to be free from filth and living creatures like insects, etc.); we should drink water, which has been filtered (through a clean cloth); we should speak only those words, which have the sanction of the *satras*; and do that act which we have carefully considered.
3. He who desires sense gratification must give up all thoughts of acquiring knowledge; and he who seeks knowledge, must not hope for sense gratification. How can he who seeks sense gratification acquire knowledge, and he who possesses knowledge enjoy mundane sense pleasure?
4. What is it, that escapes the observation of poets? What is that act, women are incapable of doing? What will drunken people not prate? What will not a crow eat?
5. Fate makes a beggar a king and a king a beggar. He makes a rich man poor and a poor man rich.
6. The beggar is a miser's enemy; the wise counsellor is the fool's enemy; her husband is an adulterous

wife's enemy; and the moon is the enemy of the thief.

7. Those who are destitute of learning, penance, knowledge, good disposition, virtue and benevolence are brutes wandering the earth in the form of men. They are burdensome to the earth.
8. Those that are empty-minded cannot be benefited by instruction. Bamboo does not acquire the quality of sandalwood by being associated with the Malaya Mountain.
9. What good can the scriptures do to a man who has no sense of his own? Of what use is as mirror to a blind man?
10. Nothing can reform a bad man, just as the posteriors cannot become a superior part of the body though washed one hundred times.
11. By offending a kinsman, life is lost; by offending others, wealth is lost; by offending the king, everything is lost; and by offending a brahmana (*Brahmin*), one's whole family is ruined.
12. It is better to live under a tree in a jungle inhabited by tigers and elephants, to maintain oneself in such a place with ripe fruits and spring water, to lie down on grass and to wear the ragged barks of trees than to live amongst one's relations when reduced to poverty.
13. The brahmana (*Brahmin*) is like a tree; his prayers are the roots, his chanting of the *Vedas* are the branches, and his religious acts are the leaves. Consequently, effort should be made to preserve his roots for if the roots are destroyed, there can be no branches or leaves.
14. My mother is Kamala Devi (Lakshmi), my father is Lord Janardana (Vishnu), my kinsmen are the Vishnu-bhaktas (Vaisnavas) and, my homeland is all the three worlds.

15. (Through the night) a great many kinds of birds perch on a tree but in the morning, they fly in all the ten directions. Why should we lament for that? (Similarly, we should not grieve when we must inevitably part company from our dear ones.)
16. He who possesses intelligence is strong; how can the man that is unintelligent be powerful? The elephant of the forest having lost his senses by intoxication was tricked into a lake by a small rabbit. (This verse refers to a famous story from the *niti-sastra* called *panchatantra* compiled by Pandit Vishnusharma 2500 years ago.)
17. Why should I be concerned for my maintenance while absorbed in praising the glories of Lord Vishwambhara (Vishnu), the supporter of all? Without the grace of Lord Hari, how could milk flow from a mother's breast for a child's nourishment? Repeatedly thinking only in this way, O Lord of the Yadus, O husband of Lakshmi, all my time is spent in serving Your lotus feet.

Chapter Eleven

1. Generosity, pleasing address, courage and propriety of conduct are not acquired, but are inbred qualities.
2. He who forsakes his own community and joins another perishes as the king who embraces an unrighteous path.
3. The elephant has a huge body but is controlled by the *ankusha* (goad): yet, is the goad as large as the elephant? A lighted candle banishes darkness: is the candle as vast as the darkness. A mountain is broken even by a thunderbolt: is the thunderbolt therefore, as big as the mountain? No, he whose power prevails is really mighty; what is there in bulk?
4. ...
5. He who is engrossed in family life will never acquire knowledge; there can be no mercy in the eater of flesh; the greedy man will not be truthful; and purity will not be found in a woman or a hunter.

6. The wicked man will not attain sanctity even if he is instructed in different ways, and the *nim* tree will not become sweet even if it is sprinkled from the top to the roots with milk and ghee.
7. Mental dirt cannot be washed away even by one-hundred baths in the sacred waters, just as a wine pot cannot be purified even by evaporating all the wine by fire.
8. It is not strange if a man reviles a thing of which he has no knowledge, just as a wild hunter's wife throws away the pearl that is found in the head of an elephant, and picks up a *gunj* (a type of seed which poor tribals wear as ornaments).
9. He who for one year eats his meals silently (inwardly meditating upon the Lord's prasadam); attains to the heavenly planets for a thousand crore of years. (Note: one crore equals ten million).
10. The student (*brahmachari*) should completely renounce the following eight things—his lust, anger, greed, desire for sweets, sense of decorating the body, excessive curiosity, excessive sleep, and excessive endeavour for bodily maintenance.
11. ...
12. He alone is a true *brahmana* (dvija or "twice-born") who is satisfied with one meal a day, who has the six *samskaras* (or acts of purification such as *garbhadhana*, etc.) performed for him, and who cohabits with his wife only once in a month on an auspicious day after her menses.
13. The *brahmana* who is engrossed in worldly affairs, brings up cows and is engaged in trade is really called a vaishya.
14. The *brahmana* who deals in lac-die, articles, oil, indigo, silken cloth, honey, clarified butter, liquor, and flesh is called a *shudra*.
15. The *brahmana* who thwarts the doings of others, who is hypocritical, selfish, and a deceitful hater,

and while speaking mildly cherishes cruelty in his heart, is called a cat.

16. The *brahmana* who destroys a pond, a well, a tank, a garden and a temple is called a *mleccha*.
17. The *brahmana* who steals the property of the Deities and the spiritual preceptor, who co-habits with another's wife, and who maintains himself by eating anything and everything is called a *chandala*.
18. The meritorious should give away in charity all that they have in excess of their needs. By charity only, Karna, Bali and King Vikramaditya survive even today. Just see the plight of the honeybees beating their legs in despair upon the earth. They are saying to themselves, "Alas! We neither enjoyed our stored-up honey nor gave it in charity, and now someone has taken it from us in an instant."

Chapter Twelve

1. He is a blessed *grhasta* (householder) in whose house there is a blissful atmosphere, whose sons are talented, whose wife speaks sweetly, whose wealth is enough to satisfy his desires, who finds pleasure in the company of his wife, whose servants are obedient, in whose house, hospitality is shown, the auspicious Supreme Lord is worshipped daily, delicious food and drink is partaken, and who finds joy in the company of devotees.
2. One who devotedly gives a little to a *brahmana* who is in distress is recompensed abundantly. Hence, O Prince! what is given to a good *brahmana* is got back not in an equal quantity, but in an infinitely higher degree.
3. Those men are happy in this world, who are generous towards their relatives, kind to strangers, indifferent to the wicked, loving to the good, shrewd in their dealings with the base, frank with the learned, courageous with enemies, humble with elders and stern with the wife.

4. O jackal, leave aside the body of that man at once, whose hands have never given in charity, whose ears have not heard the voice of learning, whose eyes have not beheld a pure devotee of the Lord, whose feet have never traversed to holy places, whose belly is filled with things obtained by crooked practices, and whose head is held high in vanity. Do not eat it, O jackal! otherwise you will become polluted.
5. "Shame upon those who have no devotion to the lotus feet of Sri Krisna, the son of mother Yasoda; who have no attachment for the descriptions of the glories of Srimati Radharani; whose ears are not eager to listen to the stories of the Lord's *lila*." Such is the exclamation of the *mridanga* sound of *dhik-tam dhik-tam dhigatam* at *kirtana*.
6. What fault of spring that the bamboo shoot has no leaves? What fault of the Sun, if the owl cannot see during the daytime? Is it the fault of the clouds if no raindrops fall into the mouth of the chatak bird? Who can erase what Lord Brahma has inscribed upon our foreheads at the time of birth?
7. A wicked man may develop saintly qualities in the company of a devotee, but a devotee does not become impious in the company of a wicked person. The earth is scented by a flower that falls upon it, but the flower does not contact the odour of the earth.
8. One indeed becomes blessed by having *darshan* of a devotee; for the devotee has the ability to purify immediately, whereas the sacred *tirtha* gives purity only after prolonged contact.
9. A stranger asked a *brahmana*, "Tell me, who is great in this city?" The *brahmana* replied, "The cluster of palmyra trees is great." Then the traveller asked, "Who is the most charitable person?" The *brahmana* answered, "The washer man who takes the clothes in the morning and gives them back in

the evening is the most charitable." He then asked, "Who is the ablest man?" The *brahmana* answered, "Everyone is expert in robbing others of their wives and wealth." The man then asked the *brahmana*, "How do you manage to live in such a city?" The *brahmana* replied, "As a worm survives while even in a filthy place, so do I survive here."

10. The house in which the lotus feet of *brahmanas* are not washed, in which *Vedic mantras* are not loudly recited, and in which the holy rites of *svaha* (sacrificial offerings to the Supreme Lord) and *swadha* (offerings to the ancestors) are not performed, is like a crematorium.
11. (It is said that a *sadhu*, when asked about his family, replied thusly): truth is my mother, and my father is spiritual knowledge; righteous conduct is my brother, and mercy is my friend, inner peace is my wife, and forgiveness is my son: these six are my kinsmen.
12. Our bodies are perishable, wealth is not at all permanent and death is always nearby. Therefore we must immediately engage in acts of merit.
13. Arjuna says to Krisna. "Brahmanas find joy in going to feasts, cows find joy in eating their tender grass, wives find joy in the company of their husbands, and know, O Krisna! that in the same way, I rejoice in battle.
14. He who regards another's wife as his mother, the wealth that does not belong to him as a lump of mud, and the pleasure and pain of all other living beings as his own—truly sees things in the right perspective, and he is a true *pandit*.
15. "O Raghava, the love of virtue, pleasing speech, and an ardent desire for performing acts of charity, guileless dealings with friends, humility in the guru's presence, deep tranquillity of mind, pure conduct, discernment of virtues, realised knowledge of the

sastras, beauty of form and devotion to God are all found in you." (The great sage Vasistha Muni, the spiritual preceptor of the dynasty of the sun, said this to Lord Ramachandra at the time of His proposed coronation).

16. *Kalpataru* (the wish fulfilling tree) is but wood; the golden Mount Meru is motionless; the wish-fulfilling gem *chintamani* is just a stone; the sun is scorching; the moon is prone to wane; the boundless ocean is saline; the demigod of lust lost his body (due to Shiva's wrath); Bali Maharaja, the son of Diti, was born into a clan of demons; and Kamadhenu (the cow of heaven) is a mere beast. O Lord of the Raghu dynasty! I cannot compare you to any one of these (taking their merits into account).
17. Realised learning (*vidya*) is our friend while travelling, the wife is a friend at home, medicine is the friend of a sick man, and meritorious deeds are the friends at death.
18. Courtesy should be learned from princes, the art of conversation from pandits, lying should be learned from gamblers and deceitful ways should be learned from women.
19. The unthinking spender, the homeless urchin, the quarrel monger, the man who neglects his wife and is heedless in his actions—all these will soon come to ruination.
20. The wise man should not be anxious about his food; he should be anxious to be engaged only in *dharma* (Krishna consciousness). The food of each man is created for him at his birth.
21. He who is not shy in the acquisition of wealth, grain and knowledge, and in taking his meals, will be happy.
22. As centesimal droppings will fill a pot so also are knowledge, virtue and wealth gradually obtained.

23. The man who remains a fool even in advanced age is really a fool, just as the Indra-Varuna fruit does not become sweet, no matter how ripe it might become.

Chapter Thirteen

1. A man may live but for a moment, but that moment should be spent in doing auspicious deeds. It is useless living even for a *kalpa* (4,320,000 × 1000 years) and bringing only distress upon the two worlds (this world and the next).
2. We should not fret for what is past, nor should we be anxious about the future; men of discernment deal only with the present moment.
3. It certainly is nature of the demigods, men of good character, and parents to be easily pleased. Near and distant relatives are pleased when they are hospitably received with bathing, food, and drink; and pandits are pleased with an opportunity for giving spiritual discourse.
4. Even as the unborn babe is in the womb of his mother, these five are fixed as his life destiny: his life span, his activities, his acquisition of wealth and knowledge, and his time of death.
5. Oh, see what a wonder it is! The doings of the great are strange: they treat wealth as light as a straw, yet, when they obtain it, they bend under its weight.
6. He who is overly attached to his family members experiences fear and sorrow, for the root of all grief is attachment. Thus, one should discard attachment to be happy.
7. He who is prepared for the future and he who deals cleverly with any situation that may arise are both happy; but the fatalistic man who wholly depends on luck is ruined.
8. If the king is virtuous, then the subjects are also virtuous. If the king is sinful, then the subjects also

become sinful. If he is mediocre, then the subjects are mediocre. The subjects follow the example of the king. In short, as is the king, so are the subjects.

9. I consider him who does not act religiously as dead though living, but he who dies acting religiously, unquestionably, lives long though he is dead.
10. He who has acquired neither virtue, wealth, satisfaction of desires nor salvation (*dharma*, *artha*, *kama, moksa*), lives an utterly useless life, like the "nipples" hanging from the neck of a goat.
11. The hearts of base men burn before the fire of other's fame, and they slander them being themselves unable to rise to such a high position.
12. Excessive attachment to sense pleasures leads to bondage, and detachment from sense pleasures leads to liberation; therefore, it is the mind alone that is responsible for bondage or liberation.
13. He who sheds bodily identification by means of knowledge of the indwelling Supreme Self (*Paramatma*), will always be absorbed in meditative trance (*samadhi*) wherever his mind leads him.
14. Who realises all the happiness he desires? Everything is in the hands of God. Therefore, one should learn contentment.
15. As a calf follows its mother among a thousand cows, so the (good or bad) deeds of a man follow him.
16. He whose actions are disorganised has no happiness either in the midst of men or in a jungle—in the midst of men, his heart burns by social contacts, and his helplessness burns him in the forest.
17. As the man who digs, obtains underground water by use of a shovel, so the student attains the knowledge possessed by his preceptor through his service.
18. Men reap the fruits of their deeds, and intellects bear the mark of deeds performed in previous lives; even so, the wise act after due circumspection.

19. Even the man who has taught the spiritual significance of just one letter ought to be worshiped. He who does not give reverence to such a *guru* is born as a dog a hundred times, and at last, takes birth as a *chandala* (dog-eater).
20. At the end of the *yuga*, Mount Meru may be shaken; at the end of the *kalpa*, the waters of the seven oceans may be disturbed; but a *sadhu* will never swerve from the spiritual path.
21. There are three gems upon this earth; food, water, and pleasing words—fools (*mudhas*) consider pieces of rocks as gems.

Chapter Fourteen

1. Poverty, disease, sorrow, imprisonment and other evils are the fruits borne by the tree of one's own sins.
2. Wealth, a friend, a wife, and a kingdom may be regained; but this body when lost, may never be acquired again.
3. The enemy can be overcome by the union of large numbers, just as grass through its collectiveness wards off erosion caused by heavy rainfall.
4. Oil on water, a secret communicated to a base man, a gift given to a worthy receiver, and scriptural instruction given to an intelligent man spread out by virtue of their nature.
5. If men should always retain the state of mind they experience when hearing religious instruction, when present at a crematorium ground, and when in sickness—then, who could not attain liberation.
6. If a man should feel before, as he feels after, repentance—then who would not attain perfection?
7. We should not feel pride in our charity, austerity, valour, scriptural knowledge, modesty and morality for the world is full of the rarest gems.

8. He who lives in our mind is near though he may actually be far away; but he who is not in our heart is far though he may really be nearby.
9. We should always speak what would please the man of whom we expect a favour, like the hunter who sings sweetly when he desires to shoot a deer.
10. It is ruinous to be familiar with the king, fire, the religious preceptor, and a woman. To be altogether indifferent to them is to be deprived of the opportunity to benefit ourselves, hence our association with them must be from a safe distance.
11. We should always deal cautiously with fire, water, women, foolish people, serpents, and members of a royal family; for they may, when the occasion presents itself, at once bring about our death.
12. He should be considered to be living who is virtuous and pious, but the life of a man who is destitute of religion and virtues is void of any blessing.
13. If you wish to gain control of the world by the performance of a single deed, then keep the following fifteen, which are prone to wander here and there, from getting the upper hand of you: the five sense objects (objects of sight, sound, smell, taste, and touch); the five sense organs (ears, eyes, nose, tongue and skin) and organs of activity (hands, legs, mouth, genitals and anus).
14. He is a *pandit* (man of knowledge) who speaks what is suitable to the occasion, who renders loving service according to his ability, and who knows the limits of his anger.
15. One single object (a woman) appears in three different ways: to the man who practices austerity it appears as a corpse, to the sensual it appears as a woman, and to the dogs as a lump of flesh.
16. A wise man should not divulge the formula of a medicine which he has well prepared; an act of charity which he has performed; domestic conflicts;

private affairs with his wife; poorly prepared food he may have been offered; or slang he may have heard.

17. The cuckoos remain silent for a long time (for several seasons) until they are able to sing sweetly (in the Spring) so as to give joy to all.
18. We should secure and keep the following: the blessings of meritorious deeds, wealth, grain, the words of the spiritual master, and rare medicines. Otherwise, life becomes impossible.
19. Eschew wicked company and associate with saintly persons. Acquire virtue day and night, and always meditate on that which is eternal forgetting that which is temporary.

Chapter Fifteen

1. For one whose heart melts with compassion for all creatures; what is the necessity of knowledge, liberation, matted hair on the head, and smearing the body with ashes?
2. There is no treasure on earth the gift of which will cancel the debt a disciple owes his *guru* for having taught him even a single letter (that leads to Krishna consciousness).
3. There are two ways to get rid of thorns and wicked persons; using footwear in the first place and in the second, shaming them so that they cannot raise their faces again, thus keeping them at a distance.
4. He who wears unclean garments, has dirty teeth, is a glutton, speaks unkindly and sleeps after sunrise—although he may be the greatest personality—will lose the favour of Lakshmi.
5. He who loses his money is forsaken by his friends, his wife, his servants and his relations; yet, when he regains his riches those who have forsaken him come back to him. Hence, wealth is certainly the best of relations.

6. Sinfully acquired wealth may remain for ten years; in the eleventh year, it disappears with even the original stock.
7. A bad action committed by a great man is not censured (as there is none that can reproach him), and a good action performed by a low-class man comes to be condemned (because none respects him). Just see: the drinking of nectar is excellent, but it became the cause of Rahu's demise; and the drinking of poison is harmful, but when Lord Shiva (who is exalted) drank it, it became an ornament to his neck (*nila-kantha*).
8. A true meal is that which consists of the remnants left after a brahmana's meal. Love, which is shown to others, is true love, not that which is cherished for one's own self. To abstain from sin is true wisdom. That is an act of charity, which is performed without ostentation.
9. For want of discernment, the most precious jewels lie in the dust at the feet of men while bits of glass are worn on their heads. But we should not imagine that the gems have sunk in value, and the bits of glass have risen in importance. When a person of critical judgement shall appear, each will be given its right position.
10. Sastric (scriptural) knowledge is unlimited, and the arts to be learned are many; the time we have is short, and our opportunities to learn are beset with obstacles. Therefore, select for learning that which is most important, just as the swan drinks only the milk in water.
11. He is a *chandala* who eats his dinner without entertaining the stranger who has come to his house quite accidentally, having travelled from a long distance and is wearied.
12. One may know the four *Vedas* and the *Dharma-sastras*, yet if he has no realisation of his own

spiritual self, he can be said to be like the ladle (spoon) which stirs all kinds of foods but knows not the taste of any.

13. Those blessed souls are certainly elevated who, while crossing the ocean of life, take shelter of a genuine *brahmana*, who is likened unto a boat. They are unlike passengers aboard an ordinary ship that runs the risk of sinking.
14. The moon, who is the abode of nectar and the presiding deity of all medicines, although immortal like *amrta* and resplendent in form, loses the brilliance of his rays when he repairs to the abode of the Sun (daytime). Therefore, will not an ordinary man be made to feel inferior by going to live at the house of another?
15. This humble bee, which always resides among the soft petals of the lotus and drinks abundantly its sweet nectar, is now feasting on the flower of the ordinary kutaja. Being in a strange country where the lotuses do not exist, he is considering the pollen of the kutaja to be nice.
16. (Lord Vishnu asked His spouse Lakshmi why She did not care to live in the house of a *brahmana*. She replied:) "O Lord! a rishi named Agastya drank up My father (the ocean) in anger; Brighu Muni kicked You; brahmanas pride themselves on their learning having sought the favour of My competitor Sarasvati; and lastly, they pluck each day the lotus which is My abode, and therewith worship Lord Shiva. Therefore, O Lord! I fear to dwell with a *brahmana*".
17. There are many ways of binding by which one can be dominated and controlled in this world, but the bond of affection is the strongest. For example, take the case of the humble bee, which, although expert at piercing hardened wood, becomes caught in the embrace of its beloved flowers (as the petals close at dusk).

18. Although sandalwood is cut, it does not forsake its natural quality of fragrance; so also the elephant does not give up sportiveness though he should grow old. The sugarcane does not cease to be sweet though squeezed in a mill; so the man of noble extraction does not lose his lofty qualities, no matter how pinched he is by poverty.

Chapter Sixteen

1. ...
2. The heart of a woman is not united; it is divided. While she is talking with one man, she looks lustfully at another and thinks fondly of a third in her heart.
3. The fool (*mudha*) who fancies that a charming young lady loves him, becomes her slave and he dances like a shakuntal bird tied to a string.
4. Who is there who, having become rich, has not become proud? Which licentious man has put an end to his calamities? Which man in this world has not been overcome by a woman? Who is always loved by the king? Who is there who has not been overcome by the ravages of time? Which beggar has attained glory? Who has become, happy by contracting the vices of the wicked?
5. ...
6. A man attains greatness by his merits, not simply by occupying an exalted seat. Can we call a crow an eagle (*garuda*) simply because he sits on the top of a tall building.
7. ...
8. The man who is praised by others as great is regarded as worthy though he may be really void of all merits. But the man who sings his own praises lowers himself in the estimation of others, though he should be Indra (the possessor of all excellences).
9. If good qualities should characterise a man of discrimination, the brilliance of his qualities will be recognised just as a gem, which is essentially bright, really shines when fixed in an ornament of gold.

10. Even one who by his qualities appears to be all knowing suffers without patronage; the gem, though precious, requires a gold setting.
11. I do not deserve that wealth which is to be attained by enduring much suffering, or by transgressing the rules of virtue, or by flattering an enemy.
12. ...
13. Those who were not satiated with the enjoyment of wealth, food and women have all passed away; there are others now passing away who have likewise remained unsatiated; and in the future, still others will pass away feeling themselves unsatiated.
14. All charities and sacrifices (performed for fruitive gain) bring only temporary results, but gifts made to deserving persons and protection offered to all creatures shall never perish.
15. A blade of grass is light, cotton is lighter, and the beggar is infinitely lighter still. Why then does not the wind carry him away? Because, it fears that he may ask alms of him.
16. It is better to die than to preserve this life by incurring disgrace. The loss of life causes but a moment's grief, but disgrace brings grief everyday of one's life.
17. All the creatures are pleased by loving words; and therefore, we should address words that are pleasing to all, for there is no lack of sweet words.
18. There are two nectarine fruits hanging from the tree of this world: one is the hearing of sweet words (such as Krishna-*katha*) and the other, the society of saintly men.
19. The good habits of charity, learning and austerity practised during many past lives continue to be cultivated in this birth by virtue of the link (*yoga*) of this present life to the previous ones.
20. One whose knowledge is confined to books and whose wealth is in the possession of others, can use neither his knowledge nor wealth when the need for them arises.

Chapter Seventeen

1. The scholar who has acquired knowledge by studying innumerable books without the blessings of a bonafide spiritual master does not shine in an assembly of truly learned men just as an illegitimate child is not honoured in society.
2. We should repay the favours of others by acts of kindness; so also should we return evil for evil in which there is no sin, for it is necessary to pay a wicked man in his own coin.
3. That thing which is distant, that thing which appears impossible, and that which is far beyond our reach, can be easily attained through *tapasya* (religious austerity), for nothing can surpass austerity.
4. What vice could be worse than covetousness? What is more sinful than slander? For one who is truthful, what need is there for austerity? For one who has a clean heart, what is the need for pilgrimage? If one has a good disposition, what other virtue is needed? If a man has fame, what is the value of other ornamentation? What need is there for wealth for the man of practical knowledge? And if a man is dishonoured, what could there be worse than death?
5. Though the sea, which is the reservoir of all jewels, is the father of the conch shell, and the Goddess of fortune Lakshmi is conch's sister, still the conch must go from door to door for alms (in the hands of a beggar). It is true, therefore, that one gains nothing without having given in the past.
6. When a man has no strength left in him, he becomes a *sadhu*, one without wealth acts like a *brahmachari*, a sick man behaves like a devotee of the Lord, and when a woman grows old, she becomes devoted to her husband.
7. ...

8. There is poison in the fang of the serpent, in the mouth of the fly and in the sting of a scorpion; but the wicked man is saturated with it.
9. The woman who fasts and observes religious vows without the permission of her husband shortens his life, and goes to hell.
10. A woman does not become holy by offering charity, by observing hundreds of fasts, or by sipping sacred water, as by sipping the water used to wash her husbands feet.
11. ...
12. The hand is not so well adorned by ornaments as by charitable offerings; one does not become clean by smearing sandalwood paste upon the body as by taking a bath; one does not become so much satisfied by dinner as by having respect shown to him; and salvation is not attained by self-adornment as by cultivation of spiritual knowledge.
13. ...
14. The eating of tundi fruit deprives a man of his sense, while the vacha root administered revives his reasoning immediately. A woman at once robs a man of his vigour while milk at once restores it.
15. He who nurtures benevolence for all creatures within his heart, overcomes all difficulties and will be the recipient of all types of riches at every step.
16. What is there to be enjoyed in the world of Lord Indra for one whose wife is loving and virtuous, who possesses wealth, who has a well-behaved son endowed with good qualities, and who has grandchildren born of his children?
17. Men have eating, sleeping, fearing and mating in common with the lower animals. That in which men excel the beasts is discretionary knowledge; hence, indiscreet men who are without knowledge should be regarded as beasts.

18. If the bees that seek the liquid oozing from the head of a lust-intoxicated elephant are driven away by the flapping of his ears, then the elephant has lost only the ornament of his head. The bees are quite happy in the lotus filled lake.
19. A king, a prostitute, Lord Yamaraja, fire, a thief, a young boy, and a beggar cannot understand the suffering of others. The eighth of this category is the tax collector.
20. O lady! why are you gazing downward? Has something of yours fallen on the ground? (She replies) O fool! can you not understand the pearl of my youth has slipped away?
21. O ketki flower! Serpents live in your midst, you bear no edible fruits, your leaves are covered with thorns, you are crooked in growth, you thrive in mud, and you are not easily accessible. Still for your exceptional fragrance you are as dear as kinsmen to others. Hence, a single excellence overcomes a multitude of blemishes.

Quotes from Chanakya Neet

"A person should not be too honest. Straight trees are cut first and honest people are screwed first."

"Even if a snake is not poisonous, it should pretend to be venomous."

"The biggest *guru-mantra* is: Never share your secrets with anybody. It will destroy you."

"There is some self-interest behind every friendship. There is no friendship without self-interests. This is a bitter truth."

"Before you start some work, always ask yourself three questions—

Why am I doing it, What the results might be and Will I be successful. Only when you think deeply and find satisfactory answers to these questions, go ahead."

"As soon as the fear approaches near, attack and destroy it."

"The world's biggest power is the youth and beauty of a woman."

"Once you start a working on something, don't be afraid of failure and don't abandon it. People who work sincerely are the happiest."

"The fragrance of flowers spreads only in the direction of the wind.

But the goodness of a person spreads in all direction."

"Who don't live in company of poor men, citizens never support a weak company and birds don't build nests on a tree that doesn't bear fruits."

"God is not present in idols. Your feelings are your God. The soul is your temple."

"A man is great by deeds, not by birth."

"Never make friends with people who are above or below you in status. Such friendships will never give you any happiness."

"Treat your kid like a darling for the first five years. For the next five years, scold them. By the time they turn sixteen, treat them like a friend. Your grown up children are your best friends."

"Education is the best friend. An educated person is respected everywhere. Education beats the beauty and the youth."

Chanakya quotes (Indian politician, strategist and writer, 350 BC-275 BC)

Similarity between Lalu and Chanakya

You can imagine Chanakya somewhere near to Lalu Prasad. Lalu started his career when Indira imposed emergency. He was one the hero of Jai Prakash revolution but before that, he was a student leader of Patna University. He became Chief Minister of Bihar for fifteen years and then he made his wife the chief minister of Bihar. He is the only successful railway minister of India after the independence. His success story has been studied globally approximately more than 120 countries. His case study is extremely wonderful. He supported Indra Kumar Gujral, Devegowda, Manmohan Singh to be Prime Minister of India and he is also known as king maker.

More or less, Chanakya story has perfect resemblance with Lalu Prasad career graph. Chanakya was also from Patna and he was mentoring students. Later, he became Prime Minister. Both of them are globally known for their intelligence and successful political practice.

Death of Chanakya

Chanakya lived to a ripe old age and died around 283 BC and was cremated by his grandson/disciple Radhagupta who succeeded Rakshasa Katyayan (great-grand son of Prabuddha Katyayan, who attained Nirvana during the same period as Gautam Budhha) as Prime Minister of the Maurya Empire and was instrumental in backing Ashoka to the throne. There were three non-traditional belief paths in society those days, Jaina, Buddhist and Ajivaka. Ajivaka practising Chanakya brought about the downfall of the Jaina Nandas and their coterie of Jaina ministers. (Chanakya's uncle was Jain, too, and a group of Jains backed Chanakya in his political machinations). Later on, Chandragupta Maurya took Jainism on abdicating his throne which passed to his Son Bindusara who was an Ajivaka. Even Ashoka was practising Ajivaka who before accession to throne became Buddhist. Bindusara was born before his father ever became Emperor so the legend is definitely not true. Ashoka's daughter was married in 265 BC and his son Kunala was 18 years of age in 269 BC, which means that even the princess married early. Ashoka was born 310 BC, and Bindusara around 330 BC. Bindusara means one who encompasses all that is need to be known.

Later on, Ajivikism which was the official religion of the empire since the Kalinga War (261 BC) and for 14 years afterwards, declined and merged into traditional Hinduism. What has been left are a mish mash of contradictory Buddhist and Jaina legends which are even rejected by Sinhalese chronicles.

The classical Sanskrit play by *Vishakhadatta, Mudrarakshasa*, is one popular source of Chankaya lore. (The play has been dated between 4th and 9th century CE).

A South Indian group of *Brahmins* in Tamil Nadu called Sholiyar or Chozhiyar, claim that Chanakya was one of them. Though this may sound very improbable, considering the vast distance between present day Tamil nadu in the South and Magadha in Bihar, it finds curious echos in the *Abhidhânchintâmani*, where Hemachandra claims that Chankya was a Dramila ("Dramila" is believed to be the root of the word "Dravida" by some scholars).

There is also a claim that Chanakya belonged to the *Brahmin* group from the present day Kerala who are considered to have been brought there by Parashurama. Considering the fact that Adi Sankara who revived Hinduism by setting up four monasteries in the four corners of India also belonged to that group, now known as Nambudiri Brahmins, this claim too merits attention. This further goes to contradict the story of his death also. In true Hindu tradition, he is said to have persuaded King Chandragupta Maurya to forsake his throne and to join him in moving to the last phase of one's life viz. *Sanyasa*. Accordingly, he took the King along with him to South India where both of them carried prolonged meditation and finally achieved *Moksha*.

Kautilya was educated at Taxila or Takshashila, in present day Pakistan. The new states (in present-day, Bihar and Uttar Pradesh) by the northern high road of commerce along the base of the Himalayas maintained contact with Takshasila and at the eastern end of the northern high road (*uttarapatha*) was the kingdom of Magadha with its capital city, Pataliputra, now known as Patna. Chanakya's life was connected to these two cities, Pataliputra and Taxila.

In his early years, he was tutored extensively in the *Vedas*—Chanakya memorized them completely at a very early age. He was also taught mathematics, geography and science along with religion. Later he travelled to Taxila, where he became a teacher of politics. Chanakya taught subjects using the best of practical knowledge acquired by the teachers. The age of entering the University was sixteen. The branches of study most sought after around India at that time ranged from law, medicine, warfare and other disciplines. Two of his more famous students were Bhadrabhatta and Purushdutta.

Political turmoil in Western India at that time caused by Greek invasion forced Chanakya to leave the University environment for the city of Pataliputra (presently known as Patna, in the state of Bihar, India), which was ruled by the Nanda king Dhanananda. Although Chanakya initially prospered in his relations with the ruler, being a blunt person he was soon disliked by Dhanananda. This ended with Chanakya being removed from an official position he enjoyed.

According to the Kashmiri version of his legend, Chanakya a thorn had pricked his foot, he uprooted the tree and poured buttermilk in the roots.

Other Thought

His foresight and wide knowledge coupled with politics of expediency helped found the mighty Mauryan Empire in India. He compiled his political ideas into the *Arthashastra*, one of the world's earliest treatises on political thought and social order. His ideas remain popular to this day in India. In Jawaharlal Nehru's Discovery of India, Chanakya has been called the Indian Machiavelli.

Three books are attributed to Chanakya: *Arthashastra*, *Nitishastra* and *Chanakya Niti*. *Arthashastra* (literally 'the Science of Material Gain' in Sanskrit) is arguably the first systematic book on economics. It discusses monetary and fiscal policies, welfare, international relations, and war strategies in details. Many of his *nitis* or policies have been compiled under the book title *Chanakya Niti*. *Nitishastra* is a treatise on the ideal way of life, and shows Chanakya's in depth study of the Indian way of life.

According to a legend, while Chanakya served as the Prime Minister of Chandragupta Maurya, he started adding small amounts of poison in Chandragupta's food so that he would get used to it. The aim of this was to prevent the Emperor from being poisoned by enemies. One day the queen, Durdha, shared the food with the Emperor while she was pregnant. Since she was not used to eating poisoned food, she died. Chanakya decided that the baby should not die; hence he cut open the belly of the queen and took out the baby. A drop (*bindu* in Sanskrit) of poison had passed to the baby's head, and hence Chanakya named him Bindusara. Bindusara would go on to become a great king and to father the greatest Mauryan Emperor since Chandragupta—Asoka. When Bindusara became a youth, Chandragupta gave up the throne and followed the Jain saint Bhadrabahu to present day Karnataka and settled in a place known as Sravana Belagola.

He lived as an ascetic for some years and died of voluntary starvation according to Jain tradition.

Chanakya meanwhile stayed as the Prime Minister of Bindusara. Bindusara also had a minister named Subandhu who did not like Chanakya. One day he told Bindusara that Chanakya was responsible for the murder of his mother. Bindusara asked the nurses who confirmed this story and he became very angry with Chanakya. It is said that Chanakya, on hearing that the Emperor was angry with him, thought that anyway he was at the end of his life.

He donated all his wealth to the poor, widows and orphans and sat on a dung heap, prepared to die by total abstinence from food and drink. Bindusara meanwhile heard the full story of his birth from the nurses and rushed to beg forgiveness of Chanakya. But Chanakya would not relent. Bindusara went back and vent his fury on Subandhu, who asked for time to beg for forgiveness from Chanakya. Subandhu, who still hated Chanakya, wanted to make sure that Chanakya did not return to the city. So he arranged for a ceremony of respect, but unnoticed by anyone, slipped a smoldering charcoal ember inside the dung heap. Aided by the wind, the dung heap swiftly caught fire, and the man behind the Mauryan Empire and the author of Arthashastra was burned to death.

His main philosophy was "A debt should be paid off till the last penny; an enemy should be destroyed without a trace". He seemed to have lived—and died—by his philosophy.

Summary

In business management, controlling plays a pivotal role in getting desired success. It is very challenging because for this, we need to open our third eyes for full 24 hours. Chanakya was a fearless mentor and a great human being. He was having natural emotional management technique. He utilized this talent to make

Chandragupta the king of Magadh. He was having very strong will power and fire to achieve the self-commitment with full patient.

His fearless attitude made him a successful mentor and great politician. His planning remained error free and time bound target oriented. His team spirit mentality made him great and honesty paid him whole the life.

According to Chanakya, a woman poses a great power and she can do any thing and everything but a person who remain away from the woman lust remain very strong and targeted.

We should donate money to the needy for the sake of God and if we donate something small amount in the morning, our day remains safe and secure. Education and proper mentoring is very necessary to be a good professional and to be successful businessman.

Apart from five principles of management, planning, organizing, staffing, coordinating and controlling we should develop third eyes to tackle the setback, emotion marketing skills to get team-spirited and endless desire. Our vision should be clear and style of working should be fearless and unbiased.

Chapter Seventeen

EXIT INTERVIEW

Exit interview is one of the most widely used methods of gathering employee feedback, along with employee satisfaction surveys. This is most beneficial for the employer as it is an eye-opener and a significant review to see how the company is doing justice with the employee. The purpose of the interview is to provide feedback on why employees are leaving, what they liked or didn't like about their employment and what areas of the organization they feel need improvement.

Therefore, exit interview is the best employee retention management tool recently introduced to get feedback from the leavers regarding working environment, manager's and colleague's behaviours with the aim to strengthen and improve existing retention strategy. Through exit interview, efficiency of employees could be improved and the most importantly profitability of the organization will surely increase multifold in days to come.

More recently, the concept of exit interviewing has been revisited and expanded as a knowledge management tool, as a way of capturing knowledge from leavers. Rather than simply capturing human resources information, the interview also aims to capture knowledge about what it takes to do the job.

In fact, anything that determines the quality of the organization, both in terms of its relationship with its staff, customers, suppliers, third-parties and the general public. Many employers ignore the opportunity that exit interviews offer, chiefly because exit interviews have not been practised in the past, and starting them is a difficult initiative to undertake, given the potentially subjective and 'fuzzy' nature of the results; the time involved; and the unspoken corporate urge to avoid exposure to criticism.

Exit interview is a chance to give some constructive feedback, and to leave on a positive note, with good relations and mutual respect. Recrimination, blame, revenge and spite are destructive feelings and behaviours, so resist any temptation you might have to go out all guns blazing. Be calm, fair, objective and as helpful as possible. In the future, you may wish to return to the organization (situations and people change.), and you may cross the paths of your ex-colleagues, managers in the future. The adage about treating people well on your way up because you might meet them on the way down applies just as well on your way out. The exit interview is an opportunity to shake hands and leave friends, not enemies.

Every employee should leave the organization in a legal way so that he can come back if something happens wrong with him. It happened with me. I left the organization for Dubai by following the exit rule of the company but unfortunately, I had to return back to India due to some personal reason. Fortunately, I joined back the same organization in a better package and better respects. That time my boss and all office staff were very happy to see me back in the office because of the one thing. I had left the organization with human touch. Our commitment and professional relation plays pivotal role in shaping up professional career. Therefore, in exit interview, we should be very genuine.

Aims and Outcomes

- Exit interviews are an excellent catalyst for identifying specific mistakes and improvement opportunities in this vital area of management development and succession.
- The results and analysis of exit interviews provide relevant and useful data directly into training needs analysis and training planning processes.
- Exit interviews provide valuable information as to how to improve recruitment and induction of new employees.
- Exit interviews provide direct indications as to how to improve staff retention.

- Sometimes, an exit interview provides the chance to retain a valuable employee who would otherwise have left (organizations often accept resignations far too readily without discussion or testing the firmness of feeling—the exit interview provides a final safety net).
- Exit interviews accelerate participating managers' understanding and experience of managing people and organizations. Hearing and handling feedback is a powerful development process.
- A significant proportion of employee leavers will be people that the organization is actually very sorry to leave (despite the post-rationalization and sour grapes reactions of many senior executives to the departure of their best people).
- The exit interview therefore provides an excellent source of comment and opportunity relating to management succession planning. Good people leave often because they are denied opportunity to grow and advance. Wherever this is happening, organizations need to know about it and respond accordingly.
- Every organization has at any point in time several good people on the verge of leaving because they are not given the opportunity to grow and develop, at the same time, ironically, that most of the management and executives are overworked and stretched, some to the point of leaving too. Doesn't it therefore make good sense to raise the importance of marrying these two situations to provide advantage both ways—i.e. facilitate greater delegation of responsibility to those who want it?
- Exit interviews, and a properly organized, positive exit process also greatly improve the chances of successfully obtaining and transferring useful knowledge, contacts, insights, tips and experience, from the departing employee to all those needing to know it, especially successors and replacements.

- They provide an opportunity to 'make peace' with disgruntled employees, who might otherwise leave with vengeful intentions.
- Exit interviews are seen by existing employees as a sign of positive culture. They are regarded as caring and compassionate—a sign that the organization is big enough to expose itself to criticism.
- Most leavers are happy to help if you have the courage and decency to ask and provide a suitable method for the knowledge transfer, be it a briefing meeting, a one-to-one meeting between the replacement and the leaver, or during the exit interview itself.
- Exit interviews help to support an organization's proper HR practices. They are seen as positive and necessary for quality and effective people-management by most professional institutes and accrediting bodies concerned with quality management of people, organizations and service.

How to Conduct Exit Interview?

Exit interviews are best conducted face-to-face because this enables better communication, understanding, interpretation etc., and it provides far better opportunity to probe and get to the root of sensitive or reluctant feelings. However, postal or electronic questionnaires are better than nothing, if face-to-face exit interviews are not possible for whatever reason (although I remain to be convinced that there is never a proper excuse for not sitting down for 30 minutes with any departing employee).

In some cases perhaps, a particularly shy employee may prefer to give their feedback in a questionnaire form, in which case this is fine, but where possible, face-to-face is best.

In terms of managing the interview, listen rather than talk. Give the interviewee time and space to answer. Coax and reassure where appropriate, rather than pressurize. Interpret, reflect and understand (you can understand someone without necessarily agreeing). Keep calm, resist the urge to defend or argue—your aim is to elicit views, feedback, answers, not to lecture or admonish. Ask open 'what/how/why' questions, not 'closed' yes/no questions, unless you require specific confirmation about a point. 'When' and 'where' are also more specific qualifying questions, unless of course they are used in a general context rather than specific time or geographic sense? 'Who' should be used with care to avoid witch-hunts or defamatory risks. Moreover, many exit interviewees will be uncomfortable if asked to name people or allocate personal blame—exit interviews are not about 'blame', the allocation of which is not constructive and should be avoided for anything other than very serious complaints or accusations, which must then be suitably referred as follow-up would be beyond the normal exit interview remit.

Prepare your exit interview questions and topics that you'd like to explore, especially when you believe that the interviewee has good experience, appreciation and understanding.

Take notes and/or use a prepared questionnaire form.

Remember, simple planning aspects such as arranging a suitable time and place, avoiding interruptions, taking notes, preparing questions, being aware of the body-language and feelings of the interviewee and adjusting your own approach accordingly, etc.

Obviously, the style of exit interview is different for someone who is being asked to leave, retiring, being made redundant, dismissed, or leaving under a cloud, compared to an employee leaving whom the organization would prefer to retain. However, everyone who leaves should be given the opportunity of an exit interview, and the organization can learn something from every situation. In certain situations (where appropriate), the exit interview also provides a last chance to change a person's mind, although this should not be the main aim of the exit interview situation.

When the interview is complete, say thanks and wish the interviewee well. If there is some specific checking or follow-up to do, then ensure you do it and report back accordingly. After the interview, look at the answers and think properly—detached and objective—about what their meaning and implications.

Take action as necessary, depending on your processes for analysing and reporting exit interview feedback. If there's an urgent issue, or the person wants to stay and you want to keep them, then act immediately or the opportunity will be lost.

Process of Exit Interview

Participation in exit interviews by the employee leaving is voluntary. Do not compel departing employees to attend exit interviews. Offer a questionnaire form alternative, which again must be voluntary.

You cannot compel a departing employee to give you knowledge that is in their head; although the return of files, paperwork and material is normally something that an employer rightfully can insist happens. In any event, a positive constructive, grown-up approach is the best assurance of a happy outcome and an optimal transfer of knowledge and contact names, etc., should this be helpful, which often it will be.

If you hear any of your people using the ridiculously confrontational maxim "No-one is indispensable...", as a defense for not bothering to gather important knowledge from a departing employee, it probably suggests that all opportunities for a cooperative hand-over have yet to be explored, so encourage people to explore them, or go explore them yourself.

Ideally, the organizations should have a documented policy stating how exit interviews happen, when, and by whom. Some organizations hand the responsibility to a skilled interviewer in the HR or Personnel department. Alternatively, line-managers or even supervisors can conduct the interviews. Interviewers need to be trained to interview, just as for normal job interviews. All types of interviews are sensitive emotional situations which require ability and maturity to manage properly, especially if interviewees are anxious or volatile.

In large organizations, HR or Personnel department should be responsible for designing the process, issuing guidelines and documentation, collecting results data, analyzing and reporting findings, trends, opportunities and recommendations, especially including anything relating to health and safety, or employment law and liability.

If you design a questionnaire or exit interview form which will be used as an input document towards central analysis, it is a good idea to convert questions wherever practicable into a 'scoreable' and/or multiple-choice format, which makes analysis far easier than lots of written opinions.

Actions resulting from exit interview feedback analysis, in any size or type of organization, fall into two categories:

- **Remedial and preventative**, for example, improving health and safety issues, stress, harassment, discrimination, etc.
- **Strategic improvement opportunities**, for example, improved induction, management or supervisory training, empowerment or team building initiatives, process improvement, wastage and efficiencies improvements, customer service initiatives, etc.

The head of HR or Personnel would normally be responsible for raising these issues with the board or CEO, and the conversion of exit interview feedback into action is a critical factor in justifying and maintaining a serious priority and operation of the process.

For many organizations, exit interviews provide a major untapped source of 'high-yield' development ideas and opportunities.

Benefits of Exit Interview

- Vital knowledge is not lost to the organization when people leave.
- The learning curve of new people joining the organization is shortened.
- Exit interviews can be done relatively quickly and inexpensively.
- Exit interviews can result in the leaver having a more positive view of the organization.

Done correctly, exit interviews can be a win-win situation for both the organization and the leaver. The organization gets to retain a portion of the leaver's knowledge and make it available to others, while the leaver gets to articulate their unique contributions to the organization and to 'leave their mark'.

Who Benefits From an Exit Interview?

Responsible employers will use this information to improve their recruitment and retention policies. However, cynics may believe this information is solely captured in case of future litigation from the ex-employee. It's for this reason that advice differs on how to handle an exit interview well.

How do I Go about It?

Traditional exit interviews can be conducted in a variety of ways: face-to-face, over the telephone, using a written questionnaire, or via the internet using an exit interview management system. In a knowledge-focused exit interview, a face-to-face interview is needed.

You will need to think carefully about the information you would like to gather before the interview and start your preparations early. While the traditional exit interview will tend to collect mainly human resources information, the primary focus of the knowledge-focused interview is on knowledge that would be helpful to the next person who will do the job or to others in the organization doing similar jobs.

Start planning the handover and exit interview as soon as you know a person is leaving. Identify who in the organization might benefit from that person's knowledge and what they will need to know. Then work out a plan to capture the leaver's knowledge during the time remaining before they leave. This should include both explicit knowledge (knowledge that is already documented such as in files and e-mails, and knowledge that can be easily documented), and tacit knowledge (knowledge that is less easy to capture and that needs to be explained or demonstrated).

In the case of explicit knowledge, make sure the leaver moves relevant files—both hard copy and electronic—into shared folders or a document library. Ask them to prune and organize these files and to create role and task folders or notes for their successor.

For tacit knowledge, you will need to interview the leaver face-to-face. Prepare for the interview by reviewing the key tasks the person does based on a job description or annual performance plan. You can then use that information as the basis for discussing how they go about those tasks, what knowledge and skills they need, any problems or pitfalls to be aware of, etc. Find out about their network of contacts and sources of knowledge. If possible, create an overlap period between the leaver and their successor so that a 'live' handover can be done.

When conducting exit interviews, think carefully about who will be the interviewer. Traditional exit interviews are conducted by someone from human resources. However, this need not be the case in the knowledge-focused interview. Often a peer or a relevant subject expert will be most appropriate. Over and above the obvious interpersonal and interviewing skills needed, you will need to consider issues of trust and honesty. For example, if an employee has had a difficult relationship with a manager or colleague, that person might not be best placed to conduct the interview. Whoever you select, make sure they are appropriately skilled and trained.

Precautions During Exit Interview

- Traditional exit interviews are usually only appropriate for employees who voluntarily resign or retire rather that those who are fired or made redundant. In the case of the knowledge-focused interview, much will depend on the extent to which the organization has a culture that encourages knowledge sharing.
- Be clear about who will use the knowledge gathered and how it will be used, before you begin to gather it; the purpose of the interview is not to gather knowledge per se, but to gather useful knowledge that will actually be used.
- The less you capture knowledge on a regular basis, the more you need to capture it at exit. However, you may decide that you could gain more value from capturing knowledge at more regular intervals.

For example, The Post Office uses exit interviews as one part of a series of 'cradle-to-grave' interviews to collect knowledge, using a method called 3E.

- The three Es are Entry, Expert and Exit. Entry interviews allow you to gather knowledge when employees first join the organization when they have 'new eyes' and a fresh perspective, and also to ask them what they would like to know to help them 'get up to speed'. Expert interviews are conducted as they develop skills and become experts in a particular role or field. For more information about this wider approach.

Must I Submit to an Exit Interview?

No. It's your right to decline an exit interview. A reputable employer will respect your decision. However, a not-so-reputable employer might resent that you didn't participate and file a "would not rehire" or similar adverse notation in your personnel records. The same employer might reveal the notation during a *background check*.

Should I Participate in an Exit Interview?

Naturally, the decision whether or not to participate in an exit interview is ultimately up to you. But there are varying opinions about whether or not you should participate. Some career experts think you should, because, although it doesn't help you much, it helps a sincere employer improve working conditions for remaining employees.

But other career experts question the usefulness of an exit interview. (A better time to conduct such a meeting is while an employee is committed, not while he or she is on the way out the door and concerned about burning a bridge.) Consequently, they don't think the risks for departing employees are worth it, so they advise against participating. Alternately, they advise participants to give "generic" responses only or at least think carefully before responding.

Besides potential bridge burning, risks for departing employees include the information falling into the wrong hands and ruining *references*, the employer revealing negative information during a background check, and as previously indicated, the employer submitting either positive or negative information as evidence in a lawsuit.

Some things to consider before participating in an exit interview are listed below:

- As a departing employee, will you benefit from an exit interview?
- Is the exit interview anonymous or must you sign a questionnaire or the HR rep's notes?
- Is the reason you're leaving any of the company's business or an invasion of your privacy?
- Why did your employer wait until you're leaving to ask your opinion?
- Will the HR department really use your comments for improvements or are they just trying to find out the "real" reason you're leaving?
- Might an exit interview burn a bridge, ruin a reference or cause an adverse background check for you?
- Might you sue your former employer down the road?

Ask the Right Question—While you have a lot of questions in mind, do not ask irrelevant questions regarding personal life. Offer to help them only if you can. You can ask thousands of questions but here are some of the questions you may want to ask:

1. Why did you join this organization?
2. What did you like and dislike most about this company?
3. What prompted you to look for a new job?
4. What is most appealing about the new position?
5. How would you rate your supervisors and peers?
6. What has been frustrating/difficult/upsetting to you in your time with us?

7. How well do you think the appraisal system worked for you?
8. What suggestion would you make to improve working conditions, hours, shifts, amenities, etc?
9. What can the organization do to retain its best people (and not lose any more like you)?
10. Would you consider working again for us if the situation were right?
11. Are you happy to say where you are going (if you have decided)?
12. What are your suggestions for improving the organization?

The answers to the above will help you redefine some of your policies like appraisal, salaries, benefits, motivational tools, recruitment practices and so on.

Do not Ask to Fill Questionnaire-like Form—Make it very short and precise. Also conduct a face-to-face interview or at the most, a telephonic interview. But under no circumstances, ask the employee to fill the form and drop it in an anonymous box as it is highly impersonal and infuriating.

The Interview Should be About Them—Most people like talking about themselves and their achievements and accomplishments. Let them do so as talking about how one does their job and what they've accomplished can provide key information to the organization and make the person feel good at the same time.

Time the Interview—There are two sides to this. When a person gives a notice that he/she may be leaving, do an exit interview immediately. You may be able to change their mind. But if the person has been asked to go or is leaving due to some internal politics, there are chances that the person may be very agitated. So, conduct the interview at a later date; may be two-three months later. During this period, the person may have cooled off and will be able to give a more rational feedback.

Don't Blow Up—There are times you may not like what you are hearing about yourself or the organization. But please control yourself as saying anything that you don't really mean or hurting the departing employee will make him only feel that leaving the organization was after all the right decision.

Use the Information Collected—Once the interview is over, do not merely file the form in the personal record of the employee. Collate past information and understand why employees are leaving the organization and help change the internal policies and practices.

Brief Sample Exit Interview Questions

Exit interview forms vary widely, but here are some core questions you can expect.

- What is your main reason for leaving?
- Would you work for this employer again?
- Would you recommend this employer to friends or family?
- What did you enjoy/dislike about your job?
- What improvements would you suggest about your job/working conditions/management support?
- What do you think it takes to succeed at this company?
- What does your new employer offer different to this company?
- Any other comments?

How you handle these questions and how honestly you answer is entirely your decision. If your main reason for leaving is to escape a tyrannical boss, carefully consider how you put this into words, particularly if you want to keep your options open for returning at a later date.

Remember the HR person's notes will be on your file, for all to see. Although you may feel that reporting your boss is the "right thing to do" in an exit interview, consider whether this may be better conveyed in a private conversation with his or her superior. Beware, open-ended questions asking for improvement suggestions or generalizations. Keep your answers short and simple, and above all, remain calm if you've had less than ideal treatment. If you have any points to make, present your ideas constructively—your interviewer will appreciate this approach enormously.

Detail Sample Exit Interview Questions

These questions can be used in face-to-face exit interviews, or to compile exit interview proforma questionnaires or electronic feedback forms.

If using these questions to compile forms to be used for large scale analysis, take care to format the questions into a format which can be analysed numerically, as far as is reasonable (certain questions and answers will always be difficult to format in this way, for example the 'how do you feel about an open-ended questions seeking ideas and suggestions—such questions and can only be analysed and reported 'by exception' when something of particular note crops up, or of a particular recurring theme is spotted).

In face-to-face interviews particularly, use the word 'why' if you want to probe, especially if the first answer is vague or superficial. Questions beginning with 'what' and 'how' are better for getting people to think and convey to you properly and honestly about their views. Some of these questions samples are more suitable for management employees, although always give people at all levels the chance to comment on issues normally 'above' their remit—you'll be surprised at how informed and insightful people can be. These questions examples are not in a sequential process, although broadly there is a logic to the order of the types of questions. There are lots more questions here than you would normally ask in a typical exit interview. Pick the questions that are most relevant to the leaving circumstances, the interviewee and your organization situation.

- Tell me about how you've come to decide to leave?
- What specific suggestions would you have for how the organization could manage this situation/these issues better in future?
- How do you feel about the organization?
- What has been good/enjoyable/satisfying for you in your time with us?

- What has been frustrating/difficult/upsetting to you in your time with us?
- How well do think your training and development needs were assessed and met?
- What can you say about the way your performance was measured, and the feedback to you of your performance results?
- What suggestion would you make to improve working conditions, hours, shifts, amenities, etc.?
- How could the organization enabled you to have made better use of your time?
- What can the organization do to retain its best people (and not lose any more like you)?
- Have you anything to say about your treatment from a discrimination or harassment perspective?
- Would you consider working again for us if the situation were right?
- Are you happy to say where you are going (if you have decided)?
- What, importantly, are they offering that we are not?

Exit Interviews and Knowledge Transfer

The days, weeks (or months in some cases) between the decision for the employee to leave, and the employee's actual departure date offer a crucial opportunity for the organization to gather important information and knowledge from the employee. This is especially relevant in roles where the employee has accumulated a significant amount of knowledge and personal connections, as typically applies in sales and buying roles, and obviously business unit management. The knowledge of the departing employee commonly has immense value, and the recovery of it is often overlooked altogether by the organization, until the employee has departed, or more likely been hurried out of the door holding the contents of their desk in a cardboard box.

When any employee resigns, or a decision is made for a person to leave for any reason, always ask: Should we spend some time thinking about how to enable some sort of knowledge transfer? In other words, if we place a value on the knowledge that the departing employee holds, isn't it worth thinking about how to enable this knowledge to be passed to the appropriate people remaining in the organization?

Instead of course all too often, senior management's response to all the head-scratching after a vital person has left, is to rationalise the loss of information (and vital personal contacts often) with the old cliché, "No-one is indispensable". The adage might ultimately be true, but that's not really the point. The fact is that most people who leave do actually possess useful (often critical) knowledge and experience. Moreover, most departing employees are delighted to share this knowledge, to help a successor, or to brief a management team, if only the organization would simply ask them politely to do so (assuming their exit is handled decently of course, which the exit interview helps to enable).

This is another good reason for thinking properly about the exit procedure, and for properly organizing some form of exit interview process. So, much depends of course on the atmosphere surrounding the departure. Often, particularly in sales, there is suspicion and imagined threat on both sides, which rather weakens the chances of a helpful hand-over. This mistrust should be diffused. It really does nobody any good.

In an ideal world, the leaver should be encouraged and enabled (and arguably rewarded if necessary) to hold a briefing meeting, which all interested parties (and certainly the person's replacement if possible) can attend and learn what they need to know. Regrettably however, it is not unusual for traditional-type '*theory-X*' sales directors and managers to be so intoxicated with testosterone and the taste of blood that such suggestions rarely make it off the stony ground of the board-room. I would urge you to take a more open constructive view. Give people the benefit of doubt, and discourage the kill'em and eat'em advocates from retaliating before there's any suggestion of being attacked. There are some suggested enabling questions below. For organizations large and small, exit interviews therefore provide lots of advantages and opportunities:

Knowledge Transfer Questions

Start thinking about using these questions when the employee and the organization knows that the employee will be leaving. Don't leave these questions until the exit interview.

- How might we benefit from your knowledge, experience, introductions to your contacts, etc., prior to your departure?
- Would you be happy to take part in a briefing meeting with managers/replacements/successor/colleagues so that we can benefit from your knowledge and experience, prior to your leaving?
- What can we do to enable you to pass on as much of your knowledge and experience as possible to your replacement/successor prior to your departure?
- How and when would you prefer to pass on your knowledge to your successor?
- I realise that you'll not be happy with the situation surrounding your departure, however we would really appreciate it if you could help us to understand some of the important things you've been working on—how might we agree for this knowledge to be transferred?
- We'd be grateful for you to introduce (name of successor) to your key contacts before you go—are you happy to help with this?

As ever, you will derive most for the organization, and be able to give most help to the departing employee, by being positive, constructive, understanding and helpful, prior to and during the exit interview process. Treat people with integrity and decency, and generally they will respond in kind.

Exit Interview Checklist

Here's a mental checklist to run through to remind you how to behave in the exit interview?

- Have I chosen to attend this interview? It's not compulsory, so if you've decided to attend, do so with grace and dignity.
- Will anything change based on my comments? If so, let the feedback flow.
- Who will benefit from my honesty? Constructive feedback is useful to a company, even if it takes time to take action.
- Who will be harmed by my honesty? Remember that, bland answers are an option if you're likely to get upset during the interview.
- Do I want to work for this employer again? Burnt bridges are difficult to repair.

  The relationship with your employer can be more intense than with your romantic partner, because so many big emotions are involved—status, achievement, security etc. When this relationship ends, for good or bad, it's better to handle the final good bye in your exit interview calmly. These sample exit interview questions, answers and checklist can help you maintain that focus.

Exit Interview Format

Dept:	Venue:
Name:	Designation:
Year or Period covered:	Length of service:
Exit Interview Date & time:	Name of interviewer:

Q.1 Why did you join this organization?

Q.2 What did you like and dislike most about this company?

Q.3 What prompted you to look for a new job?

Q.4 What is most appealing about the new position?

Q.5 How would you rate your supervisors and peers?

Q.6 What has been frustrating/difficult/upsetting to you in your time with us?

Q.7 What can the organization do to retain its best people (and not lose any more like you)?

Q.8 Would you consider working again for us if the situation were right?

Q.9 Are you happy to say where you are going (if you have decided)?

Q.10 What are your suggestions for improving the organization?

Sign of leaver Sign of interviewer

Conclusion

Suggestion

Summary

Today, we are faced with a greater challenge than ever before for retaining talented employees. It's not the changing vehicle technology, insurer relationships, or even equipment and products we use, but it is the immediate need for quality people to enter our industry so that we have the human resources to repair vehicles. Most will agree that this is a critical concern for today and in days to come. It is important to manage your people. Managers should be trained in important human resources areas. One that is critical is employee evaluations and appraisals. How often do you evaluate your employees formally? I have seen many business owners evaluate employees only when they are about to "fire" them. Another important component in attracting good candidates is to always be looking. Don't wait until a crisis forces you to hire the first person who can fog up a mirror. Evaluate your work force monthly and determine its strengths and weaknesses.

It is a very common question how to retain good employees. Obviously, it not an easy task, you have to be vigilant all the time. Determine what motivates your individual employees. Remember for most employees, money is not the key issue; relationships, fulfillment and recognition are prime issues. Notice how much recognition an employee needs. Some employees can go years without praise, whereas others will leave after six months. Understand that many employees are motivated by their social network at work. Encourage activities that make your employees feel like valued members of a team. Realize that incentives don't have to be huge. Benefits are also a vital consideration in attracting and retaining good people into our industry, but many shop owners/managers think it is strictly the paycheck. Research done many times over has proven this otherwise. Benefits also have become an extremely critical concern for businesses, especially in regard to health care costs.

A surprise gift certificate for the local ice cream parlour in the weekly paycheck will generate positive feelings. Make benefits more accessible. If your company reimburses tuition for college courses, have a college administrator come to your company, so employees can find out about classes and programs. Consider telecommuting, job sharing and other flexible working arrangements. Offer profit sharing incentives to encourage longevity. Create clear career paths at the company.

BIBLIOGRAPHY

A Handbook for Measuring Employee Performance, by the US Office of Personnel Management.

Alliance for Excellent Education (2005). *Tapping the Potential: Retaining and Developing High-quality New Teachers.* Washington, DC: Alliance for Excellent Education.

Armstrong, Michael (2006). *A Handbook of Human Resource Management Practice* (10th edition ed.). London: Kogan Page.

Biswas, Sugata and Twitchell, Daryl (1999). "Mastering the Case Interview" in *Management Consulting: A Complete Guide to the Industry*, John Wiley & Sons (January).

Bono, J.E. and Ilies, R. (2006). "Charisma, Positive Emotions and Mood Contagion". *The Leadership Quarterly* 17(4), pp. 317-34.

Boreen, J., et al. (2000). *Mentoring Beginning Teachers: Guiding, Reflecting, Coaching.* York, Maine: Stenhouse Publishers.

Bourne, M., Franco, M. and Wilkes, J. (2003). "Corporate Performance Management". *Measuring Business Excellence*, 7, 3; p. 15.

Burns, J.M. (1978). *Leadership.* New York: Harper and Row Publishers Inc.

Carger, C.L. (1996). "The Two Bills: Reflecting on the Gift of Mentorship". *Peabody Journal of Education*, 71(1), 22-29.

Cecil, A. Gibb (1970). *Leadership* (Handbook of Social Psychology). Reading, Mass.: Addison-Wesley, pp. 884-89.

Chemers, M.M. (2002). "Cognitive, Social, and Emotional Intelligence of Transformational Leadership: Efficacy and Effectiveness" in R.E. Riggio, S.E. Murphy, F.J. Pirozzolo (eds.), *Multiple Intelligences and Leadership*.

Cheng, M. and Brown, R. (1992). A two-year evaluation of the peer support pilot project. Evaluation/Feasibility Report, Toronto Board of Education. ED 356 204.

Clinard, L.M. and Ariav, T. (1998). "What Mentoring does for Mentors: A Cross-cultural Perspective". *European Journal of Teacher Education*, 21(1), 91-108.

Cox, M.D. (1997). "Walking the Tightrope: The Role of Mentoring in Developing Educators as Professionals", in Mullen, C.A. In M.D. Cox, C.K. Boettcher, & D.S. Adoue (eds.), *Breaking the Circle of One: Redefining Mentorship in the Lives and Writings of Educators*. New York: Peter Lang.

Daloz, L.A. (1999). *Mentor: Guiding the Journey of Adult Learners*. San Francisco: Jossey-Bass.

Dasborough, M.T. (2006). "Cognitive Asymmetry in Employee Emotional Reactions to Leadership Behaviors". *The Leadership Quarterly*, 17(2), pp. 163-78.

Encyclopædia Britannica. "Personnel administration is also frequently called personnel management, industrial relations, employee relations".

Feder, B.J. (2000). "F.I. Herzberg, 76, Professor And Management Consultant", *New York Times*, Feb 1, 2000, p. C26. Available from: *ProQuest Historical Newspapers, The New York Times* (1851-2003). [28 October 2006].

Garavan, Thomas N., Costine, Pat and Heraty, Noreen (1995). "Training and Development: Concepts, Attitudes, and Issues". *Training and Development in Ireland*. Cengage Learning, EMEA, p. 1.

George, J.M. (2000). "Emotions and Leadership: The Role of Emotional Intelligence", *Human Relations*, 53, pp. 1027-1055.

—— (2006). "Leader Positive Mood and Group Performance: The Case of Customer Service". *Journal of Applied Social Psychology*, 25(9), pp. 778-94.

Hackman, J.R. and Oldham, G.R. (1976). "Motivation Through the Design of Work: Test of a Theory", *Organizational Behavior and Human Performance*, [Online], vol. 16, no. 2, pp. 250-79. Available from: Science Direct. [1 November 2006].

Harrison, Rosemary (2005). *Learning and Development*. CIPD Publishing, p. 5.

Head, F.A., Reiman, A.J., and Thies-Sprinthall, L. (1992). "The Reality of Mentoring; Complexity in its Process and Function" in T.M. Bey and C.T. Holmes (eds.), *Mentoring: Contemporary Principles and Issues*. Reston, VA: *Association of Teacher Educators*, 5-24.

Henry, P. Knowles and Saxberg, Borje O., (1971). *Personality and Leadership Behavior*. Reading, Mass.: Addison-Wesley, pp. 884-89.

Hoover, John "How to Work for an Idiot: Survive and Thrive Without Killing Your Boss" (Career Press) http://www.amazon.com/How-Work-Idiot-Survive-Thrive/dp/1564147045/ref=pd_bbs_2?ie=UTF8&s=books&qid=1225302124&sr=8-2

Huang, Chungliang and Jerry Lynch (1995). *Mentoring—The TAO of Giving and Receiving Wisdom*, Harper, San Francisco.

Kouzes, J. and Posner, B. (2007). *The Leadership Challenge*. CA: Jossey Bass.

Kram, K.E. (1985). *Mentoring at Work: Developmental Relationships in Organizational Life*. Glenview, IL: Scott, Foresman.

KSEEB. *Sanskrit Text Book -9th Grade*. Governament of Karnataka, India.

Legge, Karen (2004). *Human Resource Management: Rhetorics and Realities* (Anniversary Edition ed.). Basingstoke: Palgrave Macmillan.

Mione, P. (2006). "Job Enrichment", Online paper.

Montana, Patrick J. and Charnov, Bruce H. (2000). "Training and Development". *Management*. Barron's Educational Series, p. 225.

Munk, Nina and Oliver, Suzanne, "Think Fast", *Forbes*, March 24,1997, pp. 146-51.

Murray, M. (1991). *Beyond the Myths and the Magic of Mentoring: How to Facilitate an Effective Mentoring Program*. San Francisco: Jossey-Bass.

Scherer, Marge (ed.) (1999). *A Better Beginning: Supporting and Mentoring New Teachers*. Alexandria, Virginia: Association for Supervision and Curriculum Development.

Schlee, R. (2000). Mentoring and the Professional Development of Business Students. *Journal of Management Education*, 24(3), pp. 322-37.

Smit, Martin E.J.H. (2006). *HR, Show me the money; Presenting an exploratory model that can measure if HR adds value.*

Sy, T., Cote, S. and Saavedra, R. (2005). "The Contagious Leader: Impact of the Leader's Mood on the Mood of Group Members, Group Affective Tone, and Group Processes". *Journal of Applied Psychology*, 90(2), pp. 295-305. http://www.rotman.utoronto.ca/~scote/SyetalJAP.pdf

The Columbia Encyclopedia (Sixth Edition ed.). Columbia University Press. 2005. http://www.bartleby.com/65/x-/X-personne.html. Retrieved on 2007-10-17. "Personnel management - see industrial management".

Torrington, Derek, Hall, Laura and Taylor, Stephen (2004). *Human Resource Management*. Pearson Education, p. 363.

Towers, David (2007). "Human Resource Management Essays". http://www.towers.fr/essays/hrm.html. Retrieved on 2007-10-17.

Ulrich, Dave (1996). *Human Resource Champions: The Next Agenda for Adding Value and Delivering Results*. Boston, Mass.: Harvard Business School Press.

Wilkinson, A. (1988). "Empowerment: Theory and Practice". *Personnel Review*, 27(1): 40-56. Retrieved on 2007-10-17.

International Books

Blake, R. and Mouton, J. (1964). *The Managerial Grid: The Key to Leadership Excellence*. Houston: Gulf Publishing Co.

Carlyle, Thomas (1841). *On Heroes, Hero-Worship, and the Heroic History*. Boston, MA: Houghton Mifflin.

Fiedler, Fred E. (1967). *A Theory of Leadership Effectiveness*. McGraw-Hill: Harper and Row Publishers Inc.

Heifetz, Ronald (1994). *Leadership without Easy Answers*. Cambridge, MA: Harvard University Press.

Hemphill, John K. (1949). *Situational Factors in Leadership*. Columbus: Ohio State University Bureau of Educational Research.

Hersey, Paul, Blanchard, Ken and Johnson, D. (2008). *Management of Organizational Behavior: Leading Human Resources* (9th ed.). Upper Saddle River, NJ: Pearson Education.

Miner, J.B. (2005). *Organizational Behavior: Behavior 1: Essential Theories of Motivation and Leadership*. Armonk: M.E. Sharpe.

Spencer, Herbert (1841). *The Study of Sociology*. New York: D.A. Appleton.

Van Wormer, et al. (2007). *Human Behavior and the Social Environment: Macro Level: Groups, Communities, and Organizations*. US: Oxford University Press.

Vroom, Victor H. and Jago, Arthur G. (1988). *The New Leadership: Managing Participation in Organizations*. Englewood Cliffs, NJ: Prentice-Hall.

Vroom, Victor H. and Yetton, Phillip W. (1973). *Leadership and Decision-Making*. Pittsburgh: University of Pittsburgh Press.

International Journal Articles

Bandura, A. (1997). *Self-efficacy: The Exercise of Control*. New York: Freeman.

Baumeister, R.F. and Vohs, K.D. (eds.) (2004). *Handbook of Self-regulation: Research, Theory, and Applications*. New York: Guilford Press.

Carver, C.S. and Scheier, M.F. (1998). *On the Self-regulation of Behavior*. New York: Cambridge University Press.

Cervone, D., et al. (2006). "Self-regulation: Reminders and Suggestions from Personality Science". *Applied Psychology: An International Review*, 55, pp. 333-85.

Deci, Edward L. and Ryan, Richard M. (1985). *Intrinsic Motivation and Self-determination in Human Behavior*. New York: Plenum.

Fishbein, M. and Ajzen, I. (1975). *Belief, Attitude, Intention, and Behavior: An Introduction to Theory and Research*. Reading, MA: Addison-Wesley.

Galassi, J.P., et al. (1992). "Client Preferences and Anticipations in Career Counselling: A Preliminary Investigation". *Journal of Counselling Psychology*, 39, pp. 46-55.

Goldthorpe, J.H., et al. (1968). *The Affluent Worker: Attitudes and Behaviour*. Cambridge: Cambridge University Press.

Gollwitzer, P.M. (1999). "Implementation Intentions: Strong Effects of Simple Plans". *American Psychologist*, 54, pp. 493-503.

House, Robert J. (1971). "A path-goal Theory of Leader Effectiveness". *Administrative Science Quarterly*, Vol. 16, pp. 321-39.

—— (1996). "Path-goal Theory of Leadership: Lessons, Legacy, and a Reformulated Theory". *Leadership Quarterly* Vol. 7 (3), pp. 323-52.

Human Resources Management, HT Graham and R. Bennett M+E Handbooks (1993).

Kim, B.S., Li, L.C. and Lian, C.T. (2002). "Effects of Asian American Client Adherence to Asian Cultural Values, Session Goal, and Counsellor Emphasis of Client Expression on Career Counselling Process". *Journal of Counselling Psychology*, 49, 3, pp. 342-54.

Lewin, Kurt, Lippitt, Ronald and White, Ralph (1939). "Patterns of Aggressive Behavior in Experimentally Created Social Climates". *Journal of Social Psychology*, pp. 271-301.

"Leadership: Do Traits Matter?" *Academy of Management Executive*, Vol. 5, No. 2. 1991.

Lorsch, Jay W. (Spring 1974). "Review of Leadership and Decision Making". *Sloan Management Review*.

Maggie, Lu. (2002). *The Harvard Business School Guide to Careers in Management Consulting*, p. 21.

Maslow, *Motivation and Personality*, p. 66. Ormrod, 2003.

Occupational Outlook Quarterly, Summer 2002. Informational interviewing: Get the inside scoop on careers by Olivia Crosby.

Spillane, James P., et al. (2004). "Towards a Theory of Leadership Practice". *Journal of Curriculum Studies*, Vol. 36, No. 1, pp. 3-34.

Steinmetz, L. (1983). Nice Guys Finish Last: Management Myths and Reality. Boulder, Colorado: Horizon Publications Inc.

Swanson, J.L. (1995). "The Process and Outcome of Career Counselling". In W.B. Walsh and S.H. Osipow (eds.), *Handbook of Vocational Psychology: Theory, Research and Practice* (pp. 295-329). Mahwah, NJ: Erlbaum.

Swanson, J.L. and Parcover, J.A. (1998). "Annual Review: Practise and Research in Career Counselling and Development—1997". *The Career Development Quarterly*, 47, 2, pp. 98-135.

Vroom, Victor and Sternberg, Robert J. (2002). "Theoretical Letters: The Person Versus the Situation in Leadership". *The Leadership Quarterly*, Vol. 13, pp. 301-23.

Weightman, J. (2008). *The Employee Motivation Audit*, Cambridge Strategy Publications.

Wharton MBA Consulting Club (1997). *The Wharton MBA Case Interview Study Guide*, Volume I.

Wolfgang, et al. (1998). *Genetic Programming: An Introduction*, Morgan Kaufmann Publishers, Inc.